EMPIRES AT WAR

EMPIRES AT WAR

VOLUME

II

A Chronological Encyclopedia
from Carthage to
the Normans

Richard A. Gabriel

GREENWOOD PRESS
Westport, Connecticut · London

Library of Congress Cataloging-in-Publication Data

Gabriel, Richard A.
   Empires at war : a chronological encyclopedia / Richard A. Gabriel.
     p. cm.
   Includes bibliographical references and index.
   ISBN 0-313-33215-0 (set : alk. paper) — ISBN 0-313-33216-9 (v. 1 : alk. paper) —
ISBN 0-313-33217-7 (v. 2 : alk. paper) — ISBN 0-313-33411-0 (v. 3 : alk. paper)
   1. Military history, Ancient.   2. Military art and science—History—To 500.
3. Byzantine Empire—History, Military.   4. Military art and science—Byzantine
Empire. I. Title.
U29.G232 2005
355′.0093′03—dc22   2004017427

British Library Cataloguing in Publication Data is available.

Library of Congress Catalog Card Number: 2004017427

ISBN: 0-313-33215-0 (set)
        0-313-33216-9 (Vol. I)
        0-313-33217-7 (Vol. II)
        0-313-33411-0 (Vol. III)

First published in 2005

Greenwood Press, 88 Post Road West, Westport, CT 06881
An imprint of Greenwood Publishing Group, Inc.
www.greenwood.com

Printed in the United States of America

The paper used in this book complies with the
Permanent Paper Standard issued by the
National Information Standards Organization (Z39.48–1984).

10 9 8 7 6 5 4 3 2 1

For Suzi, *Ti Amo*
"Un giorno senza Lei e' un giorno senza sole!"

To the memory of
Marvin Kaufman
(1919–2004)

CONTENTS

Introduction   XV

1. War and Empire in the Ancient World
   [4000 B.C.E.–1453 C.E.]   1

Background   1
Manpower   6
Logistics and Transport   7
Strategic Mobility   8
Tactical Flexibility   9
Siegecraft   14
Artillery   15
Administration   17
Training   18
Weapons Technology   19
Armor   20
Helmets   21
Weapons   23
Battle Death   30
Wounds   32
Infection   34
Disease   36
Injuries   38
Military Medicine   40
Civilian Casualties   45

Contents

2. The World's First Empires, Sumer and Akkad
   [3500–2200 B.C.E.]   49

   Background   49
   The Sumerian Army: Eannatum's War   51
   The Empire of Sargon the Great   57
   Sargon's Army   58
   The Commanders   60
   Lessons of War   61

3. Egypt, Empire of the Sun [1479–1154 B.C.E.]   63

   Background   63
   The Army of Egypt   71
   The Battle of Megiddo (1479 B.C.E.)   78
   The Commanders   87
   Lessons of War   89

4. The Mitanni, the Chariot People [1480–1335 B.C.E.]   93

   Background   93
   The Mitannian Army   97
   Suppiluliumas's War   103
   The Commanders   104
   Lessons of War   105

5. The Hittites, the Iron People of Anatolia
   [1450–1180 B.C.E.]   107

   Background   107
   The Hittite Army   113
   The Battle of Kadesh (1275 B.C.E.)   117
   The Commanders   125
   Lessons of War   127

6. The Israelites, the Empire of David and Solomon
   [1100–921 B.C.E.]   131

   Background   131
   Canaanites   136
   Philistines   141
   Israelites   144
   Saul's Wars (1025–1005 B.C.E.)   150
   The Battle of Jabesh-Gilead   153
   The Battle of Michmash Pass   155
   The Battle of Mount Gilboa   158
   David and the Israelite Empire (1005–961 B.C.E.)   162
   The Aramean Campaign   166
   King Solomon (961–921 B.C.E.)   171

The Commanders   172
Lessons of War   174

7. **The Iron Empire of Assyria [890–612 B.C.E.]**   177

Background   177
The Assyrian Army   181
Sargon's Urartu Campaign (714 B.C.E.)   189
The Commanders   200
Lessons of War   202

8. **The Chinese Empires [1750–256 B.C.E.]**   205

Background   205
The Shang Army   207
The Zhou   210
The Zhou Army   210
The Spring and Autumn Period (771–464 B.C.E.)   211
The Battle of Chengpu (632 B.C.E.)   213
The Warring States (464–221 B.C.E.)   219
The Battle of Guiling (353 B.C.E.)   222
The Han Empire (206 B.C.E.–220 C.E.)   224
The Battle of Jingxing (205 B.C.E.)   225
The Commanders   230
Lessons of War   231

9. **Ancient India [1200–120 B.C.E.]**   235

Background   235
The Mauryan Empire (321–120 B.C.E.)   242
The Mauryan Army   244
The Commanders   248
Lessons of War   249

10. **Warfare in Classical Greece [500–338 B.C.E.]**   253

Background 253
The Armies of Classical Greece   261
The Battle of Marathon (490 B.C.E.)   268
The Battle of Leuctra (371 B.C.E.)   280
The Battle of Chaeronea (338 B.C.E.)   285
The Commanders   296
Lessons of War   299

11. **The Persian Empire and Alexander the Great [546–323 B.C.E.]**   305

Background   305
The Persian Army   308

Contents

Alexander the Great (356–323 B.C.E.) 317
Alexander's Army 323
The Battle of the Granicus (334 B.C.E.) 329
The Battle of Issus (333 B.C.E.) 334
The Battle of Gaugamela or Arbela (331 B.C.E.) 343
The Battle of the Hydaspes River (326 B.C.E.) 352
The Commanders 359
Lessons of War 362

12. **The Carthaginian Empire and Republican Rome
[814–146 B.C.E.]** 369

Background 369
Republican Rome and Carthage 373
The Carthaginian Army 382
The Roman Army 385
The Battle of the Trebia River (218 B.C.E.) 392
The Battle of Trasimene (217 B.C.E.) 394
The Battle of Cannae (216 B.C.E.) 396
Scipio Africanus (236–183 B.C.E.) 402
The Attack on New Carthage (209 B.C.E.) 404
The Battle of Baecula (208 B.C.E.) 408
The Battle of Illipa (206 B.C.E.) 409
Scipio's Africa Campaign (205–202 B.C.E.) 414
The Battle of Zama (202 B.C.E.) 420
The Commanders 424
Lessons of War 429

13. **Rome against Greece [201–146 B.C.E.]** 435

Background 435
The Antigonid Army 440
The Battle of Cynoscephalae (197 B.C.E.) 448
The Commanders 455
Lessons of War 457

14. **Caesar's Wars and the End of the Roman Republic
[100–30 B.C.E.]** 461

Background 461
The Campaigns in Gaul (58–52 B.C.E.) 462
Defeat of the Helvetii (58 B.C.E.) 463
Campaign against Ariovistus (58 B.C.E.) 465
Campaign against the Belgae (57 B.C.E.) 466
Campaign against the Veneti (56 B.C.E.) 468
Campaign against the Germans (55 B.C.E.) 470
The Invasions of Britain (55–54 B.C.E.) 471

Caesar's Army   472
The Armies of the Gauls   478
The Siege of Alesia (52 B.C.E.)   482
Caesar and Pompey: The Civil War (48 B.C.E.)   491
The Battle of Dyrrachium (48 B.C.E.)   495
The Battle of Pharsalus (48 B.C.E.)   500
The Commanders   504
Lessons of War   507

15. **Barbarians against Rome [9–445 C.E.]**   511

Background   511
Augustus's New Legions   522
The Germans   528
The Battle of the Teutoburg Forest (9 C.E.)   532
The Commanders   538
Lessons of War   540

16. **Imperial Rome [9–450 C.E.]**   545

Background   545
The Roman Imperial Army   551
The Goths   561
The Battle of Adrianople (378 C.E.)   565
The Commanders   571
Lessons of War   575

17. **The Empire of the Huns [370–468 C.E.]**   579

Background   579
The Army of the Huns   589
The Battle of Chalons (451 C.E.)   598
The Commanders   607
Lessons of War   609

18. **Korea, The Hermit Kingdom [612 C.E.]**   613

Background   613
The Chinese Imperial Army   624
The Korean Army   627
The Battle of the Salsu River (612 C.E.)   629
Lessons of War   635

19. **The Wars of Arab Conquest [600–850 C.E.]**   639

Background   639
The Army of Islam   642
The Battle of Tours (732 C.E.)   648

The Commanders   655
Lessons of War   656

20. **Charlemagne and the Empire of the Franks [741–887 C.E.]**   659

Background   659
The Merovingians   661
Charlemagne and the Carolingian Dynasty (741–887 C.E.)   667
The Army of the Franks   675
The Saxon Wars (772–804 C.E.)   687
The Commanders   696
Lessons of War   697

21. **The Vikings [780–1070 C.E.]**   701

Background   701
The Viking Army   706
1066 C.E. and All That   710
The Battle of Stamford Bridge (1066 C.E.)   713
The Commanders   716
Lessons of War   717

22. **Normans and Saxons [1066–1087 C.E.]**   721

Background   721
The Saxon Army   729
The Normans   734
The Battle of Hastings (1066 C.E.)   738
The Commanders   745
Lessons of War   747

23. **The Medieval Knight [950–1350 C.E.]**   751

Background   751
The Warrior Knight   757
War in the Middle Ages   778
The Battle of Lechfeld (955 C.E.)   782
The Commanders   788
Lessons of War   789

24. **The Crusaders [1096–1270 C.E.]**   791

Background   791
The Crusader Armies   796
The Muslim Armies   802
The First Crusade (1096–1099 C.E.)   807
The Battle of Dorylaeum (July 1097 C.E.)   808
The Second Crusade (1147–1148 C.E.)   814

The Battle of Hattin (1187 C.E.)   816
The Third Crusade (1189–1192 C.E.)   822
The Battle of Arsouf (September 7, 1191)   824
The Fourth Crusade (1202–1204 C.E.)   829
The Remaining Crusades   830
The Commanders   830
Lessons of War   833

25. **The Japanese Way of War [1000–1300 C.E.]**   837

Background   837
The Yamato State   839
The Japanese Warrior   847
The Battle of Ichinotani (1184 C.E.)   854
The Battle of Kyushu (1281 C.E.)   862
The Commanders   869
Lessons of War   870

26. **The Mongols, Empire of the Steppes [1200–1405 C.E.]**   873

Background   873
The Mongol Army   875
The European Armies   887
A Probe to the West (1221 C.E.)   892
The Russian Campaign (1236 C.E.)   898
The Battle of the Sajo River (1241 C.E.)   904
The Commanders   908
Lessons of War   909

27. **The Swiss and the Rediscovery of Infantry [1300–1600 C.E.]**   915

Background   915
Swiss Armies   917
The Battle of Morgarten (1315 C.E.)   929
The Battle of Laupen (1339 C.E.)   934
The Battle of Sempach (1386 C.E.)   936
The Commanders   940
Lessons of War   941

28. **The Hundred Years' War [1337–1453 C.E.]**   945

Background   945
The Armies   951
The English Army   952
The French Army   955
The Battle of Crecy (1346 C.E.)   957
The Battle of Poitiers (1356 C.E.)   963

Contents

The Battle of Agincourt (1415 C.E.)   971
The Commanders   980
Lessons of War   983

29. The Byzantines and Ottomans [1054–1453 C.E.]   987

Background   987
The Ottomans   989
The Ottoman Army   992
The Army of Byzantium   1000
The Battle of Manzikert (1071 C.E.)   1009
The Fall of Constantinople (1453 C.E.)   1012
The Commanders   1026
Lessons of War   1027

30. Empires of the Americas [300–1546 C.E.]   1031

The Aztecs (1168–1521 C.E.)   1031
    Background   1031
    The Aztec Army   1037
The Incas (1200–1532 C.E.)   1045
    Background   1045
    The Inca Army   1053
The Mayas (300–1546 C.E.)   1058
    Background   1058
    Lessons of War   1068

31. The Legacy of the Ancients: The Evolution of Modern War
    [1453–2005 C.E.]   1071

Weaponry   1072
The Dawn of Modern War   1077
Naval and Air Weaponry   1084
World War I   1087
World War II   1089
Post–World War II   1093
Lethality and Casualties   1098

Index   1103

12 THE CARTHAGINIAN EMPIRE AND REPUBLICAN ROME

[814–146 B.C.E.]

BACKGROUND

Carthage was founded thirty-eight years before the first Olympiad (about 814 B.C.E.) as one of a number of colonies established in Sicily, Spain, and North Africa by the Phoenician city-state of Tyre in her effort to expand her influence into the western Mediterranean. Carthage, in Phoenician, was *kart-hadasht*, meaning "new city," and it is likely that Carthage was designed from the beginning to be the leading colony even though others, Utica for example, had been founded earlier. Tyre was a Canaanite city whose name in Greek was *Phoenicia*, meaning "land of the purple," a reference to the city's production of purple dye from the murex snail found only in its coastal waters. The purple cloth manufactured in this area was so expensive it was only affordable by kings, a fact that came to identify "being of the purple" with royalty in the ancient world. The Romans called the people of Carthage *Poeni* or *Puni*, hence the name Punic Wars.

By the sixth century B.C.E. Carthage was the richest maritime power in the western Mediterranean, supported by a powerful navy and commercial fleet. In 586 B.C.E. Tyre herself came under siege by the Assyrian king Nebuchadnezzar, and the mother-city could no longer provide protection to her colonies in Sicily. The role of protector fell to Carthage, which immediately dispatched troops to counter Greek predations there and in Sardinia. With Roman and Etruscan help as well as aid from other Greek city-states on the island, Carthage successfully checked Greek expansion, gradually bringing Sicily under her control. For the next 300 years the linchpin of Carthaginian foreign policy was to retain control of Sicily and prevent it from becoming a base to interrupt her trade in the Mediterranean or from becoming a strategic platform for the invasion of Africa itself. It was during this time that the other Phoenician colonies on the African coast were compelled to recognize Carthage's primacy and submit to Carthaginian rule. With the exception of Utica, which was permitted to keep its walls, the other cities were required to demolish their fortifications, disband their armies, and pay tribute in the form of money or troop levies to Carthage, which maintained the only standing military force.

Carthage was almost unique among non-Greek states in possessing a constitution. For the first three centuries after its founding it is likely that Carthage followed the Phoenician model and was ruled by kings. As in Tyre and Sidon, however, these kings were not hereditary but elected by a powerful oligarchy of merchant princes. The authority of these kings, moreover, was not absolute and was circumscribed by tradition and legal limitations, including removal by the same oligarchy that elected them. By the fourth century B.C.E., Carthage had evolved an oligarchic republican regime based on an annually elected dual magistracy, that of the *shofets* (in Latin *suffetes*) or, translated into Hebrew, judges; the *Gerousia* or Grand Council with an inner permanent committee of thirty Elders; a high court of 104 judges selected for life by a college of pentarchs; and a popular Assembly comprising all citizens who met the minimum property qualifications. All offices were reserved for the aristocracy so that the basis of political privilege in Carthage was wealth and land ownership, not heredity. Carthage was a commercial society where war and the military took second place to profit, where military adventures were subjected to the test of cost-benefit analysis, and where generals were distrusted and kept on a short leash.

In 580 B.C.E. Carthage sent troops to put down Greek predations in Sicily and Sardinia. Although successful, one of her commanders had performed badly and was refused the right to return to Carthage with his troops. These troops were Carthaginian citizen-levies, and they refused to obey, threatening to strike at Carthage herself. The revolt was put down by a general named Mago, who then reformed the army and established the first of the great Carthaginian military families, among which were the Barcas which produced Hamilcar, Hasdrubal, and, of course, Hannibal. Carthage's newly acquired foreign policy responsibilities of protecting her sister colonies and maintaining her commercial supremacy in the western Mediterranean threw into sharp relief the inadequacy of her citizen-levies to meet these needs. The population of Carthage in the third century B.C.E. probably did not exceed 400,000 counting all classes, a number far too small to provide for her commercial and military manpower needs, even with the addition of levies from the other colonies. Moreover, Carthage's population was not comprised of hardy agricultural stock, whose absence from the land would have produced only marginal economic disruption. Carthage's population was mostly freemen who were merchants, tradesmen, and artisans whose absence from economic activity was costly to Carthage's revenue. It was, then, simply a question of economics and numbers. It was cheaper to hire soldiers than to conscript them, and by the fourth century B.C.E. the citizen-levy had been abandoned and replaced with mercenaries.

Carthaginian recruitment agents became a common fixture throughout the Near East, Italy, Greece, Gaul, and Africa, where they hired individual soldiers and complete military units from princes and kings. A small number of Carthaginian citizens continued to serve in the military, but their numbers were insignificant. The last date for which we have evidence of Carthaginian units participating in war outside Africa is in 311 B.C.E. It was around this time that Carthage created a new unit called the Sacred Band comprised of elite citizen-soldiers. This unit, Polybius tells us, was 3,000 strong and was armed like Greek heavy infantry, by which we suppose he meant the infantry of Alexander and not classical Greece, although we cannot be certain. Other sources suggest the unit was a training battalion for young cavalry officers, but this, too, is uncertain. Whatever its composition, the Carthaginian Sacred Band could not, by law, be employed outside the *chora* of Carthage itself, suggesting that it may have been some sort of praetorian or civic guard. Why this unit was created remains a mystery. One can only say that with Alexander's victories came a desire to imitate Greek forms of warfare.

The mercenary system presented Carthage with a number of problems. First, mercenary armies were expensive. But Carthage was very rich, and as long as her armies protected her trade and metals monopolies throughout the western Mediterranean the cost was manageable. Carthage also charged her dependencies for the privilege of protecting them, sometimes, as in Iberia and Libya, requiring that they furnish specified numbers of troops and then paying them as mercenaries. Second, mercenary armies must be kept busy or they become ill disciplined and even mutinous. This problem was solved by having the army almost constantly occupied somewhere outside of Carthage itself. For more than a century Hanno occupied them with the conquest of North Africa's hinterlands, which Carthage exploited for raw materials and agriculture. Third, mercenary soldiers were one thing, mercenary commanders quite another. Command of the armies was always in the hands of Carthaginian field generals. At first this presented some problems, as a commercial people usually do not produce great military commanders. After the fourth century B.C.E., however, Carthage had begun to establish a handful of powerful families whose sons were experienced military commanders. This new military caste was established by Mago (hence the military dynasty known as the Magonids), and it soon produced others. Examined objectively, Carthaginian commanders were some of the best in the Western world.

Finally, powerful generals in command of mercenary troops can become a serious threat to civilian political authority. The Carthaginians hit upon a novel solution to deal with this problem. Prior to the reform of the army Carthaginian commanders had been high-ranking political officials. As was the Greek practice, the kings themselves in the early days commanded their armies in battle. After 300 B.C.E., military commanders were no longer permitted to hold public office of any kind. A complete separation of military from civic authority was introduced. Generals and admirals were now appointed only for specific periods of time or for specific conflicts by the Council of One Hundred Judges. Nor was it uncommon for a member of this court or even a senator to accompany the general in the field and report on his performance and, we might reasonably surmise, his political loyalty. Generals could be removed at any time by the council. When Roman ambassadors came to Carthage to demand the removal of Hannibal for his siege of Sargentum, it was to this council and the Carthaginian senate that they appealed. To make certain that its edicts were taken seriously, any Carthaginian commander who failed in the field or who otherwise failed to carry out his orders with diligence could be publicly crucified in the city's main square!

The system worked admirably, for with the exception of one Bomilar who in 308 B.C.E. attempted some sort of attack on the city with a small band of elite troops, Carthaginian commanders were completely loyal and presented no risk of praetorianism to the civil authority.

The success of the Carthaginian military system is evident in two respects. First, right to the end Carthage was able to place large forces in the field sufficient to the missions set for their commanders. Second, the quality of Carthaginian commanders was generally excellent, by far tactically superior to Roman commanders with the notable exception of Publius Scipio.

Manpower

As to the size of the armies, a few examples will suffice. The walls around Carthage were also used as barracks and stalls for animals and supplies. In the two-and-one-half-mile-long wall that protected Carthage from an assault from the mainland, there were stables sufficient for 300 elephants and 4,000 cavalry horses and barracks for 20,000 infantry and 4,000 cavalry. A force of this size represented the central core of the Carthaginian army, to be expanded in time of crisis. One advantage of a mercenary army is that its commanders can hire troops from the very country within which they are conducting operations. Thus, in 262 B.C.E. at Minoa Heraclea in the battle with Rome in Sicily, the Carthaginian commander had an army of 50,000 foot, 6,000 horse, and 60 elephants. When Hamilcar Barca (Hannibal's father) left Carthage to expand Carthaginian influence in Spain, Polybius tells us he took with him only a few elephants and a small army. A few years later when Hamilcar was killed by the Oretani in Iberia, his army numbered 50,000 foot, 6,000 horses, and 200 elephants. When Hannibal moved to cross the Alps, he had an army of 40,000 foot, 8,000 cavalry, and 37 elephants. While Carthage's military system could produce adequate manpower to deal with most military situations, what it could not do, of course, was battle a power whose manpower reserves *and* disciplined stubbornness could draw Carthage into a war of attrition. For this reason the wars with Rome ultimately could not be won.

REPUBLICAN ROME AND CARTHAGE

From approximately the eighth century B.C.E. until the third century, Rome and Carthage developed independently and without conflict as the major regional powers in the western Mediterranean basin. Rome began as a small city-state on the banks of the Tiber and gradually grew into the major land power in Italy, with little in the way of overseas contacts and no colonies or possessions outside the Italian peninsula. Rome's development paralleled that of the classic continental, albeit peninsula, power. Carthage's power was based upon its ability to secure almost unilateral access to markets and resources in Sicily, Corsica, Sardinia, the Balaeric islands, and coastal Spain. Carthage also enjoyed a rich trade with Greece and the eastern Mediterranean states. Whereas Rome developed as a land power, Carthage necessarily developed as a sea power. With access to overseas areas, its most important element of national power, Carthage developed a large commercial fleet with a large and highly skilled navy to protect its vital sea lanes. The meager contacts between Rome and Carthage were regulated by a number of treaties in which Carthage granted Rome a free hand on the Italian mainland in return for a Carthaginian trading monopoly in the western Mediterranean. As long as Carthage did not encroach on Roman ports to increase its trading outlets and Rome did not seek to expand into overseas areas of Carthaginian interest, the two states lived in relative harmony.

Rome, of course, was not yet in any position to think about expanding beyond the Italian peninsula. It took almost three centuries to expand its area of control in Italy to the point where, by 264 B.C.E., Rome controlled through incorporation or alliances most of the territory from the Straits of Messina in the south to the Po Valley in the north. With the exception of a few remaining Greek colonies in the south, by 264 B.C.E. Rome controlled most of the Italian peninsula.

The First Punic War

The conflict with Carthage started over Sicily. Carthage and Greece had long occupied Sicily, and the Carthaginians had constructed fortifications and established garrisons on the western side of the island. The eastern part was under the influence of Greek colonies and independent city-states. The Carthaginians viewed Sicily as a major strategic platform from which an invasion could be launched against Carthage itself. In hostile hands, Sicily came to resemble a dagger at the throat of Carthage, and a major goal of Carthaginian policy for centuries was to keep control of the western side of the island. Once Rome had achieved a degree of control over most of Italy, it regarded the continued occupation of Sicily by Carthage (and the Greeks as well) as a major check on its ability to expand. Expansion to the north (in Cisalpine Gaul) was difficult because of the harsh terrain and the strong

Figure 12.1 The First Punic War. Adapted from Alfred Bradford, *With Arrow, Sword, and Spear* (Westport, CT: Greenwood, 2001). Reprinted with permission.

presence of warlike Gallic tribes. Sicily, however, offered the double prize of allowing expansion into a rich and developed area of considerable commercial value while at the same time reducing the presence of a major power on Italy's border. In Rome's view, the Carthaginian presence on the strategic platform of Sicily could not be relied upon to remain defensive in nature under the press of Roman expansion. In 264 B.C.E., Rome encroached on Sicily, and the First Punic War broke out.

The war lasted more than twenty years until brought to an end by peace treaty in 241 B.C.E. It was fundamentally a war at sea, with some ground engagements fought in Sicily to expel Carthaginian garrisons. After several defeats at the hands of superior Carthaginian seamanship, Rome embarked upon a program to build a navy. Historically, the Romans had never developed a navy and did not even know how to design ships. Using a captured quinquirime as a template, the Romans built hundreds of fighting ships. Men recruited into the army were trained in rowing and tactics on land, and then deployed shipboard. Even with Rome's advantage in ships, Carthage continued to defeat the Roman navy in battle after battle. At one point Roman naval casualties and losses due to storms amounted to approximately 15 percent of the total number of able-bodied men of military age in Italy!

The problem of Carthaginian superiority at sea was finally solved by the introduction of new technology. The Roman strong suit was close infantry combat. The problem for naval planners was how to bring this talent to bear at sea. The answer was the invention and use of the *corvus*, or "raven," and the grappling iron. The Romans had been defeated by the Celts a century before in a naval engagement in the mouth of the Seine River. While Roman ships attempted to ram, the Celts used grappling hooks on ropes to bring the two ships together, then rushed aboard with their infantry, killing the Roman crews. The *corvus* seems to have been a Roman invention and consisted of a large wooden bridge with a spike at one end. The bridge was mounted at the rear of the ship, and rotated outward. As an enemy ship was caught with the grappling irons and brought into contact with the Roman ship, the *corvus* was swung out and down so that the spike stuck in the enemy deck. The superior Roman infantry rushed across the wooden bridge onto the enemy ship and massacred its crew. These new tactics began to turn the tide at sea.

Polybius called the First Punic War the bloodiest in history, and Rome alone lost over 400,000 men. Both sides became exhausted, and in 241 B.C.E. a peace treaty was concluded. Carthage surrendered its claims and garrisons in Sicily and relinquished her claims to all Italian islands between the city of Rome and Sicily. Only Syracuse, because it was an independent city-state, remained outside the Roman control of Sicily. Corsica, too, was lost to Roman dominance. The indemnity levied upon Carthage was so high that it could not pay its mercenary armies, and for three years Carthage fought a war against its own mercenaries. Near the end of the war, on the flimsy pretext that Carthaginian garrisons on Sardinia were really targeted at Rome, the Romans seized Sardinia and garrisoned the island.

Figure 12.2 The Roman *Corvus*. Courtesy of K. Barnes.

Exhausted from war, Carthage had been deprived of its most important markets and trading stations and faced economic ruin. Its navy was destroyed and the trading fleet reduced. The economic basis of Carthaginian power was severely eroded. Under the leadership of Hamilcar Barca, Carthage turned to expanding her hold on Spain as a new source of markets and resources. For more than a century Carthage had maintained a small trading port at Cadiz. Under Hamilcar's urging, Carthage sought to rebuild its power by expanding its influence in Spain.

Hamilcar was the last holdout against Roman arms in Sicily and was an accomplished general. He spent the next nine years conquering the rugged peoples of southern and central Spain. His son-in-law, Hasdrubal the Splendid, continued the campaign. With a judicious use of force, diplomacy, and diplomatic marriages, Hasdrubal secured a stable hegemony over Spain. Following the assassination of Hasdrubal in 221 B.C.E., the army chose Hannibal—the oldest son of Hamilcar Barca—as commander of the army.

Hasdrubal had concluded a treaty with Rome in which Rome and Carthage recognized the Ebro River as the northern limit of Carthaginian influence in Spain. South of that line, only Sarguntum remained an independent city. The purpose of the treaty was to assuage Roman suspicions. Rome had watched for almost two decades as Carthaginian power increased in Spain. Although deprived of its traditional markets and resource base, Carthage had staged a remarkable economic and military recovery. From Rome the growth of Carthaginian power and wealth in Spain began to look suspiciously like the establishment of a new strategic platform from which to strike at the main islands of Corsica and Sardinia, or even at the Italian mainland itself. The Romans were themselves never ones to forget a defeat, and they suspected that

Carthage was preparing for a war of revenge. Moreover, with Sicily secured, Rome could now turn its attention to expansion in the north, where it would eventually come into conflict with Carthage again.

The Second Punic War

In 219 B.C.E. Sarguntum revolted against Carthage, probably stimulated by a pro-Roman faction within the city. Despite pleas for Roman aid, Rome did nothing. In the absence of Roman pronouncements to the contrary, Hannibal assumed he had a free hand to deal with the revolt. Sarguntum, after all, was south of the Ebro, and Rome had conceded that sphere of influence to Carthage by treaty. Hannibal assaulted the city and, after an eight-month siege, destroyed it. This was the *causus belli* that Rome sought. Rome struck before Carthaginian power became even more menacing.

Roman ambassadors arrived in Carthage with an ultimatum. Either Hannibal and his officers were to be tried and punished for their actions in Sarguntum, or Rome would hold Carthage responsible and declare war. Clearly, the issue of Sarguntum was merely an excuse. Rome had already concluded that Carthaginian power was a threat and had to be reduced by military action. Roman diplomacy served these ends. The Roman ambassador, Quintius Fabius, held out two folds of his toga and said, "Here I bring you peace and war, chose what you will." Carthage chose to fight, and the result was the Second Punic War (218–201 B.C.E.), in which Rome grappled with the armies of Carthage led by one of history's greatest generals, Hannibal Barca.

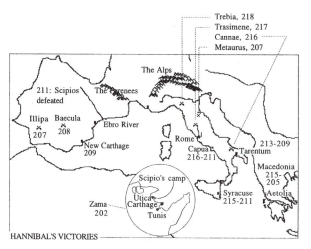

Figure 12.3 Theaters of the Second Punic War (218–201 B.C.E.). Adapted from Alfred Bradford, *With Arrow, Sword, and Spear* (Westport, CT: Greenwood, 2001). Reprinted with permission.

Hannibal's Strategy

To understand the development of Hannibal's strategy it is necessary to explore the strategic constraints under which he was forced to develop it. In any war with Rome, Carthage had three major difficulties that strongly affected the development of a successful military strategy: (1) manpower, (2) naval strength, and (3) the nature of Carthaginian rule. Each problem, moreover, was largely a reciprocal function of the other two difficulties.

The first strategic problem was the shortage of a manpower base from which to recruit and sustain the Carthaginian armies. If we can, for the moment, believe the historian Strabo that the population of Carthage at this time was approximately 700,000 people, Blodgett's method of measuring the ability of Greek city-states to raise forces from their respective manpower bases can be used to assess the manpower pool available to Carthage for military use. Approximately 37 percent of the population, at maximum, could be put to military use, which, for Carthage, meant that a maximum military effort could produce only 100,000 to 120,000 men for use in the armies *and* the fleet. Somewhere in the vicinity of 30,000 to 35,000 horse cavalry could be raised.

While these resources were not unsubstantial, they were not sufficient in light of the minimum required strategic force deployments. From its general manpower pool Carthage would have to deploy substantial contingents to Spain to retain political control of the only partially pacified tribes now being rigorously stirred to revolt by the Roman intelligence service. Failure on this front would place the rear of Hannibal's armies, and a major recruitment pool, at great risk. Moreover, trade with Spain had to continue if Carthage was to be able to raise the money needed to continue the war. Another drain on manpower resources was the need to protect Libya-Phoenicia on the African coast. This area provided the bulk of Carthage's grain and a large surplus for export, much of it to Greece, for hard currency that was needed to fight the war. Finally, manpower reserves had to be committed to defend the African coast and Carthage itself against a Roman seaborne attack in force. When taken together, these requirements stretched Carthaginian manpower resources to their limits. Under most circumstances Hannibal would not be able to count upon Carthage to provide more than 40,000 men and 8,000 to 10,000 horse cavalry for the war. An additional source of manpower had to be found if the war against Rome was to have any chance of success.

The Roman manpower situation, by contrast, was considerably better. Drawing only upon its own manpower and that of the allied companion city-states, Rome could deploy 250,000 foot and 23,000 horse within a year of the outbreak of the war. With contingents drawn from the other allied states of the Italian peninsula, Rome had a strategic manpower pool of 700,000 foot and 70,000 horse, an advantage of more than two to one over Hannibal. What this situation meant was that any attempt by Hannibal to fight a war of attrition or to engage in multiple theaters of operations would eventually fail. The Romans, on the other hand, could engage on multiple fronts, forcing the Carthaginians to react to a place and time of Roman choosing. Even when Carthage enticed Philip V of Greece to declare war on Rome to draw off Roman forces, the Romans met and continued the engagement without any significant effects on the level of forces deployed against Hannibal.

The second strategic factor limiting Carthaginian fighting power was its inability to control the sea lanes. Here was a major regional power about to engage in a war far from its shores while conceding control of the sea to the enemy. During the First Punic War, Carthage had deployed more than 300 naval ships. The basic ship of the line of the day was the quinquireme, each requiring 270 rowers and forty to fifty marines. After the war, Carthage continued to maintain and expand her commercial fleet but invested little in her naval fleet. One reason may have been the shortage in manpower required to maintain a sizeable naval arm (35,000). Rome, on the other hand, maintained a large navy after the war and had sufficient naval combatants to give it control of the sea lanes.

The inability of Carthage to protect its sea lanes placed severe limits on strategy. First, Carthage could not transport its own troops to key areas so that strategic surprise from the sea was possible. Second, resupply, reinforcement, and evacuation of troops already in position was very difficult to achieve and fraught with risk. Third, with Roman naval combatants roaming at will, the Carthaginian trade that was its main source of cash to fight the war could be easily disrupted. Fourth, without an adequate covering naval force, Carthage and the coast of Africa were open to Roman raids and invasion. Unlike the first war where most of the action occurred at sea, Carthage would have to play against the Roman advantage in ground combat. Once committed, Carthaginian ground units would have to be completely self-sustaining for the duration of the war. No help could be provided by the navy.

This requirement for self-sufficiency brought into focus the third element limiting Carthaginian strategy—the nature of its political rule over its colonies. Carthaginian rule was based on cruelty, and disputes with tribes and towns were often settled by fire and crucifixion. Carthage's own politics were based upon individual avarice and the pursuit of economic wealth and self-interest, traits cruelly buttressed by child sacrifice to Baal and public crucifixion for criminals, and the loyalty of Carthage's citizenry never went very deep. Abroad, Carthage never took pains to gain the allegiance of its subject peoples, and their loyalty to any Carthaginian cause was always suspect.

The paradox was that Carthage was heavily dependent upon these overseas areas for the recruitment of its mercenary armies, a task that was never easy. The general manpower shortage meant that, if the war dragged on, some way had to be found to continue the flow of manpower from these areas. Finally, the questionable loyalty of the subjected peoples meant that Roman gains in these areas not only deprived Carthage of the territory itself, but actually cut the legs from underneath its manpower recruitment system.

Hannibal's experience with the tenuous loyalty of Carthaginian allies in Spain probably led him to conclude that it was possible to draw off the support of Roman allies once Italy itself was invaded. If so, Hannibal failed to study the political sociology of Roman rule in Italy. Rome made great efforts to treat its allied states with fairness and justice, even to the point of extending to them Roman citizenship and law in return for troop contingents under the command of Roman officers. The situation was much more stable than what existed in Carthaginian domains. With few exceptions,

Roman allies remained loyal throughout the war despite the threats and pressures from Hannibal's army.

These three problems—manpower, control of the sea, and the nature of Carthaginian rule—placed significant constraints upon any strategy that could be developed by Hannibal to prosecute the war successfully. A number of additional limiting parameters within which Hannibal was required to develop his strategic plan can be deduced from these realities. Seven limiting parameters can be identified:

1. The war would, by necessity, have to be a ground war requiring little in the way of support by sea. Unlike the first war, Carthage could not hope to weaken Roman will by destroying large contingents of Roman manpower at sea. Every casualty would have to be caused by close combat.
2. The war would have to be fought on the Italian mainland. A war anywhere else would not sufficiently threaten Rome into a political settlement. In any case, a war in the provinces could not be sustained in light of Roman control of the sea.
3. Hannibal had to insert his army overland from his strategic platform in Spain since naval transport was impossible. To minimize losses in deployment, a strong element of strategic surprise was required.
4. Once in Italy, some way had to be found to replace combat losses or risk a war of attrition against the Romans that Hannibal could not win.
5. Once in Italy, some way had to be found to reduce the Roman manpower advantage either through battle or political means.
6. Rome had to be immobilized from striking directly at Carthage or Spain with sufficient force to bring the war to an end while Carthaginian armies were in the field.
7. Neither Rome nor her armies could be defeated in their entirety. Rome's center of gravity was the political will of the Roman Senate and her allies. The purpose of the war was to break that will so that an advantageous treaty could be concluded, possibly restoring Corsica, Sardinia, and Sicily to Carthaginian control.

Within these constraints Hannibal formulated a brilliant and risky military strategy for defeating Rome. On paper, at least, it was designed to tailor military operations to the attainment of larger political objectives. And had it succeeded and Roman power been brought to heel, one can only wonder how different the history of the West might have been.

Hannibal knew his adversary well enough to know that Rome would not have declared war against Carthage without first having in place a plan for its prosecution. He surmised that Rome was already planning to move militarily and that its strategy would probably involve a two-pronged assault on the Carthaginian position. Rome would likely mount a seaborne invasion of Spain to engage Hannibal's forces in that theater, thereby pinning him down while a second invasion, launched from Sicily, would fall on Carthage itself. With no way to interdict Roman transports at sea, the key to Hannibal's plan was to strike first. The strategic concept was to move a large army through northeastern Spain, skirt the Pyrenees along the coast, cross the Alps, and debouch on the northern Italian plain near the Po River. The shock of this deployment onto Italian soil might shake the Roman decision-making structure and paralyze Roman plans to move against Carthage. Any forces scheduled for deployment abroad would likely be shifted north to meet the invader.

The route of march (see Map 12.1) was difficult, but it had the advantage of making it equally difficult for Roman armies to interfere with it. The march over the Alps could be expected to take a heavy toll on Hannibal's army. With no possibility of reinforcement, Hannibal's plan required that he be able to recruit large numbers of Gallic tribesmen who lived on both sides of the Alps and as far south as the Po Valley itself. Given the long history of mutual hatred between the Gauls and the Romans and the frequency of slaughterous conflicts between the two antagonists, the use of advanced recruitment parties had a more than reasonable chance of replacing the Carthaginian manpower

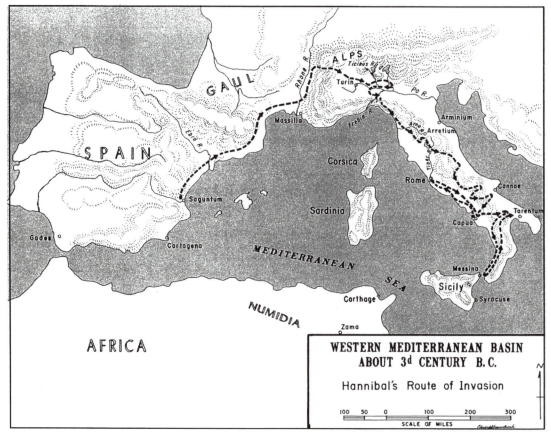

Map 12.1 Hannibal's Route of Invasion (Third Century B.C.E.). Courtesy of the U.S. Army War College.

losses incurred by Hannibal's passage of the Alps. If successful, Hannibal would succeed in placing a large and replenished army on the northern Italian plain before Rome could react. He would thus win the opening gambit.

Hannibal expected Rome to react quickly to any hostile force on its territory. The plan was to draw the Roman army far from its base in Rome, engage it as quickly as possible, and defeat it in a succession of military engagements. Hannibal knew that he would never have the manpower to defeat all the military resources of Rome. But if he could defeat the Roman army on its own soil, the Roman Senate might move toward a quick political settlement. If Rome was not quick to settle the conflict, Hannibal hoped to live off the land for as long as possible, courting Roman allied states with kind treatment and promises of freedom. Significant numbers of defections to the Carthaginian cause would deprive Rome of critical manpower assets and war supplies. More importantly, it would demoralize Roman will and confront Rome with the choice of a peace treaty or the risk of having its alliances come apart one at a time until the entire Roman dominion in Italy was threatened.

Whatever else happened, Hannibal's assessment of the comparative strength of the opposing forces made it vital that he not be drawn into a war of attrition. A series of bloody battles in which the Romans were defeated would mean nothing if the cost to his army was also high. If Rome was not stampeded into a quick settlement of the war through a series of battlefield defeats and political defections, it could recover its balance and mobilize its full strategic resources. Under these circumstances, Hannibal risked being isolated in Italy while Rome struck unhindered at Spain and Carthage. The risk was high that Carthage's political leaders might make peace to save what they could, and Hannibal and his army would become a strategic irrelevancy.

In summer 218 B.C.E. Hannibal put his plan into operation and began to move an army of 40,000 infantrymen, 8,000 cavalry, and 37 elephants over the Ebro River toward the Rhone Valley. Bypassing Massilia (modern Marseilles), Hannibal avoided Roman cavalry patrols and moved across southern Gaul. The crossing of the Alps was a brilliant and difficult maneuver. Once into Cisalpine Gaul, the tribes began to flock to his standard. By November, Hannibal had replenished his lost manpower and begun to search for the Roman field armies. The Roman reaction was almost as he had predicted. The army under Publius Scipio had moved to Massilia in late summer as a prelude to invading Spain. From here Scipio dispatched a force into Spain to restore Roman power north of the Ebro. Although the Carthaginians controlled the area south of the Ebro and the interior, Roman forces were generally successful, and within a year Hannibal's line of retreat and reinforcement from Spain were cut. Publius Scipio himself, however, returned to Rome to raise a new army to meet Hannibal on the northern Italian plain. The Roman army under Sempronius, poised in Sicily to invade Africa, abandoned its planned invasion and returned to Rome, where it linked up with Scipio's new army. By November, the Romans went hunting for Hannibal in Italy. They found him waiting on the banks of the Trebia River.

A study of the campaigns of Hannibal and Scipio during the Second Punic War (218–201 B.C.E.) has much to teach the student of the history of war. The Punic Wars can be regarded as the first in history to demonstrate one of the defining characteristics of modern war: strategic endurance. Prior to this time, wars were largely settled in one or two major battles in which the combatant states obtained or failed to obtain their strategic objectives. Battles between antagonists represented all-or-nothing affairs, and empires often changed shape and hands as the consequence of a single engagement. The Punic Wars, which together lasted more than forty years, saw the empire of Rome lose battle after battle without collapsing. Drawing on a larger pool of strategic resources than any other state in history until this time, Rome fought on until it achieved victory. Moreover, strategic endurance was demonstrated to be as much a consequence of political will and social organization as it was of material resources. Rome's eventual victory in the Punic Wars signaled a new era of international relations in which political will and the ability to marshal sufficient amounts of strategic resources in pursuit of military and political objectives became the defining characteristics of the imperial state.

THE CARTHAGINIAN ARMY

Our knowledge of the Carthaginian armies is limited. The destruction of Carthage at the hands of the Roman army at the conclusion of the Third Punic War was so complete that no Carthaginian records survived. Indeed, we do not even know what language they spoke. What we know of the Carthaginian armies comes from the accounts provided by their enemies, mostly Roman sources like Livy and Polybius. Carthage usually maintained no standing army at all, although it seems probable that there may have been a small band of citizens, about 1,500 men, permanently organized for military service. The fact that this force could not, by law, be deployed outside the *chora* of Carthage suggests that it may have been only a civil or praetorian guard. When arms were needed, the Carthaginians used their vast wealth to raise a mercenary force under the direction of Carthaginian commanders.

Infantry

Hannibal's army was comprised of the usual odd mixture of soldiers from many lands and cultures. The foot soldiers were mostly heavy infantry and came largely from Libya, Spain, and Gaul. The most loyal and talented of Hannibal's infantry were the citizens of Libya-Phoenicia, the only group subject by law to military service. Originally armed with the traditional weapons of the Greek hoplite, these units fought in the old phalanx formation. As the war wore on, they were equipped with captured Roman weapons and gradually adopted Roman tactics.

Hannibal's Spanish infantry was recruited from the Iberian tribes and included both heavy and light infantry. The heavy infantry carried the thrown javelin (akin to the Roman *pilum*) but relied mostly upon the Spanish sword, the *falcata*. Made of fine Spanish steel and stronger and wider than the Roman *antennae* sword of the period, its main features were adopted by the Romans and incorporated into the famed Roman *gladius* during the war with Hannibal. Spanish heavy infantry used the scale, lamellar, or chain mail of the day, the latter an innovation of the Celts and standard issue in the Roman armies of the period. Spanish heavy infantrymen were strong and courageous fighters and were every bit the match for Roman infantry. Spanish light infantry was armed with the standard kit of darts, javelins, light wooden shields, and slings. Some of the light infantry in Hannibal's army was comprised of Balaeric slingers who carried two slings, one for long distance and one for short. The long-range sling could fire a stone the size of a tennis ball almost 300 yards. These slingers were the finest in the ancient world, and for almost 600 years one army after another hired Balaeric slingers as mercenaries.

Hannibal recruited large cohorts of Celtic infantry from the Gallic tribes north of the Po River. Organized into clans, these tribal warriors lived for war, glory, and plunder. They used the sword as a basic weapon, wore no armor, and sometimes fought stark naked as they charged in wild groups into the enemy formations. They were incapable of any field discipline or maneuver. Hannibal often used them as shock troops to strike the enemy center before committing his cavalry. This, of course, produced heavy casualties, but they were generally expendable in any case. Their poor-quality weapons were gradually replaced from captured Roman stocks. Completing the Carthaginian mixture of forces were various African tribes, many heavily tattooed, carrying all sorts of various tribal, hunting, and agricultural implements.

Cavalry

Hannibal's cavalry was no less a mixed bag. There was a small number of elite heavy cavalry probably comprised of professional warriors drawn from Carthage itself. Additional contingents came from the upper classes of Libya-Phoenicia. The Spanish contributed the greatest numbers of heavy cavalry, armed with buckler-shield, a long and short lance, short sword, mail armor, helmet, and greaves. Reflecting their tribal origins, Spanish cavalry sometimes carried an extra infantryman aboard who dismounted into the enemy formations. The best and most reliable cavalry were the Numidian light cavalry. Sometimes enemies of Carthage, sometimes serving out of common interests, but mostly paid mercenaries, these units came from Numidia, approximately the area of present-day Morocco. They rode bareback and carried short javelins, lances, and swords. Normally armed with a shield, they sometimes wore a leopard skin over their arms in place of the shield. They were specialists

383

in maneuver warfare, often attacking, retreating, maneuvering, and attacking again at a different place on the battlefield.

Hannibal also took along thirty-seven elephants as he crossed the Alps. As an instrument of war the elephant has a long and generally unimpressive history. Alexander first encountered them in his wars against the Persians, who probably obtained them from the Indians. During the wars of Alexander's successors (the *Diadochi*), the use of the elephant in war became common among the armies of the Mediterranean area. The Carthaginians encountered the elephant in their war with Greece and took to capturing and training the smaller African elephant for their own armies.

The elephant was an important combat asset. It frightened those armies who had never seen them. For example, in the reign of Claudius, the Romans took them to Britain to impress and intimidate the local chieftains. Unless a horse had been trained around them, elephants easily spooked the cavalry mounts of the enemy. Under the control of their handlers (*mahouts*), a charge of rampaging elephants against an infantry formation could have tremendous shock effect. Elephants were used in Persia and India as platforms for archers and javelin throwers. They were also used to anchor the center or ends of infantry lines, and their height was sufficient to use them as a screen behind which to shift cavalry units.

Like all implements of war, however, the elephant came equipped from the factory with built-in disadvantages. Experienced light infantry skirmishers could meet the elephants in advance of the infantry line and hit them with darts, swords, and javelins, wounding them into a rage. Once enraged, the elephant became uncontrollable, and it had a tendency to turn back in the direction from which it came, running over the very formations that had launched it. Out of control, elephants rumbled around the battlefield, disrupting everyone's plans. To prevent this, the *mahouts* carried a large iron spike and a hammer. If the elephant could not be brought under control by normal means, the *mahout* drove the spike into the elephant's brain, killing it instantly! Another favorite defensive tactic was to move behind the elephant and cut its hamstring tendon. Once dealt with in either manner, this expensive piece of battlefield equipment had to be abandoned, since repair was impossible with existing technology.

In light of all this, it is interesting to ponder why Hannibal took elephants along on such a difficult march. Certainly the Romans were thoroughly familiar with the elephant and knew how to deal with it. The Romans had first been routed by an elephant charge in 280 B.C.E. during the war with Pyrrhus. Five years later at the battle of Beneventum, the Romans killed two and captured eight of the elephants deployed against them. Although the elephant was an expensive and prestigious weapon, the elephant represented no military advantage against the legions. Most probably Hannibal used them as instruments of propaganda. They were taken along to impress the Gauls and convince them to join Hannibal in his campaign. It is also possible that displaying them before Roman allied towns was designed to convince the inhabitants that Hannibal's army was a modern fighting force bent on serious business, and that it would be in their interest to join him.

Tactics

The Carthaginian armies of Hannibal's campaigns were such a mixture of groups, weapons, and even languages that they could not be disciplined to a standard set of tactics. It is testimony to the brilliance of Carthaginian commanders that for more than a century they were able to field these kinds of armies and still be very effective in battle. Carthaginian field commanders were known for their personal bravery and courage, traits that endeared them to tribal and clan units. They could also be ruthless in disciplining their troops with beatings and death sentences if they did not perform well. This behavior is hardly surprising among an officer corps well acquainted with seeing their comrades who failed in battle crucified in the public square of Carthage! Truly the soldiers of the Carthaginian armies often had more to fear from their commanders than from the enemy.

The nature of the Carthaginian armies made any standard tactical system impossible. Instead, the tactical brilliance of Hannibal and previous Carthaginian commanders lay in their ability to employ various types of units creatively in a given battle situation to obtain maximum collective effect. At the same time, the battlefield tapestry still had to be woven into some sort of tactical whole if victory was to be achieved. This was no easy task, and modern commanders might well ponder the difficulties involved.

Still, Hannibal placed most reliance upon cavalry as his arm of decision, with infantry used as a platform for maneuver or as shock troops. This development is hardly surprising. In the first place, close contacts with the Greeks in the eastern Mediterranean made the Carthaginians thoroughly familiar with Alexander's military system, one that also used cavalry as the arm of decision and infantry as a platform of maneuver. Second, Numidia bordered Libya-Phoenicia, and Carthage had to defend Libya and its valued grain crop frequently against the lightning raids of Numidian cavalry. The size of the border made fixed fortifications expensive and impractical against the nomadic Numidians. Thus, Carthage developed its own indigenous cavalry force to deal with the problem. One consequence was the development of a tactical doctrine that stressed the use of the horse over infantry, exactly the reverse of the Romans. Taken together, Hannibal's armies were fragile entities subject to a lack of discipline and fragmentation if events got beyond the control of their commanders. The brilliant Hannibal never let this happen.

THE ROMAN ARMY

An analysis of the Roman military system that Hannibal faced is a study in contrasts. The traditional Roman military formation from the time of the

Figure 12.4 Roman Legionnaire

Republic's founding (circa 500 B.C.E.) was essentially modeled on the Greek hoplite phalanx. The weaponry of the Roman citizen-soldier was also essentially Greek, as were the short spear, round shield, helmet, armor, greaves, and sword. In the usual case of set-piece battles on level ground against armies using similar formations, the phalanx worked well enough. However, in uneven terrain, the phalanx could not maneuver. In the wars against the Samnites (340–290 B.C.E.), fought in the rugged Appenine hills, valleys, and glens, the phalanx proved unworkable and terribly brittle to surprise attack. Moreover, the wars with the wild Gauls demonstrated how easy it was for the highly mobile formations of the Gallic armies to envelop the open flanks of the phalanx and crush it from all sides once the cavalry was driven from the field. Given that Roman cavalry was never very good, driving it from the field prior to surrounding the phalanx was not usually very difficult.

Tactical Organization

The basic tactical unit of the new Roman army was the maniple (literally, "handfuls of men"), somewhat equivalent to the modern infantry company, with a strength of 120 men. Each maniple was divided vertically into two centuries equivalent to platoons of sixty to eighty men each. Originally, the centuries had been comprised of a hundred men, but the number proved too large to be controlled effectively by a single centurion. The number was reduced to eighty, although the name "century," meaning "one hundred," was retained.

It was during and after the Samnite wars that the phalanx legion had been gradually replaced by the manipular legion. Also during this war the Romans replaced their heavy Argive-type shields with the larger but lighter wooden *scutum* shield. The Romans also adopted the famous *pilum* from the Samnites. Both pieces of equipment remained standard Roman issue until the end of the imperial period. The manipular legion was the basic fighting formation of the Roman army throughout the Punic Wars; however, Scipio Africanus, son of Publius Scipio, found that the new legion was sometimes too fragile against the massed attacks of Hannibal's heavy Spanish infantry. Gradually, he strengthened the maniples, increasing their numbers to 600 men. These new *cohorts* gradually replaced the maniples until, around 100 B.C.E., the Romans adopted the cohortal legion as their basic fighting formation. Ten *cohorts* comprised a legion of 6,000 men.

The Roman army was also reorganized on the basis of age. The youngest, most agile, and least trained men (*velites*) served as light infantry. Armed with

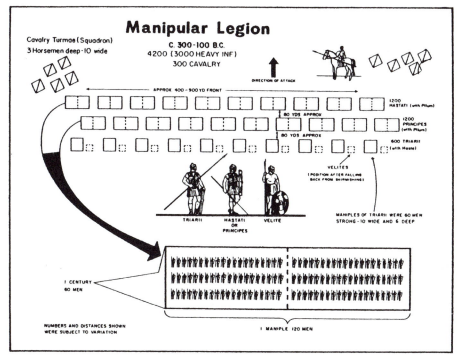

Figure 12.5 The Manipular Legion. Courtesy of the U.S. Army War College.

darts and small javelins, they acted as skirmishers. The front line of the legion was occupied by a second class of men, the *hastati*, who were somewhat older and more experienced. Armed with the sword, two *pila*, and the *scutum* shield, they formed the first line of heavy infantry. The center line was comprised of the best and most experienced veterans (*principes*). Averaging thirty years of age, these were the battle-hardened veterans. The third line was comprised of older men (*triarii*) and constituted the last line of resistance. Armed with the long spear, they lent stability to the formation and, in times of retreat, remained in place and covered the passage of the other ranks through their lines.

Tactics

The key to the flexibility of the legion lay in the relationship between the maniples within each line and between the lines of heavy infantry. Each maniple deployed as a small independent phalanx with a twenty-man front and a six-man depth. The spacing between each soldier allowed independent movement and fighting room within an area of five square yards. Each maniple was laterally separated from the next by twenty yards, a distance equal to the frontage of the maniple itself. In line, the maniples were staggered, with the second and third lines covering the gaps in the lines to their front.

Each line of infantry was separated from the next by an interval of one hundred yards. The result was the *quincunx* or checkerboard formation that permitted maximum flexibility for each maniple and for each soldier within it.

Flexibility was increased by the relationship between the lines of infantry. If, after the first line engaged, it was unable to break the enemy formation or grew tired, it could retire in good order through the gaps left in the second line. The second line then moved to the front and continued to press the attack, while the first rank rested and regrouped. This maneuver could be repeated several times, with the effect that the Roman front line was always comprised of rested fighting men. This was an important advantage. Modern studies demonstrate that men engaged in phalanx close combat could sustain the effort no more than thirty minutes (if that!) before collapsing from exhaustion. The *triarii* remained in place in the last rank, resting on one knee with their spears angled upwards. The *triarii* represented the organic reserve for the legion to be employed at the commander's will.

The ability to pass through the lines of infantry in planned fashion offered another advantage. In most armies of the period, defeat in the front ranks often turned a battle into a rout. Until the Romans, no army had learned how to break contact and conduct a tactical retreat in good order. The manipular formation solved the problem. Upon command, the first line of infantry formed into close-order maniples, turned, and withdrew to the rear through the gaps left in the other two lines. The second rank followed. The *triarii* covered the retreat with their spears, and the *velite* light infantry deployed to the front to engage the enemy while the main body withdrew in good order. The ability to conduct an ordered retreat represented a major revolution in infantry tactics.

Tactical flexibility was further enhanced by the ability of each maniple to fight and maneuver independently. This flexibility allowed Roman commanders to make maximum use of the element of surprise. It was not unusual for a commander to position a few spare maniples in hidden positions, often at the flanks, or even attempt to insert them to the rear of the enemy position. Once the main forces were engaged, these maniples could be brought into action, surprising the enemy with an attack from an entirely unexpected direction. Often the sight of a few maniples marching on the main force from an unexpected direction was sufficient to cause the enemy to break. The capability provided the legions of Rome with a new tactical dimension of ground warfare.

The Roman soldier was the first soldier in history to fight within a combat formation while at the same time remaining somewhat independent of its movements as a unit. He was also the first soldier to rely primarily upon the sword instead of the spear. The Roman sword of this period was a short, slashing sword of Italian origin (*antennae* sword). During the Punic Wars, the legions gradually adopted the famous *gladius*, a short sword incorporating many of the features of the Spanish *falcata*. The *gladius* was twenty inches long and approximately three inches wide and was made of tough Spanish steel that held a fine edge and narrow point. It was stronger in composition than any existing sword and, because it would not bend or break, provided a psychological advantage to the Roman soldier. To use it well required skill and a high level of training. The Roman army introduced military training programs in the use of the *gladius*, and in 100 C.E., the army was still being trained in the same methods used in the famous Roman gladiatorial schools.

The *gladius* was primarily a stabbing weapon, and Roman soldiers were trained not to use it as a slashing weapon, the common method of sword use in most armies of the day. The shield parry, followed by a sharp underthrust to the chest, became the killing trademark of the Roman infantry. In the hands of the disciplined Roman soldier, the *gladius* became the most destructive weapon of all time prior to the invention of the firearm. If the phalanx formations of past armies armed with the spear can be described as resembling spiked pincushions, then the Roman legion, with its reliance upon the *gladius*, resembled a buzz-saw.

A legion had the strength of approximately 5,000 men and usually deployed with an allied counterpart of the same size and generally the same organization. The allied legion usually had a heavier cavalry section of approximately 600 horses, the Roman legion commonly possessing only 300 horses. Deployed, the combined legions numbered 9,000 to 10,0000 men. Two Roman legions and two allied legions under the same command comprised a consular army of 20,000 men and deployed across a combat front of 1.5 miles.

The legion commander had a staff of professional officers who handled administrative, supply, medical, veterinary, and training matters. Combat command rested in the hands of six senior tribunes, two for each infantry line. Below them were the combat unit commanders of the maniples—sixty centurions, two for each maniple. The real combat leadership was provided by the centurions. Promotion of centurions through the ranks was based on demonstrated bravery and competence. The most noble soldiers of Rome were the First Centurions (*primus pilum*, literally "the first spear") of the legions, and, until the end of the empire, they remained the best combat commanders the nation could field.

The Roman legion had two significant weaknesses, and Hannibal exploited them both time and time again. The first was the lack of a professional senior officer corps. Roman senior officers were civilians, often state officials or politicians appointed to command the legions during time of war. Worse, this counselor system required that the same army have *two* appointed senior commanders who rotated command each day. Despite the best military organization in the ancient world, the practice of divided command often made it difficult for the legions to maintain good command direction. Moreover, changing senior commanders on a daily basis made it impossible for the army to become the instrument of a single commander's will. Hannibal studied his adversaries in detail, and he frequently chose the time of battle to coincide with the daily command of a specific adversary, always to Hannibal's advantage.

The second weakness of the Roman armies was the terrible quality of its cavalry. Like the Greeks, the Romans regarded service in the cavalry as little better than tending animals. The best soldiers from the best families refused to serve in the cavalry, and it was the most poorly trained of the combat arms. Even through the Punic Wars Roman cavalry often retained the old habit of using their mounts to arrive at the battlefield, only to dismount and join the fray as infantry. Roman cavalry seemed ill-suited to maintain the direction of the charge and showed a tendency to break up into small clusters of loose formations and wander all over the battlefield. They used no special armament, preferring instead to carry the weapons of the infantry. Hannibal's arm of decision, on the other hand, was superbly trained cavalry, and in battle after battle he drove the Roman cavalry from the field, turned, and massacred the Roman infantry. Eventually the Romans gave up trying to develop cavalry and simply hired it from allied units.

The new Roman armies had to learn two additional lessons before they could deal with Hannibal. Roman units usually did not provide for camp security. During the wars against Pyrrhus and the Gauls, the Romans were often caught in morning or evening surprise attacks while in camp. The solution was to construct the famous Roman fortified camp every evening. A fortified encampment not only prevented surprise attacks but provided the Roman commander with the tactical option of attacking from the base camp or using it as a defensive redoubt. The Romans were also slow to learn the need for security on the march, and in the early battles against Hannibal, they were often surprised while still in column. Hannibal's penchant for appearing from nowhere eventually led the Romans to stress the value of tactical intelligence. Later, under the empire, Roman tactical intelligence capabilities reach the state of a high art.

Just as the organizational structures of the Carthaginian and Roman armies were vastly different, so were the tactical dynamics of their combat units. The Roman arm of decision was its heavy infantry, and Roman tactics centered upon using the infantry for "simple bludgeon work." The idea was to commit the infantry to the center of the line and let it hack away until the center of the enemy formation broke. Given adequate room to stab with their swords, and if organizational integrity was maintained, the Roman infantry would eventually hack its way through any infantry formation in the world.

Against the open formations of the Gauls, the fighting was often man to man. But whereas the Gaul and other tribal soldiers fought as individuals, the Roman soldier could depend on the man to his left or right for help if he was not otherwise engaged. Against the Macedonian phalanx formation with its long spears, the Romans simply hacked off the spearpoints and moved inside the spear shafts to close with the enemy. Once the Romans were inside the phalanx, the individual Macedonian spearman was helpless, and the Roman buzz-saw did its deadly work. Since Hannibal often used Gallic units in open formations as shock troops in the center of the line and

Spanish infantry arrayed in traditional phalanx formation, the Romans almost always had the advantage in the heavy fighting at the center of the line.

As previously mentioned, unlike Gallic and Spanish swordsmen, the Roman soldier was trained to stab and not slash with his weapon. The legionnaire was trained to engage the man not directly in front of him but the opponent to his immediate right. Using the sword as a slashing weapon required the soldier to raise it above his head and away from his body, exposing the whole right side of his body as a target. The shield, held in the left hand, became useless as a protective device. Training the Roman soldier to strike to his right thus allowed him to cut down the enemy soldier while simultaneously raising his shield against the opponent directly to his front. Interestingly, the British army at the battle of Culloden Moor rediscovered this technique after being hacked to pieces in two successive battles by the warriors of the Highland Scottish clans. Instead of the sword, however, the British infantry employed the bayonet.

Stabbing to the right provided yet another tactical advantage in close combat. Having struck a target to his right, the Roman infantryman stepped back to pull out the sword. As he did, he moved slightly to his right to get new footing for the next assault. As a result, the Roman line tended to move to the right and slightly to the rear. This forced the enemy line to move to the left and forward, having to step over the bodies of the dead and wounded. The dynamics of the two lines resulted in the Roman soldier always being prepared to meet the next opponent, who had to stumble over the dead while watching his footing. Hannibal eliminated this Roman tactical advantage when, at the battle of Cannae, he placed his troops on a slight rise, forcing the Romans to attack uphill as his infantry gradually fell back.

A typical Roman battle opened with light infantry skirmishing in front with darts, javelins, and slings. As the lines closed, the skirmishers fell back through the gaps in the checkerboard and were usually never used again. When both lines were within range, about twenty-five yards, the front rank threw its *pila* and rushed to close the gap quickly, smashing into the enemy front. The Roman lines would fight, retire, and reenter the battle until the enemy center broke and the slaughter could begin. The flanks were anchored by the cavalry, always a risky business unless it was hired from a reliable ally. The combat strength of the legion lay in its tactical flexibility and the determination, courage, and training of its heavy infantry.

As already noted, the mix of Carthaginian armies made it impossible for Hannibal to develop a standard tactical system. The trick was to use the various types of units in a manner that maximized the effectiveness of each, while sustaining an overall tactical plan specific to each battle situation. It is possible, however, to discern some "tactical constants" or general rules that apparently governed Hannibal's battle tactics. The first of these rules was always to maximize shock and surprise. Hannibal frequently engaged while the enemy was still deployed in column of march. Another rule was to engage only after the enemy was made to work hard to transit some obstacle like a river, stream, or forest. A third rule was to use the terrain and always tempt the enemy to fight uphill. Hannibal often anchored his lines of infantry with heavy formations of phalanx infantry that could swing against the pivot points of an extended infantry line, forcing the enemy into a smaller and smaller area. Cavalry tactics centered around Hannibal's consistent use of his horsemen to drive the enemy cavalry from the field as a prelude to its returning and staging a shock attack against the rear or flanks of the enemy infantry. Above all, if Hannibal secured none of these advantages, he avoided battle. If he could not fight on his own terms, he would not fight and conserved his limited manpower for another day.

THE BATTLE OF THE TREBIA RIVER (218 B.C.E.)

The Roman hunt for Hannibal began in earnest in November 218 B.C.E. Publius Scipio had failed to catch Hannibal north of Marseilles that summer and now took command of a new army at Pisa and moved north into the Po Valley. Already across the Po, he was marching east along the river as Hannibal was moving his army down from the foothills into the valley. Probably by accident, the two armies met on the banks of the Ticinus, a northern tributary of the Po. Hannibal struck the Roman army while it was still in line of march. After a brief but heavy skirmish in which Scipio was wounded and his cavalry destroyed, the Romans retreated behind the Po to wait for Sempronius's army to link up with them. Hannibal broke contact and disappeared.

Hannibal made no effort to interfere with the uniting of the Roman armies. If he was to extract the maximum political effect from a Roman defeat, the larger the Roman force he could destroy the better. Moreover, with Scipio wounded—legend has it that he was saved by his teenaged son, later to gain fame as Scipio Africanus—Hannibal knew that Sempronius would be in command of the consular army; and Sempronius was an impetuous man. The trick was to draw Sempronius into battle under unfavorable conditions.

Polybius, himself a former general and a Roman historian of the Punic Wars, noted that Hannibal chose "a place between the two camps, flat indeed and treeless, but well adapted for an ambuscade, as it was traversed by a watercourse with steep banks densely overgrown with brambles and other thorny plants, and here he proposed to lay a stratagem to surprise the enemy." Hannibal chose his youngest brother, Mago, a dashing and sometimes reckless cavalry commander, to set the trap. Under cover of night an elite force of 2,000 cavalry and infantry occupied the banks of the stream and concealed their weapons. The experienced cavalry mounts had been trained to lay prone upon command. As dawn broke, the view from the Roman camp over the Trebbia River was clear of enemy troops.

Hannibal's next step was to provoke Sempronius into attacking. Shortly before dawn, several thousand of Hannibal's cavalry attacked the Roman camp, penetrating the encampment from all sides, wheeling about, and striking again and again. Roman officers drove the troops from their sleep, hastily forming them into battle lines. Having awakened the camp, the Numidians withdrew, seeking to draw the Romans after them to a precise spot chosen by Hannibal. Hannibal's main force was several miles away. Sempronius took the bait.

The Roman commander hastily assembled his legion. Cold and wet after a night of soaking rain, and without breakfast, the Roman army moved out across the sodden plain. Between them and Hannibal was the swollen Trebia River running swiftly in the cold, gray November dawn. It began to snow. Hannibal's troops were huddled around their campfires. Having consumed a hearty breakfast, they covered their bodies with oil as protection against the snow and sleet. Hannibal had chosen the place of battle, the sloping ground on the Carthaginian side of the Trebia. If the Romans wanted a fight, they would first have to cross the river. Once they did, they would have Mago, still hidden from sight, at their backs.

Sempronius ordered his troops to wade across the river. An army of 40,000 slowly made their way into the cold waters and up the sloping ground on the other side. The Roman army was comprised of 16,000 Roman infantry, 20,000 allied infantry, and 4,000 cavalry protecting the wings in typical Roman battle formation. Arrayed in the long Carthaginian battle line were 20,000 Celts, Africans, and Spanish infantry, and 10,000 cavalry deployed to anchor the wings. In front of the regular force were the light infantry skirmishers. The elephants were positioned in front of each cavalry wing to help protect the Carthaginian flanks. The battle began with the usual Roman attack in the center.

As the Romans pressed the center, Hannibal struck with his cavalry directly at the Roman cavalry formations protecting the Roman flanks. Outnumbered almost two to one, the Roman cavalry gradually gave ground, exposing the flanks of the Roman infantry. As the infantry battle raged in the center with neither side giving much ground, the Numidian cavalry broke contact with the Roman cavalry, leaving them in disarray, and wheeled to attack the flanks of the Roman infantry. With the Romans pressed in the center and on the flanks, Mago, waiting in ambush with his men and horses below the banks of the stream, struck the Roman rear. (Map 12.2 portrays the key elements of the battle.)

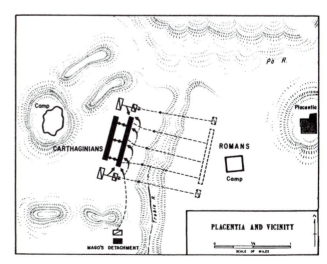

Map 12.2 Battle of Trebia (218 B.C.E.). Courtesy of the U.S. Army War College.

Each of Mago's 1,000 cavalry riders carried with him on his horse a single infantryman. As the cavalry struck the Roman rear, the infantry jumped from their horses and waded into the battle. The cavalry continued to fight on horseback. With the Roman flanks already perilously close to collapse, the shock and surprise of the new assault from yet another direction broke the Roman battle formation. A rout commenced, and the pursuing Carthaginians slaughtered thousands. Many more drowned attempting to recross the Trebia, seeking the safety of the Roman camp. Only the Roman center held. Unable to retreat and pressed from both flanks, the Roman units continued to cut their way through the Carthaginians. Punching through at last, they continued forward in good order, protecting their rear until they reached a nearby Roman fortress town. The rest of the Roman army was destroyed. Of the 40,000 Roman troops committed that day, fewer than 10,000 reached safety. Hannibal had drawn first blood.

THE BATTLE OF TRASIMENE (217 B.C.E.)

The defeat at the Trebia was met with the usual Roman *gravitas* (seriousness), and the response was immediate. Four new legions were raised, new commanders chosen, and the fresh troops deployed to block any further southern movement by Hannibal. A Roman army under Flaminius was sent to Arretium (modern Arezzo) on the western flank of the Apennines to block the road to Tuscany, and another force under Servilius Germinus positioned at Arminium (modern Rimini) to block the eastern road. It was winter, and no one expected that Hannibal would attempt to move his army over the Apennines in the harsh weather. Hannibal tried exactly that, but the harsh conditions forced him back, and his army went into winter quarters with the Gauls.

Springtime found the Roman armies still in position to block Hannibal's route to the south. Hannibal moved his army between the two blocked routes, choosing to move through the marshes of the lower Arno River valley. A number of troops and animals were lost in the difficult crossing, and Hannibal himself contracted an eye disease—probably ophthalmia—that cost him his sight in one eye. By early spring, however, Hannibal had slipped between the blockading Roman forces and moved his army into the rich agricultural area of Tuscany. If the Romans wanted to do battle, they would have to chase and catch Hannibal.

As usual, Hannibal closely studied his adversary, Flaminius, and—as both Polybius and Livy note—knew his reputation as a man given to anger and impetuous acts. The trick, then, was to irritate Flaminius and provoke him into a foolish move. As Hannibal approached Tuscany, he deliberately passed within sight of the Roman army at Arezzo but did not pause to fight. Instead, he began to ravage the countryside, burning crops, towns, and villages and slaughtering livestock. This was a calculated policy. Hannibal knew that the devastation of the lands of a Roman ally was a signal to other allies that Rome could not protect them. Perhaps they would see it to their advantage to join the ranks of the successful invader. Day after day Flaminius watched smoke rise over the fertile plains as Hannibal's army torched the countryside. Finally, unable to contain his anger any longer, Flaminius marched out of Arretium in search of Hannibal's army. He had taken the bait.

Hannibal's route took him through the small village of Passignano along the road that skirted the northern shore of Lake Trasimene. Beyond the village the terrain narrowed into a defile, with the lakeshore on one side and tall cliffs on the other. Beyond the narrow passageway the terrain opened up into a narrow valley with hills on one side and the lake on the other side. Straight ahead the road ran up a steep hill at the far end of the valley. As Hannibal moved his army over this route, he noticed that thick morning lake fog made visibility very difficult. Hannibal moved his army to the top of the hill at the valley's end and pitched camp. He waited for Flaminius.

Flaminius moved his army into the village of Passignano. His analysis of the terrain made him wary of an ambush in the narrow defile, but he concluded that the hills were too steep to conceal any large number of men. He camped for the night but failed to send reconnaissance parties into the valley. Flaminius assumed Hannibal was moving away from him, and his goal was to catch him on the line of march, engage his rearguard, defeat it, and then attack the main body before it could turn and face the Roman assault.

At dawn the next day, Flaminius moved his army through the narrow defile onto the widening plain. The thick morning mist from the lake made visibility to the right and left difficult. Straight ahead and above the mist, however, Flaminius could see Hannibal's encampment on the hill at the valley's exit. It was the rearguard of Hannibal's army, and he ordered his vanguard to assume battle formation and move quickly to engage it. With the rest of the Roman column still in line of march, 6,000 Roman legionnaires rushed up the hill to engage Hannibal's forces. At last it appeared that Hannibal had been taken by surprise.

At the top of the hill the Carthaginians turned and met the Roman charge. The fighting was furious, according to Livy, but gradually the Carthaginians gave ground, turned, and ran. The Roman advanced guard, seeking the main body of Hannibal's army, marched off in disciplined pursuit of the fleeing Carthaginians. On the valley floor Flaminius's army was now entirely through the narrow defile, its head moving up the hill at the valley's exit. The gap between the Roman advanced guard and the rest of the army had grown as the Roman units pursued the fleeing Carthaginians. Hannibal then sprang the trap.

Map 12.3 shows the disposition of the Carthaginian and Roman forces prior to the attack. Always a bold and lucky gambler, Hannibal had bet that, on the morning of the battle, the lake would produce its usual early morning fog to cover the deployment of his troops in ambush. The night before Hannibal had positioned 30,000 men on the flank of the Roman line of march. The force on the hill that Flaminius's vanguard had engaged was a ruse designed

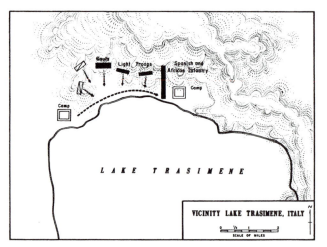

Map 12.3 Battle of Trasimene: Hannibal's Ambush (217 B.C.E.). Courtesy of the U.S. Army War College

to convince Flaminius that Hannibal's army was straight ahead in column of march, when in fact the bulk of the forces were hidden in the fog on the Roman flank. Polybius notes that the morning stillness was broken by the sound of three trumpet blasts to signal the attack. At the precise moment of greatest Roman vulnerability, Hannibal's army struck the Roman flank in overwhelming force.

The Spanish and African heavy infantry smashed into the front of the Roman column at an acute angle, while the light infantry struck the center. Within minutes the Celts and Spanish were within the Roman column, hacking from the inside. Then the Numidian cavalry smashed into the rear of the column with terrific force. The surprise was total, and the Roman units could not form their battle formations to meet the attack. Livy described the confusion thus: "Chance collected them (the Romans) into bands; and each man's own will assigned him his post; whether to fight in front or rear." The Numidian cavalry had made retreat along the road impossible. The lake precluded any depth to withdraw and form units for battle. It was a wild melee, the kind at which the Celts and Spanish infantry excelled.

In little less than an hour and a half, the Roman force was slaughtered. Flaminius himself, although he fought bravely, was struck by the lance of a Gallic cavalryman and killed. Far to the front the Roman advanced guard found itself alone as the Carthaginian forces they had been pursuing melted away into the hills. Turning back toward the valley, they came over the hill to see 15,000 Roman legionnaires lying dead on the ground. Carthaginan soldiers were stripping the dead of their weapons and armor. On the lakeshore, the cavalry was cutting down the remnants of the Roman infantry that had tried to flee into the water. Hannibal had killed 15,000 Roman soldiers at a cost of only 1,500 of his own men, a ratio of ten to one! The Roman advanced guard had finally found the main body of Hannibal's army but could only watch helplessly as it formed up and marched out of the valley. Hannibal had destroyed yet another Roman army.

THE BATTLE OF CANNAE (216 B.C.E.)

In less than two years Hannibal had met the best of the Roman legions and dealt them three catastrophic defeats. Tincius had cost the Romans upward of 2,000 men. The engagement at the Trebia destroyed 30,000 Roman and allied soldiers. And now, at Trasimene, Hannibal had killed 15,000 more Roman troops and taken the life of a major Roman commander. The Roman relief force that came late to the battle of Lake Trasimene had also been ambushed at a cost of 4,000 more men. Hannibal inflicted 50,000 Roman casualties in two years, a number equal to ten legions! Worse, with Flaminius's force destroyed and Servilius's army still at Arminium on the Adriatic coast, the road to Rome was open. If he wished, Hannibal could strike at the capital almost at will.

Rome was in mourning as news of the defeat reached the citizenry. The Senate understood that the city itself was in danger, and, according to Polybius, "abandoning therefore the system of government by magistrates elected annually, they decided to deal with the present situation more radically." Rome put the safety of its city in the hands of a dictator, Quintius Fabius, a competent general of keen intellect. Rome could afford no more rash commanders who squandered armies.

Fabius's brilliance was evident in his strategic assessment of the problem. He knew that Rome's superior manpower, naval, and economic resources would, in the end, carry the day against any opponent. Time worked to Rome's advantage, not to Hannibal's. The real threat was to the Roman resource base, and this depended heavily upon Rome being able to maintain the loyalty of its colonies and allies on the Italian mainland. Despite the quick succession of Roman defeats, not a single ally had gone over to the enemy. More Carthaginian victories, however, might tempt them to defect. The strategic objective, therefore, was not military at all, but political. Roman military forces had to be used in such a way as to maintain the loyalty of its allies. Sooner or later, Roman arms and naval power would destroy the Carthaginian base in Spain and make an attack against Carthage itself possible. Fabius's military strategy, then, was not aimed at destroying Hannibal but at containing him and keeping him on the move. Should an ally defect, Rome had the military capacity to punish it severely as an example to others who might be similarly tempted. Fabius had correctly discerned the key to Hannibal's strategy, which depended ultimately upon securing the defection of Roman allies. It was to foster this political objective that Hannibal allowed the allied soldiers at Trasimene and Trebia to go free and return to their homes.

The Senate authorized a new army of eight legions, accompanied by a similar number of allied contingents, the largest army Rome had ever put in the field. The total force was almost 90,000 men. Hannibal himself had scarcely 50,000. Under Fabius's direction, the defenses of Rome itself were strengthened. Next, he marched his army from the city and found Hannibal. For almost six months, Fabius followed in Hannibal's route of march, keeping to the high ground and always maintaining contact with the enemy. On several occasions Hannibal attempted to draw Fabius into a battle, but he never succeeded. While the Roman army had secure logistics lines, Hannibal had to forage continually for food and supplies. Occasionally, Fabius would trap and fight these foraging detachments to harass the Carthaginians, but he refused to fight Hannibal's main force. Hannibal's army was now encumbered with thousands of prisoners, cattle herds, and war booty, all of which slowed its rate of movement. Still, Hannibal continued to woo the allies. A favorite tactic was to occupy a small town or estate, identify the Romans, and kill all the Roman men of military age while carrying off their wives and children. The allied population was left alone. But the populations of the allied towns knew the Roman army was not far away. They also knew that, if they defected to Hannibal, once his army moved on the Romans would extract a terrible revenge. Rome continued to win the political battle for the hearts and minds of the allied population.

Fabius's strategy was effective, but like all strategies it ultimately depended on the maintenance of the political will of the Senate and Roman people. But political will was difficult to maintain in a social order that was accustomed to destroying its enemies by quick decisive victories. For his efforts Fabius earned the nickname *Cunctator*, meaning "The Delayer," and it was not always used affectionately in the Senate. Ultimately, he would win the name Fabius Maximus (the Greatest), and his method of delay passed into military history under the name of Fabian strategy, a strategy employed with great success by the Russians against both Napoleon and Hitler.

After six months, Fabius's term as dictator expired, and he dutifully resigned his post. Senatorial politics dominated the choice of a successor, and a popular faction rose to power on a platform of confronting Hannibal militarily. The Senate abandoned dictatorial rule and reverted to the traditional Roman system of divided military command. The elections produced two new consuls to lead the army, L. Aemilius Paulus and C. Terentius Varro. Varro, the son of a butcher, was no more talented than Rome's previous commanders who had sought to defeat Hannibal. Like them, he was hotheaded and given to taking things personally. As summer approached, Hannibal moved from his base in Apulia and attacked a small Roman garrison at the town of Cannae. His goal, as it had been for more than a year, was to provoke the Roman army into a fight. With Fabius gone, Varro obliged. On August 2, 216 B.C.E., the armies met in southeastern Italy at the battle of Cannae.

Shortly after sunrise, Varro moved his army across from the Carthaginian camp and took up a position with the Aufidus River on his right flank. Varro's army comprised nearly 80,000 Roman and allied foot and 6,000 horse. Hannibal's army numbered 35,000 infantry, 11,000 horse, and a few thousand light infantry, skirmishers, and slingers. The Roman right was anchored by the legion's cavalry under the command of the co-consul, Aemilius. The left wing was comprised of 4,000 allied cavalry. The Roman center, comprised of infantry, arranged itself in double formation. The maniples arranged themselves with a smaller front, but with many more ranks deep. Never an imaginative tactician, Varro intended to perform the traditional Roman "bludgeon work" and cut straight through the Carthaginian center. It was almost as if the enemy cavalry did not exist.

Hannibal formed up opposite the Roman mass. In front of the Roman cavalry on the right wing he placed his Spanish and Celtic heavy cavalry, some 7,000 strong. Opposite the legion cavalry on the Roman left were 4,000 Numidian horsemen. In the direct center of the line Hannibal deployed his weakest troops, Celtic and Spanish light infantry. Anchoring the ends of the infantry line were large phalanxes of heavy African infantry. After forming his infantry in a straight line, Hannibal redeployed his center units outward facing the Roman center. The Car-

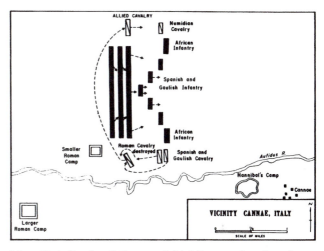

thaginian line bowed outward toward the Roman line, forming a crescent. (Map 12.4 portrays the deployment of both armies.) The Spanish and Celtic cavalry was commanded by the brave Hasdrubal (not to be confused with Hasdrubal the Splendid who was killed earlier), while Mahar-bal, the greatest cavalry commander of the war, commanded the Numidians. Hannibal himself, along with his young brother Mago, commanded the center. Upon the sound of the trumpet, the skirmishers of both armies moved into position and began throwing their javelins. The Balaeric slingers on the Carthagin-

Map 12.4 Battle of Cannae: Initial Roman Attack and Defeat of the Roman Cavalry (216 B.C.E.). Courtesy of the U.S. Army War College.

ian side rained down stone and lead shot on the Roman formations. Aemilius, commander of the Roman cavalry, was wounded. With a mighty roar of 140,000 voices, the armies moved toward one another.

The Spanish and Celtic cavalry, outnumbering the Roman horse by more than two to one, smashed into the Roman right wing. Polybius notes that the Roman force immediately came apart. During the wild melee, many were slaughtered or driven into the river. Those who fled were cut down without mercy. On the other wing, the Numidians and the allied cavalry were locked in a deadly battle, neither side able to gain a decisive advantage.

In the center, the Roman infantry gradually drove the crescent bulge of the Carthaginian line backward. First the line was hammered, even with the African phalanxes that anchored it, then it was pressed even further back. As the Carthaginian center gradually flexed under the pressure of the Roman assault, Roman units were drawn deeper and deeper into the "V"-shaped line. The Romans were fighting up a slight incline, and the further forward their units progressed, the more compressed they became. After some time, almost the entire Roman infantry was pressed into the interior of the "V," and still

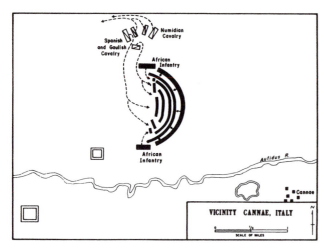

Map 12.5 Battle of Cannae: Destruction of the Roman Army (216 B.C.E.). Courtesy of the U.S. Army War College.

the Carthaginians gave ground (see Map 12.5). Hannibal was drawing them into another trap.

Having driven the Roman cavalry from the field, Hasdrubal re-formed his units and rode completely around and behind the Roman line to join the battle raging between the allied and Numidian cavalry. Taken by surprise, the allied cavalry were crushed between the two cavalry forces and fled the field. Hasdrubal re-formed his cavalry again, and this time sent the Numidian cavalry in pursuit of the allied units to ensure that they did not rejoin the battle.

The Roman infantry was now totally committed into the "V" that Hannibal's retreating infantry had created. The Roman infantry was so compressed that they could no longer maneuver in any direction. They continued to cut their way through the Carthaginian center, which, under the personal command of Hannibal himself, still held. At this critical moment, the African phalanxes that had been anchoring the infantry line turned obliquely inward and attacked the flanks of the compacted Roman formations. The Romans found themselves jammed together like packed cattle. In Polybius's words, "they were caught between the two divisions of the enemy, and they no longer kept their compact formations but turned singly or in companies to deal with the enemy who was falling on their flanks."

All that remained to complete the trap was for the Roman rear to be cut off and further compressed upon the packed formations. Having re-formed his cavalry and assured that the allied cavalry was clear of the field, Hasdrubal's heavy force struck the Roman rear with tremendous shock. With no ability to maneuver forward or toward the flanks, and with the rear cut off, the Roman army of 80,000 men was massacred where it stood. Within a few hours, the battle was over. Of the original Roman force, approximately 50,000 were dead and another 5,000 taken prisoner on the battlefield. Some 17,000 Romans managed to reach the fortified camps. But after further resistance took 2,000 more Roman lives, the surviving 15,000 surrendered. As was the Roman custom, many senators, sons of prominent families, and government officials had gone to war. When the Senate next convened, 177 vacancies had to be filled due to the casualties suffered at Cannae. The Carthaginians lost 6,000 men, most (4,000) were Celtic infantry fighting in the center of the line. Another 1,500 Africans and Spanish infantry had died, and about 500 cavalrymen as well. The total butcher's bill was over 70,000 men, heaped in an area roughly the size of Central Park. Few men, before or since, have witnessed such a sight. And it is worth quoting Livy in full to portray the battlefield at Cannae.

> On the following day, as soon as it dawned, they set about gathering the spoils and viewing the carnage, which was shocking, even to enemies. So many thousands of Romans were lying, foot and horse promiscuously, according as accident had brought them together, either in battle or flight. Some, whom their wounds, pinched by the morning cold, had roused, as they were rousing up, covered with blood, from the midst of the heaps of slain, were overpowered by the enemy.
>
> Some too they found lying alive with their thighs and hams cut, laying bare their necks and throats, bid them drain the blood that remained in them. Some were found with their heads plunged into the earth, which they had excavated; having thus, as it appeared, made pits for themselves, and having suffocated themselves by overwhelming their faces with the earth which they threw over them.
>
> A living Numidian, with lacerated nose and ears, stretched beneath a lifeless Roman who lay upon him, principally attracted the attention of all; for when the Roman's hands were powerless to grasp his weapon, turning from rage to madness, he had died in the act of tearing his antagonist with his teeth.

Hannibal had, at last, achieved the great victory he had sought for more than a year. In less than three years, he had defeated the Romans in four major battles. The cost to Rome in manpower had been horrendous. No fewer than 20 percent of the entire Roman population of military age (over seventeen) had been killed, captured, or wounded. Hannibal's army was intact and capable of further offensive action. Polybius says that, as Hannibal and Maharbal were looking out over the blood-soaked plain, Maharbal pressed his commander to strike at Rome itself. Hannibal, perhaps personally moved by the magnitude of the slaughter he had caused, refused. Although the war went on for another fifteen years, Hannibal never attacked Rome.

The failure to strike directly at the heart of the Roman political establishment and decapitate its leadership remains one of the more puzzling aspects of Hannibal's campaign. The usual answer is that Hannibal had left behind his siege machinery in Spain and, with that route of supply now cut by Scipio operating south of the Ebro River, there was no chance of provisioning Hannibal with the equipment. These reasons are hardly convincing. The siege machinery of the day was relatively simple and could have been easily fabricated from the resources within Hannibal's zone of operations. As for technical expertise, captured military and civilian experts were surely available. Why, then, did Hannibal not attack Rome?

One reason was the success at Cannae. The defeat of the Romans brought a few towns finally to the Carthaginian side. The most important of them, Capua, could provide Hannibal with 30,000 infantry and 4,000 horse. Before these defections, Hannibal could move at will; he had nothing to defend. Once a major defection occurred, he had to protect the defector from Roman vengeance, or his aim of provoking a widespread revolt by Rome's allies would never prove fruitful. Sensing this fact, the Romans besieged Capua, forcing Hannibal to protect it.

Probably a more important reason for not striking at Rome was that the Romans returned to the Fabian strategy. With multiple armies in the field shadowing his every move, Hannibal was certainly able to march on Rome, and did exactly that in 211 B.C.E., more as a stratagem to draw off Roman manpower besieging Capua. Although he could reach Rome, Hannibal could not afford to lay siege to the city. If he did, he would be tied down at a single place. Every army in Italy would make for Rome and Hannibal's army. With his movement and tactical flexibility lost, he would be forced into a battle of attrition with a superior force, a battle he must eventually lose. The refusal to attack Rome made good military sense. Still, Maharbal may have been right. The defeat at Cannae sent the Roman political leadership into shock, and although the Roman manpower base was nowhere near depletion, it still took considerable time to raise new armies. Perhaps, had Hannibal moved directly on Rome immediately after the battle, the political will of the Senate would have broken. Hannibal, the lucky and daring gambler, refused to roll the dice.

SCIPIO AFRICANUS (236–183 B.C.E.)

Publius Cornelius Scipio (Africanus) was born in 236 B.C.E., 517 years after the founding of the city, into one of the great patrician families of the Republic. His father was Publius Cornelius Scipio, who was elected consul in 218 B.C.E. to deal with Hannibal's invasion of Italy. Later, his father commanded the Roman armies in Spain. Although the young Scipio was only twenty-five when he assumed command of the Roman armies in Spain, Scipio had already seen plenty of combat, first at the Ticinus and then at Cannae. Moreover, he had been present in battles where the great Hannibal was in command. Livy suggests that Scipio studied Hannibal's victories closely and decided early on that the Roman armies would suffer defeat after defeat unless they were reformed.

For all its renowned prowess, the Roman army of Scipio's time was still essentially a citizen's militia called to duty only during times of emergency. Once mustered, the *legio* still had to be trained to the Roman system of infantry combat, a process that took considerable time. Rome's generals, although generally competent, were really annual magistrates (consuls) elected to command the armies for a year. When two consuls were in the field at the same time, command of the army switched between them on a daily basis. Chosen by politics, these men often had little military acumen or experience. The problem of semi-professional officers and troops was aggravated by the lack of good Roman cavalry units. The Romans possessed a cultural distaste for cavalry, likening cavalrymen to lowly herdsmen, with the consequence that until Scipio's time Roman armies had never developed a reliable cavalry arm. What cavalry there was tended to be poor and usually relegated to the minor role of reconnaissance.

Scipio recognized immediately that these shortcomings made victory over the Carthaginians problematic at best. In the first place, part-time Roman senior officers were fighting against true professional officers whose purpose in life was military service. Carthaginian officers had long experience in the field and were capable of innovative tactics and even brilliance. Hannibal's troops were also professionals. Comprised of mercenaries and tribal allies, the men who fought for Carthage had far more combat experience and were accustomed to fighting as units as opposed to the citizen-soldiers of Rome's legions. Carthaginian units were trained in a number of tactical maneuvers that the legion simply could not perform, a capability that gave their commanders a significant advantage. Finally, Hannibal's armies had a strong tradition of excellent cavalry that could carry out all sorts of maneuvers that were beyond the ability of the Roman cavalry. Under the command of professional officers, Carthaginian cavalry became the true arm of decision when working in close coordination with the infantry.

The Roman legion was a far different military animal. The traditional Roman military formation from the time of the Republic's founding was modeled on the Greek hoplite phalanx. The weaponry of the Roman citizen-soldier of this time was also essentially Greek: the short spear, round shield, helmet, armor, greaves, and sword. In the usual case of set-piece battles on level ground against armies using similar formations and equipment, the phalanx worked well enough. In uneven terrain, however, it could not maneuver. In the wars against the Samnites (340–290 B.C.E.), fought in the rugged Apennine hills, valleys, and glens, the phalanx proved unworkable and terribly brittle to surprise attack. Moreover, the wars against the wild Gauls demonstrated how easily the highly mobile formations of the Gallic armies could envelop the open flanks of the phalanx and crush it from all sides once the cavalry was driven from the field. And since the Roman cavalry was not very good, driving it from the field proved not very difficult. The result of the Roman experience with the Samnites and Gauls was the replacement of the phalanx legion with the manipular legion described earlier (see Figure 12.5), which served as the basic Roman infantry formation throughout the Punic Wars.

Although the Roman legion could advance or retire, it could do little else. Once engaged it tended to become a compact mass. The security of the whole army depended upon its legions remaining in close order. Once set to the task, it could not change direction or shape. Nor could it wheel or turn. This limitation led Roman commanders to employ the legion the same way again and again regardless of the circumstances in which it had to fight. The problem was that Carthaginian commanders could depend upon exactly this inflexibility, in the same way that they could depend upon not having to deal with the threat of Roman cavalry. And given that the Carthaginian armies had been trained to wheel, turn, extend and close ranks, and use its cavalry to devastating effect, it is not surprising that, until Scipio took command, Roman armies met one defeat after another. Scipio saw the problem clearly and began to reshape his armies immediately upon taking command in Spain.

Along with introducing new weapons, strengthening the maniple, and introducing regular weapons drill, Scipio also trained his army to match the tactical capabilities of his Carthaginian adversaries. He trained his legions to extend and close ranks, to redeploy from checkerboard to line to overlap the length of the enemy line, to redeploy the maniples one behind the other in a compact mass, and to do it all at the sound of a horn or drum or the sight of a signal flag. Most amazingly, Scipio trained his army to carry out these maneuvers while still engaged with the enemy. Next he turned his attention to the cavalry. He often used Spanish cavalry, among the best heavy cavalry in the world, and later, in Africa, he integrated Numidian light cavalry as well. Scipio trained and employed his cavalry in the Carthaginian fashion: in close coordination with his infantry. Scipio refashioned the legions of Rome in the image of Hannibal's army and, in truth, employed them in much the same way. His use of the fixing attack, although he employed it more often and, perhaps, with greater effect, was right out of Hannibal's bag of tricks. Scipio would often ask his legions to strike the enemy and hold their attention while sending his cavalry or the other legions to envelope or strike from the flank. General George Patton once instructed his subordinate commanders to employ the same maneuver. They were, Patton reportedly said, "to grab the enemy by the nose and then kick him in the ass!"

THE ATTACK ON NEW CARTHAGE (209 B.C.E.)

Scipio arrived in Spain by ship in 210 B.C.E., landing just inside the Spanish frontier and marching overland to Tarraco (modern Tarragona), where he set up his base of operations. He spent the winter training his troops and establishing contact with Rome's Iberian allies. Polybius reports that he spent many hours learning about the Celt-Iberian tribes that were fighting on both sides. His father and uncle had been killed when they were betrayed by some of these tribes. Although Scipio made fine use of them in his campaigns, he seems never to have trusted them completely. Scipio set his intelligence service to collecting everything of interest. In this, Scipio sought to correct one of the major failures of previous Roman armies. Time and again these armies had been unable to locate the enemy, stumbling around only to be surprised and ambushed by Hannibal. More than once Hannibal had drawn Roman armies into battle on terrain unfamiliar to Roman commanders and always to his own advantage. Once, when the Romans thought they had Hannibal trapped in a valley, he escaped at night precisely because he knew the location of the trail leading from the valley, of which the enemy was unaware. Scipio's use of tactical intelligence was unrivaled by any Roman commanders. Never did he move his army without sound knowledge of their route, nor did he ever attack a city without knowing its weaknesses, nor did he ever offer battle without knowing precisely the location and disposition of the enemy.

Scipio spent considerable time establishing Tarraco as his main base of operations in Spain, including procuring sufficient food for his army. A secure logistical base from which to launch and sustain field operations was another characteristic of Scipio's campaigns. He was an effective organizer and administrator of commissary matters in every respect, and his Spanish campaign surpasses the Spanish campaigns of Napoleon and Wellington, who found to their great regret that Spain is a terrible place in which to fight if an army has to live off the land. To move overland in Spain without planning for adequate food and water forces an army to disperse into small groups to find it, making it impossible to sustain any rate of advance or even to maintain strategic direction. Never in any of Scipio's campaigns do we hear of him encountering supply problems. His habit of establishing a secure base of operations also permitted him a place upon which to fall back should defeat rear its ugly head and the army need a respite to repair itself.

By early summer Scipio's army was ready, and he had already formulated a plan. The immediate problem was that Scipio was greatly outnumbered. To risk battle and lose so early in the game would remove the last obstacle to a second Carthaginian invasion of Italy and the reinforcement of Hannibal's army. Besides, his army was as yet unbloodied, and he dared not risk it in a major battle. It was at this time that his intelligence service served him well. Roman agents reported that the Carthaginian force was divided into three areas of operations. One army under Mago's command (Hannibal's youngest brother) was garrisoned in Gades (modern Cadiz). A second army commanded by Hasdrubal, son of Gisco, was operating near the mouth of the Targas River. The third element was under the command of Hasdrubal Barca besieging a city in central Spain somewhere near modern Madrid. Not one of them was within ten days march of their main logistical base of New Carthage. Scipio, on the other hand, could reach New Carthage in seven days.

Roman intelligence had also discovered that New Carthage was lightly defended by fewer than a thousand Carthaginian troops. The city was the closest port to Carthage itself and the main point of embarkation for reinforcements from Africa. In addition, the city held the war treasury of the enemy armies, along with most of the important hostages taken by the Carthaginians. Taking New Carthage by storm would strike a powerful moral blow against the enemy and seriously weaken his logistics and resupply capability. Time, of course, was of the essence. Scipio reasoned that, if he could arrive outside the city undetected, it would take at least a week for the news to reach Hasdrubal and another week for Hasdrubal to turn his army and reach the city to deal with Scipio. Even with luck, Scipio would have no longer than three weeks to breach the city's defenses and prepare to meet Hasdrubal's relieving attack, a very near thing indeed. It was the first of many times when Scipio would calculate the odds and take a daring gamble. He ordered his army to attack New Carthage.

Scipio did nothing to stop the rumors that ran through Tarraco as the army prepared to march. Better to let a hundred stories reach the enemy than one truth. And so it was that Scipio entrusted no one with his plans but his old friend Gaius Laelius. Scipio did not even inform his field commanders until the march was well underway, with the result that it was impossible for the enemy to learn his intentions. Scipio left 3,000 men behind to keep Tarraco safe and embarked some of his army aboard ship to sail for New Carthage under the command of Gaius Laelius. Scipio took the remainder of the army overland by foot. Scipio's army numbered 25,000 men and 2,500 horse. Seven days later, both armies arrived before the objective on the same day, a marvel of land-sea coordination. Scipio had achieved complete surprise.

New Carthage sat on a peninsula surrounded by a small bay and connected to the mainland by a narrow causeway. Scipio established his camp on the landward side and sent a small force of 2,000 men with scaling ladders against the walls. It was, in fact, a reconnaissance in force to draw the enemy commander out and focus his attention upon Scipio's camp. Predictably, the enemy commander sallied forth through the main gate to drive the Romans off. Scipio's troops pulled back, and the Carthaginians followed. When they had come some distance from the safety of the city's walls, Scipio counterattacked with a larger force that broke the Carthaginian attack and drove it back toward the open gate. So fierce was the counterattack that the Romans narrowly escaped missing the open gate. But the attack had accomplished what Scipio wanted. The attention of the enemy commander was now completely focused on Scipio and his army, positioned in front of the city.

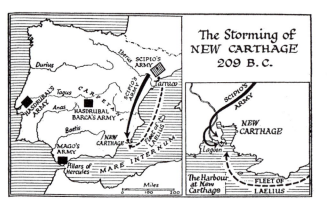

Figure 12.6 The Storming of New Carthage (209 B.C.E.). Courtesy of J. Dunn. Adapted from Leonard Cottrell, *Hannibal* (New York: Holt, Rinehart, and Winston, 1960).

What happened next is testimony to Scipio's brilliant planning and ability to use intelligence. Even before he had left Tarraco, Scipio had learned that the bay protecting the city was very shallow, and that when the tide ran out, it could be easily forded on foot. Later, Scipio told his troops that the low water had been a gift from Neptune and the gods who had foreordained his victory. Scipio set loose a ferocious ground attack against the front walls, drawing the defenders to the point of attack. With the attack under way, Scipio sent a small force of only 500 men with scaling ladders across the lagoon. They reached the city walls undetected, scrambled over the top, and took the few defenders by surprise. They cleared the top of the walls of resistance, fought their way to the landward gate, fell upon the defenders from behind, and threw open the doors. Ready at the head of his troops, Polybius says Scipio himself led the assault through the gates. Within minutes the Romans were inside the city. The enemy commander and his remaining troops fled to the citadel, determined to make a last stand.

Scipio now showed how thoroughly Roman he was. He was unwilling to risk more casualties in an assault of the citadel. And with time of the essence, he could ill afford to wait until the Carthaginian defenders were starved out. Instead, Scipio ordered the slaughter of the townspeople in full view of the holdouts. Polybius describes what happened next.

> Scipio, when he judged that a large enough number of troops had entered the town, let loose the majority of them against the inhabitants, according to Roman custom; their orders were to exterminate every form of life they encountered, sparing none, but not to start pillaging until the word was given to do so. This practice is adopted to inspire terror, and so when cities are taken by the Romans you may often see not only the corpses of human beings but dogs cut in half and the dismembered limbs of other animals, and on this occasion the carnage was especially frightful because of the large size of the population.

The horror of it all reached the heart of the Carthaginian commander, who surrendered himself and his men.

Having achieved his military objective, Scipio now turned to exploiting its political benefits. Scipio understood that Rome would triumph more quickly by gaining the respect and support of the Iberian tribes, a task made somewhat easier by the long Carthaginian practice of harsh rule over the Spanish. Scipio seems always to have understood the political context in which his battles were fought and always to have taken care to obtain maximum political benefit from his military actions. With these things in mind, Scipio freed the townspeople and returned their property to them. He sent most of the Spanish soldiers back to their tribes, where they would no doubt carry the tale of the great Roman victory and, not incidentally, of Roman fairness and mercy. Most of the Carthaginians he impressed into his navy. He spared the life of the enemy commander, sending him on to Rome as a prize of war. Scipio spent the next few weeks repairing the walls of the city and training his army in weapons drill, perhaps preparing them to deal with Hasdrubal should he suddenly arrive. We might expect that Roman intelligence kept close watch for the Carthaginian, but he made no move toward New Carthage. When the walls were repaired, Scipio embarked his army aboard ship, with the rest on foot, and returned to Tarraco. He left behind a detachment adequate to guard the city. Scipio had drawn first blood. The Carthaginians never occupied New Carthage again.

THE BATTLE OF BAECULA (208 B.C.E.)

The fall of New Carthage was a great blow to Carthaginian strength. Perhaps more importantly, the Roman victory caused three of the most powerful Spanish chieftains to desert their Carthaginian allies and come over to the Roman cause. Hasdrubal watched helplessly as Scipio courted the Spanish tribes with ever-increasing success. This was no ordinary Roman commander, he must have thought. Best to deal with him quickly. And so it was that Hasdrubal began to move his army into position for a battle with Scipio.

Scipio welcomed the opportunity to engage the Carthaginian army piecemeal. As outnumbered as he was, being able to take on one segment at a time made it more of a fair fight. Roman intelligence, no doubt, had kept a close eye on Hasdrubal's whereabouts. When he went into encampment near the town of Baecula to prepare his army, Scipio snatched the offensive away from the Carthaginian. Scipio approached Hasdrubal's camp by forced march, debouching close enough to threaten his line of retreat. Hasdrubal moved to some high ground that provided sufficient depth for maneuver and anchored his rear on the nearby river. Scipio followed quickly and encamped before his adversary. As at New Carthage, time was working against him. He guessed that the two remaining Carthaginian armies might already be on the move, converging on Baecula. If he could not bring Hasdrubal to battle and effect a quick decision, Scipio risked being pinned against Hasdrubal's army as against an anvil and being hammered by the advancing Carthaginian armies. With little time to prepare, Scipio went immediately into the attack.

Hasdrubal had taken up positions on top of a plateau. Below the frontal approaches lay a small ridge that served as a step leading to the top. Scipio sent all of his light infantry, supported by a few *cohorts* of heavy infantry, against the steppingstone ridge, gaining it quickly. Reinforcing the attacking force with more heavy infantry, he sent it against the frontal crest of the plateau. Hasdrubal, thinking the main blow to be falling on the front of his positions, brought up reserves to reinforce his front line. As the battle raged, fully occupying the attention of the Carthaginian commander, Scipio divided his remaining legions into two task forces, one under his command and the other in the hands of the trusted Laelius. Scipio moved his men around to the left of the plateau, climbed the ridge, and took the enemy in the flank. Now the enemy was engaged on two fronts, and Hasdrubal quickly threw his remaining reserves into the fight. The battle turned more violent as both armies fought for their lives. Meanwhile, Laelius and his men had been making their way up the right side of the plateau. The ground was broken and much steeper than on the left side, and it took Laelius considerably longer to reach the crest. Once over the top, Laelius's men smashed against the flank and rear of the Carthaginians, taking them completely by surprise. The whole Carthaginian army was at risk of being caught in a double envelopment, and many turned to flee; but it was too late. Laelius closed the escape route, and a terrible slaughter ensued. Some Carthaginians did manage to escape down the rear of the plateau, but Scipio had brilliantly closed off this route by sending a few *cohorts* around the plateau. Those who made it off the plateau were either captured or killed.

By day's end the Romans counted 8,000 slain and 12,000 prisoners. Hasdrubal and his staff had made good their escape. But the defeat of the Carthaginian general had been complete. His army was gone. It took Hasdrubal two years to recruit and train a new army, delaying by two years his attempt to relieve Hannibal in Italy. For the moment, the victory at Baecula left Hannibal to fight on by himself with no hope of immediate reinforcement. Once more Scipio acted to gain the friendship of the Iberians. He freed all the Iberian soldiers he had captured and permitted them to return to their homes without ransom. And then, once again, he fell back on his base at Tarraco. Scipio could, of course, have pursued Hasdrubal and what was left of his army. But his instincts told him there was danger in that course. He still did not know the location of the other Carthaginian armies, and he dared not risk bumping into them while pursuing Hasdrubal. And so Scipio returned to Tarraco. He had no sooner left Baecula than the other two Carthaginian armies arrived and joined Hasdrubal. Scipio's instincts had been correct.

THE BATTLE OF ILLIPA (206 B.C.E.)

Scipio now set out to exploit his victory at Baecula by convincing the Spanish chieftains that their future lay with Rome. In this effort, Polybius says, he was very successful, and many came over to him. But if Scipio expected a respite from the pressure of Carthaginian arms, he was to be disappointed, for in late summer a new general, one Hanno, arrived in Spain with a fresh army to replace Hasdrubal Barca. Mago, who had been in the Baelerics recruiting, also returned, so the Carthaginians were once more ready to take the field. Hanno immediately moved his new army into the interior, daring Scipio to give battle. The wary Scipio sensed a trap. The army under Hanno was but a part of the larger army, and his intelligence service had lost sight of it. Under these circumstances, Scipio was hesitant to risk a major battle lest the greater part of the Carthaginian army come up and surprise him. Scipio resolved to remain in Tarraco with the bulk of his army, sending instead 10,000 foot and 5,000 horse under the command of Silanus to deal with Hanno. As events worked out, Silanus dealt the enemy a crushing defeat, capturing the luckless Hanno in the bargain. Scipio decided that the time for battle had passed and went into winter quarters.

Scipio's success in wooing the Iberian chiefs to the Roman cause had not gone unnoticed by the Carthaginians, and as spring of 206 B.C.E. arrived, the Carthaginians made a great effort to rid Spain of Scipio once and for all. Hasdrubal had raised a fresh army that, Polybius tells us, numbered 70,000 foot, 4,000 horse, and 32 elephants. In early spring, Hasdrubal moved north to the area of modern Seville hoping to draw Scipio out of his base. Scipio readily obliged and moved south from Tarraco. The two armies met at Illipa. Scipio's victories to this point had been won by daring, good planning, and surprise. But none had required that his army execute complex maneuvers, operate in concert with his cavalry, or fight on level ground. Ever since he had assumed command, Scipio had been training his army in these new skills. Now, as he moved toward Illipa, Scipio would learn for certain whether or not his army was a match for the Carthaginians on open ground.

As his army marched to battle, Scipio was forced to consider two additional difficulties, either of which might easily have convinced a less confident and imaginative commander to change his mind. First, he was badly outnumbered. Deducting the force left behind to garrison Tarraco, the Roman army had 45,000 foot and 3,000 horse. Hasdrubal, as already noted, had almost twice that number. Of more concern to Scipio were the contingents of Iberian troops drawn from his new Spanish allies. Never one to ignore history, Scipio remembered that his father and uncle had gone to their deaths precisely because they had trusted their Iberian allies, only to have them desert on the field of battle, leaving both Roman consuls and their legions to their fate. Scipio could ill afford not to use them, but he knew better than to trust them. Scipio's solution to this difficulty ranks as one of the most brilliant in military history.

Scipio approached Illipa and found Hasdrubal waiting for him encamped on the low hills of a valley. Scipio encamped on the near side, the battlefield set between the two armies. As Scipio's troops began constructing the camp, young Mago, the bold and often reckless Carthaginian cavalry commander who had made the Romans suffer at the Trebia, took the opportunity to carry out a harassing attack. Scipio had foreseen such a possibility and had placed some of his cavalry under the shelter of a hill to deal with just this circumstance. Mago attacked, only to have his cavalry itself taken in the flank by the Romans. Scipio sent some infantry *cohorts* into the fray and drove the Carthaginians back to their camp to lick their wounds. Scipio had won the first round. More to the point, his cavalry had performed superbly.

The two camps lay facing each other across a valley between two low ridges. Every day for three days running, always in mid-morning, Hasdrubal led his army out onto the valley floor to offer battle. Scipio always followed suit, but always after the Carthaginians had deployed. For hours the armies stood in the sun, neither side making a move to engage the other. Then, as the day turned to dusk, the armies would return to their respective camps, the Carthaginians always being the first to return. Each day Hasdrubal set out the same order of battle, his center comprised of African and Carthaginian regulars and his wings of Spanish allies and cavalry. He located his elephants between the wings and the center. Scipio, too, showed the same order of battle each day, the center comprised of Roman legion infantry and the wings of his Iberian allies and cavalry. Day after day Scipio formed up his army in this manner, until he was convinced that he had baited the trap sufficiently. Like Hannibal at Cannae, Scipio set out the trap in plain sight. And when Hasdrubal did not detect it for three days, Scipio decided that the time to fight was ripe.

On the night before the fourth day Scipio ordered that the army was to rise, eat, and arm before daylight. The cavalry were instructed to be saddled and ready to move before the sun broke the horizon. As the sun rose over the Carthaginian camp, Hasdrubal and his army were surprised to find themselves under attack by Roman cavalry and light infantry units. The camp was filled with noise and confusion as men stumbled from their beds still half asleep and half naked. With the Carthaginians busy with the attack, Scipio sent his legions onto the battlefield. When Hasdrubal was told of this deployment, he feared that he would be attacked in force. He ordered his men to form for battle. None had been fed, and more than a few were only partially armed as they assembled in their usual order and prepared for battle.

One can imagine Scipio looking out over the battlefield and smiling to himself as his adversary stumbled into the trap. He ordered the signaler to sound retreat and recall the cavalry and light infantry. Following the dictum that Napoleon later made famous, Scipio did not want to hinder a man who was making a mistake and so did nothing further to hinder the Carthaginian deployment. Neither Livy nor Polybius tells us what was going through Hasdrubal's mind that day or whether he recognized that he was caught even before the battle had begun. For although Hasdrubal's men were arranged as before, Scipio had completely altered his order of battle. Now the heavy Roman infantry were on the wings, along with his heavy cavalry and light

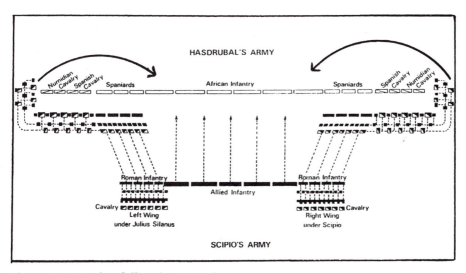

Figure 12.7 Battle of Illipa (206 B.C.E.)

infantry who deployed behind and to the oblique of the legions. In the center Scipio had placed his least reliable troops, the Spanish allies!

It is a testament to both Scipio's daring and his confidence in his training that he was willing to risk everything in a battle where he was badly outnumbered by employing tactics that depended upon his army executing complex maneuvers against the very army that was already the master of those maneuvers. Scipio ordered the Iberians into the attack, but ordered them to move slowly and to delay reaching the Carthaginian line for as long as possible. With himself in command of his right wing and Silanus of the left, Scipio ordered the legions and the accompanying cavalry to march quickly forward, aiming at the Carthaginian wings opposite them. Within a few minutes, the Roman wings were well forward of its center. As the wings approached the enemy, Scipio and Silanus maneuvered to the oblique and overlapped the ends of the Carthaginian line. Turning quickly inward, the legions fell on the flanks with great fury. Scipio now brought his cavalry into play. He ordered the cavalry to break from the rear of the legion's wings and to ride around and strike the enemy rear. His light infantry he ordered to turn inward and take the enemy deeper in the flank. The Roman war animal began chewing on the flanks of its Carthaginian prey.

And what of the center? Still the Iberian troops had not reached the Carthaginian line. Their slow rate of march had permitted Scipio to "refuse" the center, something that had never been attempted before. Although not yet engaged, the approach of the Iberians forced the Carthaginian center, comprised as it was of the best troops, to remain in place. If they advanced, they exposed their flanks to the Roman cavalry. If they stayed where they were, they were effectively out of the fight and risked being completely enveloped from the rear as Scipio's legions and cavalry decimated both flanks. It was Cannae in reverse! Scipio had carried out a complete double-envelopment. The legions proceeded to drive the enemy flanks in upon the center and began the slaughter.

Hasdrubal, to his great credit, did not panic, even after the Roman cavalry had spooked his elephants and driven them into the Carthaginian center, shattering it. The Carthaginians began cutting their way through the back of the Roman envelopment and withdrew in relatively good order, hoping to gain their camp. Luck then favored Hasdrubal. Polybius says a great cloudburst suddenly broke overhead, turning the ground to mud and preventing the Romans from storming the Carthaginian camp. The arrival of darkness prevented further action, and Hasdrubal took the opportunity to slip away, only to discover that Scipio had placed a few *cohorts* across his line of retreat. Still, large remnants of the Carthaginian army fought or slipped through the Roman noose. But having brought the enemy to hand, Scipio was not of a mind to let it go so easily. He sent the cavalry in pursuit with instructions to attack and harass the enemy and to slow down its withdrawal. He then ordered his legions on to the march and with great speed set out to catch the retreating Carthaginians. As events turned out, the Roman cavalry performed flawlessly once more and harassed the retreating army so that the legions could overtake it. And when this was accomplished, Scipio's legions fell on the weary enemy and made a great slaughter of it all. Polybius says of this final engagement, "After this it was no longer a fight, but a butchering of cattle."

With brilliant tactics and battlefield daring, Scipio's well-trained army had proven itself at last. It had destroyed an army of 70,000 men. Livy reports that Hasdrubal escaped with only 6,000 men. The rest were dead, wounded, or sold into slavery. Hasdrubal reached the Carthaginian stronghold at Gades (modern Cadiz), and he and Mago took ship for Carthage. There is no more classic example in military history of a battle in which a weaker force gained so complete a victory over a stronger one than Illipa. And it was won by innovative tactics, daring, and concentration of force. Much of Spain remained to be pacified. But after Illipa, the Carthaginians in Spain ceased to be a threat to Roman control. They held fast to Gades but could not prevent Scipio from pacifying the Iberian tribes either by slaughter, as he did on more than one occasion, or by diplomacy, as he did most of the time. Spain no longer served as a source of Carthaginian manpower or wealth. More important, Scipio's victories had removed the threat of a second invasion of Italy. Although it was true that Hannibal could fight on, after Illipa it was now just a matter of time.

Scipio returned to Rome in time for the consular elections of 205 B.C.E. Scipio's grasp of grand strategy revealed itself in his insistence that an invasion of Africa was the key to defeating Hannibal in Italy. A Roman advance on Carthage would force Hannibal to retire to Africa to take part in the defense of the city. If Hannibal remained where he was and Carthage fell, then his presence in Italy would be, at best, a strategic irrelevancy. Scipio was alone in recognizing that the "center of gravity" of the war was not Hannibal's army at all but the political will of the Carthaginian leadership to continue the war. And the surest way of weakening that will was to take the war to Carthage itself. Scipio was elected consul upon his return and presented his plan to the Roman Senate, only to have it rejected. His political enemies charged Scipio with concocting the plan to create an opportunity for gaining personal glory. Others thought it too risky. But Scipio had strong support among the tribunes and even some senators. The result was a compromise. Scipio was given command of Sicily with the task of defending it against a Carthaginian attack! If, however, in carrying out his duties he should decide that military matters required him to cross over into Africa, then he was permitted to do so. Since he was denied the authority to levy troops, just how any of this might be accomplished was left uncertain. Not for the last time in his career, Scipio's ability to act was hampered by his political opponents.

SCIPIO'S AFRICA CAMPAIGN (205–202 B.C.E.)

Scipio left for Sicily with thirty warships and 7,000 volunteers. Upon arrival he took command of the remnants of the fifth and sixth legions that had been decimated at Cannae and been banished to Sicily as punishment for their poor performance. He had no cavalry worth its name. His experience in Spain had taught him that the Carthaginians were likely to fight ferociously to defend their homeland and that his army would have to be as tough and well trained as the one he had left behind in Spain. Scipio set immediately to the task, focusing first on the recruitment and training of the heavy cavalry that was the key to fighting the Carthaginians on open ground. In the end he was able to raise only small numbers of cavalry. Next he turned to fashioning the infantry into a reliable instrument of war. As he had done in Spain, Scipio introduced weapons drill and training in new tactics and maneuvers. Scipio, himself a veteran of Cannae, appealed to the honor of the men of the fifth and sixth legions who had fought with him that day. Cannae was not, he told them, their fault. They had fought well, but the fates had been against them. Now he offered them an opportunity to redeem their honor and to show their courage in the face of the enemy. By such appeals and other skills, Scipio rebuilt his army.

By the late summer of 204 B.C.E., when he prepared to sail for Africa, Scipio had only 16,000 men and 1,600 horse under his command. It was, by any measure, a puny force and totally inadequate for the task set before them by their commander. Most troubling was the shortage of good cavalry. Without it, Scipio would have little chance of victory against the Carthaginians on open ground. But Scipio had other cards to play. Always cognizant of the connection between political and military objectives, Scipio gambled that he could redress the military imbalance through political means. And now he played his ace.

Years before, at the battle of Baecula, Scipio had captured a young Numidian nobleman who was the nephew of Masinissa, the great Numidian chieftain and brilliant cavalry commander who had fought for the Carthaginians. Scipio had treated the young man courteously and had him returned to his uncle with his compliments. Even before Scipio had left Spain he had opened negotiations with Masinissa, urging him to change sides. While Masinissa had been away at war, political changes in his kingdom had brought forth challengers to his position. Before Masinissa left Spain to deal with the problem, Scipio had promised him that Rome would help him deal with his enemies and regard him as the true king in exchange for his loyalty to Rome. Livy suggests that there was some kind of informal agreement between the two men. And now Scipio was prepared to find out whether Masinissa would reciprocate. While he raised his army in Sicily, Scipio sent Laelius to conduct a reconnaissance of landing sites on the African coast. Laelius landed at Hippo, 150 miles from Carthage but close to Numidia. The landing threw the Carthaginians into a panic, for they believed Scipio had finally come. Once they realized that it was only a small force and that Scipio himself was still in Sicily, they returned to preparing their defenses for the invasion they believed would surely come soon. Laelius, meanwhile, made contact with Masinissa and secured from him his promise to provide cavalry once Scipio had landed. In exchange Masinissa secured Roman support for his claim to the Numidian throne.

So it was that in the spring of 204 B.C.E., Scipio set sail from Lilybaeum (modern Marsala) with 40 warships and 400 supply transports, 16,000 infantry, and 1,600 horse. Polybius tells us that the army carried rations sufficient for fifty-five days, fifteen days of which were already cooked. Always the meticulous planner, Scipio had personally overseen these preparations in detail. The amount of supplies suggests that Scipio was prepared to go immediately over to the offensive and not rely upon local supplies, at least not at the outset. Should things go badly and he was unable to quickly capture a major city to serve as a main base, or should the army be forced to maneuver on the open plain against the enemy, Scipio's army could operate independently for two full months on its own resources. Scipio intended to compensate for his army's small numbers with flexibility, maneuverability, and sustainability. If all else failed, he could retreat in good order back to the coast where his ships could take his army out of harm's way. The crossing went well enough, and Scipio landed at the Fair Promontory (modern Cape Farina), a few miles from Utica and a hundred miles from Carthage itself. Utica commanded the fertile plain that was a major source of Carthage's food. Scipio moved immediately to invest Utica. True to his word, Masinissa arrived to join Scipio but did so with only 200 horse, far fewer than the thousands Scipio had hoped for. Until Masinissa could raise more men, Scipio would have to rely on his infantry.

The Carthaginians reacted quickly and sent a force of 4,000 men under Hanno to Salaeca, a town fifteen miles from the Roman camp. They were to attack Scipio and hold him in place while the larger army under Hasdrubal and the allied chieftain, Syphax (a Numidian rival of Masinissa), came up in force. Scipio moved quickly to deal with the advance elements. He sent Masinissa and his light cavalry to make contact with Hanno and draw him after him in pursuit. Scipio then placed his cavalry behind two small hills separated by a saddle that lay across Masinissa's line of withdrawal. Hanno took the bait, and his men passed in route of march before the saddle. Scipio's cavalry poured through the opening and took Hanno's column violently in the flank. Masinissa now wheeled about and struck Hanno's column from the front. The first line of Hanno's men went down quickly, a thousand of them slain on the spot. Another 2,000 were captured or killed in pursuit. With Hanno out of the way, Scipio moved quickly to improve his position. For seven days his army stripped the countryside of cattle and other supplies, destroying what they could not carry. Scipio returned to his camp and continued the siege of Utica, which was proving to be a very tough nut to crack.

Hasdrubal arrived a month later with an army of 30,000 men and 3,000 horse. But his previous encounters with Scipio had made him cautious, and he waited for Syphax to arrive with another 50,000 men and 10,000 horse. This was an enormous force, and its presence near Utica forced Scipio to raise the siege after forty days and prepare to deal with the Carthaginian army. Hasdrubal continued to wait. Scipio moved his army into a new camp, Castra Cornelia, and heavily fortified it. Still Hasdrubal did nothing, until he finally went into winter quarters in an encampment along the Bagradas River seven miles from Scipio. Scipio's supplies were adequate for the winter, but his situation was desperate. The truth was that he was bottled up by an immensely larger force only a few miles distant. He could expect no reinforcements by sea, for Rome still regarded his invasion as folly. Masinissa, though loyal, was unable to raise more men. All in all, time was working against him. Either Scipio must find some way to alter the circumstances of his situation, or spring would find him at the mercy of the enemy.

There are few commanders possessed of an imagination sufficient to solve the problem in the manner in which Scipio did. His scouts had reported that the huts of the Carthaginian camp were made of wood. The Numidians fashioned their huts of interwoven reeds and matting. Unlike the Roman camp, neither enemy camp was laid out in orderly fashion; rather, the huts were often jumbled together, wall against wall. Dirt streets and paths ran among the huts, creating alleys and cul-de-sacs everywhere. Wooden palisades ringed the perimeter of the camps, permitting access only through a few gates. Scipio now lured the enemy commanders into another trap. On the pretext of trying to end the war, Scipio opened negotiations with the Carthaginians. He personally selected experienced centurions and scouts dressed as attendants to accompany the negotiators inside the enemy camp, where they noted the important details of the camp's defenses and its interior arrangement. Day after day Scipio kept the negotiations going until his plan and arrangements were complete. The Carthaginians finally grew weary of it all, and the negotiations stopped.

Scipio moved quickly to deceive the enemy as to his intentions. He issued orders for his troops to prepare for an attack against Utica so that the enemy would know his intentions. Next he put his ships to sea with siege equipment in full view and anchored them offshore of the city. To complete the deception, Scipio sent 2,000 infantry to seize a key hill overlooking the city. All this activity was arranged so that the Carthaginians would not be disturbed at the commotion in the Roman camp. When all was in readiness, Scipio ordered his officers to feed the army its evening meal early. Once darkness had fallen and the bugles had sounded the last call of the evening, as was the Roman custom before retiring, Scipio assembled the army and marched quietly over the seven miles to the enemy camp, arriving there completely undetected. Now Scipio divided his force, placing half under the command of Laelius who, along with Masinissa, was instructed to attack Syphax's camp. Scipio himself commanded the legions outside the Carthaginian camp. At the signal, Laelius's men attacked the gates of Syphax's camp in strength and sealed them off. The Roman scouts, familiar with the camp's arrangement from previous visits as attendants to the negotiators, ran through the camp setting it aflame. Within minutes, the reed and matting huts were engulfed in an enormous conflagration. The enemy, thinking the fire accidental, rushed from their huts and tried to put out the flames. As the flames raged out of control, Syphax's men tried to escape through the gates. Here they were met by the Romans, who slaughtered them without mercy. Forced back into the blazing camp, thousands were burned alive.

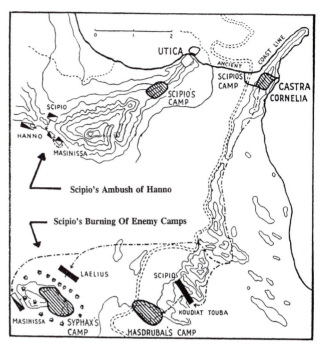

Figure 12.8 Scipio's Ambush and Burning of Enemy Camps

The commotion in the camp awakened the Carthaginians, who also thought the fire an accident. Many sought to give assistance to their allies. But as they attempted to leave the camp, Scipio's soldiers attacked them and drove them back. It was now that Scipio ordered his scouts into the Carthaginian camp to set it aflame, his main units following quickly behind and entering the camp in force. As in the other camp, thousands were slain or forced back into the flames where they were burned alive. Polybius describes the horrible sight.

> The two generals contrived to make their escape with a small body of cavalry; but of all the rest, thousands upon thousands of men, horses, mules perished miserably and piteously in the flames, while others of their comrades died a disgraceful and dishonorable death at the hands of the enemy as they strove to escape the fury of the fire, for they were cut down naked and defenseless, not only without arms but without even their clothes to cover them. The whole place was filled with the wails of dismay, confused shouting and cries of terror which mingled in an unspeakable din, while above all this rose the roar of the raging fire and flames which overcame all resistance. It was the combination and unexpectedness of these elements which made them so frightful, for indeed any one of them alone would have been enough to strike terror into the human heart.

According to Polybius, 40,000 soldiers died by the sword or the flames that day. Thousands more, no doubt, were burned and perished of their wounds later, and thousands more were scarred for life. A mere 5,000 were taken prisoner to be sold later as slaves.

It was a terrible defeat, but the Carthaginians were defending their homeland. Within a few months Hasdrubal and Syphax had raised a new army augmented by the arrival of 4,000 Spanish infantry from Iberia. Scipio, who had returned to trying to bring Utica to heel, received news that the new army was encamped only a few days' march away at a place called the Great Plain. He broke off the siege, assembled his army, and force-marched five days, bringing his army within sight of the Carthaginians. Scipio went into camp three miles from the enemy camp and immediately began harassing Hasdrubal to draw him out into battle. Scipio's eagerness to engage is easily explained by his own experience in commanding green troops in Spain. The Carthaginian levies were only recently raised and had little time to train. Except for the corps of Spanish infantry veterans, these levies were unreliable. Scipio intended to strike them before they had time to become prepared.

The two armies met in a set-piece battle on the open plain, and Scipio's sense that the new levies could be easily driven from the field proved correct. The Roman infantry fell on the Carthaginian center, comprising the veteran Spanish infantry, and held it in place. Laelius and Masinissa's cavalry quickly stripped the center of its wings and drove them from the field. Now Scipio's army showed its training. Instead of using the second and third ranks of the line to reinforce the first line in the center, Scipio sent them around the ends of the enemy center, completely enveloping it. Surrounded, the Spanish veterans fought on only to be slain to a man. The rest of the army took flight, including Hasdrubal and Syphax. Scipio recognized the opportunity before him and sent Masinissa in hot pursuit of Syphax, while Scipio himself cleansed the countryside of its supplies. Laelius joined the Roman pursuit, and Syphax himself was taken prisoner. Masinissa and Laelius took Syphax back to his capital and installed Masinissa as the new king. With the capture of Syphax, Scipio had landed a major strategic blow against Carthage. Syphax had been one of Carthage's most important allies, the source of much of its manpower and excellent cavalry. All this was now gone. To make matters worse, Masinissa now placed these resources at the disposal of Scipio.

The victory on the Great Plain proved that Scipio had been right all along in his assessment that the goal of military operations was to break the will of the Carthaginian *political* leadership to resist. The removal of Syphax from the strategic equation finally drove home the point to Carthage's leaders that the balance of resources had shifted dramatically. By invading Africa and inflicting several defeats on the Carthaginians, Scipio had reduced Hannibal's presence in Italy to a strategic irrelevancy. Hannibal could no longer affect the outcome of the war. Hannibal's original objective of breaking Rome's will to fight was no longer attainable if, indeed, it ever really was. In a battle of strategic endurance and political will, Rome had triumphed.

While powerful factions in the Carthaginian senate still opposed peace, others gained the ascendancy and sent envoys to Scipio to begin negotiations for peace. Scipio accepted their entreaties, and in a short time the outlines of a treaty were agreed to. The agreement was remarkable for its moderation and justice. Carthage then sent its envoys to Rome to negotiate a formal agreement with the Roman Senate. Rome was prepared to agree to the terms outlined by Scipio, but not until Hannibal and his army were withdrawn from Italy. Hannibal, of course, had anticipated the Roman objection and had already withdrawn his army into Italian ports and prepared ships for transporting it to Africa. While these events transpired, the war party regained control of the Carthaginian senate. They sent word to Hannibal that he was to depart immediately with his army. Hannibal arrived in Africa, expecting the war to be over. He was horrified to learn that the politicians expected him to continue the fight and march against Scipio. Ever the loyal son of Carthage, and against his better judgment, Hannibal Barca prepared to do just that.

When Scipio learned of these developments he was furious. Thinking that events were well in hand, he had made the mistake of sending ten *cohorts* of infantry with Masinissa to bolster his claim to the throne of Numidia. Now he sent word that Masinissa was to raise a large cavalry force and return quickly to Scipio. Hannibal, meanwhile, had landed at Hadrumetum on the coast with 24,000 veterans of his Italian campaign. He was immediately reinforced with 12,000 Carthaginian infantry and 2,000 horse. A contingent of 4,000 men sent by Carthage's ally, Philip V of Macedonia, arrived as well. Scipio knew that he dare not permit Hannibal's army to reach Carthage, where, using the city as a base of operations, it could hold out for months. But he was short of both infantry and cavalry and could not bring Hannibal to battle without great risk of defeat. How, then, to delay Hannibal without fighting a battle?

Once more the imaginative Scipio hit upon a brilliant plan, although not one without substantial risk. Scipio seized the offensive. He broke camp and marched his army along the Bagradas River, through the fertile farms and fields that fed Carthage, and began to destroy the towns and estates as he went. He refused to accept the surrender of any of the towns, taking them by fire and storm, causing great death and destruction, and selling their citizens into slavery. It was a classic demonstration of Roman anger and the might of Roman power and readiness to enforce its will. Scipio's campaign of terror had the predictable effect, and howls of protest rose from the seats of the Carthaginian senate. Powerful factions pressured Hannibal to take the offensive and bring Scipio

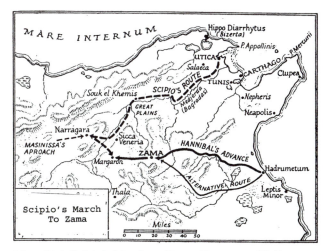

Map 12.6 Scipio's March to Zama. Courtesy of J. Dunn. Adapted from Leonard Cottrell, *Hannibal* (New York: Holt, Rinehart, and Winston, 1960).

to heel. After resisting for as long as he was able, Hannibal stirred his army and marched out of Hadrumetum in pursuit of Scipio. Once more, the great Carthaginian had been forced to act against his better judgment.

Hannibal was too good a general not to see what Scipio was up to. Scipio was marching *away* from Carthage but in a direction that closed the distance between him and Numidia, shortening the distance that Masinissa would have to travel to arrive with the needed cavalry reinforcements. Scipio was playing for time, and Hannibal knew it. But Hannibal had his own troubles. The core of his army was comprised of his Italian veterans. But the rest, including his cavalry upon which he depended so much, was made up of recent recruits with no experience. Even the terrain conspired against him, offering no opportunities for surprise. If there was to be a battle, it would take place in the open where cavalry would be vital to its outcome. But if he delayed much longer, the odds were good that Masinissa would arrive to reinforce Scipio. If this were to happen, defeating Scipio was almost out of the question. And so it was that Hannibal resolved to close the distance with Scipio and bring him to battle. The two armies met outside a small town that has been famous ever since—Zama.

Scipio had run out of time and running room. He drew his army into camp and prepared to fight. Once more Scipio played for time and succeeded in delaying battle for several days until, at last, Masinissa arrived. Both Polybius and Livy present an account of the meeting between Hannibal and Scipio that they say occurred the night before the battle. The accounts differ as to what was said, but both historians agree that nothing came of the meeting except, perhaps, that both commanders met face-to-face for the first time, each trying to take the measure of the other. But neither man was truly the master of his own actions, each trapped by the demands of his respective country. Later, the vision and humanity of both these great generals would play a part in the inevitable peace. But for now, the fate of Carthage would be decided by swords.

THE BATTLE OF ZAMA (202 B.C.E.)

Hannibal's army was built around the 24,000 veterans he had taken with him from Italy. These were combat-hardened soldiers, the equal of the best Roman infantry. Around this core were 12,000 Ligurian infantry, also experienced, and 4,000 Macedonians sent by Philip V of Macedon. The force was completed by the addition of 4,000 cavalry and contingents of Carthaginian citizen infantry. Hannibal's total force numbered approximately 55,000 men, including skirmishers and elephant troops. Scipio's force was much smaller. His campaigns in the Carthaginian countryside had cost him men and supplies, and he was desperately short of cavalry. The addition of 6,000 infantry and 4,000 Numidian cavalry brought Scipio's total force to no more than 36,000 men.

When Hannibal deployed from Carthage, Scipio had not yet received his units of Numidian cavalry. Seeking to delay the battle, Scipio moved toward Zama near the Bagradas River, a fertile area that supplied food to Carthage. As Hannibal moved toward him, Scipio withdrew, buying time until the Numidians arrived. After a few days, both armies were camped four miles apart on the plain behind the village. Hannibal sent out a scouting party to discern the Roman camp. Three of the party were captured. Much to the surprise of Hannibal, the scouts were allowed to return. They told a fantastic tale about being shown around the Roman camp by Scipio. The Roman commander, confident of victory, wanted them to report everything they had seen to Hannibal. In response, Hannibal suggested to Scipio that they meet in the evening, and hence, the meeting mentioned earlier that was recorded by both Livy and Polybius. Polybius says that Scipio ended the meeting with the challenge to Hannibal to "either put yourselves and your country at our mercy or fight and conquer us." The next day the two generals, among the best commanders in history, met in battle.

Scipio arranged his army in a slightly different formation than was usual for the Romans (see Figure 12.9). Although the infantry was arrayed in the usual three lines, Scipio abandoned the checkerboard formation and massed his maniples one behind the other, leaving clear lanes between them running through the entire formation from front to back. Hannibal's front line was thick with elephants, and the gaps between the Roman maniples were designed to give the animals a clear lane to run through when they charged. The lanes also permitted the light infantry skirmishers to withdraw quickly. Those being pursued were ordered to run outside the lanes and into the Roman infantry ranks. Outnumbered, Scipio sought to conserve as much manpower as possible. The left wing was anchored by Roman cavalry under the command of Laelius, the admiral of the fleet! The right wing was comprised of Numidian cavalry, probably 4,000 strong, under the command of Masinissa.

The mixed quality of Hannibal's troops, as always, determined his battle plan. This time, however, many of his troops were citizen levies or marginally experienced men. As at Cannae, Hannibal deployed his weakest and most expendable mercenary troops in the first of three infantry lines, accompanied by light troops. Behind them, but separated by a greater than normal distance, stood a line of Carthaginian and African levies, citizens pressed into service

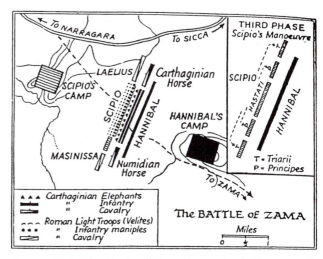

Figure 12.9 The Battle of Zama (202 B.C.E.). Courtesy of J. Dunn. Adapted from Leonard Cottrell, *Hannibal* (New York: Holt, Rinehart, and Winston, 1960).

in defense of their country. Behind them, but 200 yards to the rear, were Hannibal's veterans under his personal command. The Carthaginian cavalry deployed opposite Laelius, and the hired Numidian cavalry (some units remained loyal to Carthage even after Numidia changed sides) was positioned opposite Masinissa's 4,000-man force.

Hannibal attacked with eighty elephants, the greatest number he had ever used in a single battle. As the elephants closed, hundreds of Roman trumpets exuded a sudden roar of noise. At the same time, the skirmishers attacked the beasts with javelins, darts, and spears. The combination of fear and pain drove the elephants into a panic, and they stampeded back toward their own lines. Some of the animals crashed into Hannibal's Carthaginian cavalry, breaking their formations and scattering the mounts. As the cavalry was trying to re-form, Laelius, the Roman cavalry commander, struck the Carthaginians and began to drive them into flight. The elephants were still out of control and now wheeled into Hannibal's Numidian cavalry wing. Thrown into disarray, the cavalry broke apart and fled when Masinissa, seeing his opportunity, struck them with his 4,000 horses. Livy notes that "the Punic battle-line had been stripped of its cavalry when the infantry clashed."

But Scipio's cavalry was already engaged, and he had to face a numerically superior enemy with his outnumbered infantry. The Roman infantry fell on the Carthaginian first line, driving through it and sending it reeling back toward the second line. Hannibal had anticipated this and ordered that the second line not open its ranks. Met by a wall of shields and weapons, the remnants of the Carthaginian first line fled down the line and escaped on the flanks. Hoping to take advantage of the tired Roman first line, Hannibal ordered his second line to attack. The Roman line wavered, held, and moved its ends around the flanks of the Carthaginian line, pressing it from both sides and the center until it cracked. Once again, the remnants of the line were not allowed through the third line, but had to find refuge on the flanks.

The third phase of the battle now began when, says Livy, "the Romans had penetrated to their real antagonists, men equal to them in the nature of their arms, in their experience of war, and in the fame of their achievements." In the last line stood Hannibal's Imperial Guard, the survivors of almost twenty years of war against the Romans. They numbered 24,000. But Scipio recognized a replay of the battle of Cannae when he saw it. He discerned that Hannibal's plan was to allow the Romans to waste their strength on the weaker troops, become exhausted, and then be struck with Hannibal's freshest and most elite force. Hannibal gave the order for his veterans to attack.

There are times in war when all the training and discipline pays large dividends, and Zama was one of those times. With the enemy troops advancing toward them, Scipio ordered his men to shift battle formation. With the centurions barking orders, the men of the legions turned, retreated a small distance, abandoned the three-line formation, and formed a solid extended line with no gaps between the maniples. The extended Roman line now overlapped the flanks of the Carthaginian line. Moreover, the last two lines had not yet engaged and still had their *pila*. Upon command, they let fly a deadly shower of missiles into the enemy ranks. Scipio knew, however, that if the cavalry did not arrive in time, his thin line risked being penetrated and chopped up piecemeal.

For what must have seemed like a long time, the Roman line met and fought the charging Carthaginian formation . . . and held. Then, somewhat later than Scipio had planned, the Roman and Numidian cavalry returned to the field and struck the Carthaginians in the flank and rear. Gradually, the Roman infantry line encircled the enemy formation and proceeded grimly to hack the Carthaginian army to death. At the end of the day, 20,000 Carthaginian soldiers lay dead, and another 20,000 were taken prisoner. Hannibal, after leading charge after charge, escaped death and returned to Carthage. The battle of Zama had destroyed the last significant Carthaginian force left in the war and had brought to an end to the Second Punic War.

Within the Roman Senate there was a strong faction that opposed the peace with Carthage on the grounds that the eastern Mediterranean could not accommodate two great powers. Sooner or later, one or the other would have to be destroyed. But Scipio's views carried the day, and a peace treaty was signed ending the Second Punic War. Over the next decades the anti-Carthage faction continued to plot to provoke a war with Carthage. In 149 B.C.E. the anti-Carthage faction led by Marcus Pocius Cato saw its opportunity. A long-brewing dispute between Numidia and Carthage broke out into open warfare. Rome quickly sided with Numidia. Upon Roman demand, Carthage ceased military operations against Numidia, gave 300 hostages to Rome, surrendered most of its weapons, and dismantled the battlements of Carthage itself. These demands met, Rome pressed Carthage further. Rome now demanded that Carthage abandon the existing city altogether and move the populace inland. Carthage refused, and Cato had his war.

The initial Roman land and sea efforts against Carthage were repulsed by a vigorous defense of the city. Rome appointed Scipio Aemilianus (adopted grandson of Scipio Africanus) in 147 B.C.E. to command the Roman armies. He immediately undertook an invasion of Africa, bringing Carthage itself under blockade. For almost a year the population of the city suffered terribly from starvation and disease. In 146 B.C.E., the Romans attacked the city in force and carried the battlements. They then undertook a house-to-house battle for the capital. When it was over, nine-tenths of the population had perished. By order of the Roman Senate, the city was completely destroyed, and the survivors sold into slavery. Cato's famous statement made after the Second Punic War that "I am of the opinion that Carthage must be destroyed" ("*Carthago delenda est*") had come to fruition. Fortunately, neither Scipio nor Hannibal had lived to witness the terrible tragedy that befell beautiful Carthage.

THE COMMANDERS

Hannibal Barca (247–183 B.C.E.) was always portrayed by Roman writers as a harsh, semi-civilized, tribal brute. In truth he was a truly civilized Hellenic man of his times, well educated and religious in the fashion of his day. He spoke his mother tongue (Punic) as well as Greek, which he learned along with Greek history from a tutor provided by his father. Over his lifetime he became fluent in a number of tribal tongues and could often negotiate with tribal leaders in their own languages. He was religious, at least insofar as he paid the necessary obeisance to the gods of Carthage, and on a number of occasions sought the intercession of the gods to secure victory. In Roman eyes, of course, this was nothing more than the usual Punic duplicity. Perhaps. But how insincere could Hannibal have been in religious matters if, on the eve of his invasion of Italy, he traveled 700 miles from New Carthage to Gades to worship at the temple of Melkart, renew his vows to the gods, and beg for their intercession to bring him victory?

Hannibal spent most of his life in Iberia and grew to love the country and the people he knew better than those of his native Carthage. He refused the dress of the Carthaginian nobleman, preferring instead the simple garb of the Spanish soldier with its more durable woolen trousers and tough leather boots, what today we would call military field dress. Hannibal did pride himself on possessing the very best horses and weapons, however, a weakness easily understandable for a professional soldier of African origins where horses and horsemanship were highly regarded. Being accustomed to the military camp from his earliest years, Hannibal loved the military life and mingled comfortably with his troops. Livy says he often ate with them, preferring the common fare of the soldier to more exotic foods. Like Napoleon, Hannibal could sleep whenever he wished and wake refreshed, ready for action. He had the habit of the common soldier of dropping to the ground, wrapping himself in his warm woolen cloak, and falling asleep. When in the field he often slept among his men, waking and breakfasting with them on many occasions. He was in the prime of his life, physically strong, and capable of enduring extremes of heat and cold as he demonstrated many times during his crossing of the Alps and on the march across Italy. He was tireless as long as there was work to be done, and he supervised the planning of his campaigns in great detail rather than trust them to his staff. In this regard, Hannibal was one of the greatest logistics officers of the ancient world, managing to transport, sustain, and fight an army for sixteen long years while living off the land and having no external source of supply. Livy reports that Hannibal had a good sense of humor, which he displayed during stressful situations to calm his officers and men.

By birth and experience Hannibal was more a tribal chieftain than a staid military professional. From his father he had learned how to gain the loyalty of mercenary troops, but his manner of command was truly his own, a mix of Hamilcar's fierce discipline and Hasdrubal's patient and reasonable diplomacy. Hannibal was prone to a highly personal style of leadership, as befits a tribal chief who must lead by example, and more in the mold of the Greek warriors of the Heroic age than the Roman military professional that he fought. Like Philip of Macedonia, Alexander's father, Hannibal's men followed him because they trusted him not to squander their lives, knew that he would suffer whatever fate befell them, and admired his bravery in battle and his military skill. So successful was Hannibal in gaining the loyalty of his troops that in almost two decades of constant campaigning there were few instances of his men deserting him or betraying their loyalty toward him. And when he left Italy, he took his Spanish and African veterans with him, men who remained faithful to their commander right to the end.

The Romans always portrayed Hannibal as motivated by a hatred of Rome and point to the oath he had sworn as a boy as proof. There is no doubt that so solemn an oath taken at one's father's request had some effect on Hannibal's thinking, especially given the seriousness with which he regarded his word. But the Romans portray Hannibal's contempt for Rome as almost pathological, and that was surely not the case. There were many other reasons why Hannibal regarded Rome as dangerous. He certainly believed as did Hamilcar that another war with Rome was inevitable and that when it came Carthage's very survival would be at stake. In this he proved to be all too correct, although the great man did not live to see his beloved city destroyed at Roman hands. Psychologically, Hannibal was too complex a man to be understood by a single incident that occurred when he was little more than a child. Hannibal's war with Rome had much deeper roots.

Hannibal's entire life had been spent in the close company of soldiers, weapons, and war. There was no place more familiar or more comforting to him than the camaraderie of the military camp. He had trained all his life to be a soldier and to fight wars, that grand and terrible game but one that he enjoyed and at which he excelled. Those inexperienced in war often fail to appreciate how attractive it is, especially to the young. War is, after all, the ultimate test, the place where one risks all against the fates. If one survives, the experience shapes one's life forever. For a small group of men, like moths drawn to the flame, the experience beckons again and again, their reward always the respect of a chosen few. Hannibal was the warrior scion of a noble family of Carthaginian warriors, and he lived in a world where the pursuit of fame and glory was regarded, no less by the Romans who hated him, as a legitimate goal for a man to seek. It was quite natural that he should seek them.

With Hasdrubal dead, Hannibal found himself in command of a powerful army and governor general of all of Iberia. He could have chosen to stay on in Spain and live a comfortable life. Had he chosen to do so, his future would have fallen into a predictable pattern of suppressing one tribal revolt after another, supervising the construction of cities, and expanding Iberia's trade with Carthage—all, to be sure, worthy goals for a businessman seeking wealth, but ill-suited to a combat soldier still in the prime of life whose goal was glory. But Rome! Now there was a worthy adversary! A general's glory is measured by the quality of the enemies he faces, and in Rome Hannibal's enemies would be formidable indeed. As a philhellene tutored in Greek, Hannibal was no doubt aware of the parallels between himself and Alexander the Great. Both men had achieved high command at comparatively young ages, and although Alexander was younger by three years when he did so, Hannibal had by far the more combat experience. Both men followed famous warrior fathers whose reputation, perhaps, both may have felt they had to exceed to achieve a full measure of glory. The fathers of both men bequeathed to their sons ready-made reasons and plans for war, Philip for a war against Persia, and Hamilcar for a contest with Rome. And both men were handed the appropriate instruments by their fathers to pursue their ambitions, in Alexander's case the new Macedonian army and Hamilcar's army of Spain for Hannibal. Finally, both Alexander and Hannibal lived at a time when their adversaries where in dynamic motion, when for either man to do nothing placed him and his ambitions at great risk. Sooner or later there would be a war between Persia and Greece and between Rome and Carthage. The only question was who would fight it and win. In both cases the world itself conspired to present Alexander and Hannibal with tempting opportunities for glory and fame. It seems pointless to condemn either man for seizing them.

No general in Western history ever remained in the field for so long, fought so many battles, and won so many victories as did Hannibal, who kept his army together and fighting in a hostile country and was still able to extricate his men successfully from the war zone. He was, by this standard, "greater than Napoleon" and greater than Frederick the Great, Wellington, and even Alexander. As a field general, Hannibal Barca has no equal in ancient or modern history. His talent arose from many sources but none more important than his clear intellect. Hannibal was a first-rate strategic thinker, and he thought strategically on a very grand scale indeed. His plan to invade Italy was breathtaking in its sweep and daring, and no Roman statesman or general ever imagined the war with Carthage would be fought on Italian soil. It was a strategy that Hannibal pursued from beginning to end, never wavering from its objectives. To the last he tried to shatter the Roman confederacy with diplomacy and cunning. Hannibal was also a tactical genius. Time and again he lured the Romans into a trap, always making the terrain, rivers, or weather conditions work for him. Except for Zama, he always chose his battlefield, refusing combat when he could not control its location. His superb tactical brilliance was evident at Cannae, where he turned the open plain into a trap in full sight of his opponent. He even took advantage of his opponent's character, tailoring his movements and tactics to exploit his rival's weaknesses of personality. Few officers then or since have possessed such a complete array of tactical skills.

As a logistician and administrator, Hannibal has few peers. He roamed

Italy for sixteen years, always provisioning and equipping his army from the enemy's stores and trying not to alienate the cities and towns upon which the ultimate hope of his strategy depended. And he did it without the aid of mechanical devices or a professional staff upon which modern commanders rely. That he was a leader of great skill is clear enough from his ability to maintain the loyalty and trust of an army that was comprised of so many divergent peoples and customs. In the long years of war, only one Carthaginian officer left him. There are no reports of his troops ever having refused an order or committing mutiny. He was an audacious and opportunistic leader, always willing to take chances and run risks. Again and again he gambled, winning almost always and never losing to the degree that further action was impossible. Against him Rome offered the best military men they possessed, and he defeated all who dared do battle with him. It was only when Hannibal faced a general who had studied his own success and abilities that he was defeated in the field, and then only under conditions so unfavorable that it is unlikely any general could have succeeded. It is unlikely that we will ever look upon the likes of Hannibal Barca again.

Publius Cornelius Scipio (236–183 B.C.E.), also called *Africanus* in gratitude for his victory over Hannibal in Africa, stands in the center of the history of Republican Rome. Before Scipio no Roman would have dreamed of empire. Scipio himself would have regarded such a vision as dangerous to his beloved Republic. And yet the paradox remains that it was Scipio's victories that gained Spain and Africa for Rome and established Roman influence over the eastern Mediterranean and forced it to eventually confront the power of Greece and Syria as threats to the new Roman security perimeter. In short order Greece and Syria were reduced to Roman will, and the empire was being born even before Scipio died. In his personal life Scipio was a proponent of the new cultural and intellectual forces emanating from Rome's contact with Greece that were challenging the old Roman ways. It was a long time before these cultural strains emerged into a new blend that eventually became the Graeco-Roman culture of the imperium. These strains were in their embryonic stages during Scipio's lifetime. Nevertheless, he seems to have been a strong proponent of their integration into Roman life.

Scipio was one of Rome's greatest commanders, if not the greatest of them all. He ranks with the Duke of Marlborough as one of history's few commanders who never suffered a defeat in battle while he was in command of the army. It was Napoleon who remarked that, "in war, it is not men, but the man, that counts." This is surely a fitting description of Scipio, for few generals in history displayed such daring, imagination, and innovation as he. He fought against some of the best generals of the ancient world and defeated every one of them, including the best of them all, Hannibal Barca. Indeed it was Hannibal himself who said that had he defeated Scipio at Zama, he would have considered himself to be a general even greater than Alexander!

Publius Cornelius Scipio was born in 236 B.C.E., the eldest of two sons, into one of the great patrician families of the Republic. His father was Publius Cornelius Scipio, who was elected consul in 218 B.C.E. to deal with Hannibal's invasion of Italy. Later, his father commanded the Roman armies in Spain. He no doubt received the usual education for a Roman patrician of his day. What was unusual in this young Roman was Scipio's fondness for things Greek. It seems certain that he was instructed in Greek history and literature, and the fact that he spoke and wrote Greek is beyond doubt. At some point, perhaps shortly after Cannae, Scipio married Aemilia, the daughter of Aemilius Paulus, consul in 216 B.C.E. who fell at Cannae. He fathered two sons, Publius and Lucius, and two daughters, only one of which, Cornelia, has come down to us by name.

A sense of what Scipio looked like can be drawn from an examination of the few surviving busts of the man. It can be assumed with some confidence that he was of average height, about five feet seven inches or so, and of stocky muscular build common to Romans of the day who lived an active life. Likenesses of Scipio on coins show his hair cut in moderate length in the usual Roman style. Later, he is portrayed as bald but with a thick ring of hair running around his neck and ears. He is clean-shaven in Roman military fashion. His facial features, marked by a high forehead, thick eyebrows, and deep-set eyes protected by prominent ridges and high cheekbones, seem to reveal strength and determination. There is a seriousness in his face, a Roman *gravitas*, that reveals a man confident in himself, willing to endure, and, if need be, willing even to suffer to achieve his ends. Although a true Roman in his love for tradition and custom, Scipio was possessed of a brilliant intellect sharpened by his training in Greek rationalism.

Scipio understood soldiers and their need for something to believe in that was greater than themselves. He understood that a soldier's trust in his commander bordered upon the mystical, almost a religious faith in itself. And if the soldier's belief in the gods sustained his faith in his commander, it would be a foolish commander who neglected the gods. Both Scipio's faith and intellect spoke to him thus. Perhaps because of his faith and intellect, Scipio's troops trusted him implicitly and were steadfastly loyal. They thought him to be a fair man who could be relied upon not to take unnecessary risks or to squander their lives through incompetence. Paradoxically, this belief was rooted in Scipio's reluctance to expose himself to death. Having gained a reputation for bravery as a young officer at the Ticinus, Scipio never again risked his life without first calculating the odds and making certain they were always in his favor. He realized, as his men did, that his life was more important to the larger goal at hand than personal heroism. Scipio was more the modern commander than the Homeric hero. His troops appreciated his caution, for it extended to them as well. He could be daring in war, but only when daring was supported by a careful plan. He sent men again and again into harm's way, but only after he had calculated the odds of success. Soldiers may respect personal heroism in a commander, but they value more his competence, caring, and record of success; for these qualities are what increase the chances that they, too, will survive the battle to fight another day.

The character evident in his command of men in battle revealed itself even more clearly once he relinquished the sword and returned to civilian life. Because of his achievements in war, the people and the Senate clamored to make him a consul for life. Some even suggested he become a dictator. But Scipio was a republican to his core and loathed regal power for the threat it presented to liberty and law. Polybius tells us that Scipio refused the honors, rebuking those who offered them as creating a threat to their own liberties. Later, when elected a senator, he put a stop to numerous efforts to raise statues to him. In one case he prevented a Senate decree that would have installed his image in the temple of Jupiter. Like Cincinnatus before him, he refused all such honors as dangerous to the Republic. Few men in history have been able to resist such temptations at so young an age as Scipio.

Scipio continued to remain active in public life even as his political enemies plotted against him. He worked tirelessly to prevent vengeful Roman politicians from imposing additional punishments on Carthage. Some of these, like Cato, plotted to provoke another war with Carthage to destroy her once and for all. These machinations led to trumped-up charges of bribery against Scipio, who showed his contempt for his accusers by refusing to attend the trial, which, in any event, found him innocent. He retired to his estate and never again entered public life, preferring instead to write an account of his military exploits. Scipio Africanus died in self-imposed exile in 183 B.C.E. at the age of fifty-two. Across the Mediterranean, at the age of sixty-five, his great rival, Hannibal Barca, died in the same year.

LESSONS OF WAR

Strategy

1. Political objectives direct political and military strategy. The Romans used diplomacy to begin the war, to guide its military commanders, and to secure the removal of Hannibal from Italy. Political leaders ought never to abandon control of military policy to generals. Carthage did just that and allowed its field commanders to set political policy. In the words of Clemenceau, "War is much too important a business to be left to generals."

2. The center of gravity in war is often the political will of the adversary. Military strategy always serves the political objective of overcoming the will of the adversary to resist. General Lee fought the battle of Gettysburg for precisely this reason. So did the Viet Cong at Tet.

3. Strategic endurance is a central calculation in war. Endurance includes human will as well as material resources. Often, human will and dedication to a religious or ideological cause is the more important factor. Remember Vietnam. Remember Iraq.

4. Military ventures depend ultimately on the ability to sustain popular support for a war. This is especially true in the open and periodically unstable political systems inherent in democracies.

5. The advantages enjoyed by a commercial empire with large holdings abroad can become, in time of war, enormous liabilities if it does not command the sea lanes. A maritime power that cannot control the sea will cease to be a great power.

6. There is no substitute for a large navy if you are a maritime power.

7. Modern wars depend heavily on the integration of ground, air, and sea power. Hannibal fought a war a long way from home without sufficient command of the sea. Joint operations are the future.

8. Be alert to the development of new technologies; they can often have devastating impact. The introduction of the *corvus* and the grappling iron tipped the naval balance against Carthage.

9. Always keep a close watch on a defeated power. How one ends a conflict will have an impact on the nature of the next conflict. If no effort is made to adjust a state's changing interests to the status quo ante, it is likely to develop feelings of revenge. Sooner or later, when it feels able, it will mount challenges to the status quo. There is little difference in this regard between Carthage after the First Punic War and Germany in the interwar period.

10. There are severe limits on the extent to which military brilliance in the field can compensate for eventual shortages of strategic resources. Japan forgot this lesson in 1941 when it attacked Pearl Harbor. So did Carthage when it attacked Rome. The South in the Civil War made the same mistake.

11. A nation's reputation for fairness, steadiness, morality, and loyalty often pays significant dividends over the long run. These desirable national characteristics, however, are not a substitute for policy. Avoid becoming committed on sentimental grounds.

12. Diplomatic skill can often obtain what force cannot. A nation ought never to rely totally upon military solutions to political problems. Beware of Yugoslavia!

13. Some problems have no immediate solutions. The passage of time often creates new realities.

14. Avoid wars of attrition. Victory tends to be Pyrrhic.

15. Remember Fabius! Sometimes the denial of battle is the most effective military strategy. Napoleon and Hitler both learned this important lesson when they tried to subdue the Russian colossus.

Tactics

1. Use guile, surprise, and maneuver to offset numerical advantage. In every battle until Zama, Hannibal fought outnumbered and won.

2. If you are not ready for battle, follow the example of Scipio at Zama and delay. Never be rushed into committing yourself to a fight.

3. Train, train, train! Scipio's example suggests there is no substitute in preparing for war other than difficult and realistic training to instill discipline and familiarity with weapons. The best time to prepare for war is in peacetime.

4. Think creatively. Once the weaknesses of your adversary have been discerned, continue to use your imagination until you have found ways to exploit those weaknesses. Hannibal brilliantly exploited the Roman weakness of tactical security time and time again.

5. Never let the "system" get in the way of tactical innovation. At Trebia, Trasimene, and Cannae, Roman commanders continued to use the tactical system in the same manner even though it produced defeat after defeat. The "system" is only a tool, and it must be used differently in different situations to ensure success.

6. There is almost no substitute for tactical surprise.

7. Choose and use terrain to maximum advantage. Constantly study the terrain. Always look for an edge.

8. Be careful if you divide command. A combat army in the field is an instrument of a single commander's will. Unclear directions risk disaster.

9. In the same manner that Hannibal utilized his various types of units to weave a tactical tapestry, modern commanders must integrate various types of units and integrate them into an overall design of battle. Learn to play to the strengths and weakness of *all* combat assets.

10. Avoid employing cavalry (or armor) without infantry support, especially in difficult terrain. The Israeli Defense Force in Lebanon, as well as Varro at Cannae, learned this lesson the hard way.

11. Maintain tactical security at all times. Flaminius forgot this at Trasimene, and it cost him his army and his life.

12. Learn the elements of battle and how they fit together before developing a tactical plan. Make maximum use of all your resources.

13. Stress and use tactical intelligence!

14. An army on the march or moving into position is at its most vulnerable and tempts an enemy commander to strike.

15. Learn how to conduct a retreat in good order.

16. In the words of Napoleon, "never stop an adversary from making a mistake." Hannibal allowed the armies of Scipio and Sempronius to link up so that he could destroy them both.

17. Remember Mago's ambush. Sometimes even a small force used at the critical moment can have an enormous impact on the battle.

18. Think things through clearly. Do not be moved by anger or hatred; they cloud the intellect. Sempronius forgot this fact.

19. Keep the troops in good health and fighting trim. Look after their needs—provide them with oil for their bodies on a cold day.

20. Hannibal fought in the center of the line. Avoid the tendency to "manage systems" or "orchestrate the battle." A combat commander's job is to lead men. Be seen on the field of battle. Remember Rommel and Patton.

21. Be aware of how the weather alters the battlefield. It creates both dangers (Flaminius) and opportunities (Hannibal).

22. The success of campaigns often hinges on the struggle for the "hearts and minds" of the civilian populace. This is especially true in unconventional environments. Be sensitive to the consequences of your actions on people and property. Recall the Soviets in Afghanistan and the Americans in Vietnam.

23. Make good and frequent use of your combat reconnaissance units. They are your eyes and ears.

24. The reputations of military men are *always* subject to changes in political fortune at home. Fabius and Patton knew this well.

25. When things are going too well or the battle is progressing too easily, as with the Romans in the opening phases at Cannae, this is the time to be most alert. *War is never easy. . . . There are no easy victories.*

26. Be aware of the human cost of war. Stay the hand of violence when circumstances permit. Read Livy's account of Cannae . . . often!

FURTHER READING

Arnold, T. *The Second Punic War.* London: Macmillan, 1886.

Bagnall, Nigel. *The Punic Wars: 264–146 B.C.* London: Osprey, 2002.

Boardman, John. *The Oxford Illustrated History of Rome.* London: Oxford University Press, 2001.

Cornell, T. J. *The Beginnings of Rome: Italy and Rome from the Bronze Age to the Punic Wars.* New York: Routledge, 1995.

Cottrell, Leonard. *Hannibal: Enemy of Rome.* New York: Holt, Rinehart, and Winston, 1960.

Daly, Gregory. *Cannae: The Experience of Battle in the Second Punic War.* New York: Routledge, 2001.

De Beer, Gavin. *Hannibal: Challenging Rome's Supremacy.* New York: Viking, 1970.

Delbruck, Hans. *History of the Art of War within the Framework of Political History.* Vol. 1, *Antiquity.* Westport, CT: Greenwood Press, 1975.

Dodge, Theodore A. *Hannibal: A History of the War among the Carthaginians and Romans down to the Battle of Pydna, 168 B.C., with a Detailed Account of the Second Punic War.* New York: Da Capo, 1995.

Fuller, J. F. C. *A Military History of the Western World.* 3 vols. New York: Da Capo Press, 1954.

Gabba, Emilio. *Republican Rome, the Army, and Allies.* Berkeley: University of California Press, 1977.

Grant, Michael. *The Army of the Caesars.* New York: Charles Scribner, 1978.

Harris, William V. *War and Imperialism in Republican Rome.* London: Clarendon Press, 1985.

Holland, Tim. *Rubicon: The Last Years of the Roman Republic,* Garden City, NJ: Doubleday, 2003.

Lamb, Harold. *Hannibal: One Man against Rome.* Garden City, NJ: Doubleday, 1958.

Lancel, Serge, and Antonia Nevill. *Hannibal.* London: Blackwell Publishers, 1998.

Liddell Hart, B. H. *Greater Than Napoleon—Scipio Africanus.* London: Blackwood and Sons, 1926.

O'Connell, Robert. "The Roman Killing Machine." *Quarterly Journal of Military History* (Autumn 1988): 30–41.

Polybius. *The Histories of Rome.* London: William Heinemann, 1922.

Prevas, John. *Hannibal Crosses the Alps: The Invasion of Italy.* New York: Da Capo Press, 2001.

Santosuosso, Antonio. *Soldiers, Citizens, and the Symbols of War: From Classical Greece to Republican Rome.* Boulder, CO: Westview, 1997.

Sekunda, Nick. *The Roman Republican Army.* London: Osprey, 1996.

Starr, Chester G. *The Roman Imperial Navy.* Cambridge: Heffer, 1960.

Titus Livius (Livy). *The History of Rome.* London: G. Bell and Sons, 1919.

Vegetius, Renatus Flavius. *The Military Institutions of the Romans.* Harrisburg, PA: Stackpole, 1960.

Warmington, B. H. *Carthage.* New York: Praeger, 1960.

Watson, George R. *The Roman Soldier.* Ithaca, NY: Cornell University Press, 1969.

Webster, Graham. *The Roman Army.* London: Grosvenor Museum, 1956.

Williams, J. H. C. *Beyond the Rubicon: Romans and Gauls in Republican Italy.* London: Oxford, 2001.

Wise, Terrence. *The Armies of the Carthaginian Wars, 265–146 B.C.* London: Osprey Series, 1988.

———. *Hannibal's War with Rome: The Armies and Campaigns.* London: Osprey, 1999.

ROME AGAINST GREECE

[201–146 B.C.E.]

BACKGROUND

The fundamental weakness of the empire forged by Alexander the Great was its lack of an institutional base that could manage the transition of power after Alexander's death. The empire was, at its end, what it was at the beginning, the product of one man's dream. While there is little doubt that Alexander planned to create formal governmental institutions that would manage the empire after his death, his demise occurred before any of these plans could be put into effect. When Alexander died, his empire died with him.

From the very beginning, there had always been those within Alexander's personal retinue that cared little for his dream of a pan-Hellenic empire in which non-Greeks lived as equals with their Greek conquerors. Many of Alexander's generals, including Parmenion, were strongly attached to the traditional Greek idea that men fought for glory and plunder and not to create idealistic political orders. Having conquered Asia, these senior officers saw no reason they should not enjoy the privileges of conquest. The tension between these two points of view continued for years within Alexander's army and, in one instance, culminated in an assassination plot against Alexander. With Alexander's death, the dream of a pan-Hellenic empire was abandoned among Alexander's successors. The future of the empire was settled in traditional Greek fashion, by a series of wars among would-be successors for control of the spoils.

The result was the Wars of the Successors, a period from 323 to 280 B.C.E., where Alexander's generals and their heirs fought one another to carve out spheres of influence within which to establish their own dynasties. The political entities that finally emerged from these wars were mostly defined by the territories occupied by the various contending armies at the end of the wars.

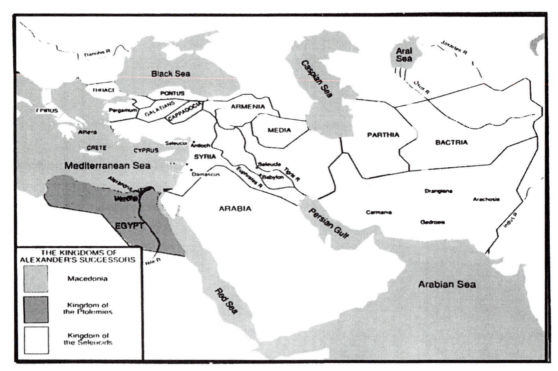

Map 13.1 The Kingdoms of Alexander's Successors

When it was over, three major imperial realms came into existence. The Antigonids ruled mainland Greece and Macedonia, The Ptolemies ruled Egypt, and the Seleucids controlled most of southwest Asia, an empire that ran from the Aegean to the Hindu Kush. Map 13.1 portrays the territories included in each of the Successor empires.

The nature of these empires was fundamentally different from the type of polity envisioned by Alexander. The Successor empires represented the imposition of Greek military oligarchies upon various conglomerations of native populations conditioned to docility by centuries of foreign occupation by one power or another. Greek rule was perpetuated by establishing military garrisons at key points throughout the respective realms and settling these garrisons with Greeks, sometimes through forcible resettlement policies. The general docility of the populations of the Ptolemaic and Seleucid empires was not, however, characteristic of the populations of Greece under Macedonian Antigonid control.

The Greek city-states had long regarded Macedonian domination of Greece as conquest. Even under Philip and Alexander, the Greek states regarded the Macedonian presence in mainland Greece as the imposition of a foreign power whose influence was maintained by military force. The Greek states continually attempted to reduce Macedonian influence by increasing their own freedom of action in foreign and domestic affairs. Macedon controlled Greece by the military occupation of key garrisons. Three of these garrisons—

Demetrias, Chalcis, and the Acrocorinth—were so important to continued Macedonian control that they were known collectively as "the fetters of Greece," and many of the policies of the Greek city-states were designed to lessen Macedonian control of these critical garrisons.

Within and around the periphery of Macedonian-controlled Greece there remained a number of states that were relatively independent and capable of resisting Macedonian control with military force. Rhodes and Pergamum were two such states. Within Greece itself, smaller states formed into collective leagues—the Achaen League was one example—to press their interests for more freedom of maneuver. These leagues were essentially political alliances to provide leverage against Macedonian policies. They were, as well, potential military alliances that could act in collective self-defense.

The Macedonian grip on Greece was fragile. Macedon was continually forced to deal with the political machinations of individual and collective city-states attempting to loosen the bonds of Macedonian political control. The ability to bring these states to heel in a particular case was effective only at the extremes, namely in the case of war. On a day-to-day basis, however, Macedonian power was far more limited. The cost of standing armies and the destruction wrought by war made the utilization of military force a last resort. The propensity of the Greek states to attempt to forge alliances with the Ptolemies and the Seleucids also represented a threat to Macedonian control. Overriding it all was the fact that the three major empires continually viewed one another with suspicion and often fought each other over one issue or another. From the Macedonian perspective, the greatest danger lay in the propensity of the smaller states to attract one of the other great powers to come to their aid with military force. The entire political and military arrangement of the Antigonid empire was fraught with danger and likely to explode at a moment's notice.

The period from 280 to 197 B.C.E., the year of the battle of Cynoscephalae, was a transitional period in the political and military history of Greece and the eastern Mediterranean. When it began, Alexander's Successors (the *Diadochi*) held the entire area in a firm military and political grip. Greek values remained the dominant cultural form of the area, and Greek arms dominated the practice of military science. When this period ended, however, the three Successor empires were in ruins, Greek culture was held prisoner to Roman *gravitas*, and the Greek influence on military history was swept from the historical scene, never to emerge as a major force again. Simultaneously, the Macedonian military system, which had remained unchallenged for more than a century and a half, also met its death at the hands of a new military system, the legions of Rome. The new Roman system of war continued in the area in one form or another for more than 1,600 years until it finally was destroyed at the siege of Byzantium by the Turks in 1453 C.E. It is difficult to find any other period in ancient history that was more momentous for the development of warfare in the West.

For most of the period from 280 to 197 B.C.E., however, the Macedonian system of war and the "military monarchies" that constituted the imperial legacy of Alexander's Successors ruled with little challenge from any power except that which they routinely posed to one another. During this period Rome was preoccupied with expanding its hold on the Italian peninsula. It was also during this time that Rome fought the First (264–241 B.C.E.) and Second (219–201 B.C.E.) Punic Wars in which Italy itself was invaded by Carthaginian armies that stretched Roman resources to the breaking point. The Romans, however, were well aware of the Greeks and their tendency to interfere in events on the Italian peninsula. Between 280 and 275 B.C.E., Pyrrhus, king of Epirus in northwestern Greece, invaded Italy. In 260 B.C.E., Rome had to deal with the machinations of another Greek state, the Illyrians, by military force. After the battle of Cannae (215 B.C.E.) in which Roman armies were slaughtered at the hands of Hannibal, Philip V of Greece sought to take advantage of the weakened Roman position and entered into an alliance with Hannibal. Although little came of this alliance, it had the effect of heightening Roman concerns about the intentions of the great Greek power that lay just across the narrow straits of the Adriatic. With the final defeat of Hannibal by Scipio at Zama in 202 B.C.E., Rome was able to turn its attention to the Greek threat.

This period was also one of significant transition in military systems. In the case of the Roman army, the Punic Wars had provided it with the opportunity successfully to transform the old phalanx legion into the more flexible and deadly manipular legion. The old legion had proven too brittle to withstand the attacks of tribal armies and was gradually reformed. The Romans had also learned to use cavalry with some skill in concert with their infantry, and the Punic Wars provided Rome with a cadre of battle-hardened officers and troops. Under Scipio at Zama, the new legions had proven to be a formidable instrument of combat. As regards the Macedonians, the armies and military system brought into existence by Philip and Alexander had, for more than a century, provided the world with the most effective combat force in the ancient world. But the Macedonian army that fought at Cynoscephalae was not the army of Alexander, although its reputation as the most successful military system remained intact. The battle of Cynoscephalae brought about the clash of two rival military systems, one with a proven record of success (Macedon) and the other (Rome) relatively new.

The battle of Cynoscephalae, then, is important to military history in two major respects. First, it signaled Roman intentions to expand its control to the eastern Mediterranean. It was the first battle in a campaign of new Roman imperialism, and when the campaign ended, the Greek world and its culture were superseded by a new world order dominated by Roman values, culture, and military forms. The influence of all things Roman remained for the next millennium and a half. Second, Cynoscephalae was the first clash of two rival military systems and introduced to the world a new form of combat and military organization that dominated the West for more than a thousand years. For more than three centuries, cavalry had played an important role on the battlefield as an arm of decision. Cynoscephalae represented the return of disciplined infantry as the dominant arm of decision. Cynoscephalae was the first battle in a campaign of Roman conquest, and when it was over neither military history nor the history of the Western world was ever the same.

Prior to the events leading up to the battle of Cynoscephalae (197 B.C.E.), Rome had a long, and mostly unpleasant, history of dealing with the Greek states across the Adriatic. The problems were mostly with the small states located on the periphery of the Macedonian empire rather than with the great Antigonid power itself. Map 13.2 shows the general geographic area of Roman-Greek conflict for the period under examination. During the First Punic War, Rome established a military fortress at Brindisium on the heel of the Italian boot to control Carthaginian shipping through the narrow straits of the Adriatic. The Illyrians, however, saw the Roman base as constricting their trade through the straits, and for sixteen years Illyrian pirates harassed Roman shipping and murdered Roman merchants. After repeated Roman requests to stop, Rome sent an army in 230 B.C.E. to put an end to this state of affairs. This was the first direct Roman military contact with a state across the Adriatic. Rome established a protectorate over a number of Greek coastal towns.

Map 13.2 Area of Roman Operations in Greece

A decade later (220 B.C.E.), a Greek adventurer named Demetrius attempted to formulate a rebellion against Roman control, and Rome sent troops to crush the revolt. Demetrius fled to the court of Philip V of Macedon who provided refuge. In Roman eyes, this act of sanctuary increased their suspicion of Macedonia. Thus, just prior to Hannibal's invasion of Italy, Rome was already involved in a minor conflict with one of the three major Greek powers.

Philip's distrust of the Romans also deepened. He realized that any conflict with Rome over territories on the Adriatic conferred upon Rome the advantage of geography. Moreover, the nature of Macedonian rule meant that there was no shortage of city-states within Greece that would exploit a Roman initiative by joining it as a way of weakening Macedonian control over the Greek mainland. After the battle of Cannae, Philip entered into an alliance with Hannibal. The intention was to provide Hannibal with supplies (and, if events proved fortuitous, perhaps troops), but Hannibal had no fleet to transport these supplies and Philip's fleet was no match for the Roman naval presence off Brindisium. Philip's hope for a Roman defeat at the hands of Carthage came to nothing, and, after the Carthaginian defeat at Zama, Philip attempted to improve relations with Rome.

Although relations improved, Roman suspicions of the Greek power on their flank prompted Rome to make an alliance with the Aetolian League, a group of states in central Greece that resisted Macedonian rule. This was the first formal alliance that Rome concluded with a state on Greek soil. It was an ominous portent. In Philip's view, it was nothing less than the beginning of a Roman policy to destroy Macedon by encouraging rebellion from within the empire. In 203 B.C., Philip concluded an alliance with the Seleucids who were engaged in a campaign against the Ptolemies in Egypt. Philip was attempting to use the Seleucids as a counterweight to Rome.

The Greek city-states were concerned lest the new alliance by two of the major powers of the area be used against them as well. Both Rhodes and Pergamum felt especially threatened, and both states appealed to Rome to force the Seleucids and Macedonians apart as the only way of maintaining the regional balance of power and guaranteeing their own freedom. The Roman Senate delivered an ultimatum to Macedon demanding that Rhodes and Pergamum be granted independent status and that Macedon abstain from any further interference with the Greek states. The demands were impossible to meet, and the result was war. Roman troops embarked for Greece, and for three years a series of indecisive military skirmishes occurred among Macedonian forces, the armies of the rebellious city-states, and the Romans. In 197 B.C.E., the two major antagonists met in battle at Cynoscephalae, literally, the "Dog's Head."

THE ANTIGONID ARMY

The general structure of the Macedonian armies under the Antigonids during the period of the Successors remained essentially as it had been during the

Alexandrian period—a force comprised of the central phalanx organized into *taxeis* of infantry, coupled with *ile* or squadrons of cavalry. As the structure of the Alexandrian armies has already been explored in some detail in a previous chapter, it is sufficient here to examine only the departures from the Alexandrian model that appeared during the period of the Successors. While the general structure of the army remained, it is important to note that the manner in which the Macedonians tactically employed their armies was significantly different from the manner in which Alexander had used them.

Tactics

The major difference between the Macedonian model and the armies of Alexander was that the role of infantry in tactical application changed substantially. Alexander used the infantry phalanx as a platform of maneuver to pin the enemy in place until he exploited the development of the battle with his cavalry. The Alexandrian cavalry, then, was typically the arm of decision. Under the Macedonians, the roles were reversed, with infantry used as the primary striking and killing force, while the cavalry was relegated to a secondary role. It is difficult to find a battle of the later Successor period where cavalry played a decisive role.

A number of factors contributed to this reversal of tactical roles. First, unlike the Seleucid empire, the Macedonians quickly lost interest in affairs in Asia where the enemy armies consisted mainly of cavalry. The Macedonians fought mostly against the former city-states of Greece proper, which, following the Alexandrian model, had relinquished the old hoplite phalanx and adopted the weapons (*sarissa*) and formations of the Macedonian phalanx. Great improvements in siegecraft made the city-state more vulnerable than ever before, and the social system that supported the old hoplite system collapsed. More and more often the armies of the smaller city-states were comprised of mercenaries and professionals who adopted the phalanx as the more effective form of ground warfare. As a consequence, Macedonian armies fought mostly infantry battles against fellow Greeks armed with similar weapons and arrayed in similar battle formations. The result was a renewed emphasis on infantry as the primary arm of decision.

A second reason for the reemphasis on infantry lay in the fact that the Macedonians generally perceived these conflicts more as police actions than as genuine wars. A similar development occurred in the other Successor empires. The role of the imperial armies was more domestic suppression than combat against foreign enemies. Under these conditions, trained infantry were considerably cheaper and more effective than the use of expensive cavalry. Finally, generals of the ancient world had no less tendency than their modern counterparts to fight the last war all over again or to learn the wrong lessons from previous battles. In 217 B.C.E., Antiochus III of the Seleucids and Ptolemy IV of Egypt, rival monarchs of the other two Successor realms, fought a great battle at Raphia. In this battle the cavalry forces of the two armies canceled each other out, and the battle was ultimately decided by infantry. The lessons of Hannibal's campaigns during the Second Punic War seem to have taught the Greeks a similar lesson. Hannibal had excellent cavalry, while that of the Romans was traditionally poor. Yet, it was Roman infantry that finally won the war. The lesson the Macedonians drew from both these wars was that cavalry was no longer the decisive arm it had been. The future lay with infantry.

By the battle of Cynoscephalae, the Macedonian emphasis on infantry had changed the combat power of the phalanx. It became a cumbersome thing that had lost almost all the flexibility it once possessed under Alexander. Under the Antigonids, the phalanx grew considerably heavier, and it is possible that the *syntagma* (Figure 13.1), a unit of about 800 men, had replaced the *taxeis* as the basic component of the phalanx. Smaller organizational units would have made the phalanx somewhat more manageable. Alexander deployed his phalanx in various depths depending upon the demands of the tactical situation. At its heaviest, the Alexandrian phalanx was sixteen-men deep. The Macedonian phalanx ranged in depth from sixteen- to thirty-two-men deep and, in some instances, even denser than that. This increase in depth

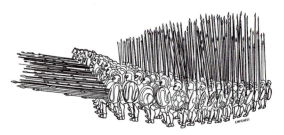

Figure 13.1 The Antigonid *Syntagma* (197 B.C.E.)

adequately demonstrates the change in tactical concept for the use of infantry. When used as a platform of maneuver, it was the stability and training of the phalanx that was most important. But when used as a decisive arm, the bulk and momentum of the phalanx became most important. The increased density of the phalanx reflected its changing combat role under the Macedonians.

The weaponry of the Macedonian phalanx also changed. Alexander's infantry carried the *sarissa*, and while there is some debate as to its length, it is generally held that the Alexandrian spear was no longer than twelve to fourteen feet. It was sufficiently light to be wielded at the balance with one hand. The length and weight of the Alexandrian *sarissa* made it possible for the phalanx to shift formations to meet an attack from any direction. By the time of Cynoscephalae, the Macedonian *sarissa* had grown in length such that it required two hands and considerable strength just to hold it out straight. The length of the infantry spear, when coupled with the denser phalanx, deprived the phalanx of any tactical flexibility. It could move in only a single direction, forward, and the propensity of the longer spears to tangle when moved about made it next to impossible for the phalanx to shift to meet an attack from the flank or rear.

Only the first five rows of the phalanx could actually engage the enemy with their spears, and it is possible that the two front rows carried shorter spears. The rest of the ranks in the phalanx held their spears upward at a forward angle to provide some protection against arrow and missile fire. No matter how many ranks were arrayed in depth, all but the first five remained essentially reserves. To increase the bulk of the phalanx even further, the Macedonians reduced the gap between individual soldiers to only 1.5 feet. To protect the soldiers within the phalanx, the technique of "locking shields"—used by Alexander at the Hydaspes—became a standard maneuver. With both hands holding the spear and with the shield held by a shoulder strap, the man of the phalanx pressed against the man to his right in an effort to permit his shield to overlap the other's right side. In this formation, it was impossible for the phalanx to maneuver in any direction except straight ahead. The press of the mass of humanity within the phalanx decreased the speed of movement to a very slow crawl.

This cumbersome body of men could hold its ground and slowly advance forward only as long as the ground was level. Even the slightest unevenness in terrain tended to throw the ranks of the phalanx out of alignment. There was an additional tendency for the wings of the phalanx to move outward from the center as it moved and to create gaps between the individual *syntagmae* within it. This was a dangerous condition. A first-rate commander could easily use his cavalry to exploit these gaps, as Alexander exploited them at Issus and Gaugamela. As the Romans demonstrated at Pydna, it was also possible to insert an infantry maniple into the gaps and to hack at the phalanx from within. But the experience of the Macedonians was largely against armies that used phalanxes and had equally poor cavalry, and though the risk of creating gaps was recognized, few of the opposing forces in the Macedonian military experience were capable of exploiting this vulnerability.

The inability of the phalanx to maneuver made it extremely vulnerable to flank or rear attack. The Macedonian phalanx fought four major battles against the Romans—Cynoscephalae, Pydna, Magnesia, and Corinth—and in every instance the phalanx crumbled to flank or rear attack. Alexander had clearly recognized this particular vulnerability of the phalanx, and he used his light infantry and cavalry to protect the flanks of the phalanx at all costs. The paradox of the Macedonian phalanx during the time of the Successors was that the decline in cavalry resulted in the rise of an infantry formation that was even more in need of flank protection at precisely the time when the new cavalry doctrines could not provide this vital combat function.

The Macedonian solution to the problem of flank vulnerability was to create two modified forms of the phalanx, the articulated phalanx and the double phalanx. The articulated phalanx may have been introduced by Pyrrhus in his wars against the Romans (281–275 B.C.E.). The idea was to make the phalanx more flexible by compensating for its tendency to spread out and create gaps between its component battalions. Companies of *sarissa* carrying phalangites were interspersed with companies of lighter armed and more loosely organized units. These units acted as flexible joints connecting the various battalions to the main body when the phalanx began to spread. The idea may have been derived from Alexander's use of the *Hypaspists* that acted as connecting joints between his cavalry and the main body of the phalanx.

Yet another way of protecting the flanks and rear of the phalanx was to use the double phalanx. The main phalanx was protected by a reserve line, sometimes a double line, of phalangites deployed behind or to the rear oblique of the main body. This formation was probably first used in 222 B.C.E. at the battle of Sellasia. While the articulated phalanx and the double phalanx represented workable solutions against another infantry phalanx, they were, at best, poor compromises to solving the problem of cavalry attack against the phalanx. In the end, the problem of the phalanx's vulnerability was never satisfactorily solved.

Finally, it might be added that the quality of the phalanx infantryman under the Macedonians had fallen considerably when compared with the soldiers who fought under Alexander. The truly national army of Alexander, comprised of men with long terms of service that produced discipline and cohesion, ceased to exist under Alexander's Successors. Even in Macedonia, the most nationally conscious of all the Successor states, the system was impossible to maintain. It cost too much and took manpower from the land and economy, just as it had during the period of the early city-states. Now, however, there was no treasury of conquest to finance the military system.

The national army motivated by patriotic fervor and long professional experience disappeared under the Macedonian Successors. It was replaced by a small national force comprised mostly of mercenaries who served full time in return for the promise of a farm upon retirement. These mercenaries were also used as garrison forces throughout the empire and could be called to service in times of trouble. The Macedonian army in essence went back to what it had been before Philip and Alexander reformed it, a levy of peasant farmers called to the colors for urgent situations. In less urgent situations, mercenaries were used, and the national troops saved for dire emergencies.

Manpower

The decline in the quality of the Macedonian army was paralleled by a decline in quantity. In 334 B.C.E., Alexander could draw 24,000 phalangites from Macedonia and 4,000 cavalry to take with him on campaign. By the time of the battle of Cynoscephalae, Philip V could only raise 16,000 phalangites, 2,000 cavalry, and 2,000 mercenary peltasts from Macedon itself. Even this number required enrolling sixteen-year-olds and recalling retired veterans to national service. Philip attempted to reconstitute the manpower base of Macedonia by requiring families to produce children, forbidding the traditional practice of infanticide and even resettling large numbers of Thracians in Macedonia proper. Twenty years later (171 B.C.E.) when Persus raised an army to resist the Romans, he could field only 21,000 phalangites, 3,000 cavalry, and 5,000 peltasts. This was the largest army led by a Macedonian king since Alexander's time.

The problems of quantity and quality of manpower worked to reinforce the Macedonian emphasis on infantry over cavalry. In the same manner that Napoleon adopted the column formation as a solution to controlling troops of poor quality with little training, so, too, the phalanx had the singular advantage of not requiring much training for its members. As in the old hoplite phalanx, very little skill was required of the phalanx soldier except that he hold his ground and move along with his comrades. While the phalangite also carried the sword to use in desperate situations, the degree of training in using this weapon was universally poor. In a fight with the Roman legionnaire who used the sword as his primary weapon, the Macedonian soldier was a poor match.

Cavalry

The transformation of infantry in the Successor armies was paralleled by a transformation in the quality, numbers, and tactical use of cavalry. The same forces that worked to emphasize the importance of infantry likewise worked to reduce the importance of cavalry on the battlefield. Alexander's Companion cavalry had been drawn from the Macedonian nobility, and during long years of fighting together had worked to make cavalry the decisive striking force in Alexander's army. The key to its effectiveness was its strong national spirit and cohesion, long years of operating together as units and with infantry, and the generalship of Alexander himself. The wars of the Successors destroyed any national spirit that remained after Alexander's death, and the expense of cavalry led the Successors, especially the Macedonians, to recruit cavalry from the populace in much the same way mercenaries were recruited. The monarch retained around his person a squadron or two of elite cavalry, but in numbers and in the ability to recruit and train cavalry, the cavalry forces of the Macedonians were but a pale copy of what they had been during Alexander's time.

The tactical employment of cavalry changed as well, especially in Macedonia. Wars in Macedonia were between phalanxes of heavy infantry, and the one thing cavalry could not do was successfully charge a disciplined line of spear infantry. Alexander had managed it, but only by timing his attack to exploit gaps in the rival infantry. This type of tactical sophistication, however, required a skill and discipline on the part of cavalry that no longer existed. Instead, the Macedonians reverted to the traditional uses of cavalry common during the hoplite era. Cavalry actions were now largely confined to the wings of the army, with cavalry attacking cavalry and generally with no significant influence on the outcome of the battle. As it had been for earlier centuries, the defeat of the enemy's cavalry became an end in itself with little regard for how it affected the overall tempo or direction of battle.

Further, it became almost a tactical stereotype to open the battle with a cavalry attack rather than to wait until events unfolded and use the cavalry to exploit or create exploitable situations. This regression to cavalry tactics of the pre-Alexandrian era precluded the effective use of cavalry on the battlefield, and cavalry in Macedonia ceased to be the decisive arm it had been in the hands of Alexander. Macedonian cavalry doctrine also played directly to the strong suit of the Romans who always had poor cavalry and used it in the same unimaginative and indecisive manner as the Greeks. Cavalry doctrine remained static for more than two centuries until the Parthians redesigned it entirely with horse-archers that defeated the Romans at Carrhae and with the heavy *cataphracti*, the armored knights that could break even the most disciplined body of infantry.

The Successors were, however, responsible for one significant innovation in the art of Western warfare, the use of the elephant. The time between Alexander's death and the battle of Pydna (168 B.C.E.) was the only time in Western military history when the elephant played an important role in warfare. Alexander had first come into contact with the elephant at the battle of the Hydaspes and had introduced them in a very small way into his own army. It fell to the Successors, particularly to the Seleucids and Ptolemies, to acquire elephants in large numbers, and, in a short time, every major power from Macedonia to Carthage had integrated them into their respective armies.

Figure 13.2 One of Pyrrhus's Elephants. Adapted from Alfred Bradford, *With Arrow, Sword, and Spear* (Westport, CT: Greenwood, 2001). Reprinted with permission.

The most common use of the elephant was to screen the deployment and maneuver of cavalry and, on rare occasion, to lead attacks against infantry. Rarely were they used against fortified positions, and then almost always with failure. In concert with light infantry, elephants could be used to protect the flanks of the phalanx, and, indeed, a new and important combat role for light troops was to distract and destroy enemy elephants. Given the expense and difficulty associated with acquiring, training, and employing elephants, these animals seem to have been among the most expensive and least effective instruments of warfare. The last serious use of elephants by Western armies was at the battle of Magnesia (190 B.C.E.), and they failed to prevent the defeat of the Seleucids at the hands of Roman infantry.

The Roman Army

The Roman army that marched into Greece with the objective of destroying the army of Philip V was essentially the army that for almost twenty years fought and eventually defeated Hannibal. That army has been described in detail in an earlier chapter. It remains only to focus upon the advantages it enjoyed in its wars with the armies of the Successors. The experience of the Roman army against Hannibal made it the most reliable killing machine in the era of muscle-powered warfare. Its superbly trained legions of swordsmen relied upon an excellent logistics system that kept the soldier physically healthy and well supplied when in the field. The Roman army was a well integrated triad of ferocity, skill, and logistics.

The war with Hannibal forced the first reforms in recruitment, which expanded the manpower base of the Roman army away from the aristocracy to the landed middle classes. Roman skill at diplomacy and the willingness to extend Roman citizenship to her allies in Italy further expanded the recruiting base. The result was the ability to field army after army, even in defeat, until victory was achieved. Polybius records that, at the time of the wars with Philip V of Macedon, Rome's military manpower stood at 700,000 legionnaires and 70,000 cavalry.

Roman training, typically with weapons and shields twice an individual's normal weight, and the psychological disposition that may have evolved as a result of the introduction of the gladiatorial games (264 B.C.E.) created a skilled, cold-blooded soldier accustomed to death and killing. The horrible wounds inflicted by the *gladius* often shocked the enemy. This mental aptitude for war often had a devastating psychological effect upon the enemy. Livy records an interesting incident in this regard. In 200 B.C.E., Philip V of Macedon was engaged in war with Athens. Rome had sent a few contingents of infantry in support of Athens. In an insignificant engagement, the Roman cavalry armed with the *gladius* clashed with some of Philip's cavalry. Philip attempted to whip up enthusiasm among his troops by holding a funeral for those soldiers who had fallen in the engagement. The Macedonians, accustomed mostly to neat wounds inflicted by javelins and spears, were not prepared for the sight of what was left of their countrymen after meeting the Roman buzz-saw. Livy recorded the horror of the Macedonians upon seeing their dead: "When they had seen bodies chopped to pieces by the Spanish sword, arms torn away, shoulders and all, or heads separated from bodies . . . or vitals laid open . . . they realized in a general panic with what weapons, and what men, they had to fight." Philip's army was never the same.

The comparative advantages and disadvantages of a battle between Roman infantry and the Macedonian phalanx, such as occurred at Cynoscephalae, were summed up by Polybius, himself a Greek soldier who fought in the phalanx against the Romans in the Macedonian wars. Polybius says,

> In the front nothing can stand up to the *sarissa* phalanx; the individual Roman with his sword can neither slash down nor break through the ten spears that simultaneously press against him. But the Roman legionary is adaptable to any place at any time and for any purpose. The *sarissa*-bearer can fight only as a member of the entire phalanx and not even in small units and not as an individual fighter. Furthermore, the phalanx can move only on very level terrain; every

ditch, every hill, every hole, every clump of trees causes it to fall into disorder. But if it has fallen into disorder at any place at all or if Roman maniples should fall upon it from the flank, which can be easily done with the echelon formation of the Romans, then it is lost.

It was just this sort of confrontation between the phalanx and the legion, an engagement between the Macedonian spiked pincushion and the Roman buzz-saw, that occurred at the battle of Cynoscephalae. And when it was over, the future and the domination of the ancient world belonged to Rome.

THE BATTLE OF CYNOSCEPHALAE (197 B.C.E.)

In the summer of 200 B.C.E., Rome raised six new legions to deal with the problems in Greece and Macedonia. Two of these legions were sent under the command of Consul Galba to Greece and landed at Appollonia in Illyria late in the year. Along with the legions, Galba brought a few elephants and a thousand Numidian cavalry, legacies of the recently concluded Punic Wars. The Roman march inland continued for only a short time as Philip V moved his forces toward western Macedonia to counter the Roman presence. There were no encounters between the two antagonists until spring.

In less than a year, however, the political situation confronting Philip changed. The Greek states of Aetolia, Dardani, and Illyria saw their chance to weaken Macedon, and they joined in the Roman effort against Philip by providing troops to fight along with the Romans. Philip moved quickly to put down the revolt in Illyria, but the Romans placed a fleet off the Illyrian coast, and Galba marched to meet Philip's army in the field. Outmaneuvered, Philip was forced to withdraw. A small battle was fought in a nameless mountain pass, but nothing significant resulted. Galba proved to be a timid commander and did little to carry the war to Philip. For two years not much of any military significance occurred. Then, in 198 B.C.E., command of the Roman forces in Greece was assumed by Titus Quinctius Flaminius, the new twenty-nine-year old consul. Flaminius was intelligent, diplomatic, and aggressive.

Flaminius made one last diplomatic effort to call a council among the Greek states, Philip, and himself as representative of Rome. In typical Roman fashion, Rome preferred to achieve by diplomacy, bluff, and threat of force what it had not yet achieved on the battlefield. Rome's terms were too high, amounting to nothing less than that Philip cede control of Macedonia's foreign policy to the Roman Senate. Nonetheless, envoys were sent to Rome to seek a solution while a truce held in Greece. The Senate refused to alter its terms, and the truce expired. The rival armies once again took to the field in the spring campaign season of 197 B.C.E.

Flaminius moved first and quickly seized Thebes near the Macedonian border. Philip had a much-deserved reputation for ravaging towns and farms during his previous campaigns in Greece, and Flaminius seems to have preferred to fight the war on Macedonian soil. Next, Flaminius marched northward into Thessaly in an effort to catch Philip on his own ground. Learning of the Roman movement, Philip moved his army directly at the Romans in an effort to engage. Philip encamped his army four miles from the town of Pherae, while the Romans were encamped only a few miles to the south of the town. While it was clearly the intention of both commanders to find the adversary and bring him to battle quickly, neither side knew the position of the other. Both armies sent out reconnaissance patrols that stumbled into one another. Both reconnaissance forces held their respective positions close to the crest of a nearby ridge while sending messengers back to their commanders seeking instructions. Both commanders ordered their reconnaissance forces to withdraw, and there was no engagement.

The next day both sides sent substantial cavalry forces into the area, and there was a brief skirmish between the Aetolian cavalry serving with the Romans and Philip's units. Philip's cavalry seems to have received the worst of the skirmish, and it withdrew. The Romans did not pursue. Although Flaminius and Philip were eager for battle, both commanders recognized that the terrain was unfavorable. The area around Pherae was agricultural, and many of the roads were bordered by high hedges. The hilly and wooded countryside was not favorable for maneuver. Both sides broke contact and moved south toward the town of Scotusa.

Scotusa was a small agricultural town that possessed significant grain stores. Philip needed the grain to feed his army, and the Romans sought to deprive him of these supplies by getting to the town first. As both armies moved southward in parallel, they were separated by a long ridge of hills and high craggy peaks. The next day and the following day, the armies moved, encamped, moved, and encamped again. Both commanders failed to gain contact with their adversary, so that, as the armies moved along a parallel route, neither had any idea where the other one was.

On the third day the armies broke camp opposite a ridge of hills called Cynoscephalae. The morning dawned with heavy rain followed by a dark grey fog that shrouded both the hills and valleys. The Romans remained in camp, fearful that any attempt to move might make them vulnerable to an ambush. Philip needed to reach the grain supplies at Scotusa, so he broke camp and set his army on the move toward the town. Livy and Polybius both recorded that the fog was so dense that the standard-bearers could not see the road ahead. The soldiers following in column of march often became disoriented and drifted off the packed trail. It was a slow and confused column that moved toward Scotusa that morning. After a short interval, Philip concluded the army could no longer move safely and ordered a halt.

The Romans remained in camp, but Flaminius was becoming concerned that his failure to determine the position of Philip's army was more dangerous now that the weather provided an opportunity for the enemy to conduct an ambush in force. The Roman commander ordered a reconnaissance in force consisting of ten troops of cavalry and one infantry troop. Their mission was to find the enemy. Philip, stalled in column of march along the fog-shrouded road, also became concerned about an ambush, and he, too, ordered a reconnaissance in force. It had finally dawned upon both commanders that the adversary was somewhere on the other side of the hills that separated the two armies. Moving up opposite sides of the ridge, the advance units of the reconnaissance forces met in the fog and clashed in a brief skirmish. The commanders of both the Roman and Macedonian reconnaissance units quickly committed the remainder of their forces to the engagement. Both sent messengers back to their commanders to inform them what was happening. As often happens in war, the reports from the reconnaissance parties greatly exaggerated the size of the enemy and the significance of the engagement. Nonetheless, both commanders now faced the prospect of events having overtaken them. Both had to decide whether to fight at a time and place that neither had chosen.

Philip had not planned on a battle, especially in the dense fog. During the halt, he had sent some part of his army into the countryside to forage for supplies. With less than full combat strength at his disposal, Philip delayed and did nothing. As the fog cleared near the crest of the ridge, Philip could see the infantry of his reconnaissance force deployed in phalanx, attempting to hold off an attack of Roman cavalry. The Romans had sent a strong cavalry force to reconnoiter the ridgeline, and it was this unit that had made contact with the light skirmishers acting as advance guard for Philip's reconnaissance force. The Romans charged the light infantry and chased it without caution over the crest of the hill, only to run right into the Greek infantry deployed in phalanx. The Macedonian cavalry that accompanied the infantry on reconnaissance accepted the Roman attack, drove it back, and pinned it against the infantry phalanx. The Roman cavalry broke up into small units and began a headlong rout down the hillside, with the Macedonian cavalry in full pursuit.

The Aetolian cavalry that had been sent along with the Roman cavalry had not pursued the Greek light infantry over the crest of the ridgeline but had remained just below the crest. As the Roman cavalry came galloping back over the crest in disorder and retreat, a thousand Aetolian horsemen held their ground and counterattacked the pursuing Macedonians, breaking up the charge. The Roman cavalry was saved, and the Macedonians retreated. Wisely, the Aetolian cavalry did not pursue.

As these initial engagements were taking place, both Philip and Flaminius were worried that neither knew the strength or disposition of the other. The dense fog increased the concern regarding ambush for both commanders. Neither was so foolish as to risk an attempt at withdrawal in the face of the unknown tactical situation. Both commanders decided that they had no choice but to accept the reports of their reconnaissance units at face value and assume the enemy was approaching over the ridgeline to take their armies in the flank. For a moment the fog at the crest of the ridgeline rose sufficiently to permit Philip a view of the engagement. What he saw was his reconnaissance infantry arrayed in phalanx, attempting to hold off the attacking Roman cavalry. If he chose to fight at this time and place, one thing was sufficiently clear. The control of the crest of the ridgeline was vital, and the army that gained the crest first would have a significant advantage in the coming battle. Philip decided to seize the ridge.

A substantial part of his army was still in the countryside foraging for supplies. Philip began to commit the forces he had readily available. He ordered Athenagoras, the mercenary commander, to take the Macedonian and Thessalian cavalry and move rapidly to the crest of the ridgeline. Athenagoras reached the top of the ridge in time to drive off the remnants of the Aetolian cavalry that was acting as a rearguard for the fleeing Roman cavalry. The news sent back to Philip was confusing. In the fog Athenagoras mistook the fleeing Aetolian cavalry and the remnants of the Roman reconnaissance party for the Roman main force and reported that the main body of the Roman army was in full retreat. He urged Philip to commit the main body of his army and crush the invader. Philip, believing these reports were accurate, did exactly that.

Part of Philip's army was already in battle formation and ready to move up the ridge. He took personal command of this force and moved it toward the crest. Upon reaching the top, he deployed it to his right. The rest of the army, some still straggling back from foraging, was not yet ready to move. Philip placed Nicanor in command of these remnants and ordered him to form up as quickly as possible and follow him to the crest. Upon reaching the top, Nicanor's force was instructed to deploy to the left and become the left wing of the combined army. Philip was committing his forces to battle piecemeal.

As Philip approached the top of the ridge, he saw the ground littered with Roman corpses that had fallen in the two previous skirmishes. The sight confirmed Athenagoras's reports. As Philip reached the crest of the ridge and looked over and down the hill, however, he saw the entire Roman army formed for battle. Flaminius had ordered the legions to form as soon as he had been informed of the cavalry clash with his reconnaissance units. Although the legion could form more quickly than the phalanx, they had longer to travel from their camp in the valley to the crest of the ridgeline. Flaminius had arrayed his army for battle in the valley and was moving them uphill in battle formation in a race with Philip to reach the crest. Even if he failed to get there first, Flaminius had no intention of being taken in column of march. He was ready to meet any enemy attack, even if he had to fight uphill.

Map 13.3 depicts the deployment of Philip and Flaminius's forces on and below the ridgeline. Philip was caught in a dilemma. His left wing under Nicanor had not yet arrived at the crest and was still making its way up the hill in column of march. His own force, buttressed by cavalry, light infantry, and peltasts, stood opposite the Roman left wing. Livy records that Philip's army

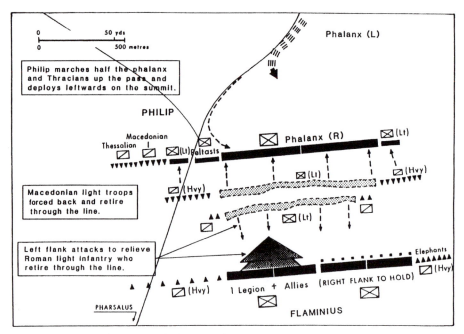

Map 13.3 Battle of Cynoscephalae: Initial Movements (197 B.C.E.)

was comprised of 16,000 phalangites, 2,000 peltasts, 2,000 hoplite infantry, 1,500 Thracian tribesman (javelin throwers), and no more than 2,000 cavalry. The Roman force numbered about the same but with about 3,000 cavalry counting that of its Greek allies. About two-thirds of Philip's army was in position on the crest of the ridge.

Philip feared that, if he waited too long for Nicanor to come into position, both wings of the Roman army might breach the crest. While his own force was engaged directly against the Roman left, the Roman right wing might catch Nicanor in column of march, destroy his force, and then turn on Philip's flank and rear. If this happened, Philip's army would be annihilated. Philip had little choice but to attack. The ground to his front was smooth and sloping downhill, perfect terrain for the phalanx in the attack. If he attacked now, the sheer momentum of the downhill attack against the Roman wing might easily shatter it. If Philip was able to break the Roman left in one blow, Nicanor might reach the crest in time to attack downhill against the Roman right, finishing the battle. Philip ordered his cavalry to take up positions on his extreme right. He positioned his skirmishers to the front and ordered them to engage. They were quickly driven back by the Roman cavalry. Some units, apparently accompanied by cavalry, pressed the Roman left with some success, forcing Flaminius to commit some of his forces to hold the line. But these were all preliminary actions. Philip ordered his phalanx to form at double depth, shortening his front like a hammer, and instructed his troops to arrange themselves in close-order "shield lock"

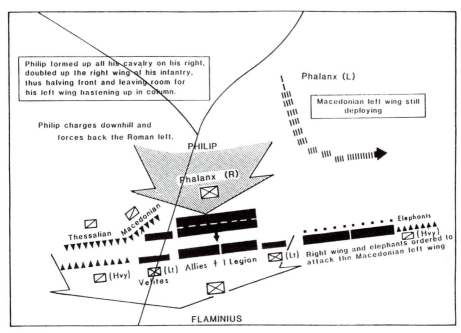

Philip formed up all his cavalry on his right, doubled up the right wing of his infantry, thus halving front and leaving room for his left wing hastening up in column.

Philip charges downhill and forces back the Roman left.

Phalanx (L)

Macedonian left wing still deploying

PHILIP

Phalanx (R)

Thessalian Macedonian

Elephants

(Hvy)

(Hvy) Right wing and elephants ordered to attack the Macedonian left wing

(Lt)

(Lt) Allies + I Legion

(Hvy) Velites

FLAMINIUS

Map 13.4 Battle of Cynoscephalae: Philip's Attack (197 B.C.E.)

formation. Then he ordered the phalanx and cavalry to charge straight down the hill into the Roman left wing.

Flaminius saw the charge coming directly at his left wing (see Map 13.4). He gave the order for both wings of the army to advance and meet the charge. With no one in front of them, the Roman right wing moved up the hill directly toward the crest of the ridgeline, while the left wing took the full brunt of the Macedonian charge. The open formation of the legion allowed it to flex and bend in the face of the momentum of the phalanx. Resistance slowed the Macedonian charge in much the same manner, Livy notes, as a tree branch bends but does not break before the wind. In circumstances such as these, Roman training paid huge dividends. Almost as if on command, the legion broke into small groups and sidestepped the charge of the phalanx. As the phalanx tried to pass through the legion, small units of swordsmen fell on its flanks and began to slash it to pieces. Attacked from the flanks, the phalangites could not move their long *sarissae* to meet the assault, and their spears became entangled. Livy notes that someone gave the order to abandon the spears and fight on with swords, but under these conditions of close combat, the phalangite was no match for the legionnaire.

As the legion and phalanx clashed, Nicanor was reaching the crest of the hill on the Macedonian left. He had marched his phalanx up the hill in column of march rather than battle formation and needed time to deploy the phalanx opposite the Roman right. To Nicanor's front the Roman wing continued to advance toward him with contingents of elephants to their front.

The Romans intended to engage Nicanor before he had time to deploy the phalanx and attack downhill. Nicanor, with no time to form his phalanx, ordered an immediate attack.

The terrain in front of Nicanor was uneven. As the partially formed phalanx began its hurried attack, it began to spread and come apart even before it made contact with the Roman right wing. The elephants led the Roman attack, closely followed by the infantry. The elephants made first contact, plunging into the phalanx and scattering the phalangites in every direction. Close behind the elephants came a volley of *pila* thrown by the closing ranks of the legion. Seconds later, at the run, the legionnaires were in the midst of the phalanx killing everything within reach. The phalanx broke, and its men turned and ran. What remained of the Macedonian left wing fled the field in terror to avoid being annihilated.

At this point Philip's phalanx had all but broken through the Roman left, although remnants of the legion were still attacking its flanks. Philip was now fully engaged and completely cut off from his left wing. There was no chance of reinforcement. A Roman tribune fighting on the Roman right saw the enemy turn and run. Glancing to his left and rear, he immediately grasped the peril that faced Philip. On his own authority, the tribune ordered twenty maniples from the Roman right to stop, pivot, and turn obliquely to the left rear (see Map 13.5). This force now faced downhill at an oblique angle to the rear of Philip's heavily engaged phalanx. Without hesitation, the tribune

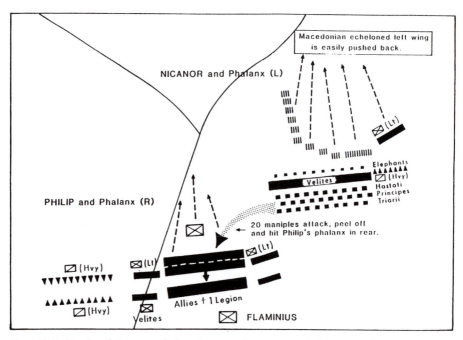

Map 13.5 Battle of Cynoscephalae: Roman Counterattack (197 B.C.E.)

ordered his men into the attack. The Roman force slammed into the phalanx, and the great slaughter commenced.

When it was over, more than half of Philip's army, 13,000 men, were killed. The Romans lost only a few hundred men. Philip fled the field with a few remnants of his army and was never again a threat to Roman rule in Greece. The initial clash of two military systems was a clear victory for the Roman legions. On three more occasions in the next sixty years the legion fought the phalanx, always with the same result. In less than the span of a single generation, Rome destroyed all three Successor empires and reigned supreme in the eastern Mediterranean. The last embers of the fire ignited by Alexander's armies almost two centuries before were crushed under the heel of Roman imperial rule. For almost the next millennium, the history of military science in the West was written by a Roman hand.

THE COMMANDERS

Philip V of Macedon (238–179 B.C.E.) was a genuinely popular king and an able field general. Adopted by his father's cousin, Antigonus Doson, he succeeded him to the throne of Macedonia in 221 B.C.E. Philip had already gained combat and command experience during the Social Wars and border skirmishes that plagued Macedonia from time immemorial, so he came to the throne, like so many of his predecessors in Macedonia, an already tested military commander. He had been king for less than a year when events forced him into war with Sparta, the Aetolian League, and Elis. The Greek city-states had always viewed the Macedonian empire as the result of conquest and, since Philip II's hegemony, had resented its presence on its soil and continually maneuvered to remove it from their territories. Foreign powers, most particularly Rome, maneuvered to establish relations with these recalcitrant Greek city-states as a means to reduce Macedonian power on the Greek mainland and as a prelude to increasing Roman power and influence.

Philip was an excellent strategic thinker and knew well enough that a clash between Roman and Macedonian power was inevitable. Perhaps in the hope that he could preempt Roman policy by a show of arms, in 206 B.C.E. Philip attacked the Roman client states in Illyria (Yugoslavia), provoking a war with Rome. Rome provided military aid to the Greek city-states already allied with her, and the war dragged on for three years with Philip finally bringing the city-states to heel. Philip now moved to consolidate his hold on Greece, with the result that Rome declared war and sent an army to Illyria in 200 B.C.E. Three years later, at Cynoscephalae, Philip was defeated and signed a peace treaty with Rome.

Philip retained his crown since Rome was not yet prepared to occupy all of Greece to ensure order. Instead, it strengthened Philip at the expense of the city-states by reducing his tribute and recognizing some of his claims against the city-states. Philip became a solid Roman ally. He spent the next twenty years governing Macedonia with a just and efficient hand, building roads, consolidating the kingdom's finances, and defending his kingdom against the interminable border incursions from the barbarians. He remained a soldier to the end, taking field command in the border wars, and he died in 179 B.C.E. while planning yet another military campaign against the barbarians in the northwest.

Philip V was every bit a Macedonian king, a tough and experienced soldier first and a political leader second. This said, in every maneuver he undertook to preserve Macedon from Roman influence the clear connection between political and military objectives and means can be seen. Soldier though he was, Philip always used military means in service to political ends, never the reverse. In this he was a solid strategist as well as a field commander. One sees in Philip that trait of cold-eyed realism that seems to have been a characteristic of Macedonian kings since Philip II.

T. Quinctius Flaminius (228–? B.C.E.) was not yet thirty years old when appointed to assume command of the Roman armies in Greece in their war against Philip V. He replaced Sulpicius, a grim soldier whose lack of diplomatic skills was unsuited to the task of wooing the Greek city-states from the Macedonian orbit. Polybius, who is our only source on Flaminius, says that he possessed a good balance of diplomatic and military skills and was determined to set up a Roman protectorate in Greece. But, Polybius says, "he was also vanity itself, thirsting for honor and glory, and above all for the praises of the Greeks which fervent admiration for Hellenism caused him to set above everything." The pursuit of public fame was not, however, a character trait Romans would have found unappealing.

Flaminius spoke fluent Greek and was very successful in enticing many of Philip's allies away from his alliance, promising the city-states freedom and Roman commercial ties to weaken Macedonian influence with the ultimate goal of removing it from Greece entirely. In this he was very successful, so that when Flaminius finally committed the Roman army to an invasion from the north, Philip was placed at a great disadvantage.

Flaminius showed himself an able field general at Cynoscephalae. Finding himself lost and unaware of where Philip's army was, Flaminius kept his head and used his intelligence assets to great advantage. The result was one of the greatest victories in Roman military history. Cynoscephalae was the Jena of Macedonia. The Roman buzz-saw destroyed the Macedonian pincushion. Greece and the world learned to their stupefaction that the famed Macedonian phalanx had found its master. The heavy phalanx of the Antigonids had proved too heavy and unwieldy as a tactical weapon against the legion. Warfare was changing, and the future belonged to the more mobile and flexible legions of Rome. As a consequence of Flaminius's political skill and military ability, all the Greek allies of Macedon had either been forced into submission to Rome or won over to her side as allies. T. Quinctius Flaminius was both the architect and builder of this great and important victory.

LESSONS OF WAR

Strategy

1. Great powers seeking to maintain spheres of influence must find and be willing to utilize appropriate means to control or strongly influence the foreign affairs of the smaller states within their sphere of influence. Failure to accomplish this invites other great powers to use these smaller states as tools of their own national interests. Macedon failed adequately to control the foreign policies of Rhodes and Pergamum in much the same way as the United States failed to control Cuba. In both instances, other great powers used the smaller states to harass the dominant power in the region.

2. Objective conditions of relative power define security concerns more than common cultural, historical, or even political heritage. The Successor states shared all three of these elements in common, and still they fought one another. This might give pause to those who argue that democracies do not fight one another.

3. Geography often defines objective security concerns and promotes conflict. Greece and Rome faced each other across the narrow straits of the Adriatic. Two great powers cannot live for long in geographical proximity without provoking rival security concerns.

4. Be wary of entangling alliances with minor powers. Such alliances present the risk that great powers will be drawn into local or regional conflicts, even when they have only marginal interests at stake. Rome and Greece were drawn into conflict over Illyria in just this way.

5. Commitments to minor states ought to last only as long as there is a clear confluence of interests. The commitment *per se* should never become the reason for the alliance.

6. Stability is enhanced among rival power blocs when the dominant powers recognize the nature of the blocs and do not interfere in the domestic affairs of a member state. The Cold War was stable for precisely these reasons. Relations between Rome and Macedon were unstable for precisely the opposite reasons.

7. Nations have no permanent friends or enemies. Great powers have only national interests. Despite long years of mutual suspicion, when Philip failed to use Hannibal to check Rome, he moved directly to improve his relations with Rome itself. Be willing to examine the costs and benefits of even radical policy shifts if they appear to protect or advance national interests.

8. Shifts in the power balance among great powers are likely to have unforeseen effects on the loyalty of smaller states. Philip pursued the primary objective of counterbalancing Roman power by concluding an alliance with the Seleucids, only to frighten the smaller states of Rome and Pergamum and drive them directly into Roman arms.

9. In planning defense strategies, know the difference between implements of war and "cathedrals." A weapons system that is expensive, exotic, and prestigious may not be useful in battle. Remember the Macedonians and don't purchase too many elephants. The Successors had many of these high-cost, exotic, and prestigious weapons, and they lost.

10. Remember Flaminius. Always attempt to obtain what you want by diplomacy and threat of force rather than war. Always be prepared to fight if diplomacy fails.

Tactics

1. Military capabilities are always relative to the enemy and are in constant flux as a consequence of technological development and human resource management. Greece died at the hands of Rome because it failed to maintain an army proficient in meeting a new type of threat.

2. Beware the universal propensity to fight the last war. The Macedonian tactical doctrines of infantry and cavalry were drawn directly from its past military experience with little concern for their applicability under new circumstances.

3. There is a tendency for force structures to be driven by a multitude of factors quite beyond any rational calculation of military effectiveness. Macedonian culture and economics, more than concerns of military effectiveness relative to the threat, shaped the force structure of its military with disastrous consequences.

4. The quality and training of combat manpower assets are important combat multipliers and are often decisive in battle. Develop and conserve the quality of your unit's manpower.

5. Prepare your troops psychologically for battle through rigorous and realistic training. The Romans always observed this axiom with great success.

6. When given a mission, take the initiative in battle. Do not be timid like Galba or, like him, you will likely fail or be removed from command.

7. Seek the enemy out and carry the battle to him. Both Philip and Flaminius were excellent commanders in this regard.

8. At Pherae, both Flaminius and Philip broke contact because the terrain and circumstances were not right for battle. Do not be hurried into a fight. Exercise as much choice as to time and location as circumstances permit.

9. Always maintain contact with an army on the move. Both sides forgot that maxim in their marches to Cynoscephalae and stumbled into a battle for which neither was prepared.

10. Be very suspicious of early reports of engagements. They tend to be inaccurate and to exaggerate the scope and intensity of the engagement. In any case, initial reports of contact rarely reveal the larger tactical situation. Both Flaminius and Philip ignored this truth with the result that Philip lost control of his own tactical design.

11. Exploit the weather. Do not allow it to exploit you . . . as the fog at Cynoscephalae did to both commanders.

12. Never commit your forces piecemeal into an escalating battle as Philip did, especially if you do not have a clear picture of the overall tactical situation. Wait, think, formulate a plan, and then commit decisively. Do not rely upon your ability merely to react to events as they develop.

13. Be especially alert while on a movement to contact. Flaminius's movement to contact, although he was at a terrain disadvantage, was conducted in such a manner that he was always prepared to react immediately to an enemy initiative. Never expect the enemy to allow you to move into an advantageous position without opposition.

14. Be flexible. Follow the example of Flaminius and be ready to change plans in the midst of battle to exploit opportunities.

15. Force the enemy to react to your initiative. The commander of the Roman right wing at Cynoscephalae forced Nicanor into the attack before he was prepared. The result was slaughter.

16. Once contact has been made, increase the tempo of violence against the enemy. The commander of the Roman right wing did exactly that by striking first with his elephants, following closely with a volley of *pila*, and then attacking rapidly with his infantry. Be aggressive.

17. Take the initiative on your own authority to exploit an opportunity presented by the enemy. The commander of the twenty Roman maniples who reversed course and ordered the attack against the rear of Philip's phalanx crushed the enemy in a single decisive blow. Be aware, as well, that there are a number of career risks if things do not work out.

FURTHER READING

Adcock, F. E. *The Greek and Macedonian Art of War.* Berkeley: University of California Press, 1957.

Berthold, Richard M. "The Army and Alexander: The Great's Successors." *Strategy and Tactics* 152 (June 1992): 45–47.

Cambridge Ancient History. Cambridge, UK: Cambridge University Press, 1955.

Delbruck, Hans. *History of the Art of War within the Framework of Political History.* Vol. 1, *Antiquity.* Westport, CT: Greenwood Press, 1975.

Jouquet, Pierre. *Alexander the Great and the Hellenistic World: Macedonian Imperialism and the Hellenization of the East.* 2 vols. London: Ares Publishers, 1978.

Livy. *The History of Rome.* Book 33. London: Penguin, 1967.

Polybius. *The Histories.* London: Penguin, 1963.

Seaton, Stuart. *The Successors.* London: Charnwood, 1987.

Tarn, William W. *Hellenistic Civilization.* New York: Dutton, 1989.

———. *Hellenistic Military and Naval Developments.* London: Ares Publishers, 1975.

Wallbank, F. W. *Philip V of Macedon.* Cambridge, UK: Cambridge University Press, 1940.

14 CAESAR'S WARS AND THE END OF THE ROMAN REPUBLIC

[100–30 B.C.E.]

BACKGROUND

Julius Caesar stands out in the military history of the ancient world as one of the greatest military commanders ever to plan a campaign or lead men in battle. This is true for a number of reasons, not the least of which is because he was one of only a handful of ancient personages who left a personal record of his life and its accomplishments. In his *Commentaries*, Caesar seems to have anticipated the dictum of Winston Churchill "that history would always be kind to England . . . for I intend to write it." In analyzing the life and accomplishments of Julius Caesar, it is impossible to ignore his own account of events. And so, Caesar himself has shaped most modern perspectives of his life, even from his grave.

The three battles offered for analysis here are Alesia, Dyrrachium, and Pharsalus. The siege of Alesia was the last great battle in the suppression of the Gallic revolt of 53–52 B.C.E. and sealed for all time the fate of Gaul as an adversary of Rome. It was one of the few battles against the Gauls in which Caesar faced a tribal general, Vercingetorix, of some skill and training. The battle of Dyrrachium (48 B.C.E.) pitted Caesar against Pompey in an engagement whose strategic and operational complexities have few equals during this period. Both armies were Roman trained and led, making the difference between victory and defeat a product of the intelligence of the rival commanders. Dyrrachium is one of the few battles in which it can be asserted with some confidence that Caesar was out-generaled and defeated. The battle of Pharsalus (48 B.C.E.) represented truly a set-piece battle of Roman infantry in which the outcome was decided by generalship and tactical brilliance. At Pharsalus Caesar defeated Pompey, the beginning of the end of the civil war for the control of the Roman state. The selection of these three battles is essentially arbitrary, except for the reasons noted, and it is likely that other historians wishing to stress other aspects of Caesar's military talents could just as arbitrarily choose other battles as points of analysis.

THE CAMPAIGNS IN GAUL (58–52 B.C.E.)

In Caesar's day Gaul included the whole of France and Belgium and parts of Holland, Switzerland, and all of Germany west of the Rhine. Map 14.1 portrays the relevant geography of Caesar's Gallic theater of operations. The population was of mixed origin, although the Celts were in a majority, and probably numbered between 15 and 20 million people. The population was divided into 200 to 300 tribes with some tribes held as vassals—Caesar called them *clientela*—to the larger ones. The tribes lived in villages scattered around a central town that was often fortified, although usually without a moat. These towns were frequently located on appropriate high ground for defensive reasons. The Gauls practiced extensive agriculture and cattle breeding, and their tribes were more stable than the largely nomadic and pastoral Germanic tribes across the Rhine. The country was relatively well developed in terms of bridges, dirt roads, frequently used river fords, docks, and relatively heavy river traffic.

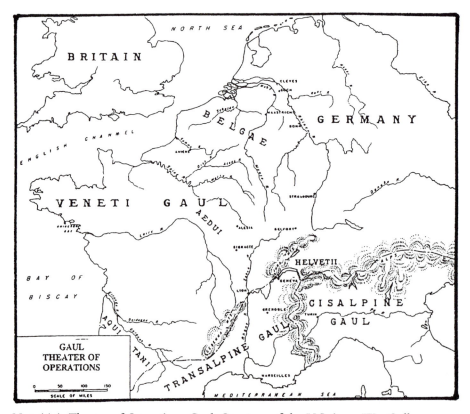

Map 14.1 Theater of Operations, Gaul. Courtesy of the U.S. Army War College.

Accordingly, Caesar found a significant transportation and economic infrastructure upon which he could draw to sustain his armies in the field.

Caesar was sent to Gaul as proconsul in 58 B.C.E. His term of office was fixed at five years, and his military complement consisted of four legions. He had no military experience to speak off and certainly none in the art of command at the general officer level. It was in Gaul that he learned his trade as a military commander. Between 58 and 51 B.C., Caesar conducted almost constant military operations in Gaul with the objective of bringing the area under Roman domination and incorporating it as a province of the Roman Empire. But that was hardly the most important reason for Caesar's wars. Caesar cannot be correctly seen solely as a loyal soldier given the operational mission to conquer another province for Rome. More accurately, Caesar was a *condottieri* general given wide responsibility and power for military conquest that he intended to use first and foremost to increase his own wealth, reputation, and political power so that they

Figure 14.1 Roman Legionnaire

could be used as weapons against his rivals in the struggle to control the Roman state. It was personal ambition that lay at the root of Caesar's genius.

It is impossible to describe here in any significant detail the major battles fought by Caesar in his Gallic campaigns leading up to the suppression of the Gallic revolt in October 52 B.C.E. This section provides the reader with only a general sketch of each of those battles and the campaigns (Map 14.2) of which they were a part. The description is offered only to provide a general sense of the events leading up to the siege of Alesia. The specific strategic situations concerning the later battles at Dyrrachium and Pharsalus are described in the relevant sections dealing directly with those battles.

DEFEAT OF THE HELVETII (58 B.C.E.)

Shortly after Caesar assumed his post as proconsul, the entire Helvetiian people, a Gallic tribe living in the area of modern Switzerland, began a migration westward toward the fertile lands of the Rhone Valley. The tribe comprised (by Caesar's count) 368,000 people, including 92,000 warriors. Fearing that this movement would pose a threat to Italy, Caesar hurried from Rome to Geneva. Caesar had only one legion in Transalpine Gaul, so he ordered the recruitment of a large force of auxiliary troops from loyal Gallic tribes that feared being overrun by the tribal migration. He destroyed the bridge the Helvetii had constructed over the Rhone and constructed a nineteen-mile-long chain of fortifications across the Rhone Valley migration route to stop the Helvetii. The Helvetii, deflected from their route of march, moved westward across the Jura country north of the Rhone.

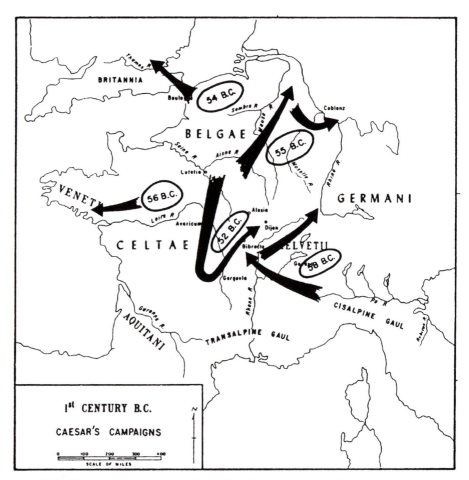

Map 14.2 Caesar's Campaigns in Gaul (First Century B.C.E.). Courtesy of the U.S. Army War College.

Upon learning of the westward movement of the Helvetii, Caesar left his legate in charge of the barriers near Geneva and traveled back to Cisalpine Gaul to raise more manpower. He raised two new legions from the province and called in three from Illyria. With this force he moved from near Turin, crossed the Alps, advanced through Grenoble, and crossed the Rhone near Lyon. East of Lyon he was joined by the Tenth Legion and a body of Gallic cavalry. His force numbered 30,000 men and 4,000 cavalry. During his march from Italy to Gaul, Caesar averaged sixteen miles a day over rough mountain tracks.

Caesar's reconnaissance learned that the Helvetii were crossing the Saone on boats and rafts a few miles above Lyon. He waited a half day's march from the crossing point. When most of the Helvetii were across the river, Caesar broke camp at midnight, conducted a rapid night march, and struck the enemy remaining on the east bank at daylight. He overwhelmed and annihilated more than 30,000 Helvetiian warriors trapped on the near bank. He then bridged the river at the battlefield and cautiously followed the main body of Helvetii as it withdrew.

Caesar's army was running low on supplies, and he turned northward to the town of Bibracte to resupply his army. The Helvetiians thought that Caesar had lost his nerve, turned back toward the Romans, and fell on their rear-guard. To check the Gallic attack, Caesar ordered his cavalry force (4,000 horse) to engage the Helvetiian infantry near the Armecy ridge. Using his cavalry as a screen, Caesar deployed his four veteran legions in triple line on the ridge, with the two newly raised legions behind them in reserve. Caesar awaited the attack.

The Helvetiian army was encumbered by thousands of men, women, and children that accompanied them on the migration. Operating from a wagon *laager*, the Helvetiians attacked up the slope. Wave after wave was repulsed by *pilum* and *gladius*. At last, the Romans moved off the ridge and down the valley, driving the Helvetii before them, only to be attacked in the flank. While the Romans were dealing with the flank attack, the Helvetii launched another frontal assault. The fighting was desperate, and losses on both sides were high. As Caesar wrote, "There was no rout for throughout the action, though it lasted from the seventh hour to eventide, no one could have seen the back of the enemy." Gradually, the Romans moved toward the *laager* and, reaching it, continued the assault against warrior and civilian far into the night. Amid great slaughter (Caesar says 238,000 were killed), the Helvetii were driven from their wagons. Deprived of their sources of food and having been almost annihilated, they had little choice but to surrender. The battle of Armecy was Caesar's first military engagement in Gaul, and he had conducted it brilliantly and emerged victorious.

CAMPAIGN AGAINST ARIOVISTUS (58 B.C.E.)

No sooner had Caesar dealt with the problem of the Helvetii than he had to confront the problem of a Germanic incursion under the leadership of Ariovistus. Representatives from a number of tribes near the Rhine approached Caesar for help in stopping the rampages of the Germanic chieftain. Caesar saw the opportunity to cast himself in the role of savior of all Gaul. Moreover, he felt strongly that sooner or later the German problem would have to be dealt with forcefully. It was Caesar's uncle, Marius, after all, who had saved Rome from a Germanic invasion fifty years earlier.

Caesar requested a meeting with Ariovistus, who advised Caesar to stay out of the quarrel. Caesar responded by informing Ariovistus that any further encroachments in Gaul would be met by force of Roman arms. Ariovistus's response was to assemble thousands of Germanic Seubi tribesmen on the Rhine who threatened to cross and reinforce Ariovistus in Gaul. To prevent this reinforcement, Caesar broke camp and marched to make contact with Ariovistus.

Three days into the march Caesar learned that Ariovistus was planning to seize the town of Vesontio (Besancon). This town was a well-fortified Sequani arsenal. Caesar changed direction and moved to seize it first. Having seized the town, Caesar rested his troops and replenished his supplies. Within a few days, he was on the march again in search of Ariovistus. Seven days later, Caesar's scouts found Ariovistus twenty-four miles from the van of Caesar's army. A meeting between Caesar and Ariovistus settled nothing, and two days later, Ariovistus maneuvered to cut Caesar's supply line. Caesar had to bring Ariovistus to battle or risk the starvation of his army.

For five consecutive days Caesar marched his army onto the open plain to draw Ariovistus into a fight. Except for minor cavalry skirmishing, the German chieftain refused. Tribal shamans had warned Ariovistus that the time was not propitious for a fight until the new moon had turned. Finally, Caesar marched all six of his legions in triple line to the ramparts of the enemy camp. Ariovistus had no choice. He drew up his army in seven tribal formations, behind which he posted the wagon *laager* that contained his supplies and the wives and children of his warriors.

The battle opened with both sides simultaneously charging directly at one another. So rapidly did both sides close that the Romans had no time to launch their *pila*. Observing the disposition of forces prior to the battle, Caesar spotted a weakness in the enemy left wing in that it "appeared less steady" than the other. Caesar took command of his own right wing and waited for both sides to engage. After some time, the Roman right began to break through the German left. At the same time, however, the Roman left began to falter as the sheer weight of German numbers began to take its toll. At this point, Publius Crassus, the cavalry commander, took the initiative and brought up a line of cavalry from the rear to reinforce the Roman left wing. With its last opportunity to break the Roman line gone, the German center wavered and broke. The rest of the army turned on its heels and fled.

Having caught his enemy at last, Caesar refused to disengage. He ordered a relentless and ruthless pursuit. Some of the Germans succeeded in swimming the Rhine, but many others drowned. The remnants of the 75,000-man army were trapped between the legions and the swift waters of the Rhine. Working in concert, the Roman infantry and cavalry slaughtered most of it. When news of Caesar's victory reached the Seubi on the east side of the Rhine, they abandoned any plans for a river crossing and returned to their homes. As Caesar wrote, "Two campaigns were thus finished in a single summer." Within one year, Caesar had gained central and southern Gaul for Rome.

CAMPAIGN AGAINST THE BELGAE (57 B.C.E.)

The Belgae—the collective name for the tough, Gallic-Germanic peoples of northeastern Gaul—were alarmed that Caesar's successful campaigns might be a prelude to their own conquest. They assembled a force of "300,000" warriors (this number is according to Caesar and clearly an exaggeration) and marched south. In Italy at the time, Caesar quickly raised two more legions and, in the early spring, returned to his camp at Vesontio. He made logistical preparations and, with an army of 40,000 legionnaires and 20,000 Gallic auxiliaries, set out to invade the land of the Belgae.

Within a fortnight, Caesar reached the borders of the Belgae on the Marne River. He surprised the Remi, a Belgic tribe, so completely that they went over to his side. The Remi told Caesar that Galba, the king of the Suessiones, was in supreme command of a Belgic coalition comprised of the Bellovaci, the Suessiones, and the Nervii. Meanwhile, Caesar's intelligence had located the main body of the enemy in route of march toward him. Caesar rapidly moved his troops across the Aisne River by constructing a bridge and built a forti-fied camp on the northern side of the river. With the river to his back and his supply line secure over the bridge, Caesar waited for the arrival of Galba.

The two armies engaged in cavalry skirmishes for several days, and a Bel-gic raid on the fortified bridge was repulsed as well. But no significant battle occurred. Instead, the typical failure of the Gallic tribal armies to provide for logistical support forced Galba's army to withdraw because of its inability to feed itself while investing the Roman camp. Caesar saw his opportunity and followed the army, harassing the rearguard and advancing into the various tribal lands, meeting and defeating the tribal contingents piecemeal. Having ravaged the lands of the Suessiones, the Bellovaci, and the Ambiani, Caesar prepared to deal with the fiercest of the Belgic tribes, the Nervii.

Caesar's army halted at a point ten miles from the Sambre River, where he learned that somewhere on its far side the Nervii were waiting for him in coalition with the Atrebates and Viroman-dui. Caesar's difficulty was that he did not know the strength of the enemy (about 75,000 as it turned out) nor its disposition across the river. As was his normal practice, Caesar sent his cavalry ahead to locate a camp for his legions. They selected a spot on a hill overlooking the woods on the other side of the Sambre. Because he expected to contact the enemy, Caesar moved his bag-gage train to the rear of the column under the guard of two legions. The rest marched in light field order toward the camp, ready to engage (Map 14.3).

When the six leading legions reached the camp area, they began to cut timber and construct the camp. It was normal Roman practice to provide security for the construc-tion elements. Perhaps Caesar thought his cavalry was sufficient force to deal with an

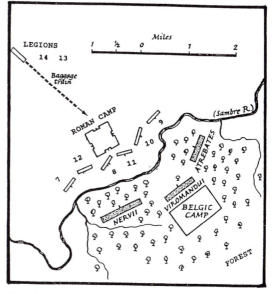

Map 14.3 Battle of the Sambre River. Adapted from J. F. C. Fuller, *Julius Caesar* (New York: Da Capo, 1965).

ambush. In any event, he did not post a strong security force. This was a serious error and almost caused a catastrophe. The Nervii attacked from out of the woods, struck the Roman cavalry screen, routed it, and then raced up the hill and attacked the legionnaires at work on the camp. The surprise was complete and nearly lethal. Fortunately, the legions' commanders had been ordered by Caesar not to leave their legions until the camp was completed, so there were officers to direct the resistance. Second, these legions were highly disciplined veterans. Their centurions immediately grasped the danger, and instead of allowing the men to seek their own *cohorts*, the centurions assembled the troops around the nearest standard and began to fight. Now the rest of the enemy force engaged. Caesar was with the Tenth Legion on the left flank. When he saw the Atrebates closing with the flank, he gave the order to attack.

The Ninth and Tenth legions engaged fiercely, stopped the enemy advance, threw it back down the slope, and without losing contact, followed it over the Sambre. At about the same time the legions in the center held their ground and began to drive the enemy force back toward the river. The whole Roman line began to swing on a hinge comprised of the Twelfth and Seventh legions, which were under strong assault by the Nervii. Gradually, the Nervii compressed the two legions in upon one another and began to envelop Caesar's right flank, the end of the Roman line.

Things were desperate. When Caesar arrived he found the Twelfth so closely huddled together that the men could not raise their swords against the enemy (a similar situation happened at Cannae). Many of the legion's centurions were already dead, and many others were wounded. Caesar, by his own account, grabbed a shield from a soldier in the rear rank and pushed his way to the front. He called upon the centurions by name to force the men to open ranks to better wield their swords. Then Caesar personally led the counterattack. As events would have it, the Thirteenth and Fourteenth legions that had been with the baggage train now came over the hill and entered the battle. This was enough for the Belgae, who began to retreat.

At this point Caesar's most trusted officer, Labienus, who had led the Tenth Legion across the river and captured the enemy camp, turned his legion back toward the river and fell upon the enemy's rear. The Belgic army stopped in its tracks. The massive column of Nervii was trapped on three sides. In a desperate fight, the enemy column was hacked to pieces. Roman casualties were heavy, but the Nervii lost 60,000—almost seven out of every eight men who took the field that day. The destruction was so complete that Caesar noted in his writings that "this engagement brought the name and nation of the Nervii almost to utter destruction."

CAMPAIGN AGAINST THE VENETI (56 B.C.E.)

In the spring of 56 B.C.E., Caesar invaded the Brittany Peninsula to conquer the Veneti. The pretext for the invasion was the mistreatment of Roman ambassadors by the tribal leaders. In fact, the Veneti, a skilled seafaring people who monopolized the lucrative trade with Britain, had learned that Caesar was planning a campaign against Britain and that Rome would thereby threaten the traditional livelihood of the tribe. The Veneti had reckoned correctly. Caesar used the incident as a pretext to seize and subdue the vital channel ports he needed to support his invasion of Britain.

The Veneti would have to be brought to heel either by defeating them at sea or by capturing their coastal strongholds. Neither was an easy task. The Venetian ships were made of stout oak that the Roman galley rams could not penetrate. These ships had shallow keels that allowed them to run in shallower water than the Roman galleys. In addition, their large square leather sails and the considerable height of their decks above the water made them fast and difficult for the lower Roman galleys to grab successfully using pike or grappling hooks. The coastal towns of the Veneti were well fortified and difficult to approach from land or sea. Any garrison in danger of succumbing to land attack could be easily evacuated by sea, a tactic used by the Veneti against Caesar on several occasions.

After several attempts to reduce the coastal cities by force with only mixed success, Caesar determined to fight a naval campaign. He ordered a sizeable fleet of ships to be built on the Loire. When completed and manned, the Roman fleet assembled in Quiberon Bay under the eyes of Caesar and the Roman army and awaited the arrival of the Veneti fleet. The enemy fleet arrived with 220 ships, approximately twice the number of the Roman ships on hand!

The Roman naval commander, Decimus Brutus, had thought through his plan of action. The problem was how to stop the enemy ships from using their superior speed and invulnerability to the Roman galley's ram. Using the galley's superior short-range sprint speed, the Roman ships could easily maneuver next to the larger Veneti ships. Roman engineers, who had revolutionized naval warfare in the Punic Wars by inventing the *corvus* (the swinging boarding platform) and using the grappling iron, now introduced another new piece of naval technology that was to see service for at least another millennium in the navies of the world: the sail-cutter. Using long poles to which scythes were attached, Roman sailors cut the leather sails of the enemy ships. Grappling irons were then used to grasp the halyards, which attached the yards to the masts, and the force of the rowers moving the galley away from the enemy ship snapped the halyards, collapsing the sails and immobilizing the Veneti ships.

With the enemy ships unable to move, the conflict, as Caesar wrote, "became a question of courage." Roman infantry boarded ship after ship and killed the crews. The battle lasted from about four o'clock to sunset and it "finished the campaign against the Veneti and the whole seacoast." Without ships, the coastal towns could neither be evacuated nor supplied, and the Veneti were forced to surrender. Ground operations continued for a few more months, especially against the Morini and Menapii of northwestern Belgica, but by the winter, aside from some small areas in the swamps of the Low Countries where rebel remnants held out, all of Gaul was now under Roman domination. So that no one would miss Caesar's point that Rome intended to brook no rival in Gaul, the entire membership of the Veneti senate was executed and most of the rest of the population sold into slavery. Caesar had gained complete control of his strategic platform from which to launch his invasion of Britain.

CAMPAIGN AGAINST THE GERMANS (55 B.C.E.)

During the winter, news reached Caesar that two Germanic tribes, the Usipetes and the Tencteri, had crossed the Rhine into Gaul in an attempt to establish themselves in a new homeland. Caesar correctly guessed that there were many Belgae who would welcome these tribal kin and seek to form a new alliance against Rome that was more formidable than anything Caesar had previously faced. The new tribes comprised 430,000 people, with more than 100,000 warriors. If the invasion succeeded, Roman control in Gaul would be usurped. Caesar determined to prevent these circumstances in the most dramatic manner possible.

In May, Caesar gathered his legions, marched to the Meuse River, and entered into negotiations with the Germans. During the negotiations, Caesar's army slowly moved closer and closer to the enemy position until they were so close that some kind of contact was almost inevitable. With negotiations underway, a small unit of Germanic cavalry attacked Caesar's Gallic cavalry, perhaps by accident and certainly not with command authorization. Caesar immediately seized and detained the chiefs of the enemy army with whom he had been talking. He then ordered his army into the attack against the entire enemy force and trapped it in a cul-de-sac near the junction of the Moselle and Rhine rivers. The entire people, some 430,000 men, women, and children by Caesar's count, were slaughtered. There were no survivors in this deliberately calculated act of political butchery designed to send a clear message to any other tribal people, Gallic or Germanic, who might consider resisting the will of Rome. Even in Rome the massacre provoked shock and outrage. One writer called the slaughter "unquestionably the most atrocious act of which any civilized man has ever been guilty."

Caesar, for his part, answered his critics with the argument that the massacre was necessary to deter further German inroads into Gaul.

After the battle, Caesar marched his armies down the Rhine. Near the site of modern Bonn, Caesar decided to cross the Rhine in a display of Roman power and will. When the Ubii offered him boats for the crossing, he refused. Instead, to impress upon the barbarians the Roman ability to cross the river at will, Caesar ordered a long suspension bridge constructed across the river. In ten days a wooden roadway forty feet wide hung from a trestle suspension bridge from bank to bank. Caesar crossed the Rhine. Once inside Germany, he left a strong rearguard to secure his line of retreat and then, for eighteen days, ravaged the countryside in a display of military power. Caesar returned to Gaul and destroyed the bridge, having made it clear to the Germans that any future attempt to cross the river would be met by the punishment of Roman arms, even in their homeland if circumstances required.

THE INVASIONS OF BRITAIN (55–54 B.C.E.)

Caesar's expedition to Britain in August 55 B.C.E. was more a reconnaissance-in-force than an invasion. With less than half the summer left, Caesar loaded the Seventh and Tenth legions and their cavalry into eighty infantry and eighteen horse transports and set sail from Boulogne for the British coast. The expedition landed near Dover, where it was strongly opposed by the Britons. After a spirited battle, the Britons sued for peace. Four days after the battle, Caesar's flotilla was scattered by a strong storm. This event encouraged the Britons to renew the fight. Again the Romans defeated them, and again a peace was declared. Caesar then returned to Gaul. Before leaving for Italy for the winter, he ordered the legion commanders to construct as many ships as possible over the winter for use in a spring invasion of Britain. In the spring of 54 B.C.E., Caesar rejoined his army. Six hundred new transports and twenty-eight galleys had been readied for the invasion. In July, after a delay caused by the need to put down a local revolt, Caesar launched the invasion with almost 700 ships carrying five legions and 2,000 cavalry. This would be the largest fleet of warships deployed in the English Channel until the invasion of Normandy in 1944.

The force landed unopposed northeast of Dover. Caesar quickly debarked his legions and began a march inland, seeking to bring the enemy army to battle and destroy it as quickly as possible. Again Caesar neglected to protect his fleet from harsh weather, and a severe storm destroyed and damaged a large number of vessels. A large force of Britons had assembled under the command of a chieftain named Cassivellaunus. Caesar marched inland, sweeping aside a number of minor attacks, crossed the Thames somewhere west of modern London, and struck at the Britons' main force. After a number of battles in which Caesar carried the day against fierce fighting, Cassivellaunus and the Britons sued for peace. After receiving the formal submission of the Britons, Caesar returned across the channel to Gaul where, Caesar wrote, he had learned "of a sudden commotion in Gaul."

In less than seven years Julius Caesar had conquered Gaul, a country of 15 to 20 million people, with an army that numbered less than 50,000 men. The cost to the Gauls of the Roman victories was enormous. Plutarch recorded that, in the conquest of Gaul, Caesar "had taken by storm about eight hundred towns, subdued three hundred states, and of the three millions of men, who made up the gross sum of those with whom at several times he had engaged, he had killed one million and taken captive a second." Caesar now had his own province that he could begin to exploit to produce the kind of vast wealth he needed if he were to make a serious bid to seize control of the Roman state.

The Roman conquest of Gaul required almost seven years of constant warfare. There had been, however, no time between engagements to organize the peace. There was no effective peacekeeping mechanism or law operating on a day-to-day basis. The tribes that had been conquered or that went over to the Roman side still retained their arms, and the ability of these tribes to raise armies remained generally intact. The Gauls, as Caesar noted several times in his writing, were fast learners. Years of warfare against the Romans had taught them a number of lessons in how to fight the enemy. These wars produced a new generation of warriors and leaders who had extensive experience in dealing with the occupier and who were not prone to accept Roman authority as a permanent condition of their lives. Finally, although Caesar's brutality in dealing with some of the conquered tribes was designed to preempt future resistance through fear, it often had the opposite effect. Gaul was full of warriors who hated the Romans and who welcomed the opportunity for revenge. Gaul was seething with resentment, and it did not take much to fan this resentment into a general conflagration of hatred and resistance that threatened to reverse all of Caesar's accomplishments.

CAESAR'S ARMY

Manpower

The legions that Caesar took with him into Gaul were the result of major reforms in the Roman army brought about by Caesar's uncle, Gaius Marius. Marius had been elected consul in 107 B.C.E. to deal with the problem of the Numidian war. He recognized that Roman society had long since ceased to be a republic of free landholders (the traditional source of Roman soldiers), and that unless the recruitment system of the army was reformed, Rome would be unable to produce the level of military manpower required to sustain its emerging empire. To deal with the problem Marius thoroughly reformed the legions of Rome. He carried out the most significant series of military reforms the Roman army had seen in 250 years and bequeathed to future generations of Romans the most effective and efficient killing machine ever devised in the ancient world.

As mentioned, Marius's most significant reform was to change the basis of military recruitment. The traditional middle-class landowners who had provided the base of military manpower from the very founding of Rome could no longer meet the expanded manpower requirements of Rome's military efforts. Decades of war had taken farmers from their land on extended tours of military duty. Unable to keep their farms productive, many of the farmers sold their land to speculators who combined the farms into large estates (*lattifundia*). Roman conquests provided adequate supplies of slaves to work the land, further dispossessing even the tenant farmers. The result was an enormous growth in landless urban proletariat.

Marius opened the ranks of military service to the urban proletariat of Rome. Roman citizenship was still technically required, but after the Social Wars (90 B.C.E.), citizenship was extended to all Italians, expanding the manpower base even further. The quality of manpower drawn from the proletariat was below the hardy peasant farmer stock to which the legions were accustomed. To bring manpower quality up to standards, Marius introduced new drill and training regimens. Every training program from sword drill to road marches was upgraded and standardized, and a strict discipline was imposed. In 105 B.C.E., the training methods used in the Roman gladiatorial schools were introduced throughout the army. The result was a tough, disciplined, professional soldier who bore only scant resemblance to the old citizen-soldier.

Prior to the Marian reforms the legions were assembled on an ad hoc basis as military necessity required. Once the military urgency passed, the legions were disbanded. Unlike the old farmer-soldier, the new proletariat soldier had no farm to which to return for his livelihood. Moreover, the new legions were raised not by the state but by *condottieri* generals, who paid the soldier from plunder accumulated in successful campaigns. Accordingly, the legions were never disbanded, and, gradually, Rome came to have a permanent standing army of full-time professionals. The old militia army was allowed to die a natural death. When Marius made the legion organizations into permanent structures and provided each legion with its own standard, he was formally recognizing the new permanent status of the army. Later, Caesar provided each legion with a number, and, under Augustus, each legion acquired a name.

Tactical Organization

Marius also introduced major tactical innovations. The decline in the quality of fighting men had reduced the level of discipline below what was required to make the old maniple system work. Moreover, the wars against the tribal armies, first in Spain under Scipio and later against the Celts, Gauls, Teutones, and Cimbri, demonstrated that the maniple had to be sturdier to withstand the ferocious frontal massed assaults of these enemies. To strengthen the legion, Marius combined the maniples into *cohorts*, an innovation first attempted by Scipio in Spain (Figure 14.2). Three maniples comprised a 600-man *cohort*. Ten *cohorts* comprised a legion of 6,000 men. All soldiers were armed with the same weapons, the *pilum*, the *gladius*, and the *scutum* shield. This weaponry had been used by some lines of the legion since the Punic Wars. It was Marius's innovation to arm all soldiers of the cohort with the same weaponry. Tactically, the *cohorts* could still fight in open or closed order, and the checkerboard (*quincunx*) formation of the maniple tactical system was retained. But instead of the old battle order of three lines, the new *cohort* was strong

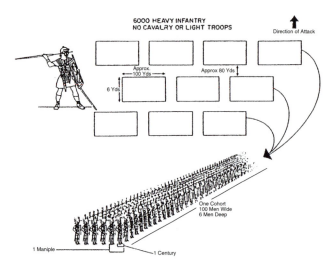

6000 HEAVY INFANTRY
NO CAVALRY OR LIGHT TROOPS

Direction of Attack

Approx. 100 Yds

Approx 80 Yds

6 Yds

One Cohort
100 Men Wide
6 Men Deep

1 Maniple — 1 Century

Figure 14.2 Roman Cohortal Legion (circa 100 B.C. through Imperial Rome). Courtesy of the U.S. Army War College.

enough to assemble in any combination of lines, squares, rectangles, or circles. The use of the same weaponry throughout the formation allowed the *cohort* to confront an attack in any of these formations with the same type and level of combat power. The result was a legion that increased its combat power while retaining and even increasing its tactical maneuverability and flexibility.

Logistics

Marius greatly improved the army's logistical system. His logistical reforms closely paralleled those introduced by Philip of Macedon two centuries earlier. The size of Roman baggage trains was reduced by the simple expedient of having troops carry much of their own rations and equipment. A Roman soldier carried fourteen days' rations instead of the usual three-day supply. He also carried two sharpened wooden stakes to be used in building the encampment each night. Armor and helmets were often worn on the march, and the soldier carried his own weapons and other equipment. The Roman legionnaires carried about sixty pounds and called themselves "Marius's mules."

Further reforms in the logistical system removed the ox-cart from the baggage train and replaced it with mules, horses, and even camels, greatly increasing cross-country mobility. On average, a legion had a standard complement of 1,200 mules for first-line logistical transport, a very small number even by Alexander's standards.

The Roman foot soldier received new boots, a major innovation that greatly reduced foot injuries. Marius positioned the baggage train of each legion directly behind the legion in the line of march, a practice that did much to reduce the vulnerability of the supply train to attack.

Despite these reforms, one notes that Caesar seems to have had considerable difficulty making the system work well in Gaul. In his *Commentaries*, Caesar constantly complained that his supply system could not keep pace with his army or supply it with sufficient food, and in a number of instances, he had to break off a campaign to search for supplies.

The new Roman armies were thoroughly professional, almost mercenary in fighting quality, but were still comprised of Roman citizens who had the right to vote. Comprised of the landless, the army now became a career. The central problem was what to do with the veterans. With no way to sustain themselves after military service, these tough former soldiers could become a danger to the Republic, and, indeed, they eventually did. Marius's solution was to force the state to grant his veterans land in conquered territory. Increasingly, however, soldiers became more loyal to their commanders, who provided booty and land, than to the state. Inevitably, the armies became military instruments for the political ambitions of their commanders.

Tactics

The Marian reforms concentrated the combat power of the legion in the heavy infantry to the almost total (and usual) neglect of cavalry and light infantry. The Roman army was a one-armed (infantry) fighting machine. It was one of the curious aspects of Roman military history that, for a people who liked horse racing and raising horses, the Romans never developed the cavalry arm into a significant combat force. (Interesting as well is that Italy, a country with water on three sides, never developed a serious professional naval force.)

A legion had approximately 300 cavalry divided into ten squadrons of thirty (*turma*) horsemen organically attached to it. Each squadron was commanded by a *decurio*. The squadrons deployed in either line or checkerboard formations in the same manner as the infantry. The troopers were armed in Greek fashion with helmet, armor, shield, spear, and sword. The heavy cavalry charge perfected by Alexander, where engagement occurred in mass and at the gallop to deliver maximum shock, was unknown to the Romans. Instead, cavalry usually engaged at a trot or even a brisk walk, forgoing any shock value. Worse, cavalrymen preferred to dismount and fight alongside the infantry after becoming engaged. Despite Roman experience in the Punic Wars and against the Greeks, Roman cavalry never developed into an arm of decision. Instead, it was used in the traditional manner, to protect the infantry's flanks, to reconnoiter, to forage, and, sometimes, to pursue. It was a paradox of the first order that such great Roman generals as Scipio, Sulla, Marius, and even Caesar himself never saw the need to develop Roman cavalry to a level where it could be a decisive combat asset.

Marius introduced the practice of hiring the famous military mechanics of the Mediterranean—the Balaeric slingers, Cretan archers, and other specialized military practitioners—and integrating them into the legions. The old practice of utilizing Italian allied legions in concert with Roman legions was abandoned. The extension of citizenship to all peoples of Italy made it possible to form legions entirely of Romans and to arm and train them in similar fashion.

Perhaps because of his own military experience against tribal armies, Marius gave considerable attention to the problem of preventing surprise attack. The combat formations of pre-Roman armies were reflections of a less sophisticated style of warfare that was incapable of conducting surprise attack. Accordingly, the art of castrametation—building fortified camps when deployed in the field—was never developed by these armies. But the size, diversity, and mobility of the armies against which Rome fought, especially the tribal armies, made the prospect of surprise attack a horrifying reality. The Romans thus introduced the practice of building a fortified camp at the end of each day's march. The camp gave the commander the advantage of choosing between offensive and defensive action and also provided a secure rallying point around which a routed legion or army could regroup.

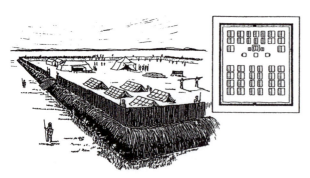

A typical Roman field camp was an 800 meter square or rectangle with rounded corners, surrounded by a ditch twelve feet wide and nine feet deep (Figure 14.3). The earth from the ditch was used to construct a three-foot-high earthen parapet. Three-and-one-half-foot-long sharpened wooden stakes were inserted into the parapet to provide the exterior wall with a spiked front. If the legion remained in an area for an extended time, further fortifications were added. Inside the perimeter the tents of the soldiers and officers were arranged in a symmetrical fashion. Each unit always occupied the same location in the camp, and units were grouped into their normal combat formations for rapid deployment in case of attack.

Figure 14.3 Roman Field Camp under Construction. Courtesy of the U.S. Army War College.

The ability to protect their armies in the field represented a major military advantage for the Romans. But the price of security was a reduction in mobility. It required four to five hours each day to construct the camp, a time that could not be used for marching. The Romans were great marchers when moving along their secure paved roads on the way to the battlefield. Indeed, under these conditions they could move twenty-five miles a day. Once in the field, however, their rate of movement was slowed by their reliance upon the spade to provide security. The Romans were obsessed with flank security, and even went so far upon occasion to protect the flanks of the legion by digging trenches along their flanks to guard against enemy cavalry attack. That reliance was tied directly to the Roman failure to develop adequate dependable cavalry that could have been used, as Alexander did, to provide security for the legion in the field.

Administration

Marius thoroughly modernized the organizational structure of the Roman army. War had become so complex that complex organizational structures were required to fight it. Although the organizational sophistication of the military bureaucracy reached its highest point around the first century C.E., it was Marius who set in place the prototypes for this further development. To deal with the problem of tactical security, Marius created a contingent of ten scouts—*speculatores*—within each legion to give the legion its own tactical intelligence capability. Even in Marius's day each senior officer had a small administrative staff responsible for paperwork, and just like modern armies, the Roman army generated a considerable amount of paperwork. For example, each soldier had an administrative file containing his full history, awards, physical examinations, training, and pay records.

Legion and army staffs included sections dealing with intelligence, supply, medical care, pay, engineers, siegers, and veterinary affairs. While armies of the past, most notably those of the Greeks, had doctors in attendance on the battlefield, the Romans were the first to attempt to systematize the provision of military medical services. Roman military medicine began with ensuring that the soldier remained in good health while in garrison. A healthy diet was combined with plenty of exercise and physical conditioning. Excellent hygiene made possible the prevention of epidemics. In addition, each legion had a full complement of medical doctors and supporting staff, including a corps of medical orderlies who served as combat medics. The Roman legion's bureaucracy and staff functions would be easily recognizable to a modern military staff officer.

Siegecraft

The Roman genius for war often resided more in organization and application than in invention, as in the case of siegecraft and artillery. The Roman contribution to siegecraft was to improve the old Greek machines, but the major innovation was to use them in a consistent, organized manner so as almost always to succeed in achieving the objective. The Romans used armored siege towers made of wood (some as high as twenty-four meters), massive iron battering rams, large iron hooks to dislodge stones, covered platforms to protect miners and assault teams, bridges, drawbridges, and elevators mounted on towers to swing assault teams over the walls. Roman catapults were much larger than the old Greek models and were powered by torsion devices and springs made of sinew kept supple with oil. The largest of these devices, the *onager* (called the "wild ass" because of its kick), could, as Josephus reports, hurl a hundred-pound stone over 400 yards. Smaller versions of this machine were also used. Vegetius noted that each legion had ten *onagi*, one per *cohort*, drawn by carts organic to its organization.

Artillery

Roman advances in the design, mobility, and firepower of artillery were significant. Smaller versions of siege machines, such as the scorpion and ballista, were compact enough to be transported by mule or horse. These machines could fire seven- to ten-pound stone shot over 300 yards. Caesar required that each legion carry thirty of these small machines, giving the legion an organic mobile artillery capability. Small machines fired iron-tipped wooden bolts. Designed much like the later crossbow but mounted on small platforms or legs, these machines could be used as rapid-fire field guns against enemy formations. They weighed about eighty-five pounds and fired bolts approximately twenty-six inches long over a range of almost 300 yards. One version of this machine fired small leaden shot that could easily kill a single man at 100 yards and hit a small group of men at 200 yards. With a maximum range of 450 to 500 yards, the small *petrobolos*, literally "stone thrower," was more accurate than the flintlock musket. Slightly larger versions mounted on a wheeled frame were called *carroballistae*. The smaller versions required a two-man crew to operate, whereas the larger machines needed a crew of ten men. These machines could fire at least three to four bolts per minute and were used to lay down a barrage of fire against enemy troop concentrations.

Overall, the strength of the Roman army lay in its training, discipline, and organization. Tactically, it was a one-armed army in that its emphasis on heavy infantry led it to neglect the development of cavalry. Its failure to develop trustworthy cavalry forced the Roman army to rely upon the shovel for tactical security when in the field, and the necessity to construct a field camp every evening reduced its ability to cover ground by four to five hours a day. When in the field, the Roman logistical system had difficulty keeping up with the army, forcing a reliance upon foraging. The comparative economic development of Gaul made foraging possible, and Caesar's armies could move relatively well on this basis. In Germany, however, the lack of agricultural development forced the army to rely upon its own logistical resources, often with poor results.

The success of the Roman army in Gaul was due in no small measure to the fact that the Gallic enemy was simply not very good at waging war. Caesar was fortunate, for example, that the Gauls never developed truly effective cavalry, although for most Gallic tribes it was their primary fighting arm and used to exploit the Roman weakness in this area. Moreover, the Gallic propensity to conduct undisciplined frontal assaults against combat-hardened Roman infantry squandered numerical superiority time and again. Finally, tribal armies tended to bring along the whole tribe when they engaged in battle. As a result, a battlefield defeat often exposed the entire tribe to massacre. While the Roman system of war was certainly more advanced than anything produced by the Gauls, it is difficult to escape the conclusion that even the Roman system might have had a difficult time if the Gauls had been able to exploit obvious Roman military weaknesses.

THE ARMIES OF THE GAULS

The military structure of the Gauls was a reflection of their larger social organization. Gallic society was governed by an aristocracy of nobles surrounded by groups of retainers who acted as a warrior class, not unlike the warrior retinues of the European Middle Ages. Most of the rest of the social order was comprised of various types of free landholders and tenant farmers, a large portion of which had been reduced almost to serf status. The Druidic priesthood constituted another social caste and, while influential, was unable to act as an organizer for Gallic society outside of its religious functions. Unlike the Germans, however, Gallic society was not primarily a warrior society. The Gauls were a relatively advanced people who practiced extensive agriculture, constructed roads, forts, and bridges, and used currency rather than the more primitive barter as a form of economic interchange. Indeed, the very sophistication of the Gallic social and economic infrastructure was what permitted Caesar to sustain his military operations within the country for as long as he did. The constant jockeying for power and shifting alliances among the rival nobilities further precluded any significant degree of national integration even to confront the common Roman enemy. One consequence was the lack of any national army or any genuine level of military sophistication that could be marshaled to defend Gaul against the Roman invasion.

Tactical Organization

Among most of the tribes of Gaul the primary fighting arm was cavalry. Although the chariot had been used in Gaul for centuries, it seems to have disappeared sometime prior to Caesar's arrival except among the tribes in Britain. Its place was taken by cavalry as the warrior nobility increased its control over other segments of the population. Caesar called these horse-borne nobles *equites*, commonly translated as "knights," and they typically constituted the tribal command structure for war. The Gallic armies had spent centuries in intertribal warfare, with the consequence that they had made few improvements in their weapons, tactics, or style of war. This was certainly true of the cavalry, which was generally poor in quality and, in any case, accustomed to fighting as individual combatants rather than as a coordinated group. When combined with infantry, significant coordination in battle was rarely achieved.

In a social order divided almost feudally between warrior knights on horseback and tenant farmers, serfs, and freeholders, it was hardly surprising that Gallic infantry amounted to little more than an untrained, temporarily assembled armed rabble incapable of any significant degree of tactical sophistication, discipline, or direction on the battlefield. The typical infantryman was armed with the long slashing sword as his chief weapon. Little use was made of spearmen or archers, although Caesar occasionally encountered javelin throwers and slingers. The infantry and cavalry carried wooden or wattle shields, and Caesar recorded that some Gallic troops fought stripped to the waist. In other instances he noted that the nobility wore bronze cuirasses, chain mail, and highly decorated helmets, more, no doubt, as signs of military status and rank than genuine defensive implements. The Gauls seemed to have been fast learners when it came to copying Roman methods of siegecraft, however, and their traditional skills as miners served them well in this regard.

The Helvetii and the Nervii, the tribes against which Caesar conducted most of his infantry battles, were exceptions to the generally poor condition of Gallic infantry. The Helvetii had refined their art of war through centuries of running battles on their borders with the Germans. Accordingly, they were first-rate infantrymen who fought in disciplined formations under good command. They seem as well to have acquired some of the Germanic skill at cavalry. The Nervii of the Sambre Valley were an infantry force of considerable skill and discipline. They had no cavalry at all. In all Caesar's battles in Gaul, it was only the Helvetii and Nervii who dared challenge the legions of Rome to infantry combat on the open field, and they consistently gave a good accounting of themselves on the battlefield.

The conduct of warfare by the Gauls left much to be desired, especially so when confronting the Roman enemy whose strong point was organization. The Gauls had almost no military organization to speak of. Long centuries of tribal civil wars made any military coalition a fragile entity. Caesar was a master at playing one tribe off another to prevent a concentration of superior military forces against him. Moreover, by engaging the Gallic armies piecemeal, an isolated victory against one contingent was often sufficient to fragment the entire coalition, whose members simply returned home. The Gauls were incapable of sustained military operations if they required sustaining a tribal political coalition for any length of time.

As mentioned, the Gauls lacked any significant military organization. When the tribe went to war, the whole tribe went, including the women and children. There was no logistical system to speak of, and after a few days in the field, when supplies ran low or the countryside proved incapable of supplying the army and its following, the army often melted away as various contingents returned to their villages. The lack of a proper commissariat conceded the military initiative to the Roman army, which could sustain itself in the field for months on end through a combination of logistical supply and foraging off the land. Even if defeated or outmaneuvered in the field, Caesar had but to keep his army moving for a few days before it became impossible for the Gallic army to follow it due to lack of logistical capability.

In the field, the Gallic army anchored itself around a ring of wagons—a wagon *laager*—within which the women, children, and supplies of the tribe were concentrated for protection. The integration of a tribal army with its larger social structure proved a terrible disadvantage in defeat. A local defeat often turned into a rout that gathered around the wagon *laager*, thereby exposing the women and children to capture and massacre. On a number of occasions, Caesar surrounded, captured, and enslaved entire tribes. In other instances, he massacred entire peoples trapped in this manner.

Tactics

In combat, the Gauls had no discernible tactical system of engagement. Led by their mounted nobles, an unorganized mob of undisciplined infantry would launch a frontal attack hoping to overwhelm the adversary with sheer numbers. These attacks were not conducted by units but by masses of individuals fighting as individuals. During the first few encounters with the Gauls, these frontal attacks unnerved the Romans and caused some *cohorts* to break under the assault. The physical stature of the Gaul was significantly more impressive than that of the average Roman. One authority suggests that the average Gaul may have been as much as seven inches taller than the average Roman! These huge people attacked the Roman infantry with their long swords held above their heads. Upon smashing into the Roman formations, the broadsword was brought crashing down on the heads of the Roman infantry to great effect. The Roman shield, made entirely of wood, frequently proved unable to absorb the force of the sword blow and broke apart on impact.

After an engagement or two, the Romans learned to cope with the challenges of Gallic infantry. First, the shield was reinforced with a metal rim capable of taking the force of the sword stroke. Second, the front line of the infantry was trained to raise their shields above their heads and permit the enemy swordsman to bring his sword down directly upon the shield. As the blow struck, the Roman infantry absorbed the blow by gradually bending to one knee. At this point the enemy infantryman was defenseless, with his sword on top of the Roman shield and the force of the blow expended. Now the Roman soldier sprang upward and forward from his crouched position, driving his *gladius* into the unarmored body of his adversary. Once engaged, the long sword of the Gaul proved to be no match for the Roman short sword, especially so since the Roman infantryman was a trained professional fighting against a part-time tribal warrior.

The problem in dealing with Gallic infantry was usually numbers. Wave after wave of howling swordsmen crashed into the ranks of the legion. If the legion had possessed good-quality cavalry, it could have made short work of the Gallic infantry by attacking and enveloping the flanks. Fortunately, the only cavalry worse than the Roman cavalry was Gallic cavalry—a fact that led Caesar to hire German mercenary cavalry whenever he could. The Romans solved the problem of numbers by utilizing the flexibility of their infantry lines inherent in the open *cohort* formation. The initial line of Roman infantry engaged the adversary and held up the assault as long as it could. Then, upon command, the first line was reinforced and gradually replaced by the second line, and the first line withdrew through the third line to rest. The third line then moved into position to relieve the second line upon command. The flexibility of infantry lines permitted the Roman infantry to place the maximum number of fighting men in the front ranks at all times and to ensure that there was a continual source of rested replacements and reinforcements to deal with the attack.

It is difficult to read Caesar's *Commentaries* without reaching the conclusion that much of Caesar's brilliance in command had to do with exploiting the obvious weaknesses of his enemy to good effect. Certainly Caesar was fortunate in not having to deal with an enemy that had efficient cavalry. Indeed, for most of its history Rome rarely fought enemies who excelled at cavalry. In Gaul, the problem was how to deal with hordes of tribal infantry armed with poor-quality weapons and even fewer combat skills and direction. For this, cavalry was not absolutely required. At the operational level, Caesar was always fighting an enemy that could not bring its numerical superiority to bear on the battlefield either because it could not achieve political unity or, more commonly, because it lacked any significant logistical capability for sustained operations. In fighting the Gauls, the Roman army, like Roman society, was years ahead of its adversary in developing the organizational skills for effective maneuver, supply, and tactical capabilities. In Caesar, moreover, the Gallic armies had to deal with a field commander who had few equals anywhere in the Western world at the time. As a consequence, the wars between the legions of Julius Caesar and the tribal armies of Gaul were never really a serious contest.

Caesar's battles against Pompey and other Roman and Eastern antagonists were another matter. Against Pompey Caesar faced an adversary who was every bit as good a general as he was and, at times, even more capable of leading and directing men in battle. The army of Pompey was, after all, a Roman army, and it brought with it all the advantages that Caesar's army possessed.

In regard to cavalry, Caesar's cavalry generally consisted of hired Gallic and German horsemen, whereas Pompey's cavalry arm was of considerably better quality, being drawn from the horsemen of Rome's eastern provinces. In the battles between Pompey and Caesar, it was more the quality of generalship than the nature of the armies that decided the issue.

THE SIEGE OF ALESIA (52 B.C.E.)

Caesar returned from Britain in early fall of 54 B.C.E. and was greeted with the news that the harvest in Gaul was a poor one. To facilitate the supply of food to his troops for the winter, Caesar dispersed his ten legions into eight camps scattered across northern Gaul. The camps were all within one hundred miles of one another, and two were within sixty miles of each other. It seems to have occurred to several Gallic chieftains that it might be possible to strike at the dispersed Roman camps, destroying them one by one. One of these chieftains, Ambiorix of the Eubrones, struck the first blow. If he could destroy a Roman army in its camp, then perhaps the rest of Gaul would rally to the standard of rebellion.

Ambiorix mounted a tentative attack against the Roman garrison near Aduatuca. When the Romans resisted, Ambiorix broke off the attack and sought negotiations. In these talks Ambiorix explained he had attacked the garrison under pressure from his people to join the larger movement of Gallic rebellion. He told the Roman commander that in a few days all eight of the garrisons would come under attack simultaneously. Ambiorix urged the Roman commander to abandon the camp and join the other legions in the nearest camp sixty miles away. Ambiorix guaranteed the Romans safe passage through his territory.

The Roman commander took the bait and marched out of the fortified camp the next morning. Ambiorix ambushed the Roman column from both ends when it was trapped deep within a defile in the forest. All day and into the evening javelins rained down on the Roman column until, finally, weakened from casualties, it was overrun and the Gauls closed in for the kill. Most of the Roman legion was killed in battle, and at the end of the day, "seeing that all hope was gone, every single man committed suicide." In fact, however, a few soldiers survived to reach the Roman garrison sixty miles away and warn them of an impending attack.

Ambiorix had his first victory, and with it he convinced some of the other tribes to join him for an attack on the Roman garrison near Binche. Within days, a 60,000-man Gallic army laid siege to the town, trapping another Roman legion within its walls. When Caesar was informed of these events, he immediately sallied from his base near Amiens with a relief force of 7,000 infantry and approximately 1,500 horse. When Ambiorix learned of Caesar's movement, he left a small garrison to continue the siege and moved his main army into the path of Caesar's approaching army. Near the Sabis River, the Romans encountered the Gauls in battle and, after a bitter fight, drove them from the field. Caesar moved on to relieve the siege. He was amazed at the Gallic siegeworks, virtual copies of the Roman machines and methods. Caesar noted in his writing of the Roman garrison that "not one man in ten remained unwounded."

The revolt simmered throughout the winter as Caesar remained with his army, keeping up a steady pulse of reconnaissance and diplomacy to stay abreast of what the tribes were doing. Revolt was constantly in the air. During the winter, Caesar swept down on the Nervii and ravaged their lands in a preemptive strike. In the spring, Caesar used all ten of his legions to conduct a campaign of intimidation against the Belgae. He crossed the Rhine again to dissuade the German tribes from coming to the aid of Ambiorix or giving him sanctuary. Caesar's campaign involved no major battles. Instead, it was a counter-insurgency campaign designed to terrorize those who might support the rebellion. Caesar painted a vivid picture of this campaign when he described the operations against the Eubrones, the people of Ambiorix. They were shown no mercy.

> Every hamlet, every homestead that anyone could see was set on fire; captured cattle were driven from every spot; the corn-crops were not only being consumed by the vast host of pack-animals and human beings, but were laid flat in addition because of the rainy season, even if any persons succeeded in hiding themselves for the moment, it seemed that they must perish for want of everything when the army was withdrawn.

The destruction was pointless. Ambiorix was never caught. But the spirit of Gallic rebellion was wounded, and open revolt ended. After a while, Caesar became convinced that things had returned to normal, and in the fall, he set out for Italy.

During all this activity, central Gaul had remained peaceful. But the extraordinary degree of Roman brutality in dealing with the revolt angered the Gauls and, for the first time, forced upon them the realization that they would have to act in concert if Roman oppression was to be overthrown. Tribal leaders throughout the country held secret meetings to discuss an uprising. With Caesar in Italy, the Roman army was without its head, and the Gauls began to plan an uprising that would strike at several Roman garrisons at once. What was needed was a sudden and violent event to detonate the revolt and bring the tribes to arms. In the winter of 52 B.C., the Roman merchant community at Cenabum (modern Orleans), the capital city of the Carnutes, was slaughtered in the streets by the Gauls (Map 14.4). Within a day all Gaul had heard of the massacre, and one after another, the tribes flocked to the standard of rebellion. The leader of the general revolt was a young Avernian chief, Vercingetorix, known for his intellect, discipline, and brutality.

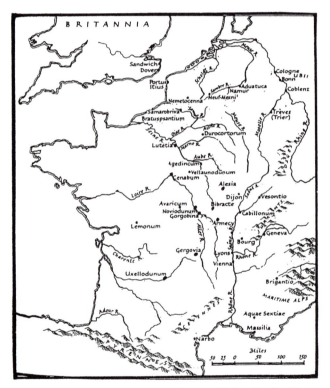

Map 14.4 Vercingetorix versus Caesar: Major Battle Sites

Task forces from the assembled Gallic army began to move on several Roman garrisons simultaneously to bring them under attack. A separate force moved south toward Narbo to block Caesar's return to Gaul. Most of Caesar's army was in north-central Gaul around Lutetia (modern Paris). Accompanied by his bodyguard and a small provincial levy from Narbo (modern Narbonne), Caesar crossed the snow-covered Cevennes Mountains. His sudden appearance in front of the Gallic force threw it into a panic, and they retreated. Caesar broke contact and swung eastward along the Rhone toward Vienna on the Saone River, where he was joined by Roman cavalry units garrisoned in the vicinity. He then moved north outside of Alesia, where two of his legions were posted in winter quarters. The rest of Caesar's army was in the vicinity of Paris, readying to move south to join him.

Quite by accident, Vercingetorix found his own army between the two Roman forces. He moved southwest and struck at the town of Gorgobina, a major town of one of Rome's loyal tribal allies that had not joined the revolt. Caesar left his baggage at Agedincum near Alesia and marched toward Gorgobina to relieve the assault against his allies. Vercingetorix's movement left the towns of Vellaundodunum and Cenabum defenseless, and Caesar moved quickly to attack both towns. This placed Caesar behind Vercingetorix, who raised his siege of Gorgobina and turned toward Caesar in an effort to make contact with the Roman army. Caesar continued to advance and occupied the town of Noviodunum (modern Nevers). The two armies brushed by each other with only sporadic contact between their cavalry forces. Caesar then moved on to Avaricum.

Vercingetorix's operational plan had failed. He had not succeeded in preventing Caesar from joining his army in Gaul. Once in command, Caesar had moved so audaciously and rapidly that the less organized tribal armies of the Gauls could not react quickly enough to prevent Caesar from seizing a number of key towns. The attempt to grab Gorgobina and punish a Roman ally had failed. Worse, Vercingetorix realized that his defensive strategy conceded the initiative to Caesar, who exploited it brilliantly with maneuver and speed. If the revolt was to succeed, another strategy was required. Vercingetorix decided upon a war of attrition in which a scorched earth policy deprived the Roman army of its supplies until the Gauls could pin it down and destroy it. After a meeting with the other tribal chiefs, the area around Avaricum—the land of the Bituriges—was set to the torch. Caesar wrote that "in a single day more than twenty cities of the Bituriges were set on fire. The same was done in other states, and in every direction fires were to be seen."

Vercingetorix seized Avaricum (modern Bourges), the last fortified and supplied town in a barren and burnt province. Caesar, seeing his chance finally to do battle with the Gallic army, laid siege to the town. For twenty-five days the Romans constructed an earthen ramp 300 feet long and 80 feet high. Then, on a rainy grey day, the Roman assault carried the ramparts, and a garrison of 40,000 men, along with their wives and children, was massacred. Vercingetorix and his bodyguard escaped, and Caesar lost his chance to capture the leader of the rebellion. Caesar rested and resupplied his armies in Avaricum for several days, then secured the nearby town of Noviodunum and established a large supply base there to support his further operations in the area.

Word reached Caesar that the northern tribes had joined the revolt. He split his army into two commands. Four legions under Labienus were sent north to contain the tribes. Caesar, in command of seven legions, moved down the eastern bank of the Allier River to strike at Gergovia (modern Georgovie). Vercingetorix moved his army into the area around the town hoping to draw Caesar into the attack. Caesar took the bait. Vercingetorix's plan was to hold Caesar in place and use his cavalry to harass and kill Caesar's foraging parties until Caesar's army was weakened by lack of supplies. This activity went on for almost a month, during which time each side conducted attacks against the other's fortifications, but without result. Vercingetorix renewed his diplomatic efforts to attract even more tribes to the standard of revolt with significant success. Caesar, meanwhile, concentrated on the siege of the city. Suddenly, a Gallic army moving south struck and captured Noviodunum in Caesar's rear. This was a catastrophe. Noviodunum was Caesar's main logistical base. With its capture went his reserve supply of food for the army, his war treasury, most of the army's baggage, and a large supply of extra horses. The Gauls massacred the small garrison in the town. The news of the attack rallied even more tribes to the cause, including some that had remained loyal to Rome from the beginning of the revolt.

Caesar's position was critical. His tribal allies had been wooed away, and new military forces were being assembled across his rear. The Bituriges, their land already in flames, were burning for revenge. Ahead, Vercingetorix's army barred the way to the safety of Cisalpine Gaul. The scorched earth policy had its anticipated effect, and Caesar's army was desperate for supplies. Worst of all, four badly needed legions were off to the north chasing tribes through the woods to no practical effect. Desperate as his situation was, Caesar never panicked. Instead, he broke contact from the siege, wheeled his army about, and slipped through the Gallic armies that were still moving into position to entrap him. He crossed the Loire River, swung around Cenabum, and reached Agedincum (modern Sens), the logistical support base of the four legions operating in the north. As luck would have it, Labienus heard rumors of a catastrophe befalling Caesar to his south. Fearing that the rumors were true, Labienus fell back to his administrative base at Agedincum. He thus joined forces with Caesar coming from the other direction just outside the town. Caesar had once again united his army. The eleven legions rested and replenished at Agedincum before they set out again in search of Vercingetorix.

Vercingetorix kept to his plan to avoid a pitched battle against the superior Roman infantry, to deprive the Romans of supplies, to use his cavalry to harass Roman foragers and supply lines, and to engage the enemy only in defense or ambush. Vercingetorix had 80,000 infantry and 15,000 cavalry in the field, a force only slightly larger than Caesar's eleven legions (55,000 men) and 3,000 cavalry (not counting his German mercenary horsemen). Vercingetorix selected the fortified town of Alesia as his main base of operations. He suspected that Caesar might make for Cisalpine Gaul with his army, where he could replenish it and return with a larger force. Vercingetorix was determined to keep Caesar bottled up in Gaul until he could wear down his army, force it to battle, and kill it. Soon, Caesar began to move his army down the Soane Valley. Vercingetorix deployed his cavalry along the valley to harass Caesar's movement and threaten his lines of communication. The idea was to ambush Caesar in column of march with his baggage.

Vercingetorix set the ambush at a location near Dijon. He deployed his infantry in three strong camps directly astride Caesar's route of march so that the vanguard of the army would advance directly into his troops. Once Caesar's column had halted, Vercingetorix planned to use his cavalry to strike the column in the flanks and rear, cutting it into isolated segments that could be dealt with piecemeal. Caesar failed to use his cavalry to provide sufficient reconnaissance and security, and the vanguard of his army clashed directly with Vercingetorix's force. Caesar was taken completely by surprise, as he had been at the Sambre River previously, and, by all odds, his army should have been trapped and annihilated. For some unknown reason, however, the Gallic cavalry did not engage in force but contented itself with skirmishing. Delbruck suggests that this may have been because Caesar bolstered his cavalry with infantry, but Caesar makes no mention of this. The failure of the Gallic cavalry to press the attack permitted Caesar sufficient time to use his own horse to keep the enemy at a distance, while he assembled his infantry in battle formation. The result was that the ambush did not strike decisively at Caesar's column but allowed it time to redeploy to meet further attack.

When Vercingetorix saw that the ambush had failed, he remained true to his operational plan and broke contact, withdrawing back toward his base at Alesia. This withdrawal opened the road to Italy for Caesar, who could now retreat without opposition. Instead, Caesar wheeled to his rear, assembled his army, and pursued Vercingetorix back to Alesia. The Romans fell on the Gallic rearguard and killed 3,000 men. More importantly, Caesar now had Vercingetorix and his army on the defensive, and for the first time since the rebellion had begun, Caesar could come to grips with the enemy main force and its wily commander.

The town of Alesia (modern Alise Ste. Reine) was situated on an elevated plateau almost 1,500 feet above the valley floor, through which ran two minor rivers, the Ose and Oserain. On three sides, across the valley, were hills. Vercingetorix withdrew to the town and encamped his army on the surrounding hills, with forward positions along the approach to the valley. Caesar realized that the only way to take the position was by siege, and he invested the town (Map 14.5). The fortifications constructed by Caesar around Alesia were some of the most extensive and complex in all antiquity. He enclosed the entire hill upon which the city stood with a wall of circumvallation designed to keep Vercingetorix within it. This wall ran for sixteen kilometers. The outer wall of circumvallation was twenty kilometers long and was designed to keep any relief army from breaking through to the besieged town. Between the two streams in the valley across from the forward positions of the enemy, Caesar constructed a twenty-foot trench with perpendicular sides to prevent any attack through this weak area. Beyond the outer wall, two concentric trenches were dug—each fifteen feet wide—and the inner trench filled with water diverted from the stream. Behind the inner trench was a twelve-foot-high earthen rampart crowned by a wooden palisade, with turrets of wood placed at eighty-foot intervals. In front and in between each layer of defensive belts were anti-personnel devices such as pits

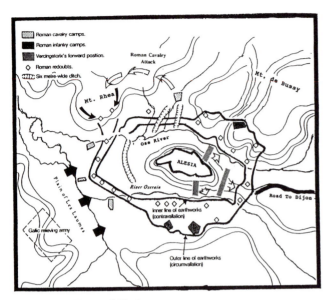

Map 14.5 Siege of Alesia

with spikes at the bottom, iron pikes in large wooden logs pointing directly at the enemy, fallen and tethered trees to make movement difficult, sharpened wooden stakes, *stimuli* (a fishhook type trip device), and various other obstacles. Covering it all were ballistas, crossbows, and field guns that could rain missiles with deadly accuracy on any troops making their way through the obstacle belt. Twenty-three forts or strong points were placed at strategic locations along the outer wall, and eight major camps—four infantry and four cavalry—completed the system. The siegeworks around Alesia were truly formidable and required five weeks to construct.

Caesar had just begun to construct these siegeworks when Vercingetorix went over to the offensive. He sent a large force of cavalry (Vercingetorix had 10,000 to 15,000 cavalry at hand) against Caesar's army. Caesar countered with his own cavalry forces, and a large cavalry battle ensued. Vercingetorix was remaining true to his plan and using his cavalry to make it difficult for Caesar to forage for supplies. The attack was designed to massacre the Roman cavalry and make foraging even more dangerous. As Caesar recorded it, his Spanish and Gallic cavalry did not perform well and were in danger of being destroyed. Caesar committed his German cavalry squadrons at the propitious moment, and the enemy cavalry broke. As Vercingetorix's cavalry fled toward the town, the narrow gates of the outlying fortifications could not accommodate the sudden onrush of thousands of cavalry horses. A great jam occurred, and Caesar's German cavalry fell on the enemy and killed large numbers.

Within the city Vercingetorix had less than a thirty-day supply of food. Perhaps because of this, he abandoned his original plan to harass the Roman foragers and starve Caesar's army. Instead, he sent most of his cavalry away from Alesia with instructions to raise an enormous army among the tribes and come to the relief of Alesia. His plan was to keep Caesar in place until the relief army could be assembled and attack Caesar from the rear. The immediate effect of this change in plans was to allow Caesar complete freedom to construct his siegeworks and to range far and wide in search of food for his army.

Feeding the Roman army was no easy task. The countryside had been picked over, and foraging units had to range farther and farther afield to find grain. Caesar also realized that once the Gallic relief army arrived, there would be no more foraging. He ordered his commissariat to build a thirty-day reserve of grain. It is important to note that, had Vercingetorix not changed his plans and thus given up his harassment of Caesar's foragers, Caesar would never have been able to feed his army nor, as it turns out, been able to construct the complex siegeworks around Alesia. Vercingetorix had been correct all along in his original plan, but he changed his tactics at a critical moment in the campaign. It was a costly mistake.

It took five weeks for the Gauls to assemble a relief army and move it to Alesia. Caesar says this army numbered 250,000 infantry and 8,000 cavalry, but clearly this is an exaggeration. An army of that size could not move along the dirt tracks of Gaul nor feed itself. Judging from the manner in which it maneuvered once in place around Alesia, Delbruck concludes that the Gallic relief army comprised probably 80,000 men and horse. By the time the army arrived, food supplies were down to starvation levels within Alesia itself. One proposal from a Gallic chieftain was that the old be slain and their bodies cannibalized by the warriors. Vercingetorix chose instead to send all the old, women, and children from the city to offer themselves as slaves to the Romans. Caesar refused to permit them to pass, and these wretched people were forced back into the city.

A few days after this incident, the relief army arrived and camped on the heights west of the town. They next deployed their entire force into the valley and up to the Roman walls, where they began to fill in the moat. To put a stop to this activity and to test the mettle of the newcomers, Caesar sent out a strong cavalry force to engage the enemy cavalry. The Gauls had dispersed some foot archers among their cavalry, and a large number of Roman horsemen were wounded by arrows. For hours, "from noon almost to sunset," 12,000 cavalry fought in front of the Roman walls. Again Caesar held his German squadrons in reserve until the right moment. When they attacked, the German cavalry struck first at the enemy horsemen covering the archers. Driving them away, the cavalry then fell on the archers and massacred them. As the Gallic cavalry fell back, the infantry that had been filling in the moat was exposed. It also took flight and, along with the cavalry, retreated to the hillside. The first attempt to break the siege of Alesia had ended in failure.

The Gauls tried again the following night. Units of sappers with ladders and hurdles moved silently toward the outer wall. Under cover of arrows and sling shot from support troops, the sappers began to fill in the outer ditches. Simultaneously, Vercingetorix's forces assaulted the wall from the city. This force was driven back by a hail of missile fire of javelins, ballista shot, and sling shot. A third Gallic force attacked the fortifications on the opposite side, but in the darkness many fell into the spiked pits or were otherwise killed or wounded by the anti-personnel devices that protected the outer walls. The three-pronged assault was poorly coordinated and floundered until daylight, when the attackers were ordered to withdraw.

The Gauls planned still another assault. This time they conducted a reconnaissance and discovered that the line of circumvallation was not complete at a point along the Ose River at the foot of Mount Rhea. This soft point was garrisoned by two legions whose camps were overlooked by high ground. During the night, the Gauls moved 6,000 hand-picked warriors under one of their best field commanders around Mount Rhea to a location in the hills above the Roman camps. Once in place, the force rested until midday. At noon, they swept down the hill and attacked the Roman camps. In a simultaneous and coordinated attack, the main body of Gallic cavalry moved across the Plain of Laumes and struck the main Roman force guarding the wall. This maneuver provided screen and cover for a large follow-up infantry force. From the town itself, Vercingetorix launched yet another assault at the Roman wall covering the gap between the streams. In addition, several smaller assaults were conducted at various points along the Roman line in an effort to pin down the enemy and prevent him from shifting his forces along interior lines within the fortified walls.

Atop a siege platform, Caesar had an excellent view of the entire battlefield, and he quickly discerned that the critical point in the battle was the attack on the two legion camps at the base of Mount Rhea. After the initial assault, the Gauls supported their attack with strong reinforcements. Caesar sent six *cohorts* under Labienus to shore up the Roman position. A major attack was also conducted across the plain, and the fighting was bloody. Despite heavy casualties, the Gauls were able to fill in some of the ditches and dismantle other obstacles. Twice Caesar had to send reinforcements to the positions opposite the wall to hold it. Once assured that this secondary front could resist the enemy pressure, Caesar turned his attention to the attack on the two legion camps.

Caesar took command of four *cohorts* of infantry and personally led them to reinforce Labienus, who was now engaged in a desperate fight. Caesar ordered some cavalry units to maneuver outside the walls and to swing around the rear of Mount Rhea to get behind the enemy force attacking the legion camps. When Caesar himself arrived with his infantry to reinforce the camps, the men recognized him in his red cloak and immediately took heart. They began to fight with greater effort. Caesar had analyzed the situation well. From the beginning of the battle he had recognized that the main assault would fall on the legion camps. Once he had assured himself that the rest of his positions could hold, he personally reinforced the threatened position. Since the main Gallic army was engaged around the legion camps, Caesar had sent his cavalry around its rear. At the height of the infantry battle for the legion camps, the Roman cavalry suddenly appeared in the rear of the enemy army and went into the attack.

It was Napoleon who said that "there is a moment in an engagement when the last maneuver is decisive and gives victory; it is the one drop of water which makes the vessel run over." The appearance of Caesar's cavalry behind the Gallic army produced a panic, and the enemy turned and fled. The cavalry pressed the attack, and in the pursuit, a great number of the enemy were slain. High above the battle in Alesia, Vercingetorix witnessed these events from his command post in the city. He broke off the secondary attack that he had launched against the inner wall. As these forces began to withdraw, the forces that had been left on the heights in reserve began to panic. Within a short time, the entire relief army broke up into tribal contingents, as effective command and control disappeared. By evening, many of these contingents began to wander away and make their way home. Caesar ordered his cavalry into a night attack against these reserves to ensure that the enemy kept on the move away from the battlefield. By morning, it was over.

Vercingetorix surrendered himself in the hopes of avoiding a massacre of his people, and, in fact, Roman terms were generally lenient, consisting of hostages and large indemnity payments. Vercingetorix was taken to Rome for Caesar's triumph and executed in a Roman dungeon by strangulation. The siege of Alesia is regarded one of the most remarkable examples of military brilliance and campaign sophistication in the ancient world. A single army besieging an enemy was itself besieged, only to destroy both armies—the besieged and the relief army—in a single engagement conducted by one of antiquity's most audacious and brilliant generals.

For the rest of the year and into the spring and summer, Caesar conducted a number of small campaigns to crush the embers of the revolt. For the most part, these forays were against brigands and renegades, most of the major tribes having submitted to Rome. By late summer all Gaul had again been pacified. The destruction that Caesar wrought over a decade of war and conquest had deprived the Gauls of any real possibility of resistance for a generation. By then, of course, it was too late, and Gaul was well on its way to full integration and Romanization into the new world order of imperial Rome.

CAESAR AND POMPEY: THE CIVIL WAR (48 B.C.E.)

Caesar's campaigns in Gaul endowed him with a reputation that overshadowed Pompey. Caesar trained a large army that was devoted to him and would do his bidding. He amassed great wealth that could be used to support his political ambitions, and he added a vast new province to the Roman Empire. All of these accomplishments made Caesar's enemies in Rome nervous, and in 50 B.C.E., Pompey convinced the Senate to order Caesar to relinquish his command, disband his legions, give over his province, and return to Rome to stand for election to the consulate as a private citizen. Caesar recognized the summons for what it was, a death sentence, and refused. At the time of the summons Caesar was in Cisalpine Gaul at Ravenna. Roman law forbade a Roman general to bring his military forces into Italy itself without the consent of the Senate. The southern boundary of Cisalpine Gaul and Italy was the tiny Rubicon River just south of Ravenna. On January 11, 49 B.C.E., Caesar conducted a night crossing of the Rubicon. Rome had its answer. Caesar intended to seize power by force of arms, and Rome was plunged into a civil war.

Caesar, who had fought only against barbarians or semi-civilized peoples, was now engaged in a more serious struggle, with legion against legion. Caesar had only the Thirteenth Legion with him when he crossed the Rubicon, but the Eighth and Twelfth legions were on the march to join him. Caesar could muster a total force of eight legions, 40,000 first-rate, battle-hardened veterans, plus some 20,000 auxiliary troops and cavalry. Pompey, the legal chief of the Roman state, had three legions in Italy, seven in Spain, and the authority to raise eight more in Italy. One of the legions in Italy consisted of raw recruits, and the other two had fought for years with Caesar before being sent from Gaul two years earlier. Pompey did not considered the latter trustworthy. Caesar chose Italy as the first arena of the contest, and in that arena Pompey was at a severe manpower disadvantage. The bulk of Pompey's loyal veteran legions were in Spain, too far away to affect the outcome of any battle in Italy in a timely manner.

Caesar moved quickly to exploit his advantage. He advanced rapidly down the coast of the Adriatic, seizing the rich towns as he went. Within a few weeks, he had advanced a considerable distance and was joined by his legions from Gaul. In town after town local garrisons joined him. Caesar's conduct of the campaign clearly reflected his awareness that this was a civil war and not a foreign war, and that it was a war that demanded different techniques. Caesar understood that the most important asset in a civil war was the support of the populace, and he took great pains to minimize battle damage and to treat his captives leniently. Long before Clausewitz, Julius Caesar recognized the essentially political character of warfare, and he changed his military tactics accordingly. His central strategic goal was to convince the populace, the property owners, and even the enemy legionnaires that his cause was the more desirable one for their own interests.

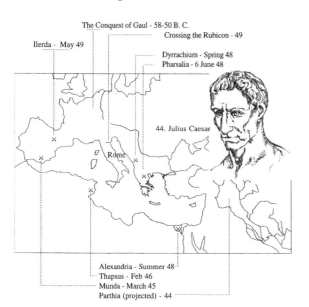

Figure 14.4 Civil War Campaigns of Caesar. Adapted from Alfred Bradford, *With Arrow, Sword, and Spear* (Westport, CT: Greenwood, 2001). Reprinted with permission.

Pompey's ability to react was hindered by his lack of reliable manpower. If he relied upon the two legions at hand to defend Rome, he had to accept the grave risk that they might go over to Caesar, their former commander. If this happened, the war would be over before Pompey could bring his forces to bear. Whereas Caesar had sole command of his troops, Pompey was the legal creation of the Roman Senate and required their consent to act. Worse, while Caesar acted as his own field commander, Pompey was saddled with two elected consuls to command the armies. Caesar's forces and popular support increased almost daily, and he made ready to move on Rome itself. The Senate panicked and fled to Capua in such a haste that they forgot to take the treasury with them! Caesar tried to cut them off, but they fled again to Brundisium (modern Brindisi). Pompey's single asset was his control of the fleet, some 500 warships and a large number of light galleys. As Caesar's army approached Brundisium, Pompey used the fleet to evacuate 25,000 troops and most of the Roman Senate across the Adriatic to Epirus in Greece, from where he expected to continue the fight. In February 49 B.C.E., less than two months after crossing the Rubicon, Caesar entered Rome, master of all Italy.

The strategic situation confronting Caesar was curious. He held Italy, the central position between Pompey in Greece and his major political and military base of support in Spain. But Pompey controlled the fleet and thus the sea. Although Pompey's force in Greece was but a skeleton and would be easy prey, there was no easy way to get at it. Without sufficient ships, an attack on Pompey would force Caesar to go overland through Illyricum (Yugoslavia), a route that left a long line of communications through Cisalpine Gaul greatly exposed to Pompey's legions in Spain. With great strategic insight, Caesar realized that the way to defeat Pompey in Greece was first to defeat his legions in Spain. Caesar expressed the situation clearly in his *Commentaries*: "I am setting forth to fight an army without a leader, so as by and by to fight a leader without an army." In March, Caesar set off for Spain.

Caesar started for Spain via a land route along the northern shore of the Mediterranean. Short on finances, Caesar adopted the novel method of paying his soldiers with money borrowed from his officers. This ensured the good will of the former and the adherence of the latter. The route ran in front of the important and historic fortress town of Massilia (modern Marseilles), which supported Pompey. Caesar invested the town with three legions and sent the main force forward to seize the passes over the Pyrenees, which it did just in time to prevent their occupation by an army of Pompey loyalists under the command of L. Afranius and M. Petreius. Unable to trap Caesar in the mountains, the two commanders awaited Caesar at Ilerda (modern Lerida). Caesar moved toward the confrontation with 37,000 men against an army of 65,000 with reserves of two additional legions of 45,000 Spanish auxiliaries.

In truth, neither side wanted to fight. Caesar was wary of the enemy's numbers, and the enemy commanders had little stomach for engaging a commander of Caesar's reputation. Consequently, both armies moved around one another and engaged in little more than cavalry skirmishes, each side seeking to entrap the other in some untenable defensive position. A month later, diminishing supplies forced the Pompeyian commanders to withdraw to the Ebro River. Caesar anticipated the movement, crossed the river first, and cut their line of retreat. Now Caesar showed his brilliance. He kept the enemy bottled up and cut off its water supply, but refused to attack. He hoped to avoid spilling Roman blood. Both armies faced each other from their respective camps. Gradually, the men of both sides began to fraternize regularly. Eventually, the idea of Roman fighting Roman seemed ridiculous, especially so in light of Caesar's superior disposition of forces, which would have made any battle a single-sided slaughter in favor of Caesar. The enemy commanders, rather than attempt to fight their way out of the trap, surrendered. Caesar treated the enemy with leniency and respect. Most of the enemy legions were simply disbanded, but Caesar accepted many legionnaires into his own army. Leaving two legions to hold Spain, Caesar returned to Marseilles, where the siege was brought to a successful termination. With his back secure, Caesar prepared to attack Pompey in Greece.

Caesar mounted his invasion of Epirus in western Greece from Brundisium where he assembled twelve legions and 10,000 cavalry. Pompey's control of the Roman fleet left few ships in which to transport Caesar's troops. There was sufficient transport for seven legions (2,000 men each, as noted by Caesar) and some cavalry. Even this small force could only be accommodated if food supplies and baggage were left behind. Mark Antony, left in control of Brundisium, was ordered to find more ships as quickly as possible and follow the invasion force across the Adriatic. In today's world it would be considered strategic suicide to attempt to transport a major force by ship without first securing control of the sea (and air). Caesar attempted a bold gamble.

Caesar reckoned that the enemy would never expect him to mount an invasion in mid-winter, and he was correct, for the enemy fleet was safely anchored in its coastal harbors. The distance to be crossed by sea was approximately one hundred miles, a crossing that would take only twelve to fifteen hours with favorable winds. If Caesar made the crossing safely, he could fall upon the undefended coastal cities of Epirus. Although these cities were rich in supplies, Pompey's army was still moving into position and had not garrisoned the southern coastal cities. They were rich prizes and still undefended. At this point Caesar's intelligence reported that Pompey had not reached Epirus (the report was incorrect, however) and that the enemy army still had no head. Caesar reckoned that Pompey's absence would slow the reaction of his army to the invasion sufficiently to allow Caesar to secure the beachhead.

Map 14.6 Caesar's Theater of Operations in Northern Greece

All this aside, however, Caesar still faced an army of considerable size. Pompey controlled the entire eastern half of the empire with its rich sources of supply in Egypt and the Levant. His command comprised 36,000 men, but recruiting was continuing and his army was growing every day. Metellus Scipio was on his way from Egypt with two veteran legions, and Pompey's cavalry, drawn from the eastern provinces, was far superior numerically and qualitatively to that of Caesar, who seems to have still been using the same mercenary Gallic and Germanic squadrons used previously. At the time of the invasion, then, Pompey's army had nine legions of infantry, 7,000 cavalry, 3,000 archers, and 1,200 slingers. On January 4, 48 B.C.E., Caesar sailed out from Brundisium on a night tide with favorable winds bound for Epirus. Shortly after daybreak, Caesar's army landed at Palaeste, one hundred miles south of his objective, Dyrrachium (Map 14.6).

THE BATTLE OF DYRRACHIUM (48 B.C.E.)

Caesar debarked his troops and sent the ships back to Italy to transport the rest of the army. Without waiting, he moved northward and quickly occupied Oricum, Valona, and Apollonia (Map 14.7). Alert now to Caesar's landing, Pompey moved south of Dyrrachium and took up a position at Kuci astride Caesar's route of advance at the Apsus River. Pompey's admiral, Bibulus, having been caught sleeping during the original crossing of the Adriatic, was now awake and alert. His squadrons overtook Caesar's transports on their return trip and captured thirty ships. The crews, with their ships, were burned alive. Caesar was cut off from his base in Italy. At the same time he faced a numerically superior army that had more and better-quality cavalry deployed to use interior lines close to its base of supplies. Had Pompey attacked, it is likely he would have easily defeated Caesar. As it was, he decided to do nothing and wait for the arrival of Scipio and his legions. Pompey's failure to take the offensive was a grievous tactical and strategic error.

For more than a month the armies faced each other. Sometime in February, after being given an order by Caesar to disregard the risk of Pompey's fleet, Mark Antony set sail at night with four legions and 800 cavalry, half the force assembled for the follow-up invasion. The army was carried by favorable winds beyond the point where both armies

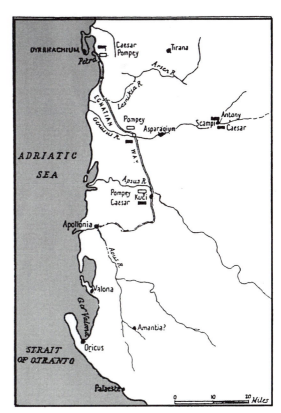

Map 14.7 Battle of Dyrrachium: Tactical Area of Operations

were entrenched to the town of Nymphaeum, north of Dyrrachium. When Pompey learned of Antony's landing to his rear, he broke contact with Caesar and moved to intercept Antony's legions. Caesar moved northeastward toward Tirana and sent messengers to warn Antony. Antony, always an excellent field commander, avoided the ambush, and both Roman armies linked up at the town of Scampi. Pompey had failed to prevent the joining of the two armies, allowing Caesar to achieve local superiority of force against him.

The strategic and logistical situation prevented Caesar from exploiting his advantage. He sent two legions toward Macedonia with the mission to find Scipio and his legions and prevent them from joining Pompey. Another legion and a half were sent inland to forage and to establish relations with the local inland towns for the provision of supplies. Then disaster struck. Pompey's son, Gnaeus, commanding the Egyptian naval squadron off the coast, attacked Caesar's naval and supply base at Oricum. Using shipboard catapults, Gnaeus forced the blockaded harbor and turned his fire on the city walls. Covered by shipboard artillery, his infantry scaled the walls and took the city. Gnaeus burned the city, Caesar's supplies, and all Caesar's remaining ships. In an almost simultaneous attack, Pompey's navy attacked Antony's support base at Lissus and burned all his ships. With these attacks, Caesar's two naval supply bases were neutralized, and every ship at his disposal was destroyed. Not even a single galley remained with which Caesar could communicate with Italy. With no way to return to Italy, Caesar was trapped.

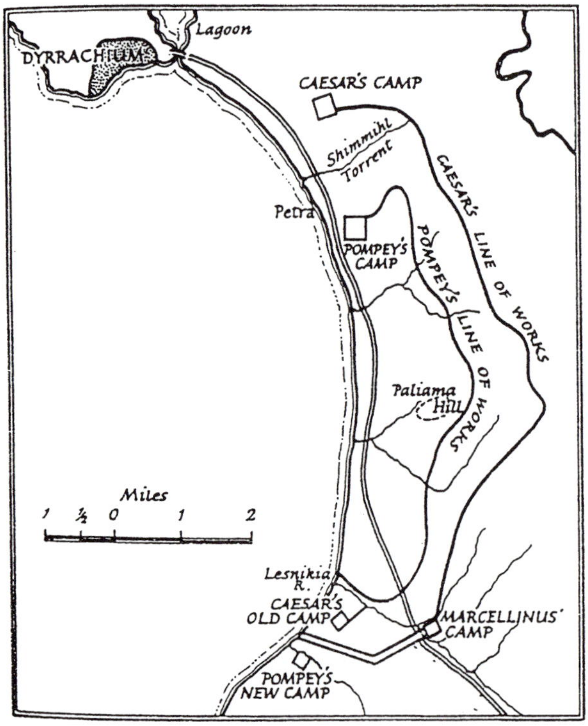

This state of affairs would have unnerved most commanders. Instead, Caesar began to move. He shuffled his army northward, attempting to gain the road to Dyrrachium before Pompey discerned his intentions. Pompey moved parallel to Caesar. Although Caesar reached the road to Dyrrachium an hour before Pompey, the proximity of Pompey's army to Caesar's lines made an attack on the city impossible. Pompey deployed his army around Petra south of the Shimmihil torrent (Map 14.8), with Caesar deployed opposite him. Caesar's numerical inferiority and lack of siege machinery, in addition to the strong fortifications of the city, made

Map 14.8 Caesar's and Pompey's Fortifications around Dyrrachium. Adapted from J. F. C. Fuller, *Julius Caesar* (New York: Da Capo, 1965).

an attack on Dyrrachium unrealistic. Pompey, although cut off from his base in the city, could resupply his army by sea and, should events require it, move or evacuate his army at will. Pompey, again cautious, decided to remain in place and await Scipio.

Caesar's position was far worse. He was cut off from his main base in Italy, his naval bases in Greece were gone, and he had no ships. Supplying the army with forage and purchased supplies became difficult. Somewhere to his south was Scipio with two legions that might show up at any moment. Pompey's army was larger than his, and Caesar feared having to fight a battle in open country where Pompey's superior cavalry represented a deadly threat. With nowhere to go and insufficient force to bring about a decision, Caesar held Pompey's army in place as the best way of neutralizing Pompey's military advantages. Caesar began to invest the enemy.

Caesar constructed a wall of contravallation around Pompey's fortified position that extended from Petra in the north to the Lesnikia River in the south. A continuous line of small hills naturally formed much of the ring, and the armies skirmished over control of these hills. When completed, Caesar's wall extended fifteen miles in length and enclosed within it Pompey's line of fortifications, which was eight miles long and 1.5 miles inland from the beach. Pompey's line had twenty-four redoubts along it, and the meadows within the wall provided forage for Pompey's cavalry.

The supply situation on both sides was serious. The surrounding countryside had been picked clean, and Caesar's men subsisted on a bread made from a root (*Chara*, as the bread is called, is still eaten in Albania). Pompey resupplied his army by sea, drawing on the substantial stocks in Dyrrachium. Caesar had diverted the streams, and Pompey was forced to dig wells, which proved inadequate to supply his men with water. Pompey's cavalry horses had eaten what grass there was in the meadows within the ring of fortifications and were beginning to die of starvation. Eventually, Pompey transported his cavalry by ship to Dyrrachium, where they had sufficient food and were well placed to attack Caesar's rear. Like Vercingetorix at Alesia, Pompey was in an excellent position to use his cavalry to harass Caesar's foragers and engineers. Why he did not is a mystery, but it was a serious error to permit Caesar to maneuver unhindered. The situation on both sides was less than ideal, and it was Pompey who took the initiative to change the circumstances.

Pompey guessed that Caesar was desperate for some sort of solution to the problem (as, perhaps, was he), so Pompey decided to provide Caesar with one. Pompey arranged for "a certain man of Dyrrachium" to approach Caesar and offer to betray the city and open the gates, the stratagem by which many cities in ancient warfare had succumbed. Inexplicably, and perhaps as a sign of his desperation, Caesar took the bait. In one of Caesar's most bizarre decisions, he decided to lead the infiltration force himself! Late into the night, Caesar and his small force moved through the marshes surrounding the lagoon near the city. As Caesar moved through the "narrowest point," he was suddenly attacked from the front and rear by "large forces which had been conveyed along the shore in boats and suddenly fell upon him; thus he lost many men and very nearly perished himself."

While Caesar was floundering about attempting to extricate himself from the ambush in the marshes, Pompey launched three coordinated attacks against Caesar's positions. In one engagement, four legions were thrown against a redoubt in the center of the Roman line held by a single *cohort*. The legionnaires in the redoubt fought like lions until two legions could be brought up in support. After the battle, Caesar noted, 30,000 enemy arrows that had been fired at the position were picked up and counted; one legionnaire had no fewer than 120 holes in his shield. Every member of the original garrison who survived had been wounded. In another attack, a Pompeyian legion assaulted a position held by three Roman legions and was driven back. The third attack was also repulsed by Caesar's German cavalry, presumably fighting dismounted. Although these assaults failed to break Caesar's line, Pompey's plan was brilliantly executed and almost worked.

Pompey's intelligence service had, meanwhile, acquired two Allobrogian deserters from the Roman camp, and they provided Pompey with a detailed knowledge of Caesar's fortifications. Caesar had carried his entrenchments across the plain south of the Lesnikia River. To protect his army from envelopment and rear attack, Caesar had constructed another wall of contravallation along much of his left line. The two walls were about 200 yards apart and ran to the sea. These walls were not completed, however, and there was no transverse wall connecting the two. It was possible for a significant sized force to insert itself between the walls and follow them into Caesar's main position. Informed of the nature of Caesar's fortifications, Pompey attempted an assault against Caesar's left.

The plan was brilliant and clearly demonstrated Pompey's ability as a general. Sixty *cohorts* comprising the main assault force passed through Pompey's fortified line, crossed the Lesnikia River, and seized Caesar's old camp (now deserted) across the river (Map 14.9). None of this action was difficult since the area through which the assault force had to move was between the two lines of fortifications and generally unguarded. Once inside the old camp, this force prepared to attack Caesar's line of circumvallation (the interior line). Simultaneously, an amphibious force of light infantry and archers moved by sea against the second line of fortifications. The larger part of the amphibious force landed south of the second line, whereas the smaller force landed between the two walls and pressed its way inland. The idea was to take

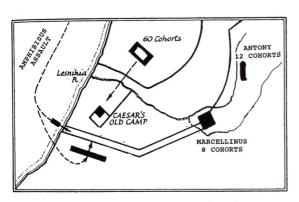

Map 14.9 Pompey's Attack on Caesar's Left

Caesar at once in the front, the rear, and in the flank. If it worked, Pompey intended to roll up Caesar's left flank. The land and sea attack was launched under cover of night, and just before dawn, the light infantry was put ashore on the beach.

The two Caesarian *cohorts* manning the wall were caught in the act of changing the morning guard. Although these *cohorts* manned their stations and fought well, the amphibious assault had caught them completely unprepared. The defenders finally panicked and fled down the lane between the two walls. The nearest Caesarian reserves consisted of eight *cohorts* under the command of Marcellinus who, although hindered by soldiers fleeing in the opposite direction, rushed his troops into the fight. Elements of Pompey's main force moved from their position in Caesar's old camp along the interior wall and were on the verge of overrunning Marcellinus's camp when Antony arrived with twelve *cohorts* and drove them back. Shortly thereafter, Caesar himself arrived with thirteen *cohorts* and engaged the attackers. While the fighting continued, Pompey landed large troop contingents (almost five legions) to the south of the defensive wall and began constructing a fortified camp. The camp provided security for his ships passing near the shore and guarded the plain to the south, where Pompey could graze his cavalry. Pompey's attack broke Caesar's control of the coastal plain.

With Caesar now in command at the place of the attack, the Romans rallied and pushed Pompey's troops back to within a half mile of the coast. Caesar worried most about the sixty enemy *cohorts* that occupied his old camp on the coast, and he launched an attack in force to regain the camp (Map 14.10). Ever the gambler, Caesar left only two *cohorts* to hold the entrance to the path between the walls and organized his thirty-three *cohorts* of infantry into two columns. One column assaulted the eastern face of the camp and quickly pressed the garrison back through the camp. The second column advanced and struck the connecting wall between the camp and river.

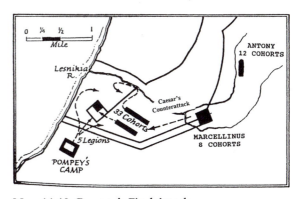

Map 14.10 Pompey's Final Attack

Finally, they broke through near the end of the wall on the bank of the river and entered onto a broad plain between the rampart, the river, the sea, and the camp.

Pompey realized that Caesar had committed all his available forces in one throw, and he maneuvered to counterattack and trap the attackers. Caesar's left column had breached the camp walls and driven the garrison back against the northern wall, where it was hacking it to pieces. Suddenly, from across the double fortified wall, Pompey's legions fell on the Roman column with tremendous force, overwhelming it. At the same time, Pompey committed his cavalry over the river and across the plain to attack Caesar's right column, now trapped between the attacking cavalry and the rampart wall connecting the camp to the river. Within minutes, both columns collapsed in panic, as they were hammered by superior forces attacking from an unexpected direction. The rout was complete. Caesar described it this way: "Every place was full of disorder, panic, and flight, so much so that when he [Caesar] grasped the standards of the fugitives and bade them halt, some without slackening speed fled at full gallop, others in their fear even let go their colors, nor did a single one of them halt."

Caesar's army was in great danger. His left flank was in complete collapse. The battle at the camp had cost him thirty-two tribunes and centurions, 960 rank and file, and thirty-two unit standards. The wounded numbered in the thousands. Many of the dead had not been killed by enemy action but had been trampled to death in the panic. The reserves of Marcellinus and Antony had already been committed, and there were no reserves left to stabilize the situation. Pompey had out-generaled Caesar, badly mauled his army, and placed him in a tight spot.

Fortunately for Caesar, Pompey did not reinforce the attack, and both sides broke off the engagement. Caesar was in no position to continue the fight and decided to withdraw. At nightfall the next day, Caesar set his baggage train and the wounded, along with one legion as an escort, on the road to Apollonia. A few hours later, four more legions set out upon the same road. Finally, acting as a rearguard, two final legions moved into the darkness. Having learned of Caesar's movement, Pompey sent his cavalry in pursuit. Caesar reinforced his rearguard with 400 hand-picked light infantry. Over the next four days, Pompey's cavalry caught up with Caesar's guard at least twice, but the rearguard held them at bay. Caesar had lost the battle for Dyrrachium, but he and his army were still in the field. And they were still dangerous.

THE BATTLE OF PHARSALUS (48 B.C.E.)

Caesar rested his army for a few days, then began to withdraw inland toward Macedonia. Before the engagement at Dyrrachium, Domitius Calvinus had been sent into Macedonia with two legions to find and check Scipio, who was on his way from Syria with two legions to reinforce Pompey. Domitius had been successful in maneuvering around Scipio and preventing him from linking up with Pompey. Caesar's withdrawal from the coast, however, uncovered Domitius's rear and forced him to break contact with Scipio. Scipio slipped away and made for Larissa, where he joined up with Pompey.

Caesar attempted to join up with Domitius's army. He had sent Publius Sulla inland before the battle of Dyrrachium to develop good relations with the towns and establish them as supply bases. Sulla had been successful in obtaining the loyalty of these towns; however, as news of Caesar's defeat spread, a number of these towns and vital supply points declared for Pompey and closed their gates to Caesar. Caesar completed the link-up with Domitius at Aeginium and moved southeast toward Gomphi. A formerly friendly town, Gomphi now shut its gates to him. Caesar stormed the town and sacked it, turning it over to his troops to plunder. Next, he moved toward Metropolis, which, having seen the lesson of Gomphi, complied with Caesar's request for supplies. Caesar moved on toward the Pharsalian plain just below Cynoscephalae, where he crossed the Enipeus River and took up positions on its northern bank.

Within a few days, Pompey and his army arrived and camped three miles northwest of Caesar on the slopes of Mount Dogndiz. Both armies faced each other, but only Caesar seemed eager for combat. Caesar formed up his armies for battle outside his camp several times, attempting to draw Pompey down from the high ground. Pompey refused. After a while the shortage of supplies forced Caesar to consider moving south to Scotussa to replenish his stores. On the day Caesar formed his army for the march to Scotussa, Pompey deployed his army closer to Caesar's camp on more level ground. Caesar stopped his march, wheeled his army into position, and readied it for battle.

There remains considerable debate as to the number of troops that fought at Pharsalus. In Caesar's account, he understated his own strength and overstated that of his opponent to make the victory seem even greater. Caesar said he had eighty *cohorts* or, as he calculated it, some 22,000 men and 1,000 cavalry. Caesar put Pompey's forces at 110 *cohorts* or 47,000 men and 7,000 cavalry. The analyses conducted by Delbruck and Fuller of these numbers leads me to accept Delbruck's numbers for the battle of Pharsalus. Thus, Delbruck states that Caesar had about 30,000 infantry and Pompey about 40,000. The real difficulty lies in calculating the number of cavalry. The idea that Caesar's 1,000 cavalry defeated Pompey's 7,000 horsemen, cavalry that were not only numerically superior but considerably superior in quality to Caesar's Germanic and Gallic tribal cavalry, is unacceptable. Delbruck is probably more correct when he suggests that Pompey had 3,000 cavalry, all of which is listed by Caesar in describing Pompey's order of battle, and Caesar had about 2,000 horsemen. Although Caesar was outnumbered in both infantry and cavalry, the numbers were not as one-sided as Caesar's account of the battle would suggest.

Pompey anchored his right flank on the steep banks of the swift Enipeus River. He placed 600 Pontus cavalry along the riverbank to anchor the flank and probably to protect against any surprises from light infantry or archers that might attempt to cross the river. In typical Roman fashion, he deployed his infantry in three lines. The front was broken into three sectors: the right wing was commanded by Lentulus, the center by Scipio, and the left by Ahenobarbus. On the extreme left of the line he marshaled his cavalry, now 2,400 strong, interspersed with units of slingers and archers. This heavy cavalry assault force was commanded by Labienus, Caesar's old chief-of-staff from the wars in Gaul who had gone over to Pompey when the civil war first began. Labienus was a first-rate officer, a combat veteran of many battles, and in command of the main attack force of Pompey's army. Pompey's battle plan was to use his infantry to engage and hold Caesar's infantry line in place, then use his superior cavalry to smash Caesar's right flank, turn it inward, and envelop Caesar's army. It was a simple plan, and it played to Pompey's strength and Caesar's weakness.

Caesar formed up his infantry in the usual three-line formation of the Roman legion. The numerical disparity between the armies meant that Caesar's *cohorts* were not as deep as Pompey's. Had Pompey chosen to lighten the depth of his *cohorts*, he could have produced a longer line that would have overlapped Caesar's. As things were, Caesar could match the length of Pompey's line using thinner *cohorts*. Caesar probably reckoned that his army of veterans could use their experience to compensate for the disparity in manpower. Caesar's left wing was commanded by Mark Antony, the center by Domitius Calvinus, and the right by Publius Sulla, all veteran commanders. As Caesar was moving his men into position, he observed Pompey's disposition of forces, quickly deduced Pompey's intentions, and changed his deployment.

With Pompey's cavalry massed on his left, Caesar moved all his cavalry to his own right to accept the inevitable charge. In the process, however, he followed the instructions of Xenophon, the old Greek cavalry commander, who noted that it was possible to hide infantry behind a cavalry force because the height of the horses and horseman blocked the ability of the enemy to see the hidden infantry. Caesar did precisely this. He drew up his 2,000 cavalry directly across from Labienus. From the last line of his infantry Caesar took six *cohorts*, 3,000 men or 1,800 men depending upon whose account is believed, and placed them at an oblique angle behind the cavalry (Map 14.11). The remainder of the third infantry line was re-formed and ordered to remain back from the main engagement. They were to act as a reserve and to commit only on Caesar's personal command. The two front infantry ranks would be forced to bear the brunt of Pompey's infantry attack.

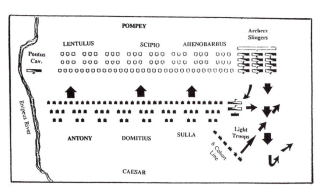

Map 14.11 Battle of Pharsalus

Caesar augmented his cavalry force with light infantry, presumably archers, javelin throwers, and slingers. He placed them behind the cavalry and in front of the hidden force of infantry, although they were clearly to engage when the rival cavalry units clashed. It is intriguing to ask why Caesar mixed the force in the manner he did. Caesar had first encountered this type of mixed unit when the Gauls used it against him at Alesia with some success. This mix of forces was common among German cavalry, and much of Caesar's cavalry was German. It is clear, however, that after the battle of Dyrrachium Caesar had reinforced his rear cavalry guard with light infantry forces to hinder Pompey's pursuit. Finally, this mixing of cavalry and light infantry forces had been common in the East since Alexander's day, and since Pompey's cavalry was mostly of Eastern origin, it was no surprise to discover that his cavalry was supported by integrated light infantry as well. Caesar's use of mixed cavalry and light infantry units was important from another respect. It provided the entire force with an agility it might not otherwise have had and, at the same time, protected the cavalry from enemy infantry until it could maneuver through the enemy and envelop it.

Caesar ordered his infantry into the attack first, perhaps hoping to offset his numerical disadvantage in infantry with the *elan* of his superior veteran troops. The Caesarian infantry attempted to close the 200 yards between the infantry lines at the run. Halfway across the gap, it was noticed that Pompey's men did not meet the attack. Instead, they remained steadfastly in place. Caesar's centurions ordered the infantry to stop running and catch its breath. After a short period, the infantry began to close again. This time, however, they were met by Pompey's infantry at the run.

Just seconds before the infantry lines smashed into one another, Labienus launched his cavalry against Caesar's right and smashed into Caesar's Gallic and German cavalry squadrons. The Germans and Gauls absorbed the initial shock intact, but the press of numbers gradually drove Caesar's cavalry back beyond the ranks of his infantry. As Labienus's cavalry pressed the enemy further and further backward, they exposed their own right flank to infantry attack from the six *cohorts* hidden from their view. As the enemy cavalry passed, Caesar's infantry fell on its flank with devastating lethality. At about the same time, Caesar's cavalry, as if on command, turned and reengaged Pompey's cavalry. This support of cavalry by heavy infantry required excellent discipline, training, and leadership. The flexibility of the *cohort* system was also needed to make this superb maneuver work correctly, as were the disciplined combat veterans of Caesar's army that carried it out.

The surprise and force of the flank attack by the hidden infantry *cohorts* shattered Labienus's cavalry, which turned and fled the field. The Roman infantry made short work of the archers and slingers left unprotected by their fleeing cavalry comrades. Caesar's cavalry pressed the pursuit only to the end of Pompey's infantry line, at which point the heavy infantry and the cavalry fell on the enemy flank. The more agile and swift light infantry swept around the flank and began to envelope the infantry line. It was quickly joined by elements of the cavalry who completed the envelopment.

At the same time, the two infantry lines were fully engaged on the field. Caesar's infantry was barely holding its own and was nearing exhaustion. Shortly after the cavalry fell on the flank of Pompey's infantry line, Caesar committed his third line reserve infantry. The flexibility of the *cohort* system permitted the nearly exhausted front line infantry to disengage, pass through the rear ranks, and be replaced by the third line of fresh, rested troops. As these troops moved to the front, they fell on Pompey's tired infantry. The infantry line sagged and was pressed back until it broke. As Pompey's infantry began to scatter, they were greeted by the sight of Caesar's cavalry running rampant in their rear. A panic broke out. The third line reserve pressed the attack, broke through, and headed for Pompey's camp.

Once it was clear that Labienus's cavalry attack had failed, Pompey retreated to his camp to await the outcome of the battle. When his infantry broke through Pompey's line, Caesar ordered it to continue the attack until it stormed Pompey's camp. As Caesar's men broke through the ramparts, Pompey threw aside his general's cloak, mounted his horse, and, with a few retainers, fled to Larissa. Although Caesar's men were nearly exhausted, he pressed them on into the mountains to hunt down Pompey's broken army. At the head of four legions Caesar trapped a large number of enemy units, surrounded them, and cut off their water source. They surrendered the next day. According to Appian's account, Caesar lost 30 centurions and 2,000 men killed. Of Pompey's army, Caesar said that "15,000 appeared to have fallen," and 24,000 surrendered. In addition, 180 standards and nine eagles were presented to Caesar. Pompey's army ceased to exist. Pompey himself fled to Larissa and then to the coast. A month later, while attempting to establish relations with the Ptolemies in Egypt to raise another army, Pompey was assassinated. When, in October, Caesar was offered the embalmed head of his adversary, he refused it . . . and wept.

THE COMMANDERS

Julius Caesar (100–44 B.C.E.) was one of the most complex personalities to emerge from the pages of ancient history. As a general he was personally courageous and always clearly present on the field of battle, easily identified by the red cloak he wore when in command of his armies. On a number of occasions Caesar plunged directly into the battle at a crucial point to rally his men to the attack. He was an excellent horseman and could handle a sword and shield with the best of his centurions. He, along with Alexander, understood that soldiers fight for many reasons, not the least of which was the trust, faith, and confidence they had in their commander. Although a firm disciplinarian, Caesar always saw to the welfare of his men, and they loved him for it. He repeatedly drew on their sense of affection and trust when in a tight spot in battle, and he was never disappointed in the willingness of his soldiers to follow him into danger.

But Caesar was far more than a technically proficient soldier and general. He was also a remarkable orator capable of moving crowds of civilians and soldiers to the heights of emotion. His speaking and writing skills served him well in his role as accomplished politician in the violent scramble for power that followed his conquest of Gaul and the crossing of the Rubicon. Caesar was also a first-rate strategic thinker in all he attempted and accomplished. Encumbered by few scruples, Caesar always clearly perceived the linkages between ends, ways, and means and was very flexible in devising tactics to make these linkages function correctly. He rarely allowed personal anger or hatred for an enemy to cloud his thinking or judgment, and he meted out clemency and slaughter with equal ease depending only upon what tactic at the time served the larger end. In his intellectual determination of strategy, Caesar saw all situations—political, military, social, and personal—as amenable to the same type of solution: do what must be done to achieve your goal.

Examined purely from a military perspective, a study of Caesar's campaigns suggests a number of shortcomings in strategy and command that are sometimes overlooked by modern students of military history. For example, Caesar rarely seems to have planned a campaign in sufficient detail to ensure adequate logistical support for his armies. By his own account, time and again he was forced to divert his march, withdraw, alter his plan, or change his tactics because he had failed to ensure an adequate food supply for his troops. At Dyrrachium, for example, his army subsisted on whatever roots they could find. In other instances, Caesar's failure to pay sufficient attention to intelligence about the enemy and/or to provide for adequate security almost cost him his life. The battle of the Sambre, for example, almost ended in as great a disaster as the battle of Teutoburgerwald because of Caesar's failure to take adequate security precautions. It is no exaggeration to suggest that in some instances Caesar's bold strokes were more the products of desperation brought about by his own previous failures than of planned military design.

Whatever his military operational shortcomings, however, Caesar's brilliance was clearly evident in his ability to shape military operations to function as a means to larger political ends. It was political strategy that shaped military strategy, and never the reverse. Thus, although the manpower reserves of the Gauls far exceeded anything Caesar could match with his army, it was only rarely that Caesar fought a battle in which he was outnumbered. Clever use of diplomacy, ruse, treachery, and bribery served to make it impossible for his adversary to fight within a larger coalition of tribal forces. Clemency or cruelty against the Gauls was for Caesar always a choice to be made on political grounds, never an act of emotion, hatred, or anger. Probably what was most instructive to the modern soldier-strategist about Julius Caesar was that he successfully conducted military operations in an extremely complex military, social, and political environment, made even more complex by the deadly nature of the domestic political arena of the Roman state. The modern statesman and soldier has much to learn from Caesar's ability to deal with the various aspects of his complex environment.

Caesar's uniqueness, complexity, and importance make it difficult to treat his military experiences adequately in the short space allowed by this chapter. His achievements were enormous. The pacification of Gaul by force of arms was one of the most important events in Western history. It was Caesar who established the Roman frontier at the Rhine, the line that marked the boundary between two different cultures for the next half millennium and laid the basis for the distinction between civilization and barbarian that ultimately had such tragic consequences for Rome and the West. It was Caesar who stood as the transition between the death of the old Republican order and the birth, under Augustus, of the new imperium. Caesar's life clearly reflected the inability of the old political order to deal successfully with the primary problem of any political system under stress—the ability to manage the transition of power in a peaceful manner. Caesar's short dictatorship was also noteworthy for the major administrative and economic reforms with which he reshaped the Roman state. It was upon these reforms that Augustus built the new imperial order of Rome.

Finally, any military analysis of Caesar must recognize that he fought scores of battles under widely varying circumstances. In Gaul, he fought tribal armies and conducted sieges. During the civil war, he fought a Roman army under Pompey that was every bit as good as his own, against an opponent who was an equally talented general. After his victories over Pompey, he fought battles against Egyptian, African, and Spanish armies. There are few military commanders in history who have fought so many major battles against so many different types of enemies in so many different environments in so short a time.

Gnaeus Pompeius Magnus [Pompey the Great] (106–48 B.C.E.) was one of the four great men of Republican Rome along with Caesar, Marius, and Sulla. An excellent administrator, he was a resourceful and enterprising politician and general officer. Born into turbulent and violent times, he served in the army under his father while still in his teens. He was already a general in his early twenties when he supported Sulla and marched on Rome with three legions of his own. He suppressed the revolts and *condottieri* of two major enemies of the new social order brought about by Sulla, and was elected consul at the age of thirty-six. He held this position two additional times in his career.

Married to Julius Caesar's daughter, Julia, he formed an alliance with Caesar and Crassus to create the First Triumvirate of military strongmen, who together ruled Rome. When Crassus was killed at the battle of Carrhae in 53 B.C.E., relations between Caesar and Pompey worsened, eventually breaking down completely into all-out civil war. When Caesar crossed the Rubicon River in northern Italy with his veteran legions of the wars in Gaul, the Senate responded by appointing Pompey to protect the Roman state. After Caesar's march on Rome, Pompey and his army retired to Illyria (Yugoslavia) to await Caesar's pursuit. Pompey was defeated at Pharsalus and fled to Egypt where he was murdered by one of his men. His head was presented to Caesar when he arrived in Egypt in search of Pompey.

As a young man, Pompey proved himself in battle after battle as an excellent soldier and commander of men. But his military acumen seems to have deserted him in later life. At Dyrrachium, for example, he outmaneuvered Caesar but failed to press his advantage. The sense of risk that had characterized his earlier military exploits was not in evidence. It is likely, although not certain, that he was suffering from some sort of serious illness when he fought against Caesar that may have affected his ability to command. In any case, the ancient world lost a great general when he was killed, and Rome lost the last man who was willing to fight to preserve the form and substance of the Roman Republic. After him came Caesar's dictatorship and the end of republicanism in Rome.

Vercingetorix (?–45 B.C.E.), the chief of the Gauls, is unknown to us except for what Caesar himself tells us of him in his *Gallic Wars*. He was the son of the king of the Averni tribe of central Gaul and clearly a competent soldier and general. Vercingetorix seemed to recognize the nature of Caesar's conquests in Gaul and the threat to the very core of the Gallic way of life. To prevent this, Vercingetorix took advantage of Caesar's absence from Gaul to forge a political alliance of the tribes and to create a national army under his leadership. His military acumen is clearly evident in his willingness to learn from his adversaries. Having witnessed the Roman way of war in earlier skirmishes, Vercingetorix trained his army in the Roman method of war and even copied Roman weapons. He acquitted himself well enough against the great Caesar but was eventually trapped in the city of Alesia, which the Romans besieged and captured. Vercingetorix himself was taken prisoner and displayed in Caesar's triumphal parade into Rome. He may have remained a prisoner in Roman jails for more than a year before he was executed by strangling.

LESSONS OF WAR

Strategy

1. Diplomacy is an equal partner in war. Successful diplomacy can be used significantly to alter the strategic force equation in your favor. Caesar used diplomacy continually to prevent a coalition of Gallic tribes against him. At any given time, the military manpower resources of the Gauls could have easily overwhelmed Caesar's manpower resources. It was diplomacy that was used to prevent the concentration of superior manpower against Caesar.

2. Always clearly and unemotionally delineate the connection between strategic ends, ways, and means. The formulation of a military strategy is no place to indulge illusions, anger, or hatreds. Like Caesar, always attempt to see things clearly. Never allow personal anger or hatred of the enemy to cloud your judgment in assessing strategic or tactical capabilities.

3. Caesar's life is an excellent study in the complexity of the political and cultural environment in which most wars of any size are fought. History reveals only a few wars in which military strategy was not conducted within a complex and confusing political environment. Emulate Caesar in

this regard. Recognize the complexities and the limits they impose and adjust to them. Don't waste too much time fighting the problem.

4. Always exploit the political weakness of your adversary. Caesar did this very well when he took advantage of Pompey's inability to act rapidly because of his need to secure political support of the Roman Senate in the Italian campaign. By the time the Senate had agreed to a strategy, it was too late—Caesar was successfully ensconced in Italy and moving on Rome.

5. Always remember that military actions have important second- and third-order social, psychological, and political effects that the commander must attempt to control. Caesar's victories in Gaul over nearly a decade almost came to nothing when his brutality in dealing with the conquered armies provoked the one thing he was attempting to prevent, a national uprising of the Gallic nation. Make every effort to see the big picture. Control second- and third-order effects of military operations to the degree possible.

6. Think about war termination before the campaign begins! Caesar's campaign against Pompey in Italy is a model of tailoring military operations to attain political goals in a precise manner, governed by the outcome of how Caesar wanted the campaign to end. Caesar sought to obtain an Italy in which most of its resources and, most important, the loyalty of the populace remained for him to use in future military operations. To this end, he minimized combat damage and treated the defeated leniently. The same man who brutalized the Gauls changed his military strategy during the Italian campaign because the nature and methods for how he wanted to terminate the conflict were different.

Tactics

1. A good battlefield commander learns from his own experiences. Remember that Caesar had no military experience in command of troops before taking command of his legions in Gaul. Great generals are made, not born. Keep at it. . . . There is hope!

2. Pursue, pursue, pursue! When the enemy is on the run, conduct a rapid and lethal pursuit as Caesar did against Ariovistus and Pompey. Once you have paid the price to engage and shatter the enemy force, follow that force ruthlessly until you have neutralized it as an effective combat force.

3. Remember Labienus at the battle of the Sambre. Pursue, but know when to break off the pursuit and use your forces decisively to influence the outcome of the main engagement. Be careful not to evoke too much enthusiasm.

4. Caesar took every opportunity to neutralize the enemy command structure before, during, and after the battle. If the opportunity presents itself, strike at the head of the serpent. If you can kill the head, the body dies, and the fangs cannot hurt you.

5. Caesar always took the initiative and went over to the defensive only as a temporary measure to prepare to regain the initiative. The offense knows

what goals it seeks to achieve, while the defense is always somewhat uncertain. Gain and utilize the initiative to decide the time, place, and tempo of battle.

6. When in doubt as to the enemy's size or plans, use maneuver to compensate and to change the tactical situation. Force the enemy commander to react to you. In almost every case, once Caesar had learned that there was a hostile force loose in the area, he set out to find it and move toward it. When in doubt, do something!

7. Always concentrate superiority of force at the critical point in the battle. Caesar always achieved this, as at Alesia and Pharsalus.

8. When you ambush an enemy, hurt it! Be decisive. Vercingetorix's ambush of Caesar's column near Dijon was a failure because the commander did not commit sufficient force to harm the column substantially. The result was that Caesar was able to extricate himself from a potentially deadly situation and fight another day.

9. Do not get fixated on the immediate tactical situation and lose sight of what may be happening in the larger tactical area of operations. Caesar made this mistake at Gergovia when he failed to detect a large relief army moving across his line of communication. Caesar's army was trapped and could have been annihilated.

10. Pay close attention to supplying your army. On several occasions, Caesar had to change his plans because he failed to arrange for adequate logistical support for his army. As Napoleon remarked, "An army moves on its stomach." This is still true today!

11. Care for your men. If they believe in your ability and believe that you genuinely care for them, they will follow you into harm's way. Like Caesar, let the men see you when the bullets fly. Expose yourself to the same risks and hardships that you expect your soldiers to endure.

12. Develop a close and successful working relationship with your intelligence staff. There is no substitute for good intelligence in divining the enemy's intentions. Caesar failed to use his intelligence adequately at Alesia and at the Sambre with almost disastrous results. Pompey's possession of the plans of Caesar's fortifications as a result of counter-intelligence operations is also a good example.

13. Always use your combat arms in concert when you can. Caesar's use of combined cavalry and infantry forces at Pharsalus was brilliant, as was Pompey's in his attack on Caesar's left flank at Dyrrachium. Individual combat arms contribute most to the outcome of the battle when used in conjunction with one another.

14. Deceive the enemy whenever you can. Pompey's use of intelligence assets to convince Caesar that traitors would open the gates of Dyrrachium to him was a brilliant piece of combat deception. It almost killed Caesar!

15. Be bold! Caesar crossed the Adriatic in the dead of winter at great risk to position his force in an area where he could confront Pompey. Guard against over-caution in military operations.

16. Do the unexpected. After the ambush on the road to Alesia by Vercinge-torix, Caesar reversed his withdrawal and attacked the enemy rearguard. Sometimes the most difficult thing to do in battle is to find the enemy and force him to fight. Caesar almost never avoided a battle when he could find the enemy. And once engaged, Caesar rarely disengaged until the issue had been settled.

17. Never stop harassing the enemy supply line. Caesar was in a difficult spot at Alesia and Dyrrachium. In both cases, however, the enemy commanders failed to use their cavalry to harass Caesar's supply line or hinder his construction of fortifications. Both commanders paid dearly for this mistake.

FURTHER READING

Balsdon, J.V. P. *Julius Caesar and Rome.* London: Penguin, 1971.

Caesar, Julius. *The Civil War.* New York: Penguin, 1988.

———. *Commentaries on the Gallic War.* New York: Penguin, 1982.

Connolly, Peter. *Greece and Rome at War.* Englewood Cliffs, NJ: Prentice-Hall, 1981.

Delbruck, Hans. *History of the Art of War.* Vol. 1, *Antiquity.* Westport, CT: Greenwood Press, 1975.

Dodge, Theodore Ayault. *Caesar: A History of the Art of War among the Romans down to the End of the Roman Empire with a Detailed Account of the Campaigns of Julius Caesar.* New York: Da Capo, 1977.

Fuller, J. F. C. *Julius Caesar: Man, Soldier, Tyrant.* New York: Da Capo, 1965.

———. *A Military History of the Western World—From Earliest Times to the Battle of Lepanto.* New York: Da Capo, 1954.

Gabriel, Richard A. *The Culture of War.* Westport, CT: Greenwood Press, 1990.

Gabriel, Richard A., and Karen S. Metz. *From Sumer to Rome: The Military Capabilities of Ancient Armies.* Westport, CT: Greenwood Press, 1991.

Gilliver, Catherine. *Caesar's Gallic Wars.* London: Routledge, 2003.

Greece and Rome. Vol. 4, no. 1 (March). London: Oxford University Press, 1957.

Hackett, Sir John. *Warfare in the Ancient World.* London: Sidgewick Jackson, 1989.

Holmes, Thomas R. *Caesar's Conquest of Gaul.* AMS Press, 2001.

Jimenez, Ramon L. *Caesar against the Celts.* New York: Da Capo, 1996.

———. *Caesar against Rome: The Great Roman Civil War.* Westport, CT: Praeger Publishers, 2000.

O'Connell, Robert L. "The Roman Killing Machine." *Quarterly Journal of Military History* (Autumn 1988): 36–39.

Payne, Gallwey, "The Artillery of the Carthaginians, Greeks, and Romans," *Journal of the Royal Artillery,* 58(1) (April 1931): 34–40.

Tacitus, Cornelius. *The Histories.* New York: Penguin, 1998.

Thibaux, Jean-Michel. *Vercingetorix.* London: Plon Publications, 1994.

Todd, Malcom. *Roman Britain.* London: Fontana, 1981.

Warner, Rex. *War Commentaries of Caesar.* New York: New American Library, 1997.

Watson, G. R. *The Roman Soldier.* Ithaca, NY: Cornell University Press, 1969.

Wiseman, Ann. *Julius Caesar: The Battle for Gaul.* London: Chatto and Windus, 1980.

15 BARBARIANS AGAINST ROME

[9–445 C.E.]

BACKGROUND

The civil war that destroyed the Roman Republic ended with the Battle of Actium (31 B.C.E.) with Augustus's defeat of the forces of Mark Antony, which ushered in the age of the *Pax Romana*. Rome conferred upon its empire a time of unparalleled peace, stability, and development never again seen in the history of Europe. Rome witnessed a golden age in which economic, literary, artistic, and engineering development grew rapidly. The architect of this peace was Gaius Julius Caesar Octavianus (63 B.C.E.–14 C.E.), who history knows as Caesar Augustus and who shaped the history and destiny of Rome from 30 B.C.E. until his death in 14 C.E., bequeathing to his successors the Roman imperium.

It was during the reign of Augustus that Rome finally attempted to deal with the "German problem" in a systematic manner. The roots of the German problem reached back for more than a century in Roman history. Rome's first encounter with the Germans was in 113 B.C.E. when mass migrations of the Cimbri and Teutoni moved through what is now Switzerland into southern Gaul. Four years later, these Germanic tribes invaded the Rhone Valley as a first step in breaching the Roman security frontier protecting northern Italy. The Roman army sent to stop the Germans was defeated, and after several further attempts to deflect the German line of migration, Mallius Maximus led an army of 80,000 men against the Germans in 105 B.C.E. At the battle of Arausio, the Roman army was virtually annihilated along with 40,000 noncombatants. Arausio was one of the worst disasters ever to befall Roman arms.

The defeat at Arausio left the road to Italy open, but the migrating Germans turned away from Italy and moved to conquer Spain. Strong resistance was encountered from the Celtibernians in the Pyrenean mountain passes, and the Germans were repulsed. They now turned their attention toward Italy. The time between the battle of Arausio and the redirection of the German advance toward Italy had given the Romans sufficient interval to undertake the Marian reforms and raise another army. Marius himself led the Roman army into Gaul to stop the German advance.

The primary German tribes, the Cimbri and the Teutones, divided their armies. The Cimbri marched northeast through Switzerland toward the Brenner Pass, while the Teutones marched south down the Rhone Valley. Marius repulsed a number of assaults by the Teutones at the junction of the Rhone and Isere rivers, and as the Teutone army moved down the Rhone Valley, Marius followed. Finally in 102 B.C.E., Marius drew the Teutones into battle at Acquae Sextae (modern Aix-en-Provence) and slaughtered 90,000 men, women, and children while taking 20,000 others prisoner. Meanwhile, the Cimbri had crossed the Brenner and defeated a Roman army under Catulus in the Po Valley. Marius redeployed his army to Italy and, in 101 B.C.E., defeated the Cimbri at the battle of Vercellae in which 140,000 Cimbri men, women, and children were killed and another 60,000 taken prisoner. With these two battles, the German storm died as suddenly as it had arisen.

For over forty years the Germans remained quiet behind the Rhine. In 58 B.C.E., Caesar encountered another German menace in the person of Ariovistus, who crossed the Rhine at the invitation of some of the Gallic tribes.

Figure 15.1 German Heavy Cavalryman (9 C.E.)

Caesar defeated Ariovistus, and the German threat once again receded. Caesar understood, however, that the German threat was only in temporary retreat. To firm up Rome's control of Gaul, in 57 B.C.E. Caesar defeated the tribes on the west bank of the Rhine and established Roman control there. Two years later in a demonstration of Roman power and will, Caesar crossed the Rhine and ravaged German territory before withdrawing. Caesar's successful Gallic campaign effectively established the Rhine as the Roman northern frontier. That frontier remained quiet throughout the great civil war, and when Augustus became emperor of Rome, the Rhine frontier was still undisturbed.

The Battle of the Teutoburg Forest (9 C.E.), in which a German chieftain by the name of Arminius destroyed three Roman legions under the command of Publius Quintilius Varus, was one of the most important battles in Western history. The defeat marked the end of the Roman grand strategic design to extend the empire's frontiers from the Rhine to the Elbe. As a result of the defeat, the Germanic lands beyond the Rhine remained wild, tribal, and Germanic, untouched by the Romanization that so strongly shaped Gaul and the remainder of the Western empire. Had this division of rival and hostile cultures not occurred, there would have been no Germanic tribes gradually to migrate to Britain and bring with them the Germanic roots of the English language. Indeed, there would have been no England as we know it. Had Germany between the Rhine and Elbe been Romanized for four centuries, one culture and not two in unending conflict would have dominated the West. There would have been no rival culture to eventually destroy Rome and plunge Europe into the Dark Ages. Fuller sums up the importance of the Battle of the Teutoburg Forest in Western history when he notes, "There would have been no Franco-German problem, or at least a totally different one. There would have been no Charlemagne, no Louis IV, no Napoleon, no Kaiser Wilhelm II, and no Hitler." He might have added, there would have been no military destruction of the Roman Empire at the hands of barbarians.

The Roman Empire that Augustus acquired in 30 B.C.E. had been established and enlarged by chance rather than grand design. Few of its provinces or allied territories were integrated into anything approaching a national state. The civil war fragmented Roman central control even further, and the empire's rim was in the grip of military units under the command of renegade Roman officers. In some areas, like Spain and Africa, the tribal peoples used the disruption of the civil war to throw off the Roman yoke. Bringing these peoples back under Roman control required the use of military force. At the beginning of his long reign, Augustus faced the necessary prelude of pacifying the imperial realm before creating a state bound together by a common sense of national identity and purpose.

While pacification and administration were major difficulties that had to be addressed, the most immediate and dangerous problem facing Augustus was what to do with the army. The civil war had proven that the armies could make an emperor, and their loyalty to their commanders was the fatal flaw that provoked the breakdown of civil authority and plunged Rome into civil war. When Augustus took power the Roman army consisted of between sixty-five and seventy-five full legions, some of which remained under the control of officers who had fought on the opposing side and whose loyalty to the new civic order was as yet untested. At the very least Augustus had to demobilize the army, purge it of disloyal officers, find ways to accommodate the demands of the released veterans, and, finally, reconstitute the Roman army in a manner that ensured its future loyalty to the state. Also of great importance was the problem of assuring that the army's structure reflected the new strategic realities that now confronted Rome. All depended upon the reform of the army, for if the military could not be again reduced to a servant of the state rather than its master, no grand strategy directed by political means was possible.

Strategy

The central strategic problem for Augustus was to establish effective command, control, and communications over a vast geographic area that was, in reality, not one but two distinct imperial realms. Maps 15.1 and 15.2 provide an overview of the geography of the Roman Empire in the northern and eastern theaters of operations. While Roman political and economic control emanated from Rome north to the Po Valley, the vast imperial realms of the eastern empire were geographically disconnected from the political center. Roman power extended from Libya, through Egypt, along the Palestinian land bridge inland to Syria, through the Anatolian peninsula as far as Armenia and the Black Sea, and across the Aegean Sea to include Greece, Macedonia, and the southern coastal strip of Yugoslavia, an area the Romans called Illyricum. The eastern empire was not connected to the Roman imperium by even a single road. As Caesar had discovered during the civil war, Italy was connected to Greece and Illyricum only by a single seaport. Any attempt to construct an imperial realm required that land

Map 15.1 Rome's Northern and Eastern Strategic Theater of Operations

communications be established between Italy and the East as an economic and military necessity.

Roman influence to the north and west, to Gaul and Spain, was almost totally dependent upon two roads, neither of which was securely in the hands of the Roman army. The main road to Gaul connecting Cisalpine Gaul with southern France was threatened by tribal peoples who lived in the Alps. Both the Great and Little St. Bernard passes were under the control of these tribes, and as long as this was the case, Roman access to the rich and strategically important Gallic heartland would never be secure. Augustus realized that Caesar's conquest of Gaul could not be sufficiently exploited unless Rome controlled the land routes through the Alps between Gaul and Italy. Without secure Roman control of Gaul, there was no buffer between Germany and Italy to absorb the shock of a potential conflict with the Germans. In this sense, Augustus regarded Gaul as the Egypt of the north, a strategic buffer,

Map 15.2 Roman Gaul and Germany (9 C.E.)

forward defense platform, and source of supplies for the forward-deployed armies of Rome stationed on the Rhine.

The problem of control and communication had another dimension. If Rome was to establish an overland route from northeast Italy (Trieste) through Austria and down through Yugoslavia to connect with Illyricum, Greece, and eventually Byzantium, this entire area first had to be brought under the control of Roman arms. The area around Trieste was controlled by hostile tribal armies of noted fierceness, while Austria and Bavaria (Noricum) were the homelands of a number of Germanic tribes that would also have to be brought to submission. Only then could the Roman thrust move south into Yugoslavia. The difficulty was that the extension of Roman communications into Austria-Bavaria placed this line of communications itself at great risk from an attack by those tribes living beyond the Rhine. Accordingly, these tribes would eventually have to be dealt with as well. To do this, in turn, required the extension of Roman control deep into Germany itself, a thrust that was certain to meet with military resistance. Augustus found himself in the position of having to extend the Roman defensive line from the Rhine to the Elbe, and only then down along the Danube to secure the Roman line of communication with the empire in the east. Although there had been no major conflicts with the Germans for almost half a century, this tranquility was about to end at Roman initiative.

The final geo-strategic problem confronted by Augustus was the need to redefine Roman security in the coastal Mediterranean basin. With the period of Roman conquest largely at an end, Augustus sought to stabilize the littoral frontier by adjusting Roman military dispositions to the new political reality of peace and diplomacy. Force of arms had brought Rome an empire, but Augustus was the first to understand that only peace, diplomacy, and the judicious (and infrequent) application of force could keep it. For Augustus, the administration and security of the new imperial realm was the overarching objective that guided Roman strategy. The centerpiece of Roman strategy was (1) the reduction of military expenditures to a level that the empire could afford, (2) the deployment of the legions to the imperial frontiers in a defensive posture, (3) the connection of the political and military assets of the empire to the empire's rim with a well-developed network of roads that facilitated commerce, Romanization, and the movement of military forces to troubled areas, and (4) most importantly, the use of diplomacy as the primary means of preempting and settling conflicts. The grand strategic design of Caesar Augustus was an excellent example of the preeminence of political goals and direction over military strategy, a lesson that modern strategists must relearn from time to time.

Augustus's strategic priority was pacification, and in 27 B.C.E., Rome sent military forces to Spain and Africa with the objective of bringing these two important provinces under control. It was not until 19 B.C.E., after a series of localized wars and massacres, that Rome succeeded in reimposing its will on the recalcitrant provinces. With these victories, the core of the empire—Italy, Spain, and Gaul to the Rhine—was secure. Augustus now turned to securing the eastern frontier of the Roman imperium. He understood that the Roman eastern realm was already far too large and that, since Roman power depended upon control of the Mediterranean, its logical extension inland ought not to exceed the boundaries of the coastal states. Accordingly, he established a series of fortresses across Egypt and reinforced Roman control of the Palestinian land bridge. The pivotal point of the eastern defense alignment was Syria, and its eastern border became the practical limit of effective Roman control in the area. Augustus also annexed Galatia, Pontus, and Cappadocia, thereby establishing Roman control over much of Asia Minor as far north as the area around the Black Sea between the Dniester and Dnieper rivers. Roman policy suffered from some indecision over the question of Armenia, but diplomacy prevailed, and a working arrangement was concluded between Parthia and Rome over control of the Armenian state. In less than ten years, Augustus had brought peace to the imperial realm and readjusted the southern and eastern borders of the Roman world.

During this time Augustus turned his attention to the problem of the army and its place in the new imperial state. At the end of the civil war Augustus's armies numbered almost 500,000 men. All but twenty-five legions of the former armies of the civil war were disbanded, and approximately 300,000 soldiers were pensioned off or resettled. Augustus adopted Caesar's practice of establishing military colonies for his veterans. Some of these colonies were in the provinces, so Italy was rid of many veterans who might have posed problems in the future. Augustus replaced the soldier's oath previously taken to his commander with an oath of loyalty to the Roman state, thereby placing military service upon a new legal basis. While conscription was still legally in force and remained so throughout the empire, in practice it was used only in time of dire emergency. In reality, the Roman legions were comprised of professionals and volunteers trained to mercenary quality. To encourage enlistments, Augustus legalized the terms of enlistment and established retirement benefits for the veterans of the legions. Most importantly, the adoption of a new strategic doctrine centered around the defense of fixed frontiers allowed Augustus to disperse the legions to the frontiers of the empire, thereby reducing whatever future threat they might present to the civil government of the imperium. With the exception of the Praetorian Guard, no military forces were stationed on the Italian mainland. There would be no more crossings of the Rubicon by rebellious generals at the head of their loyal legions marching on the capital. And, should it ever happen again, the Praetorian Guard was designed precisely as the protector of the Roman state against such eventualities.

Early in his reign Augustus turned his attention to the limited access Rome enjoyed to Gaul. In 25 B.C.E. Roman armies secured greater access to the Little and Great St. Bernard passes over the Alps by driving the hostile tribes from the area around the avenues of approach. In 17–16 B.C.E. Roman armies pushed east around Lake Garda, opening the way for the passage of Roman arms into Austria. In 15 B.C.E., Augustus sent Roman armies into the great block of territory that included the Tirol, eastern Switzerland, western Austria, and southern Bavaria. Part of the plan was to extend the central section of the northern frontier upward to the Danube. Two task forces, each under the command of one of Augustus's stepsons, Tiberius and Drusus, set off from Italy in 15 B.C.E. Tiberius marched eastward from Gaul toward Lake Constance to Vienna, while Drusus, beginning in Italy, moved over the Resia Pass along the valley of the Inn toward the same goal. Within a year the armies met and reduced any local opposition to the new Roman presence. Immediately Roman engineers began the construction of roads and strong points in the area.

The occupation of the Austrian-Bavarian sector and the pacification of the area around the Alps and Trieste made it possible for the Romans to attempt to achieve the most important of their strategic objectives, linking the eastern empire (Illyricum, Greece, and Turkey) with Italy by way of a secure military road. To achieve this task, most of what is now Yugoslavia had to be brought under control by force of arms. The geography of the area offered only two logical routes of advance. The first was through the Save and Drave river valleys down to the border of Illyricum. From there the Drina River could be followed to the coast. The second route moved east from the lower Save valley to the Danube and along that river to Belgrade and Byzantium. The valley of the Save and Drave rivers to the Drina nexus was the homeland of a Celtic people the Romans called Pannonians. The remainder of the Yugoslavian hill country was occupied by various other tribes. In 13 B.C.E. Roman armies under the command of Marcus Vinicius attacked Pannonia. Within a year command of the expedition passed to Agrippa, who died shortly thereafter. Command of the Roman operation then fell to Tiberius who, four years later, brought the entire area under Roman military control.

At the same time as the Roman operation against Pannonia was being undertaken, Augustus planned a simultaneous operation against Germany. This was no mere afterthought. Although the Germans had been quiet for almost half a century, Augustus was of the same mind on this matter as had been Caesar. Regardless of the Rhine frontier, sooner or later Germany would have to be dealt with, especially now that Roman strategy demanded control of Austria and Bavaria as the primary means of securing Roman overland access to the east. Moreover, Rome had few real enemies left. Most of her potential antagonists could mount only revolts or short wars at best. None possessed the geographic position or manpower base to offer anything like a life-threatening challenge to Rome.

Only Germany had the manpower and geographic assets to offer a serious challenge to Roman existence. At one point in Rome's history, Germany had done precisely that. While Gaul had been thoroughly Romanized and brought into the Roman defense perimeter, Germany remained a wild and foreign land whose tribal social structure made it difficult to use diplomacy as a means of ensuring compliance. Finally, if a war with Germany was an eventuality, Augustus may have felt that the time was ripe. The legions had been rebuilt, Roman armies held Bavaria, the legions along the Rhine were well trained and well supplied, and Gaul itself, so close to the German homeland, was an enormous logistical and manpower base to support Roman operations into Germany. In 12 B.C.E. the Romans launched a large-scale expedition against Germany under the command of Drusus, Augustus's adopted son. It was an expedition designed to subdue and thoroughly integrate Germany into the new Roman imperial world.

But Germany was not Gaul, and the conduct of military operations in Germany by the Romans presented a number of difficulties that even Caesar had not encountered in his conquest of Gaul. Caesar, for example, could move and feed his army in Gaul with some ease because the country was richly cultivated and possessed an established infrastructure of bridges and roads that facilitated the normal commerce of the country. Germany, on the other hand, was full of primitive tribes that held agriculture in contempt, that built no roads or bridges, and whose pastoral economy provoked seasonal tribal movements. The wealth of the Germanic tribes lay in cattle, not cultivated lands. Even their housing structures were so primitive—at times little more than holes in the ground covered with animal skins—that Romans found them unfit for quartering troops. The German terrain was characterized by hills and valleys overgrown with dense forests and interspersed with marshes and swamps, terrain not favorable to Roman infantry tactics, but helpful to ambushes by German tribal armies. The terrain also slowed the Roman rate of movement, depriving the legions of tactical flexibility. A Roman commander seeking to dominate the terrain, move rapidly, and supply his army had to rely heavily upon fleets of small boats, using the interior rivers to sustain his operations.

Invasion

In 12 C.E. Drusus crossed the Rhine with six legions and moved into Westphalia where he proceeded to ravage the countryside. He then moved along the coast to the Lacus Fveuvus (the Zuider Zee was then a lake), assembled a fleet of boats, and sailed to the mouth of the Ems River. Having gained the seacoast at the Weser, Drusus then prepared for his invasion of Germany proper. In 10 C.E., using diplomacy to clear his path by cementing alliances with rival tribes, much as Caesar did in Gaul, Drusus fought a number of battles with German tribal armies. Within two years Drusus had reached the Elbe and established a Roman presence between it and the Rhine.

On his way home a year later (9 C.E.), Drusus fell from his horse and died of his injuries. He was replaced by his older brother Tiberius. Tiberius conducted a number of aggressive campaigns against various Germanic tribes. In Roman thinking, these military forays, often little more than raids, were intended to have a psychological impact more than a military effect. Frequently, a Roman raid against a comparatively small tribe might be accompanied by great slaughter as a lesson to larger tribes yet to be engaged. The Romans clearly understood the psychological dimension of war and used it to great advantage throughout the imperial period. By 7 C.E., Tiberius had brought the campaign to a successful conclusion and was rewarded with a new command in the East. Over the next decade Roman authority in Germany passed through the hands of a number of different officers who tried to keep the peace within the new German lands.

The Roman occupation of Germany had gone relatively well, but the Roman presence was neither stable nor secure. The Roman invasion force had fought only tribal armies of questionable quality. Germanic weaponry was shoddy at best, inappropriate to close-order combat, and Germanic battle tactics that stressed the frontal assault played directly against the Roman strength in disciplined infantry. Equally important was that few German tribal leaders had any previous contact or experience with the Roman army and knew little about how to fight it. Over a period of twenty years, however, many German tribal chiefs served with Roman units in Pannonia, Dalmatia, and other places where they gained valuable military experience in combating Roman strengths and exploiting Roman weaknesses. Examined objectively, the Roman invasion of Germany consisted of little more than a series of raids against disorganized tribal armies resident between the Rhine and the Elbe.

Although the Romans eventually built more than fifty camps and strong points in Germany between the Rhine and Elbe rivers, few Roman forts were permanent bases where the army could remain secure and self-sufficient in garrison through the winter months. More commonly, Roman units withdrew to the secure bases near the Rhine or even behind the Rhine itself for the winter. While some efforts were made to establish a road network in Germany, the first roads were primitive affairs—often of the corduroy log variety—usually connecting only the most important military camps. In the end, the Roman occupation of Germany was so short that no appreciable road-building program was possible or attempted. No sooner had Tiberius departed Germany for his command in the East than the tribes in Germany and in the central Danube area began to create difficulties.

Shortly before the turn of the millennium, a Germanic leader named Marroboduus responded to the gradual Roman encirclement of southern Germany by moving his tribe from the valley of the Mainz to Bohemia (see Map 15.2). Marroboduus had seen service in the Roman armies and was quick to recognize the nature of the Roman threat to German independence. In these two characteristics Marroboduus was the prototype of the new Germanic tribal leader that was slowly emerging. Roman policy at this time sought to secure a land route across Bohemia and, eventually, to annex the entire area as vital to keeping open the route from the Danube to the Elbe. Roman diplomacy sought to isolate Marroboduus from his neighboring tribes who, in any event, feared the growth of Marroboduus's power. From 1 to 3 C.E. Roman armies maneuvered around Bohemia gaining the allegiance of the border tribes and defeating those whose allegiance to Marroboduus could not be bought.

Elsewhere in Germany, Roman armies under various commanders were required to put down sporadic revolts, and events threatened to slip out of control. Roman armies could not move against Marroboduus until their rear and flank bases of operations in Germany were secure. To bring this about, Tiberius was again called upon to take charge of the armies in Germany. From 4 to 6 C.E., he conducted a series of military operations, joined with excellent diplomacy, to firm up the Roman position in Germany proper. By 6 C.E., events had stabilized, and Tiberius was ready to move against Marroboduus. Twelve Roman legions marched out against the German enemy, the total force of the armies of the Rhine, Raetia, and Illyricum. Within months the legions closed in on Bohemia and Marroboduus's army. As the legions were poised to strike, news arrived from Illyricum that a general revolt had broken out against Roman authority. Tiberius, ever the political general, realized the serious nature of the crisis and quickly came to terms with Marroboduus. Marroboduus was made king of the Marcomanni and named a special friend of Rome. Tiberius now turned his armies southward to crush the revolt in Illyricum.

The Illyricum Revolt

The great rebellion in Illyricum began when native levies being mustered for the campaign against Marroboduus mutinied, revealing the danger in the Augustan policy of allowing native auxiliary units to fight under their own commanders. The incident spread into general revolt as tribe after tribe joined the movement against Roman taxation and recruitment policies. Within weeks, all of Illyricum was ablaze, and the threat of severing the eastern provinces from Roman control became very real. At the height of the revolt, the rebel armies could muster 200,000 infantry and 9,000 cavalry. Roman armies in the area had been previously depleted by the campaign against Marroboduus and, in any case, probably had never exceeded three legions. Rome attempted to meet its manpower shortage by conscription, but there was large-scale resistance to the point, as Tacitus tells us, where sons of the nobility had their thumbs cut off so as to be unable to serve in the legions. Augustus reinstated the death penalty for draft evasion (although it does not appear to have been carried out), and all veterans and retirees were recalled to their old units. Even companies of liberated slaves (*cohortes voluntariorum*) were raised for the war, and national auxiliary units from other parts of the empire were shipped to the Illyricum theater of operations.

Tiberius was a general equal to the job of suppressing the revolt with little conscience. The manpower shortage precluded fighting pitched battles, and in the few instances when such battles were forced upon the Romans (the Battle of the Volcaean Marshes for example), the result was near disaster. Tiberius's strategy was to seize every city, port, and strong point of importance and devastate the countryside in a methodical manner, depriving the enemy of food and supplies. At the same time, Tiberius used diplomacy to drive wedges among the parties to what was in essence a tribal coalition. By 8 C.E., Pannonia fell to Roman arms and, one by one, moving from north to south, the various tribal areas that comprised Roman Illyricum surrendered.

The revolt in Illyricum revealed a number of weaknesses in Roman strategic thinking. First, the need to keep the cost of the military down had reduced the Roman army to about twenty-five legions scattered throughout the empire. Even given superior Roman equipment and skill, the Illyricum revolt had shown that Roman manpower was scarcely adequate to contain a serious challenge, even from tribal armies. Second, the inability quickly to raise additional manpower levies through conscription revealed that the Roman army had little strategic depth. The lack of a strategic reserve that could be quickly moved to a trouble spot remained a major problem for two centuries. Third, Roman military manpower deployment conceded any initiative to the enemy and depended critically upon the ability of Roman intelligence and diplomatic assets to discern and defuse potential threats, without actually using the military except as a last resort. Finally, Roman imperial policy was of a single piece in that a frontier attack or breakthrough required almost all the available military assets of the empire to deal with the problem. What would happen if, say, two provinces rose in revolt simultaneously? What would have happened if Germany had risen in revolt at the same time as Illyricum?

During the troubles in Illyricum a deceptive tranquility hung over Germany. Tiberius's last campaigns (4–5 C.E.) seemed to have stabilized the situation, and the revolt in Illyricum found no echo in Germany. Even the most formidable of the German tribes, the Cherusci, seemed willing to accept the continuation of Roman rule in their lands. Roman units moved forward from the Rhine and Lippe to outposts near the Elbe every summer, only to withdraw again to their bases as winter approached. Rome's distraction in Illyricum had deprived it of the manpower and resources to begin a network of roads and fortified positions in Germany. Scarcely five days after the collapse of the Illyricum revolt, news reached Rome that three Roman legions under the command of Publius Quintilius Varus had been slaughtered by a Cheruscan army under the command of a Germanic chieftain named Arminius. Rome had received its first lesson in the meaning of strategic overreach.

AUGUSTUS'S NEW LEGIONS

The structure of the Roman legions reformed by Marius a century before Augustus and used with such skill by Caesar and Augustus remained essentially unchanged under the *Pax Romana*. Since the subject of the legions has already been treated in some detail in the previous chapter, only those reforms that can be directly attributed to Augustus are addressed here. Marius had placed the legions on a new social footing by opening their ranks to the landless of Rome and thereby establishing the beginnings of a truly professional army. Augustus placed the legions on a new political footing by relating their number, type, and social composition to policy goals controlled essentially by economic considerations. Augustus intended to use the legions to defend the frontiers of the empire and maintain domestic peace and order, and to do so with the least possible strain on the economic fabric of the Roman state.

Reforms

Augustus reduced the size of the imperial army to twenty-five legions, about 150,000 men, but retained a force of auxiliary troops of about the same number. Thus, the total military force of the Roman army in the Augustan age was approximately 300,000 men out of a population of almost 100 million. The force structure, in turn, was driven by a new strategic concept that relied upon a small military force of high cohesion, discipline, mobility, and technology to defend the imperial borders. The quality of the force took precedence over its numerical strength, a problematic distinction not unknown to modern military planners involved in debates on how to reduce and restructure their armies in light of changing strategic objectives and new technologies.

Reducing the size of the army and stationing it on the frontiers of the empire was possible only because Augustus reasoned that the nature of the threat had changed. Spain and Africa had by this time been pacified. Redrawing the security frontier in Asia had reduced the Parthian threat and made the borders more militarily defensible. Most important, Rome itself intended, at least at the outset, few offensive military operations, a policy designed to avoid provoking the fears of her rivals. The tribes beyond the Danube and the Rhine were also at peace at this time, and the reestablishment of civil peace allowed the legions to be moved from the Italian mainland, where they were no longer needed as a civil police force. The whole strategic and military structure depended upon the ability of Roman diplomacy to prevent a threat from emerging from more than one enemy at the same time. Without a central reserve to reinforce a threatened point, the empire could be strengthened at one place only, at the potential risk of weakening it in another. Accordingly, Augustus began the construction of a superb road network behind the frontiers that connected the provinces with Rome and its military bases. This road system was the military substitute for a strategic reserve.

Having demobilized much of the veteran army of the civil wars, Augustus standardized the new system of recruitment to stabilize the supply of manpower for the legions. The myth that the Roman armies were coteries of conscripts and landholders was replaced with the reality that service in the army was a career. A major source of military manpower was the legions themselves. To meet the demands of the demobilized soldiery after the civil war, Augustus established a policy of granting veterans land throughout the empire. These settlements served Rome well over the next few centuries. They provided groups of loyal men who could be called to arms in an emergency. The veterans started farms from which Roman units could contract for supplies. The sons of the veterans often entered the army, following their fathers to their old regiments as career soldiers. Augustus established a special fund, the *aerarium militare*, supported by death and auction taxes, to ensure an adequate treasury from which to pay retirement benefits to the soldiers on a sound and regular basis. A normal military career spanned twenty years.

One effect of these reforms was to change the social composition of the legions. From Augustus's time forward, more and more legionnaires were of non-Italian stock. Whereas previously non-Italians and even those not holding Roman citizenship were allowed to fight alongside the legions as "allies," under Augustus these allies came to constitute the bulk of Rome's military manpower. The division of the empire into the Greek-speaking East and the Latin-speaking West was manifest in the recruitment patterns of the legions. The Western legions were recruited in Italy and the Romanized provinces of Gaul. The legions of the East were drawn almost entirely from that region. The legions garrisoning the Danube regions drew on both eastern and western areas for their soldiers. Latin, however, remained the official language of the Roman army, and, we might surmise, many of the soldiers in the eastern legions were bilingual. The process of allowing non-Romans into the legions was greatly facilitated by a change in the law that allowed the legitimization of the social and marriage relationships between a soldier and a provincial woman after the soldier retired. This made it possible for him to achieve citizenship, legitimize his children, and remove any legal barriers to inheritance. It also meant the veteran's son could enter the army as a citizen when his turn came.

Stabilizing the legions in one place for long periods (sometimes centuries) meant that generation after generation of soldiers established strong roots in the area, something that accelerated Romanization and instilled patriotism and identification among the local populations as being a part of the great empire of Rome. It was not unusual for a soldier to remain attached to the same legion, century, and *cohort* for his entire career, and he might well spend all his military life in the same camp.

The prolonged period of peace allowed Augustus to standardize the size of the legion. In Caesar's day, *cohorts* varied in size by as much as a few hundred, and the number of *cohorts* per legion varied as well. The Augustan legion was standardized at 6,000 men comprised of ten *cohorts*. The first and tenth cohort had a thousand men each, while the remaining eight were 500 strong. The reason for this arrangement is unclear. Weaponry, training, logistics, and tactics remained essentially as they had been in Caesar's day.

The most important reform of the legion was the close integration of provincial troops, the *auxilia*, within the battle formations of the imperial legions themselves. Irregular units first became important during Caesar's wars, and during the civil wars, large contingents of troops were drawn from the provinces and fought under their own national commanders. During the Pannonian revolt, for example, seventy *cohorts* of infantry and fourteen *alae* of cavalry were provided by auxiliary troops to help Rome crush the rebellion. By the Augustan age, fully half the imperial army, approximately 150,000 men, were drawn from the provincial forces.

Auxiliary forces were organized in infantry and cavalry *cohorts* of 500 men, although units of 1,000 sometimes existed. Early on, these provincial units were allowed to fight under the command of their own chiefs and use their own weaponry. This created two major problems. First, as provincials they naturally identified with the homeland from which they came and were reluctant to serve anywhere but in the proximity of that homeland. Second, national identity and loyalty to the homeland of their garrisons made the possibility of mutiny very real. Indeed, the great revolt in Illyricum began exactly in this manner. Rome addressed this problem by making the tribal chiefs of auxiliary units Roman citizens in the hope that they would develop a greater loyalty to Rome than to the tribe. This method often worked. The case of Arminius, however, was a dismal failure. Sometimes a mixed national unit would be assigned a commander, a veteran legionnaire who had retired as *primus pili*, literally "the first spear" of the legion, whose task was to whip the unit into shape and keep it loyal to the imperial standard.

Throughout the age of Augustus the Romans never found a genuine solution to this problem, and unit mutinies and tribal revolts were a real concern. Over time, however, provincial units were shifted around from province to province to dilute traditional loyalties, sometimes with success. By the time of Trajan, it became the practice to create regular standing units of auxiliaries, comparable to the *cohorts* of the legions, where nationalities were deliberately mixed to reduce tribal identifications. These units were known by their numbers and were given the general designation of *numeri*. One effect was that large numbers of barbarians gained military experience and familiarity with the Roman system of war. Since few of the men in the *numeri* served for a career (although some did), they became a constant source of military expertise that was used to improve the military capabilities of the barbarian tribes.

As a general proposition, the legions of the Augustan age were the best Rome had ever placed in the field. They were healthier, lived longer, trained more extensively, were equipped with more advanced military technology, were generally literate, and were far more organized and organizationally articulated (they produced an excellent military medical service, for example) than any legions previously.

The one element that strikes a discordant note in this picture was the quality of the legions' senior officer corps. For the most part, the senior officer corps was comprised of amateurs who did not often acquit themselves well. From the time of the Republic the Romans had always taken great care to assure that the command arrangements of the army did not threaten the republican nature of the state. Two central mechanisms for ensuring this condition were civil control of the military (the magistracy) and frequent rotation of field commands at the highest levels. The result was that Rome never produced a professional senior officer corps, nor did it develop military colleges. What training the individual officer received he received in the legion itself. The senior officer corps was always chosen for its political credentials rather than its military ones, which were often completely lacking to begin with.

The threat of a civil war, when joined with the traditional Roman fear of military rule, produced a system of military command that relied on amateurs whose first and most important credential was their loyalty to Roman civil authority. The higher officers of the legions were anything but military professionals. Legions were commanded by a new type of public official, the *legatus*, an office created by Augustus. Although Caesar had started this practice when he placed sections of his army under the command of various *legati* chosen for their loyalty to his person, Augustus institutionalized it. The *legatus* was a well-known public official with sufficient political reputation for loyalty to allow him to be considered for military command. This officer was appointed by the emperor to legion command but was not allowed to serve with the legion for more than a year or two. After that time he returned to Rome to hold another public post or was transferred to one of the numerous provincial governorships or other posts held by men of praetorian rank. Political selection, short tenure, and rotation through the capital and then to the hinterlands made it impossible for the Roman army to develop career senior officers. By the same token, and certainly more important from Augustus's perspective, it made it very difficult for a senior commander to use his military position to strike at the state. Augustus had seen enough of this situation in the civil war, and he institutionalized a system that made its recurrence improbable.

The only other opportunity for gaining military experience was for a young political hopeful to be appointed as a *tribunus militum*, which would at least allow service with a military unit for a short time. This post seems to have been a minor one and certainly held none of the traditional powers normally associated with the old tribunate under the Republic. It was exceedingly rare for someone to go from being a *tribune militum* to a higher military post without some extended interval between assignments. An interesting possibility was the ability of a man of higher social class to request an assignment in the legion as a centurion. While more will be said of the Roman centurionate shortly, it must be noted here that such upper-class centurions served only for short times in any given legion before being transferred to another legion. This was in stark contrast to the previous practice of a centurion spending his entire career in a single legion. The policy of rotation suggests once again that the civil leadership was at pains to prevent the rise of popular senior officers with strong roots of loyalty within their military commands.

The requirement for political loyalty and the selection and rotation system combined to ensure that there would be no professional senior officer corps. In a crisis, Rome might send a man of tried ability to assume command, or as in the case of Drusus and Tiberius, commands might be assembled around them for specific operational purposes. On a day-to-day basis, however, Rome was prepared to take the risk that the security environment had changed, that most military matters could be handled by men of moderate ability, and that, if all else failed, special commands could be assembled in time to deal with the crisis.

This arrangement might well prove workable at the strategic and theater level of operations, but it could easily lead to disaster at the tactical level where army and legion commanders might have to fight with little or no training or experience. The absence of professional officers at the senior level was to some extent remedied by the institution of the centurionate. Each legion had sixty centurions, six attached to each of the legion's ten *cohorts*. The senior centurion was called the *primus pilus*, the best and most experienced soldier in the unit. The centurions began life in the ranks and were promoted on the basis of performance, which, as Livy says, was defined as leadership and courage. They served for life with the same unit and were true and well-respected professional soldiers. It was within the centurionate that the professional combat skills and institutional memory of the legion resided.

Although technically noncommissioned officers, the centurions acted more like modern company commanders in both tactical and leadership responsibilities. A long tradition had grown up in the Roman army where it had always been customary for the legion commander to consult with a group of senior centurions prior to ordering the legion into action. This group of senior centurions was called the *primi ordines* and consisted (probably) of the centurions of the first *cohort* (usually the first to engage and the anchor of the infantry line) and the senior centurion of each of the remaining *cohorts*. This meeting functioned much like the modern commander's conference, and it afforded the inexperienced legion commander the opportunity to obtain advice from men much more experienced in the art of war. Assuming that disaster could be avoided at high planning and operational levels of command, when it came to actual fighting the experienced centurions and professional soldiers of the legions of Rome could always be expected to give an excellent account of themselves. Even in defeat it was often the case that the legion fought to the last man. And it was expected that the centurions would hold to the last, even unto death.

One of Augustus's important contributions to Roman military power was his recognition of the navy as an important instrument of national policy. A credible argument can be made that until the time of Augustus, every

Roman government failed to appreciate the importance of seapower. Under the Republic, naval service ranked lower than service in the legions, and no regular naval force existed. In times of crisis Rome requisitioned ships and crews from her maritime allies. No class of naval officers existed, and even Caesar seems to have overlooked the importance of seapower.

Augustus's experience during the civil war, most certainly the importance of Actium to his victory, led him to retain parts of the fleet from that war and to reexamine the role of naval power in Roman grand strategy. Early in his reign Augustus ordered two naval bases constructed, Misenum on the Bay of Naples, and Ravenna, near the mouth of the Po River. These two installations served for centuries as the headquarters of the major Roman fleets. Smaller fleets were constructed and stationed at critical provincial ports throughout the empire, and the major rivers had regular squadrons assigned to them to patrol their waters. It will be recalled that Drusus used significant numbers of boats to move his units on German rivers during his campaign in 12 C.E. When his son, Germanicus, conducted operations in Germany in 16 C.E., he had more than a thousand ships of various types under his command. It took almost another century before Rome produced a truly modern navy, but it was Augustus who first recognized naval power as important to the conduct and success of Roman national strategy.

The Roman armies that took the field against the Cherusci in 9 C.E. were perhaps the most professional and proficient soldiers that Roman society had ever produced. Their strength, as always, lay in disciplined infantry, good training, and excellent logistics. Their weakness, as always, lay in the Roman failure to develop disciplined cavalry and integrate its use into an overall tactical doctrine. The Romans simply hired cavalry when they needed it and employed it as an adjunct combat arm. Man for man, unit for unit, however, there was not another army in the world that could go head to head with the legions of Rome and emerge victorious. When they came up short, as the legions sometimes did, it was due most often to poor leadership rather than to the quality of the Roman soldier.

THE GERMANS

The other barbarian armies that confronted Rome have already been addressed, the Iberians and Celts in Chapter 12 and the Gauls in Chapter 14. The Goths will be addressed in the next Chapter. The present chapter examines the wars between the Romans and the German tribes. The German armies that the Romans encountered in their efforts to subdue the territory between the Rhine and Elbe were products of a social order far less developed than Rome or even that of the Gauls that Caesar had fought more than fifty years earlier. It is an axiom of military history that the nature and structure of armies are determined by the nature and structure of the larger social orders that give them life far more than by military technology or any other factor. In this regard, then, it can be said that the social order of the Germanic tribes was essentially pre-modern in that it was not strongly or clearly articulated and lacked clear specialization of social roles. Accordingly, the dominant social role, the bonded male warrior group, became the dominant form of military organization as well. Every German male was first and foremost a warrior, and the entire society was formed around the conduct of war. Prowess in war was the road to social advancement, and behavior on the battlefield was the primary determinant of social rank and status.

Manpower

Tacitus's description of the Germans as "fierce looking with blue eyes, reddish hair, and big frames" recalls earlier Roman descriptions of the Gauls, and it is likely that, like the Gauls, the average German was much taller than the average Roman. The Germans had not yet reached a level of political development where state institutions had come into existence. Instead, the German peoples were divided into tribes (*Volkerschaften*); twenty-three different tribes lived between the Rhine and the Elbe. An average tribe numbered about 25,000 people living in a land area of approximately 2,000 square miles. Some of the larger tribes comprised 35,000 to 40,000 people and occupied a comparatively larger land area. The tribes were divided into extended-family clans called "Hundreds" (*Hundertschaft*) comprised of 400 to 1,000 people living in a single village and controlling an area of twenty square miles. Agriculture was not extensively practiced by the Germans, and what cultivation was undertaken was handled by women, the men contributing to the food supply by hunting and fishing. Land was held in common, as were some cattle herds, and utilization was determined by the head of the community, the *altermann* or *hunno*. Within each tribe were a small number of richer noble families who met in assembly with the clan *hunni* to address major issues, including war and peace. In wartime, however, it was common for the council to select a war chief, usually from the most powerful warrior noble families, to command the tribal army. An average German tribe could put 5,000 to 7,000 warriors in the field under the command of the war chief. The actual fighting units, however, were centered around the clans, and a Germanic army of 5,000 warriors would have at least twenty and as many as fifty subordinate unit leaders—the clan chiefs.

In assessing the fighting quality of German tribal armies, it must be kept in mind that Germanic tribes were first, foremost, and primarily warrior societies in which all other social roles were defined or influenced by the warrior ethos. Thus, Germanic men did not farm because it was beneath them (women's work), but they hunted since hunting improved their combat skills. The relationship between man and wife and family was also conditioned by the warrior ethos. It was the woman who, as a gift of her dowry, brought weapons to her husband. Germanic women acted as the tribe's "military medical corps," and it was to these *wilde weiber* (literally, "wild women") that the wounded turned for medical aid. Women accompanied their men into battle, urging them on to greater efforts by reminding them of the cost of enslavement to themselves and children. In short, the German soldier was a professional warrior whose very social existence was defined by war.

Tactical Organization

In times of war, each clan provided its own coterie of warriors under the leadership of the village *hunno*, who was also the civic leader of the clan in peacetime. The solidarity and cohesion of the family and clan was extended to and defined the warrior group, with the result that German small combat units were highly cohesive, strongly disciplined, self-motivated, well led, and well trained in the skills of individual close combat. They could be relied upon to make murderous charges upon command and to fight well in dispersed small groups. While blood ties usually assured that clan units remained loyal to the larger tribal military command, in fact there was probably only the most rudimentary command and control exercised by the war chief over the behavior of the clan units. Once the tribal levy had been assembled and a general battle plan decided upon, implementation was left to local units with little in the way of any ability to direct the battle.

German weaponry was the consequence of many years of intertribal wars, the lack of contact with any other culture from which new weapons could be acquired, and, as Tacitus and others tell us, the German difficulty in working with iron. Tacitus does not tell us why the Germans were poor iron-smiths, but clearly they were far behind the Celts and Gauls who, in the second century B.C.E., were making chain mail armor superior to the Romans. Roman sources note as well that only a few of the German warriors, probably their nobles or the best warriors, wore body armor or metal helmets. The basic protection from wounds was afforded by a large shield of wood or braided reeds covered with leather. Some troops wore a covering of leather or hide on their heads as well. The basic weapon of the German was the *framea*, the seven- to ten-foot spear of the type used by the Greek hoplite, tipped with a short but sharp blade. The spear was used in close combat or could be thrown. It seems likely as well that German units carried somewhat longer spears that might have been used by the front rank of a charging infantry formation to break through the enemy. Once inside the enemy formation, the *framea* was used as the primary killing weapon. The sword was relatively rare and not commonly used by German combat units. The German warrior also carried an assortment of short wooden javelins with fire-hardened tips that, as Tacitus tells us, they could hurl long distances. Other missiles, most probably stones and sharpened sticks, were also used to salvo the enemy. Although some German tribes developed into excellent cavalrymen, for the most part German cavalry was limited in numbers and used rather poorly. Battle accounts note that German cavalry moved at such a slow pace in the attack (perhaps a trot or even a walk) that the infantry had little difficulty keeping up. As the Romans learned more than once to their chagrin, the primary strength of the German tribal levy was infantry.

Tactics

The Germanic infantry fought in a formation that the Romans called the *cuneus* or "wedge." Vegetius, writing two centuries after Teutoburg, described the *cuneus* as "a mass of men on foot, in close formation, narrower in front, wider in the rear, that moves forward and breaks the ranks of the enemy." This formation, also called the Boar's Head formation by the Romans, was not a wedge with a pointed front. Rather, it must have resembled a trapezoid, with a shorter line in front followed by a thick formation of closely packed troops, with a rear rank somewhat longer than the front rank. Commanded from the front by the *hunno*, this wedge formation was designed primarily to deliver shock and to carry the formation through to a penetration of the enemy ranks.

The use of the wedge against the Roman open phalanx explains other Germanic battlefield habits. For example, if the object of the wedge was penetration, then there was no need to armor the men in the center of the wedge. Those German warriors who had body armor and helmets probably fought in the front rank and outside files of the wedge. Fourteen centuries later, it became the Swiss practice to armor only the front and outside ranks, while the men in the center of the Swiss pike phalanx wore only leather armor or none at all. Moreover, if the wedge did its job and broke the enemy formation, then the fight was reduced to either a pursuit or a scramble of individual combats. Under these conditions, the troops least encumbered by armor and other weighty equipment had the advantage.

Against the Roman *cohort*, however, the Germanic wedge was at a disadvantage. First, the thinner Roman depth meant that more weapons could be employed on the first battle line. Moreover, if the wedge did not achieve penetration, it was overlapped by the longer Roman line and easily enveloped. Once this happened, the individual Roman swordsman operating from open formation against a packed body of spearmen could wreak havoc. Finally, the open Roman formation could move more easily over broken terrain than could the massed Germanic wedge, which conferred the advantage of greater tactical mobility. Add to this the ability of Roman field commanders to exercise greater direction over their armies as a whole than could German tribal war chiefs, and it becomes obvious that in a set-piece battle the Roman legions were likely to carry the day.

The German strength lay in the highly disciplined and cohesive nature of its clan combat groups (*kampgruppen*). These groups could move quickly through the forest and swamps and could fall with terrible ferocity upon an enemy not yet deployed for battle. They could break contact and withdraw just as rapidly, for group discipline was central to the clan fighting unit. The Germans were particularly competent in scattered combat, surprise attacks, ambushes, feigned withdrawals, rapid reassembly, and most other aspects of guerrilla war. But it took the insight of a new type of tribal war chief to use these combat qualities in a manner that produced a major battlefield victory against an army that was in almost every way superior to the Germans. Arminius, war chief of the Cherusci, did exactly that.

THE BATTLE OF THE TEUTOBURG FOREST (9 C.E.)

No sooner had Tiberius brought order to the situation in Germany than he was called away to put down the revolt in Pannonia and Illyricum. Command of the army of the Rhine was transferred to Publius Quintilius Varus, the former proconsul of Syria. Varus was a political appointment whose ties to Augustus stemmed from his having married Augustus's grandniece. Varus's instructions were to continue the policy of conciliation with the German tribes. With Rome occupied with putting down the Pannonian revolt, Augustus wanted to avoid having to deal with a similar military situation in Germany. Arminius was a member of the noblest house of the Cherusci, the son of Sigmer the high tribal chief, and a longtime ally of Rome. At the age of twenty-six Arminius was posted to Varus's staff as head of a German troop contingent that accompanied Varus to the summer camp near Minden on the Wesser and remained with him. As a member of the staff and the son of a loyal ally, Arminius could move freely about and observe events. It was from his position inside the Roman commandatura that Arminius plotted the destruction of the Roman armies in Germany.

As autumn 9 C.E. approached, Varus began making preparations to move his army from the Roman summer camp at Minden on the Wesser to more secure winter quarters, either at Haltern on the Lippe River in the Ruhr Basin or at Xanten on the Rhine itself. Although events in Germany had been peaceful since Tiberius departed two years previously, the Roman armies deployed between the Rhine and the Elbe did not yet feel sufficiently safe to winter in their summer forts. In the fall, the armies moved back to safer positions, only to return to their summer positions again the next year. Redeploying the army to the rear required moving not only the troops but large numbers of wives, camp followers, slaves, animals, wagons, and the rest of the effluvia and impedimenta of an army in garrison. Sometime during the preparations for departure, Varus was informed, perhaps by Arminius's scouts, that rebellion had broken out among some of the tribes to the south. Varus would have to deal with the problem by a show of force. Varus apparently did not notice that it might be more than a coincidence that the area of tribal discontent was along the already planned route of march from Minden to Aliso.

The Roman army under Varus's command included the Seventeenth, Eighteenth, and Nineteenth legions along with three *alae* of cavalry. At full strength this force comprised 18,000 infantry and 900 cavalry. In addition to these forces, there were six *cohorts* (3,500 to 4,000) of allied infantry and three squadrons (600) of allied cavalry. Most probably these troops were Arminius's. But some part of Varus's command had been dispersed to other locations. A Roman army of occupation performed a variety of civil affairs functions, such as clearing roads, keeping economic records, conducting censuses, and, very importantly, serving as a local civil police force—conducting criminal investigations, holding hearings, issuing legal judgments, and carrying out sentences. In addition, some of the smaller local garrisons and strong points probably had some troops still with them, and others were probably on long-range patrol or acting as messengers. We have no idea how many soldiers were away from the main body. However many there were, however, they were easy targets for groups of German warriors waiting to attack them at the right time.

Varus began the march to Aliso with perhaps 12,000 to 18,000 combatants in the army. Another 8,000 to 10,000 noncombatants tagged along. A large number of supply and baggage wagons clogged the roads, and since the army was moving through friendly territory along a well-known route accompanied by a German guard of loyal local troops, the army moved in route-step fashion with no special security procedures. Indeed, Dio tells us that the troops were thoroughly mixed with the civilians as the column proceeded. The column stretched for nine miles.

Map 15.3 shows the route of march of Varus's army until the point of ambush at the edge of the Teutoburg Forest. The distance from Rehme/Minden (we are not certain as to the exact location of the Roman camp) to Aliso is thirty-three miles. The distance from Rehme to the Doren ravine is twenty-three miles. The route runs east of the Wesser River valley, whose flood plain and swamps make movement in the valley difficult. Movement overland from Rehme toward the Doren ravine was through deep forests; however, the route taken by Varus followed a well-worn path that was probably the normal route of movement from Aliso to Rehme/Minden. The historical accounts of the road make it clear that it was not an improved Roman road. The Romans had not occupied Germany long enough to build even a military road along this important route. However, the well-used route was probably somewhat improved with drainage ditches, rock fords, causeways, and

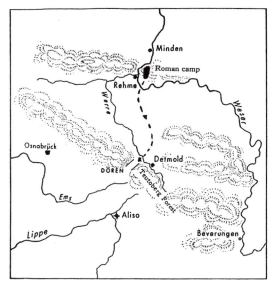

Map 15.3 Roman Route of March to Teutoburg Forest

some bridges at key points. The road ran through a thick wood as it approached the opening to the Doren ravine. The ravine itself was heavily wooded on the edges. The sandy nature of the terrain in the ravine and the swamps that lined the approaches meant that an army passing through it must place itself between a steep wooded hill on one side and the open, marshy ground on the other. It was, in short, a perfect place for an ambush.

As Varus began his march, Segestes (Arminius's uncle and a loyal Roman ally) became aware of Arminius's plot and warned Varus. He urged that Arminius be placed in chains. Varus, thinking this accusation just the result of a standing family quarrel, ignored Segestes's advice. Arminius, for his part, accompanied Varus, and his men escorted the column. Arminius remained with Varus until the evening before the revolt. On the second day out from Rehme, Arminius and his men suddenly disappeared. Shortly thereafter, reports reached Varus that outlying detachments of Roman soldiers (probably the scouts and foragers) had been attacked and slaughtered. Unbeknownst to Varus, Arminius had enlisted the aid of other Germanic tribes in his enterprise, and a number of Roman forts, including Aliso and the main camp at Minden, came under attack.

The line of march had taken Varus through open country. As the second day dawned, the army moved into heavily wooded and uneven terrain cut through by streams and gullies. In summer, movement through this area presented no problem, but during autumn, seasonal rains turned the ground into a quagmire and hindered movement to the few dry pathways presented by the terrain. It had rained the night before, and as the army began to move, the sodden soil made movement difficult and slow. In places trees had to be cut and causeways built to make any headway. As the engineers led the way, the confused column of soldiers, rabble, and baggage vehicles piled up. Despite the strange disappearance of Arminius and his men, Varus had still not ordered his men into field march formation. The column was still without adequate security. Worse, it began to rain, and the forest track turned to mud. Heavy wind accompanied the storm for, as Dio tells us, "the tops of trees kept breaking off and falling down, causing much confusion." Under these conditions, the Roman column must have resembled an inchoate mass of men, wagons, and animals without any order at all.

Suddenly, Arminius struck the Roman army's rearguard. At the same time barbarian troops emerged from the woods on the flanks and unleashed salvo after salvo of javelins into the unformed Roman ranks. Varus looked for his light-armed auxiliary infantry to engage while the legion infantry formed. The auxiliaries, Germans to a man, had deserted and gone over to Arminius. Gradually the legions formed, but not before taking significant casualties. When the van of the Roman column began to form for the attack, the German enemy disappeared as quickly as it had emerged in the initial ambush. Roman engineers found a piece of flat, dry terrain and began to construct a field camp. One by one the Roman units came up in column and reached the security of the camp. Varus pondered what to do next.

Varus ordered his supply wagons burnt and all extraneous supplies abandoned. He was less than twenty miles from Aliso, and his task was to fashion his army in a secure manner, protect the column, and proceed to Aliso. At dawn, the Romans arranged themselves in battle formation, each man armed, rested, and at the ready. With the supplies and civilians in the middle of the column, the Romans marched out of the forest into open territory. In open terrain, the Romans had the advantage and probably hoped to draw Arminius into battle. But Arminius refused to engage in force. Instead, he followed and struck the Romans with skirmishers at every opportunity. German troops hurled their javelins into the Roman ranks with good effect. Roman cavalry could keep the main body of the enemy force away from the column, but without light infantry, Varus could do little to stop the javelin attacks and small ambushes. The Roman army was dying the death of a thousand cuts.

As the Roman column slowly advanced, the trail took it once again into heavy woods where the advantage lay with the Germans. All day Arminius's troops harassed the column with javelin and small-unit attacks. Once the column entered the woods, the German attacks grew bolder, while the ability of the Romans to withstand them diminished. By the end of the day, the Roman army was mortally wounded and had "suffered their heaviest losses." Finally, night came and the army fortified itself within a second field camp to await the dawn.

The Roman column had to move forward or die. As each hour passed, more and more warriors reached Arminius's army. Soon, there would be sufficient numbers to overrun the camp with little difficulty. The Romans could expect no help from any quarter. Every major outpost east of the Rhine had been attacked, and most had been overrun. In Varus's mind, safety lay in reaching Aliso some twenty miles in front of him. There he could expect help from the Roman garrison and eventual transport for his army down to the secure winter quarters on the Rhine. Varus could not know when he formed his plan that Aliso was also under attack and that, although still resisting, the garrison was holding on by its fingertips.

The Roman camp was about a mile from the opening of the Doren ravine (see Map 15.4). Arminius had spent the night felling trees and otherwise making the floor of the ravine, already sodden with mud and crossed by swift-running streams, impassable. There was only one passage for the Roman army,

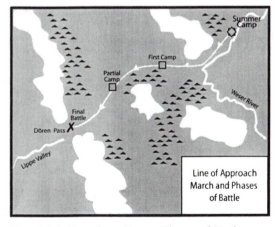

Map 15.4 Teutoburg Forest: Phases of Battle

and that was along a narrow path that placed the column between marshes, bogs, and swamps on one side and a densely wooded hill on the other. The hill was occupied by Arminius's troops. If Varus was to gain passage through the ravine, he would have to fight for every foot.

The Roman advance began sometime in the morning. Roman units pressed up the pathway, meeting heavy resistance. Some of Arminius's units had fought with the Romans in Pannonia and probably were armed with Roman *pila* and *gladius*. These could have been used in close combat. The bulk of the German troops, however, were armed and employed in the traditional manner. Occupying the dune-like hills above the path, the Germans rained down volley after volley of javelins before closing with the Romans again and again. The Romans, however, drove off the attacks, gradually gaining ground. The further they moved into the ravine in search of eventual safety, however, the more the terrain itself seemed to envelop them.

And then it began to rain again. The heavy downpour prevented the Roman soldiers "from going forward and even from standing securely." The hide shields became soaked and so heavy they could not be used. The Romans were now trapped in a sea of mud and rain. They continued to press forward, all of which had been uphill, but with diminished morale and vigor. At some point a Roman *cohort* stopped and began to move backward. Gradually, others followed as the Romans attempted a controlled retrograde maneuver back to the safety of their camp. Fatigue and discouragement ran through the Roman ranks. Arminius then gave the order for a general attack.

The German *baritus* or war cry echoed among the hills and glens as thousands of warriors poured down from the hillside and engaged the floundering Romans at several points along the column. Arminius, surrounded by his personal retinue of warriors, struck at the Roman cavalry, wounding their horses. The wounded animals, slipping about in the mire and their own blood, threw their riders and plunged among the ranks of the legions, creating havoc. Varus ordered a retreat to the base camp. But this only made matters worse, and the Roman retreat, which had begun in good order, now turned into a rout as the lead units of the column ran into those in the rear who still retained some order.

It was at this point in the general confusion that Numonius Vala, the Roman officer in charge of the cavalry, ordered his squadrons to

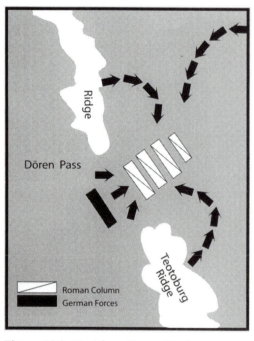

Figure 15.2 Teutoburg Forest: Final Engagement

disengage and rode away, abandoning his comrades to their fate. The rain and the nature of the terrain made it difficult for the cavalry units to remain together as they searched for an escape route. The squadrons broke up into smaller units, each seeking its own way. The German cavalry overpowered each of these units in detail. The Roman cavalry was slaughtered to the last man.

The German onslaught had taken its toll on the senior Roman officers. Varus was severely wounded and committed suicide rather than fall into the hands of the Germans, who had a reputation for human sacrifice and torture. A number of other senior officers perished bravely, while some others committed suicide. Yet, the bulk of the infantry under command of the centurions fought on steadily and stubbornly, repelling attack after attack. But as each Roman soldier fell, the small units that resisted grew weaker. Eventually, the Germans cut the column in several places, isolated the pockets of defenders, and overcame each one piecemeal. One small troop of soldiers fought on throughout the day, beating off attack after attack. The next morning they were overwhelmed by the Germans and massacred on the spot. As for the rest of the army, the Germans slaughtered their enemies with deliberate ferocity. As Vegetius notes, the Romans were "exterminated almost to a man by the very enemy whom it had always slaughtered like cattle."

Only the camp garrison still remained to be subdued. The camp prefect, Ceionius, eventually surrendered, and Arminius's victory was complete. Varus's servants had attempted to burn their master's body and hide it from the Germans. Arminius had the body dug up and the head of Varus severed from its body. The head was then sent to Marroboduus, king of the Marcomanni, who was having his own troubles with Rome. Marroboduus wisely refused to accept it and sent it on to Rome. Arminius had the heads of some of his fallen enemies impaled on spears and placed around the Roman camp. Those Romans who were captured or surrendered were crucified, buried alive, or offered as sacrifices to the Germanic gods, since the tribes practiced human sacrifice in their sacred groves.

A few years later when Germanicus led a Roman army into the area to avenge the defeat, Tacitus recalls what Germanicus found on the site of the old battlefield. "On the open ground were whitening bones, scattered where men had fled, heaped up where they had stood and fought back. Fragments of spears and of horses' limbs lay there—also human heads, fastened to tree trunks. In groves nearby were the outlandish altars at which the Germans had massacred the Roman colonels and senior company-commanders." Three Roman legions and almost 10,000 noncombatants died at the hands of an obscure Germanic chieftain who, although he did not know it, changed history.

The death of a Roman army far away in the dark forests of Germany sent shockwaves through Rome. Augustus had always feared that an uprising in Germany would spread to Gaul and, as it had a century before, result in an attack upon Italy itself. As events turned out, every Roman garrison east of the Rhine, save that of Aliso, which, after a tenacious defense, had slipped past the Germans and gained safety, fell to the Germans. Yet, many Germanic tribes remained loyal to Rome or simply chose not to exploit the situation. Within months it was evident that Arminius's revolt was not a general uprising of the Germans and that there was no threat to Gaul or Italy.

Augustus, nonetheless, could not know this immediately and reacted with alarm as he attempted to raise new legions for use on the German frontier. Military operations in Pannonia had taken a significant toll, and Augustus had great difficulty raising new manpower. Even draconian measures failed to produce the needed manpower, and in the end, companies of slaves were raised for military service. A year later Tiberius led a Roman army into Germany. This time Arminius did not engage. And so it went, on and off, for a decade. Roman armies, next under Germanicus, ravaged the area between the Rhine and the Elbe and chased Arminius and other rebel chieftains over the countryside. But Rome had lost her stomach for a military occupation of Germany, and with the succession of Augustus by Tiberius, Rome put off the occupation of Germany for at least a generation and then, as it turned out, forever.

Confronted with rebellion in Germany, there was little Rome could do. The occupation of Germany between the Rhine and Elbe had always been a tenuous thing. One thing after another interfered with Rome's ability to establish a genuine military, political, and economic presence in the area. Roman arms were never sufficient to keep order, and the process of road building and Romanization had barely begun when Arminius brought it to a halt. More importantly, Tiberius was the only member of the Roman leadership who remembered that the occupation of Germany had begun as a marginal venture to begin with. Its loss to a handful of Germanic tribes hardly constituted a strategic threat to Rome. The Elbe was no more defensible than the Rhine. The Augustan period had been one of remarkable expansion, pacification, and consolidation of Roman power in the West. Tiberius was sufficiently intelligent to recognize the propensity of a marginal state interest to transform itself into one perceived as a vital interest. This was the case with Germany, and with the reign of Tiberius, Roman power never again ventured east of the Rhine. Germany had begun as a marginal Roman interest. And so it would remain.

THE COMMANDERS

Publius Quintilius Varus (?–9 C.E.), the Roman governor of Germany and commander of the Roman army at the battle of the Teutoburg Forest, was the scion of a well-regarded Roman family, although not of the old nobility of Rome. He married the great niece of Emperor Augustus and was assigned as governor of Syria where, Florus tells us, he enriched himself considerably. From there he served as the emperor's consul in Pannonia before being assigned as consul to Germany. He had little experience as a soldier, and none in higher-level command, and apparently held his posts as a consequence of his strong loyalty to Augustus more than from any record of demonstrated military competence. Dio Cassius says of Varus that "he was a man of mild character and quiet disposition, somewhat slow in mind as he was in body, and more accustomed to the leisure of the camp than to actual service in war." He was, accordingly, more a lawyer and bureaucrat than anything else and probably quite unfit to military and political command in Germany, which, unlike Syria and Pannonia, was not yet subdued by Roman arms.

His character and experience led him to rely too heavily upon personalities and diplomacy, and he scattered his legions all over Germany trying to accommodate the demands of local chiefs for civic order. Even when he was warned that Arminius and Segimer (another rebellious chief) were planning a revolt, he refused to believe it because he personally knew both men and had frequent meetings with them. As a consequence, history has blamed Varus for the disaster that befell the Roman army in the Teutoburg Forest. That he failed to understand the German temperament is clear, but some blame must be assumed for the Roman failure by Augustus himself, who appointed such an unfit person to a position of high command.

As Arminius's troops closed in on the remnants of the Roman army, Varus committed suicide rather than be taken alive. His officers buried his body to keep it out of the hands of the Germans. The Germans found the grave, however, and disinterred Varus's corpse. Arminius ordered the head cut off and sent it to Marroboduus, another German tribal chieftain, urging him to join Arminius in his revolt against the Romans.

Arminius (15 B.C.E.–21 C.E.) was a member of the noblest house of the Cherusci, the son of Sigmer, the high tribal chief. Arminius had served as commander of a tribal troop contingent under Roman command during the revolt in Pannonia. He held Roman citizenship, spoke Latin, may have visited some Roman cities, and held equestrian rank. Arminius's brother also served in the Roman army as an officer, took a Latin name (Flavius), was given knightly rank, and remained loyal to Rome even when his brother was in open revolt. In personality, Tacitus says Arminius was headstrong ("a frantic spirit") and was given to rash action when angered ("the incendiary of Germany"). Fuller says Arminius was possessed of an inbred hatred of the Romans (as, supposedly, was Hannibal), but there is no evidence to support this assertion.

History offers no clue why after years of service to his own people and to Rome Arminius would suddenly lead a revolt against his former employers. It might simply have been that Arminius was a headstrong, angry young man who felt his time had come to do something great. Great deeds were the stuff of Germanic legend and high social status. An affair of the heart may also have had something to do with it. Arminius wanted to marry Thusnelda, the daughter of his uncle, Segestes. Segestes refused, creating bad blood between the two men. Segestes was a loyal ally of Rome and served as an advisor to Varus. On several occasions Segestes denounced Arminius to Varus as being of questionable loyalty, but the suspicions were dismissed by Varus as mere family squabbling.

Segestes's opposition aside, Arminius and Thesnelda eloped, but after the clash with the Romans, Thesnelda returned to her father's camp. After the battle in the Teutoburg Forest, Augustus sent Germanicus to Germany to deal with the revolt. Segestes, always the Roman ally, turned his daughter and her son, Arminius's child, over to the Romans who deported them to Rome. This removed any chance of a peaceful settlement with Arminius, who fought a series of indecisive engagements with Germanicus. By 19 C.E., Germany was in full revolt and the Romans withdrew, abandoning forever their plans for Germany's incorporation into the empire. For more than a century, civil war among rival chieftains consumed Germany. In one of these tribal battles in 21 C.E., Arminius was killed.

LESSONS OF WAR

Strategy

1. Great powers must be mindful of the need to redefine and readjust security arrangements in light of a changed security environment. No nation can achieve all its goals nor maintain the means necessary to attempt to do so. Augustus's major readjustment of the Roman security frontier in the Mediterranean after the civil war is an excellent example of a successful strategic readjustment.

2. The triumph of a superpower over its enemies brings in its wake a period of prolonged peace. Peace reduces the perceived need to sustain military forces at high levels since direct challenges to the victor's new status seem unlikely. Under conditions of reduced military preparedness, a nation must seek other means to protect itself. Diplomacy and intelligence are indispensable in times of peace as the primary means of preventing war. Roman strategy under Augustus relied primarily upon diplomacy and intelligence to keep the empire secure.

3. Strategic goals are ultimately dependent upon the means to achieve them. Beware the tendency of means to define and drive strategic goals. The Roman expansion beyond the Rhine was driven by the need to secure the Roman land route through Bavaria. The conquest of Germany, however, quickly became a goal in its own right.

4. Political considerations guide all aspects of strategy, including military aspects. Under Augustus, the primacy of political and economic concerns forced the decrease and complete restructuring of the army in almost every detail. There is nothing new in this!

5. Strategic means must be adequate to established strategic goals if a policy is to have any chance of success. Roman strategy in Germany never mustered sufficient means to achieve its goals. In designing strategy, always

ask if the means to be utilized are sufficient to achieve the end. President Kennedy failed in this regard in his handling of the Bay of Pigs crisis.

6. Beware the tendency of what began as a marginal national interest to transform itself into a vital national interest to appease powerful domestic interest groups or rescue a disaster in the field. Never allow "the presence of troops on the ground to become the policy," and know when to cut your losses. Remember Tiberius. After the defeat of Teutoburg Forest, he refused to redefine Germany as anything more than the marginal interest it had always been.

7. Any force structure must have sufficient manpower and equipment to deal with unforeseen reverses. There is always a need for a strategic reserve. Augustus forgot this, and when the Roman army lost three legions, even the most draconian measures could not replace them in sufficient time. If a military force structure cannot meet the requirements expected of it, then it becomes a hollow army.

8. Forward deployments of strategic ground forces are only useful as long as the lines of communication upon which they depend are secure. The Roman position in Gaul could not be fully exploited unless the passes over the Alps were controlled. The forward deployment of Varus's army over insecure lines of communication turned a force of influence into a hostage, with disastrous results.

9. In designing or pursuing a strategic plan, be ever aware of the tendency for events to throw things into disarray. Roman strategy toward Marroboduus was totally derailed by the unforeseen events in Illyricum. In strategic planning and execution, Murphy is alive and well. Things will always go wrong!

10. Understand and use the psychological dimension of war and policy. The Roman occupation of Germany failed to win the "hearts and minds" of the populace. Roman intelligence services never identified those German leaders who had to be neutralized.

Tactics

1. A good commander uses his intelligence assets to the fullest extent possible. Varus lost the battle before he left camp when he failed to fully explore the reports that Arminius was not trustworthy. Establish a working trustful relationship with your intelligence officers. This can prevent embarrassment.

2. Alliances are based upon mutualities of self-interest. When those mutualities begin to diverge, as they did between Rome and Arminius, no amount of past honor or praise will prevent an ally from pursuing his national self-interest. Allies are allies; they are not friends. A policymaker or field commander who attributes to nations or peoples the characteristics of individuals is likely to be disappointed.

3. Utilize the principle of mass. Although Varus outnumbered his German attackers, his choice of battle formations and the terrain prevented him from bringing the superiority of numbers to bear in the battle.

4. Get flexible! Varus killed his army because he never adjusted to warfare in an unconventional environment. Varus's continued use of standard Roman battle formations in an environment of repeated ambush bled his army to death. Find ways to adjust to unconventional tactics and terrain.

5. Always practice proper field security, especially when on the march. More armies have been annihilated throughout history by being taken by surprise while in column of march than one can count. As long as your command is standing on or moving through someone else's country, there is no such thing as "friendly territory." Always use security when in the field.

6. Use the weather and terrain to maximum advantage. Arminius used both perfectly with predictable results.

7. Whenever possible follow Arminius's example and inflict surprise. Force the enemy to react to your initiatives on as short a notice as possible.

8. As the battle progresses, do not allow your opponent to draw you into a new engagement at a time or place that squanders the advantages your actions have already achieved. Varus attempted to redress the balance in the battle by drawing Arminius into a set-piece battle after ambush tactics had taken a heavy toll. Arminius refused to alter his plan of battle, for to do so would have given away his tactical advantage.

9. Exploit the psychological effects of a tactical victory. Arminius's killing of the Roman enemy to the last man and nailing their skulls to trees was designed to send a psychological message to Rome that the cost of conquest was very high. It worked.

FURTHER READING

"Battle of the Teutoburg Forest." *Archaeology* (September–October 1992): 26–32.

Burns, Thomas S. *Rome and the Barbarians: 100 BC–AD 400.* Baltimore: Johns Hopkins Press, 2003.

Cambridge Ancient History. Vols. 9–10, *The Augustan Empire, 44 B.C.E.–70 C.E.* Cambridge, UK: Cambridge University Press, 1954.

Creasy, Edward Shepard. *Fifteen Decisive Battles of the World.* New York: Dorsett, 1987.

Delbruck, Hans. *History of the Art of War—The Barbarian Invasions.* Westport, CT: Greenwood Press, 1980.

Dio. *Roman History,* Books 18–25. London: Penguin, 1978.

Dupuy, R. Ernest, and T. N. Dupuy. *The Encyclopedia of Military History.* New York: Harper Rowe, 1986.

Fuller, J. F. C. *Military History of the Western World—From the Earliest Times to the Battle of Lepanto.* Vol. 1. New York: Da Capo, 1990.

Gabriel, Richard A. *The Culture of War.* Westport, CT: Greenwood Press, 1990.

Gabriel, Richard A., and Karen S. Metz. *From Sumer to Rome: The Military Capabilities of Ancient Armies.* Westport, CT: Greenwood Press, 1991.

————. *A Short History of War.* Carlisle, PA: Strategic Studies Institute, 1992.

Grant, Michael. *The Army of the Caesars.* New York: Barnes and Noble, 1997.

————. *History of Rome.* New York: Charles Scribner, 1978.

Green, Miranda. *The Celtic World.* New York: Routledge, 1996.

Rankin, David. *Celts and the Classical World.* New York: Routledge, 1996.

Shuckburgh, E. S. *Augustus Caesar.* New York: Barnes and Noble, 1995.

Suetonius, Gaius Tranquillus. *The Twelve Caesars.* New York: Penguin Books, 1957.

Tacitus. *The Annals.* London: Penguin, 1963

————. *Germania.* London: Penguin, 1968.

————. *The Histories.* London: Penguin, 1961.

Wolfram, Herwig. *History of the Goths.* Berkeley: University of California Press, 1990.

16 IMPERIAL ROME

[9–450 C.E.]

BACKGROUND

Adrianople may well be the most fought-over city in the world. The British historian John Keegan has identified no fewer than fifteen battles and sieges that have involved the city of Adrianople, the first of which occurred in 323 C.E. and the last in July 1913. The reason Adrianople seems to have attracted armies throughout history is its peculiar geographical location. The city stands at the confluence of three rivers, whose valleys provide avenues of advance through the mountains of Macedonia to the west, Bulgaria to the northwest, and the Black Sea coast to the north. These rivers flow through the most extensive plain in the southeastern tip of Europe.

Constantinople sits at the other end of this plain. Adrianople is the strategically twin city of Constantinople, and both guard and control the movement of armies between the Black Sea and the Mediterranean and between southern Europe and Asia Minor. The nature of the fortifications of Constantinople enhanced the strategic value of Adrianople. With Constantinople's face to the sea, combatants attempting to attack Constantinople were forced to land and maneuver on the plain that faced the landward side of the city. Invaders from Asia Minor had to attack Constantinople from this direction, as did those who originated on the great plain to the north of the Black Sea. Invaders from Europe proper had no choice but to cross this same plain. Adrianople sits on the edge of a geographic land bridge that controls the major land approaches to Constantinople, one of the richest and most sought-after prizes of the ancient world.

The battle of Adrianople is often cited as a watershed in the history of Western warfare, as the point where the traditional dominance of infantry gave way to the triumph of cavalry. Yet, even after Adrianople, one can point

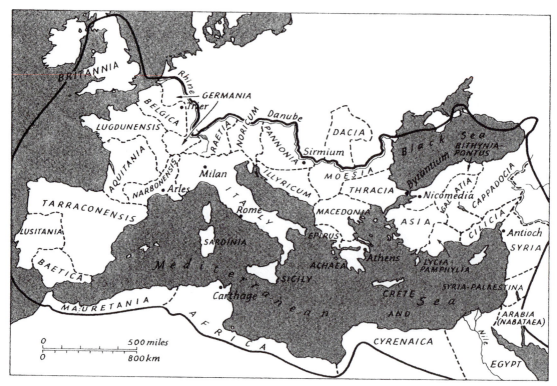

Map 16.1 The Roman Empire at Its Height (Second Century C.E.). Adapted from Arther Ferrill, *The Fall of the Roman Empire* (New York: Thames and Hudson, 1986). Reprinted with permission.

to several examples of battles in which infantry was decisive over cavalry. If we attempt to understand Adrianople as only a victory of one military technique over another, then we will have missed the point. What occurred at Adrianople was nothing less than the initial victory of *one type of social order over another.* There was nothing in the *military* events of the battle of Adrianople that were definitive in shaping the future forms of combat in the West. Rather, it was what happened to the Roman *social* order as a consequence of the defeat of Roman arms at Adrianople that determined the relative military development of cavalry and infantry over the next 500 years.

It is axiomatic that the military establishment of a society is a reflection of that society, insofar as the degree of military sophistication depends heavily upon the degree of political, social, and economic development and articulation evident in the larger social order. The defeat of Roman arms at Adrianople set in motion powerful forces that gradually led to supplanting the Roman social order by a less-developed, less-organized, and less organizationally articulated tribal social order. As the more complex Roman society gradually died, it was replaced by a form of societal organization that could not sustain any form of military organization and warfare more sophisticated than the clash of tribal armies led by coteries of warriors and nobles. As the social and military importance of tribal leaders increased, their style of warfare—mounted cavalry combat—also grew in importance. The inability of the empire to recruit and train sufficient numbers of infantry conceded the contest between rival forms of warfare to the barbarian style. Over time, the social and political triumph of warrior chieftains supported by coteries of armed nobility led to a form of warfare that prepared the way for the Medieval period in which this form of combat predominated. The battle of Adrianople may indeed have been a watershed in military history, but it was so more for sociological than for military reasons.

Strategy

The strategic threats confronting Rome in the fourth century were aimed at three geographic sectors along the imperial borders (Map 16.2). The most troublesome area, and the most unstable, was the border between Gaul and Germany formed by the Rhine. The second area of strategic concern was the province of Mesopotamia, wherein Roman power directly faced the emergent expansionist power of Persia, heir to the defunct Parthian empire. The third strategic threat was centered on the middle Danubian basin. The adversaries along the Rhine and Danubian frontiers were the armies of the emerging tribal confederations, which, more and more, found common cause to form temporary alliances against the Romans. Persian military power, on the

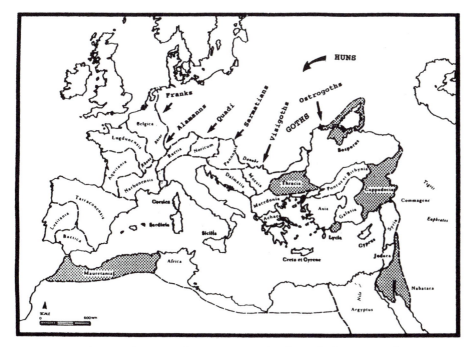

Map 16.2 Barbarian Threats to the Roman Empire (Fourth Century C.E.)

other hand, was rooted in a more traditional army of greater complexity than the tribal armies of the Rhine and Danubian tribes. In all three arenas of conflict, Rome faced grave problems. Defeat on the Rhine frontier threatened Gaul and even Italy itself. An enemy victory on the Danubian frontier could cut the empire in two, while a Persian victory ultimately meant Roman expulsion from Armenia and Syria and, eventually, from the eastern Mediterranean coast.

Constantine's accession to the imperial throne in 306 C.E. began with a flurry of military activity to regain and solidify the Rhine frontier. In two major campaigns the Roman emperor defeated the Franks and a larger Germanic tribal confederation, and even established a Roman military foothold on the east bank of the Rhine. Constantine rebuilt the frontier fortresses, established a naval flotilla on the Rhine, and increased the number of troops in that strategic sector. The coastal defenses of Gaul and Britain were also rebuilt, and a special military command was established for Britain. When Constantine left Gaul for the last time in 316 C.E., the Rhine frontiers were peaceful and militarily secure.

The civil war of 350–353 C.E. emboldened the Germans to cross the Rhine again. When Roman units were redeployed from the frontier to take part in the internal squabbles, the Germans overran the west bank of the Rhine, destroyed the defensive fortifications, and killed or captured most of the garrisons. In 354 C.E., and again in 355 C.E., Constantine's son and would-be successor, Constantius, tried with mixed success to suppress the German onslaught. It was Constantius's scholarly cousin, Julian, who in 356 C.E. drove back the Germanic invaders, winning back a great number of towns, including Cologne, which had been taken by the Franks. In 357 C.E., at the battle of Argentoratum (Strassburg), Julian defeated a coalition of seven Germanic kings. Between 358 C.E. and 361 C.E. Julian conducted more pacification operations across the Rhine and down the lower Rhine. By 361 the Rhine frontier and Gaul were again pacified and under firm Roman military control.

From 361 to 365 C.E. Rome engaged in yet another civil war over secession to the throne, with the predictable result that the Germans again crossed the Rhine and ravaged parts of Gaul. In 365 C.E. the new emperor, Valentinian, took command of an army near Paris and, in January 366 C.E., defeated the Alemanni near Chalons-sur-Mons. In 368 C.E. Valentinian led his army in a punitive expedition across the Rhine at Sulz and defeated the Germans again. Follow-on expeditions were conducted in 371 and 374 C.E. Valentinian rebuilt the frontier fortresses and added castles and watchtowers. His son and successor, Gratian, further strengthened the frontier in the West and, in the spring of 378 C.E., crossed the Rhine in force and again defeated the Alemans near Argentaria (Horburg near Comar). Paradoxically, on the eve of the battle of Adrianople in the East, Roman power in the West was stronger and more militarily secure than it had been in a century.

While Julian was suppressing the Germans in the West, the Persian emperor renewed his war with Rome in 358 C.E. by invading southern Armenia. Conflicts between the Sassanid empire and Rome over Mesopotamia had waxed and waned for almost a century, with Persia always taking advantage of Roman preoccupation with the problems on its Rhine and Danubian frontiers. Rome was paralyzed once more as Julian and Constantius struggled for control of the imperial throne. In 363 C.E. Julian invaded Persia from Constantinople with an army of 95,000 men, purportedly the largest expeditionary force Rome had ever assembled in the East. Julian detached a force of 30,000 men to march northward into Armenia, where he expected it would be joined by 24,000 troops promised by the king of Armenia. After joining forces, the combined army was to move down the east bank of the Tigris and march on Ctesiphon, the Persian capital. Julian, with 1,100 river supply ships and 50 armed galleys, marched down the east bank of the Euphrates hoping to join forces with his other army outside of Ctesiphon. Unfortunately, the Armenian king did not cooperate, and Julian's second army did not arrive in time. Nonetheless, Julian defeated the Persians in a battle before the walls of the city. As the Persian emperor fled into the interior of Persia, Julian gave chase.

Julian destroyed his fleet, lightened his baggage train, and marched east. The Persians conducted a "scorched earth" policy in front of him, however, and Julian soon ran low on supplies. Realizing the danger, Julian attempted to break contact with the enemy and withdraw up the Tigris to Armenia. As soon as the Romans changed direction, the Persian army fell on their columns with swarms of horse-archers and light cavalry. Julian was killed during a night attack on his camp, and the army elected a general, Flavius Claudius Jovian, as his successor. Jovian was in a desperate situation and elected to save his army by agreeing to Persian terms that were disastrous for Roman security policy in the East. Rome gave up all territory east of the Tigris along with a number of key fortified border towns that constituted the Roman defense in depth. All of the fortified towns in Mesopotamia were relinquished, and Rome relinquished any claims to suzerainty in Armenia and the other Caucasian regions. In return, Jovian was allowed to lead the remnants of a starving army to Antioch. The Roman security situation on the eastern frontier was suddenly altered to Rome's serious disadvantage. But before Rome could deal with the problem, disaster struck in Britain, where Saxon sea rovers and Pict and Scot uprisings had to be dealt with by military force. Closer to Constantinople, the Danubian frontier was beginning to heat up after almost a hundred years of relative peace.

In 368 C.E., the army chose Valentinian to replace Jovian as emperor. Valentinian immediately appointed his brother, Valens, as co-emperor in the East. While Valentinian busied himself with suppressing the German revolts on the Rhine, Valens turned his attention to the Danubian frontier and the problems with Persia. Since Claudius had defeated and established a peace with the Goths in 269 C.E., relations between Romans and Goths along the

Danubian frontier had been relatively peaceful for almost a century. The Goths had been converted to Christianity (German Arianism), and the West Goths (Visigoths) especially had established the semblance of a stable semi-agricultural society. Military relations between the Romans and Goths had been formalized by Claudius, who forced the Goths to pledge their status as *foederati* in return for the payment of annual subsidies (*annonae foederaticae*).

Soon after Valentinian rose to the purple, relations with the Goths along the Danubian frontier began to change. In 364 C.E. predatory bands of Goths ravaged Thrace and, almost simultaneously, there was a major incursion into Pannonia by the Quadi and the Sarmatians. In 366 C.E., a usurper attempted to seize power in Constantinople. Valens defeated the rebel army and executed Procopius, the usurper. Valens used the fact that some Gothic mercenaries had supported Procopius as an excuse to cross the Danube at the head of a Roman army and preempt any Gothic invasion by striking deep within the Gothic homeland. For two years the Romans chased the Goths in a series of indecisive skirmishes and minor battles. The war ended with a peace treaty in which the Goths renounced their status as *foederati* and both parties recognized the Danube as the boundary between the Roman and Gothic nations.

The Romans rebuilt and strengthened the border defenses along the Danube, and the peace held for a few years. With the border quiet, Valens turned his attention to the Persian threat in Armenia. Rome attempted to undermine Persian control of Armenia by creating an Armenian government and army in exile. In 373 C.E., combined Roman and rebel forces attacked Persian forces in southern Armenia. Although initially successful, it soon became apparent to the Romans that there was no military solution to the problem. After almost four years of political intrigue and indecisive guerrilla war, both sides agreed to a treaty preserving the status quo in Armenia. Valens needed to extricate himself from Armenia to deal again with the Gothic threat emerging in the Danube basin. In 374 C.E. the Quadi and Sarmatians mounted another major invasion of the border serious enough to require that Valentinian march with his army from Gaul to defeat the invaders and throw them back over the Danube. Eventually, in 390, Rome and Persia concluded a pact in which Armenia was formally partitioned between Rome and Persia, in effect making Armenia the strategic security zone between the two powers.

The central Roman security problem was how to protect the empire from a plethora of enemies lurking beyond the frontier sectors of the Rhine, the Danube, and the Mesopotamian-Armenian border zone. There were so many potential invaders, especially in the "tribal zones" across the Rhine and Danube rivers, that no truly effective military defense at a reasonable cost was really possible. Time after time Rome absorbed the invasions, contained them, threw the invaders back, and reestablished the imperial frontiers. And time after time the invaders waited a few years and again crossed the frontiers.

Roman diplomacy tried to keep the tribal societies at each other's throats to prevent the formation of political confederacies and military alliances, generally with good success. In one sense, however, Rome was its own worst enemy in failing to develop a political system that permitted the peaceful transfer of executive power from one emperor to the next. Frequently, the death of an emperor brought about a violent struggle for power in which the frontier legions were diverted from their military mission to support one pretender or another. Under these conditions, it was only a matter of time before a confederation of tribal or foreign armies dealt the Roman army a sufficiently severe blow to disrupt the fragile fabric of political control and authority and tear it beyond repair. That is essentially what happened to the Roman imperial army at the battle of Adrianople.

THE ROMAN IMPERIAL ARMY

The Roman army that fought and died at the battle of Adrianople in the summer of 378 C.E. was a far different army than the army that had been annihilated by Arminius in the Teutoburg Forest three centuries earlier. Although it has become commonplace to lay the onus of the collapse of Roman society at the foot of military defeat, in fact the armies of the empire succeeded quite well in keeping it secure for more than three centuries. Even after the disaster at Adrianople, the Roman imperium functioned for at least another century. After that, the Greek version of the imperium—the Byzantine Empire—survived for another thousand years until finally destroyed at the hands of the Ottoman Turks in 1453 C.E. As records of military success go, the overall history of the legions of Rome has yet to be equaled by any other military establishment in the world.

Figure 16.1 Roman Legionnaire (Second Century C.E.)

The military strategy initiated by Augustus and followed by his successors for more than a century was premised on the ability of the legions of Rome to prevent, preempt, and, if need be, defeat the empire's enemies before they could penetrate the frontiers and run rampant in the interior of the empire. It was the primary goal of Roman diplomacy to prevent a situation where the legions had to fight on two fronts at once. All had to be accomplished with a military establishment that did not exceed twenty-five legions, or approximately 300,000 men, and a similar number of auxiliary troops raised from the provinces and Rome's allies. In short, the military strategy was cost-effective. The spine of the Roman military machine was its infantry legions posted along the rim of the empire in permanent camps, ever ready to pounce on any enemy who ventured too close. The legions could be launched on preemptive and punitive expeditions when required by events.

By the time of Trajan (98–117 C.E.), Roman military policy had succeeded for more than a century in keeping the borders secure. Indeed, the empire had gradually expanded to the point where tight military control was becoming a problem. The sheer length of the imperial borders forced Trajan into conducting one preemptive and spoiling raid after another to ensure the security of the frontiers. His adopted son, Hadrian (117–138 C.E.), adjusted the empire's borders to coincide with extant military capabilities. The legions were positioned along natural barriers. In Germany, the lines of defense ran along the Rhine and, further east, along the Danube. The area between the upper Rhine and upper Danube was fortified by constructing a ten-foot-high, 200-mile-long wooden palisade complete with guard towers and forts along which the legions were deployed. Thus, in those places where natural defenses were insufficient or nonexistent, Hadrian constructed them, as he did in middle England where he built "Hadrian's Wall." The legions remained the bulwark of the empire and were expected to take the brunt of any attack across the borders. Behind the border posts Hadrian constructed a connecting network of military roads that allowed the legions to move rapidly along the border to reinforce any outpost under assault. As under Augustus, there was no central strategic reserve. The 5,000-man Praetorian Guard stationed in Rome could have acted as such, but it never did. As long as Rome was not required to fight on two fronts at once, as long as the legions remained of high fighting quality, and as long as the prestige of the Roman army remained sufficiently high to give pause to any tribal enemy that might contemplate an attack, Roman strategy worked well.

Manpower

The army of Hadrian's time comprised about 157,000 Roman legionnaires organized into some twenty legions and augmented by 227,000 auxiliary troops, the *auxillia* that had first been introduced by Augustus. By the middle of the second century C.E., there were 257 *cohorts* of auxiliary troops, of which 130 were mixed *cohorts*. This type of unit was comprised of infantry supported by a small cavalry squadron, and it was first used by Caesar at Alesia and Pharsalus. Caesar probably adopted it from the Gauls. This mixed *cohort* had approximately a four-to-one ratio of infantry to cavalry, with the cavalry comprising 120 horse. In addition, there were forty milliary (units of a thousand strong) units, of which twenty-two were mixed. This new type of unit was first introduced by the Flavians in the East. There were eighty-two ordinary cavalry regiments and eight milliary cavalry regiments. The total Roman army of this period was approximately 384,000 men, of which 71,000 were mounted.

Equipment

As the mix and type of military units gradually changed during this period so, too, did the equipment. The Roman helmet was now made in arms factories

Lorica Segmenta
First Century A.D.

Roman Cavalry Chain Mail
Adrianople, 378 A.D.

Roman Port Helmet
3rd Century

Roman Cavalry Helmet
1st Century

Intercisa Helmet
378 A.D.

Figure 16.2 Roman Military Equipment. Courtesy of J. Dunn.

in Gaul to take advantage of Celtic skill in iron making. A new helmet, called the Port type, originating in the Alpine area, was introduced. Its most distinguishing feature was its extended neck guard that gave substantially better protection down to the shoulders. Body armor also underwent radical changes. The chain mail that the legionnaire had worn for more than two centuries gave way to a new type of body armor, the *lorica segmentata*. This, too, was a Celtic innovation and consisted of connected steel bands held around the body by straps and hooks. The new armor weighed only twenty pounds compared to more than thirty pounds for chain mail (Figure 16.2).

The traditional oval Roman *scutum* shield, which had been in use for more than four centuries, was replaced by a shorter rectangular shield of the same name. Constructed like half a cylinder with straight sides, the new shield was made of laminated wood and covered with leather. Unlike the old shield, the new model was reinforced around the edges with metal—probably first introduced during the Gallic wars to counter the Gallic sword—and was reinforced with an iron boss and a protected hand grip. The shield weighed about twelve pounds. The straight sides of the shield probably allowed a tighter interlocking of shields with less exposed space between each shield, a considerable advantage when facing either infantry or cavalry whose primary weapon was the stabbing spear.

The traditional *pilum* remained but went through several design changes, sometimes becoming heavier and then lighter. One heavier model had a plumb weight at the base of the striking point to give it greater force in penetrating the enemy shield. The traditional function of the *pilum* was to disable the enemy's shield. As the Roman legions came to face cavalry and spear-carrying infantry more often, the *pilum* gradually gave way to the spear, a more effective instrument against both types of adversaries.

The Roman sword underwent changes that made it shorter and straighter in design. The *gladius* remained essentially the same weapon, but the nature and armament of the adversary was changing, which, in turn, forced a change in infantry tactics. More and more often the legions fought in closed lines rather than in the open formations of the past. Gradually, the *gladius* gave way to the barbarian sword, the *spatha*. Derived from the Celtic long sword, the weapon had a blade of sixty to seventy centimeters in length and functioned as a cutting, not a stabbing, weapon. Its introduction to the legions was a response to changing tactics. It was also a function of the fact that more and more barbarian infantry was being used in the legions, infantry whose native weapon was the *spatha*. Training the soldier to use a cutting weapon required less time, and the soldier needed less skill than was formerly the case with the *gladius.*

Figure 16.3 Roman Cavalryman, Battle of Adrianople

Roman cavalry underwent significant changes during the second century C.E. Although armored cavalry had been around for years in the Roman army, the emphasis on infantry had always relegated cavalry to a secondary role (Figure 16.3). It was during Hadrian's time that this situation began to change. The arrival of the Roxolani along the Danube introduced the Romans to a new type of cavalry first developed in the East. These *cataphracti* were heavy cavalry where both the horse and cavalryman were armored and the cavalryman carried the lance, the *contus*. Hadrian was the first Roman emperor to introduce units of *cataphracti* into the Roman army. The introduction of these new units, however, did not change the traditional Roman emphasis on infantry. Most cavalry still consisted of hired foreigners—such as the light Numidian horse that used the bow rather than the lance and wore no armor at all—and the role of cavalry in Roman tactics was essentially unchanged.

Traditional Roman cavalry rode small horses (almost ponies, averaging fourteen hands high) that wore no armor. The cavalryman himself wore chain mail armor, a helmet that covered the whole head except for the eyes and nose, and carried the long Celtic *spatha* as his main weapon. The standard cavalry shield was a flat oval or sometimes hexagonal-shaped device. The saddle appeared among Roman cavalry for the first time in the late first century, as well as, Connolly suggests, the horseshoe, another Celtic innovation in warfare. There is no evidence of the use of the stirrup by the Romans. The armament of the Roman cavalry during this period clearly reflected its limited tactical role in support of infantry. Roman cavalry reflected the earlier Greek pattern of cavalry employment in conjunction with the infantry phalanx.

By the middle of the third century, Roman military equipment underwent further significant changes, mostly as a result of the changing nature of the army and the kinds of enemies with which it had to deal. In general, Roman military equipment became more like that of the barbarian armies the Romans fought (Figure 16.4). By the time of the battle of Adrianople, the *gladius* had disappeared from the kit of the Roman infantryman and was replaced by the barbarian *spatha*. As Roman infantry was expected more and more to act as a phalangeal barrier to barbarian cavalry charges, the thrown *pilum* gradually gave way to the stabbing spear, a weapon much more suited for use in a wall of pikes. The straight-sided, cylindrical *scutum*, a shield designed to repel infantry attack, was replaced with the light oval shield characteristic of barbarian cavalry. The oval shield

Figure 16.4 Roman Legionnaire (First and Fourth Centuries C.E.)

permitted the soldier more striking area with his spear. As Roman infantry increasingly became light infantry valued for its mobility, body armor fell into disuse, so that by the time of Adrianople most Roman legionnaires went into battle with little or no body armor. The characteristic Roman helmet finally gave way to the lighter, cheaper, barbarian helmet known as the Intercisa type, and even the military belt, the very symbol of the legionnaire, was discarded in favor of a single broad belt with a leather baldric for holding the sword.

Despite the gradual changes in weaponry, unit structure, and tactics over the span of almost two centuries, it is important to note that the essentially "Roman" quality of the army remained intact. The extension of the franchise to all provincials by Caracalla in 212 C.E. removed any distinction between Romans and provincials, but the army continued to think of itself as Roman and observed Roman form and language. Although more and more barbarian units served within the army's ranks, there was never any question that they were subordinate to the larger sense of Roman control. Most barbarians served in the army precisely because they wanted to be subsumed under the larger rubric of Roman civilization. It was only after that rubric had manifestly collapsed that it became desirable to regard oneself as a member of a tribal army. As long as the Eternal City remained free of foreign occupiers, and as long as those provincials (and barbarians) who rose to the top continued to think of themselves and publicly act as heirs of the Caesars, the particular Roman cast of the army remained. The Roman character of the army,

Figure 16.5 Roman Officer and Legionnaire

however, depended upon the character and stability of the larger social order and its political institutions, and these were often in jeopardy from civil war.

By the beginning of the second century, the threat to Rome came not from without but from political turmoil within. The murder of Emperor Commodus, presumably with the concurrence of the Praetorians, began a period of marked domestic instability that weakened the empire. At first the corrosive effects of political murder had little effect. Septimius Severus (193–211 C.E.) even took a more active military role. He raised three new legions to deal with the Parthian problem and added Mesopotamia to the empire. Two of these new *Parthica* legions were stationed in the new province, while the third formed the nucleus of a new unit in Rome itself. Severus disbanded the old Praetorian Guard and replaced it with a new unit of ten *cohorts* of double strength (30,000 men) recruited from the frontier legions. This army was the forerunner of the Roman mobile army and was intended to be used to reinforce the frontier armies and put down any military rebellions that might occur among the frontier legions.

From 235 to 297 C.E., at the end of which Diocletian finally put down the last surviving pretender to the Roman mantle, Rome suffered through sixty years of civil war in which no fewer than sixteen emperors and more than thirty would-be emperors were felled by the dagger or the sword. The frontier legions became deeply involved in plots to raise this or that commander to the purple. As legion after legion marched out of its frontier garrisons to fight other legions supporting rival pretenders, the frontier defenses fell into shambles. Much of the trained manpower of the legions fell in civil combat with one another. As political instability continued to ruin the armies, across the frontiers the barbarians began to form tribal confederations and to act in concert militarily. The Germans began making forays along the Rhine, and the Goths pressed along the Danubian border. In the Middle East, Persia began its rise to power, replacing the old Parthian empire and becoming a worthy competitor willing to do battle with Rome.

Tactical Organization

The increased pressure on the frontiers revealed the shortcomings of a Roman army weakened by political war. The old preclusive defensive strategy no longer was possible, and Rome changed to a more elastic system of defense. The frontier legions and border garrisons and strong points were retained, but it was now recognized that the quality of the legions and the multiplicity of highly mobile threats from barbarian raiders required increased mobility on the part of the defensive forces to contain the penetrations. The legions acquired stronger cavalry components designed to run down the enemy horsemen and engage them until the legion infantry could be brought to bear. Credit is usually given to Gallienus (253–268 C.E.) for creating the first large-scale Roman cavalry force that was used as a central reserve to reinforce the border infantry garrisons. But this "prototype" did not remain in existence very long after Gallienus. A number of strong emperors—Claudius, Aurelian, and Probus—all won major victories against the invaders and managed to stabilize the Roman frontiers. In 284 C.E., Diocletian assumed the purple. He reigned until 305 C.E., the longest reign of any Roman emperor since Antonius Pius.

The major reforms of the Roman army came during the reigns of Diocletian (284–305) and Constantine (306–337 C.E.). Since it remains a matter of some debate as to what reforms were introduced by which emperor, the reigns of the two emperors are treated as a single period in the outline here on the Roman army. Diocletian restored the imperial borders in a series of vigorous campaigns on several fronts. To manage the empire more efficiently, Diocletian created the post of vice-emperor, to which he appointed Maximian; then he and Maximian took successors-designate (caesars), appointing Galerius in the East and Constantius in the West. In 293 C.E. Diocletian reorganized the empire for administrative purposes by creating a number of smaller provinces out of the older provincial boundaries. The frontiers were reorganized into four military sectors, each sector assigned as the direct responsibility of one of the caesars. Each sector had its own legions, cavalry detachments, and mobile cavalry reserves. To tie the system of forts and unit deployments together to make rapid reinforcement possible, Diocletian spent a fortune on roads, bridges, and strong points.

Under Diocletian the army grew from the 300,000 men under Severus to about 400,000 men. The number of legions was doubled from thirty-three to almost seventy, but in some instances the number of men per legion was reduced to 1,000. This process of reducing the strength of the infantry legions was completed under Constantine. The increase in manpower came in the area of the *auxilia* and the creation of new types of specialized infantry units. The old legionary infantry became a smaller proportion of the overall army. At the same time, Diocletian expanded the number of cavalry units, almost all of which were drawn from German and other barbarian tribes. A large variety of these units—*cunei, alae, vexillationes*—were raised for all segments of the army. The old legionary cavalry disappeared and was replaced by these new types of units. Despite the increases in cavalry, it is important to note that the Roman army under both Diocletian and Constantine was still predominantly an infantry army. Whereas in the early empire the cavalry to infantry ratio was approximately one to ten or twelve, by the time of Adrianople it was one to three.

The larger armies were reorganized to make the strategy of elastic, in-depth defense work properly. Diocletian stopped the old tradition of awarding military commands to powerful political personages, most often provincial governors. Instead, command was offered to professional soldiers. Under Constantine this separation of career paths became permanent. The old remnants of the legion were posted in fixed positions at key border or river points for frontier defense. Gradually, their quality declined, as it was more attractive to serve in the new elite units. These remnants were designated as *limitanei* (border guards) and *riparienses* (river guards) and were usually deployed in "legions" of 1,000 men. Diocletian formed the *comitatenses*, or mobile imperial army, comprised largely of provincials from Germany, Illyricum, Gaul, and the Danube and commanded by the emperor himself. It was stationed near the major cities and roads in the interior of the empire and functioned as a strategic rapid reaction force to expel border penetrations. The contingents of infantry within this force were largely light infantry and of provincial and barbarian origin. The cavalry was divided into 500-strong horse regiments called "*vexillationes*," and the infantry, although still called legions, were assembled in brigades of 1,000 men. There were a total of 170 legions at the end of the fourth century. Between the *comitatenses* and the field legions there was another rapid reaction cavalry force called the *pseudocomitatenses* that was used to fill in the gaps as the occasion arose.

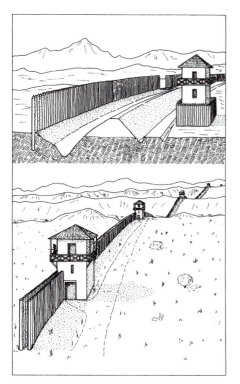

Figure 16.6 Roman Frontier *Limes*. Adapted from Arther Ferrill, *The Fall of the Roman Empire* (New York: Thames and Hudson, 1986). Reprinted with permission.

Diocletian confined the old Praetorian Guard to Rome, a city he rarely visited, and replaced it with a large Imperial Guard loyal only to the emperor. This new unit was called the *palatini*. It is not possible to say with accuracy how large the Imperial Guard was under Diocletian, but by the time of the battle of Adrianople, the *palatini* comprised twenty-four horse regiments of 500 troopers each and twenty-five infantry legions, each with 1,000 men. The Guard also comprised another 108 *auxilia* infantry regiments, each 500 strong. Some of these infantry units had specialized functions and were called *auxilium*. One group of infantry recruited from the Rhine Germans served as shock troops and were known for their savagery and bravery. This unit served as the Foreign Legion of the late Roman army. Constantine added a personal life guard, *Scholae Palatinae*, comprised mostly of Germans, to the Imperial Guard. By the end of the century the Imperial Guard consisted of 12,000 horse and 80,000 foot, nearly all cantoned around the provincial capitals of the empire.

Although Diocletian began the reforms of the army in the third century, it was Constantine who formalized and systematized the new army into a coherent military system that supported a new military strategy. The mobile reaction strategy by Constantine was not adopted because the barbarian incursions at the frontiers were wholesale tribal movements seeking to resettle within the empire. This pattern of migration only began decades after Adrianople, when the empire revealed itself to be much weaker at resisting barbarian migration. Moreover, the continued Roman practice of recruiting entire tribal armies along with their civilian populations for service in the imperial armies encouraged migration. At the time of Constantine, however, most border incursions were undertaken by bands of raiders seeking plunder. Although these raids sometimes involved thousands of barbarian soldiers, for the most part border incursions were carried out by much smaller groups.

Tactics

The old strategy of static defense centered around the infantry legions was no longer successful against sporadic hit-and-run raids undertaken along thousands of miles of border. Roman strategy recognized that the entire frontier could not be made impenetrable except at prohibitive cost. The mobile reaction strategy was based on the idea that the frontier infantry could defend the largest and most important sectors of the border. If a penetration occurred, infantry forts and border strong points served as pockets of resistance until larger forces could be rushed to the point of penetration. Since most of the raiders were horse-borne, Roman reaction forces were cavalry and light infantry. Behind the legion border forts garrisoned by the *limitanei* were the provincial forces comprised of small infantry and cavalry units capable of rapid reaction. Positioned at key points within the empire were segments of the large strategic field army, comprised of cavalry and infantry forces that functioned as the empire's strategic reserve (Map 16.3).

Roman tactics changed to accommodate both the new strategy and the nature of the threat. Legion infantry now fought in smaller contingents (about 1,000 strong compared to the old 5,000-man legion), armed with the spear and light shield. Since their opponents were essentially cavalry forces and untrained light infantry, Roman infantry required flexibility and mobility to deal with the enemy infantry and, at the same time, had to be capable of stopping a barbarian cavalry charge. To accomplish the latter, Roman infantry deployed more often in compact lines than in the old open infantry formation of the *quincunx* and functioned more like the old pre-cohortal infantry phalanx, with a hedge of spears to stop enemy cavalry. The idea was to fix the enemy until the cavalry could engage and deal decisively with it. Infantry, still the largest and strongest combat arm of the Roman army by far, was gradually reduced to a tactical platform of maneuver for cavalry, in much the same way as it had been for Alexander.

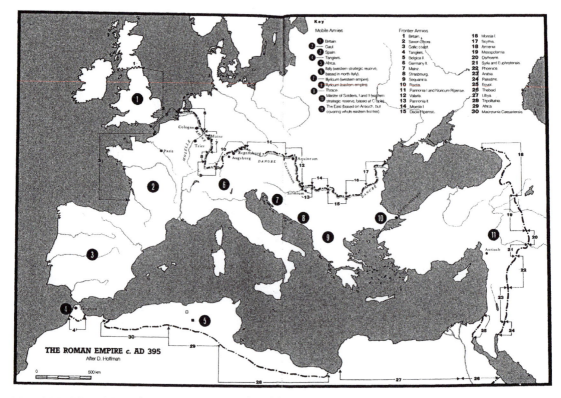

Map 16.3 Disposition of Roman Frontier and Field Armies (Fourth Century C.E.). Adapted from John Hackett, ed., *Warfare in the Ancient World* (New York: Facts on File, 1990).

The important point to understand about the Roman army on the eve of the battle of Adrianople was that it was *not* an army on the verge of collapse. Quite the contrary. The army of Rome was of more than adequate size, generally well led, and should have been adequate to the task of protecting the empire. It was certainly true that the border infantry had declined in quality, but it was equally true that the Germanic and Illyricum infantry that formed the bulk of the army's mobile front-line infantry was first rate and easily the equivalent of the infantry of any enemy it might have to fight. The quality of the Roman cavalry, although drawn largely from barbarian sources, was also excellent and, again, easily the equal in quality of any potential adversary. Moreover, the Roman cavalry was generally superior in numbers. The large mobile, strategic central reserve that gave the Roman strategic doctrine its defining combat capability was large, well equipped, well trained, and deployed in such a manner that it could adequately seal off and repulse any major breech of the frontiers. The whole system was well designed, and even after Adrianople, when Theodosius was faced with the problem of repairing the damage done by the defeat, the Roman armies were deployed essentially as they had been before the defeat.

THE GOTHS

The tribal threat to the imperial frontiers from Augustus's time to the end of the empire came primarily from the growing military power of Germanic tribes. The term "Germanic" covered a wide range of peoples that lived north of the Rhine-Danube line beginning on the North Sea and extending eastward to the Black Sea. These people varied in the degree of their social and military development, and even spoke completely different languages. Their increased pressure against the imperial frontiers over the centuries was due to three factors. First, many of these tribal societies were warrior societies so that war with the Romans fulfilled their requirements for social status, prestige, and entertainment obtained through raiding and plunder. Second, at various times tribes moved toward the imperial frontiers in a simple effort to better their lives, a situation seen today in the population migrations of Eastern Europe by people seeking better living standards in the West. Third, as was the case with the Goths in 376 C.E., encroachment on tribal lands by stronger tribal invaders forced the tribes nearest the imperial borders to cross the imperial frontiers in search of safety. Given the nature of the stimuli for tribal migration and the great length of the imperial borders, it is no surprise to discover that, from about the middle of the third century (250 C.E.) until the end of the empire, these frequent tribal penetrations constituted the primary strategic threat that Rome had to confront on its borders.

The Goths probably originated in Scandinavia and then migrated to the upper Vistula. Gradually, they moved south toward the middle Danube, then east toward the upper rim of the Black Sea (Map 16.4). By the third century, the Romans distinguished two Gothic kingdoms in this area. North of the Danube in the former Roman province of Dacia lived the Visigoths, called alternatively the West Goths or the "Wise Goths." North and east of them in southern Russia north of the Black Sea were the Ostrogoths or East Goths. Early in the fourth century, the Goths were converted to Arian Christianity. The translation of the scriptures into Gothic by Ulfilas turned the barbarian Gothic tongue into a literary language. The first serious Roman contact with these semi-nomadic peoples came in 238 C.E. in the province of Moesia (northern Bulgaria), where the Roman legate Gaius Trajanus Decius contained a penetration and defeated the Goths in a series of running battles that lasted four years.

In 250 C.E., the Goths under King Cniva attempted a large invasion of the same area. Cniva crossed the Danube in force and defeated a Roman army at Philippopolis. Cniva then plundered the entire area, slaughtering (so we are told) more than 100,000 people. Decius, now emperor, marched against the Goths, and in two major battles drove them back to the marshes south of the mouth of the Danube. With the Goths backed into a corner, Decius pressed the campaign, seeking to exterminate the Gothic threat once and for all. In 251 C.E. the Roman army under Decius met the Goths at the battle of Forum

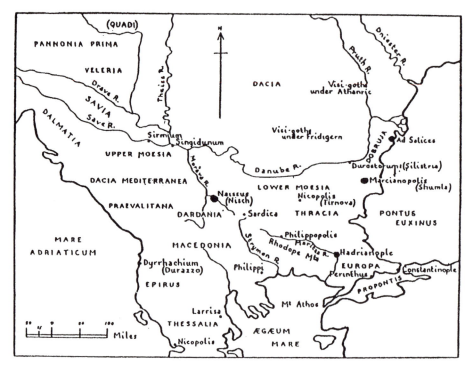

Map 16.4 Battle of Adrianople: Lower Danube Area of Operations

Trebroni. The Roman general, Gallus, failed to press the attack at a critical point in the battle, allowing the Goths to trap the Romans and counterattack. Decius himself was killed, and the Roman army shattered. Gallus became emperor and concluded a disadvantageous truce in which the Goths were allowed to retreat across the Danube and keep their booty. In exchange for a promise not to undertake further border incursions, the Romans agreed to pay the Goths an annual monetary tribute.

In 258 C.E. the Goths raided Circassia and Georgia. Four years later they mounted sea and amphibious raids against Moesia, Thrace, and northern Asia Minor. They even sacked Ephesus, where they destroyed the Temple of Diana, one of the seven wonders of the ancient world. Five years later, with 500 boats, they passed through the Bosphorus, occupied the area around Byzantium, and laid waste to Corinth, Sparta, Aregolis, and Athens. Finally, the Greeks destroyed the Gothic ships, and the Goths retreated overland out of Macedonia. In 268 C.E. Claudius, having served loyally and having effectively held the Danube frontier under three emperors, himself became Emperor Claudius II. He marched his armies to Thrace to deal with the Gothic threat. In 269 C.E., at the battle of Naissus, Claudius isolated and slaughtered the Gothic army, killing more than 50,000 men. The Goths were driven back behind the mountain passes and were starved into submission. Claudius compelled the Goths to enter Roman military service as *foederati*. Claudius was awarded the appellation "Gothicus" for his victory over the Goths. With the death of Claudius, the Goths once again tested the Roman resolve and, in 270 C.E., crossed the Danube. The new emperor, Aurelian, attacked and drove the Goths completely out of Moesia and back across the Danube. He then reached a peace with the Goths in which Rome abandoned Dacia. The peace held for almost a hundred years.

Society

As with all armies, the social structure of the Goths strongly influenced the structure, tactics, and overall combat capabilities of the Gothic armies. The Goths lived a semi-agricultural existence centered around the village, in which hunting, cattle raising, and a pastoral style of life predominated. The Goths' society did not differ much from the type of social order the Romans found among the Germans under Arminius in the first century. The Gothic social order revolved around the clan—the *hunno*, or hundred, headed by the *alderman*—which conducted most of the important political and social functions of the village. As with previous Germanic tribes with which the Romans were familiar, tribal leadership was conducted by an oligarchy of nobles. There is some evidence that a monarchy may have developed among the Ostrogoths by this time, but it is not certain that the Visigoths had reached this stage of social articulation. During wartime, a tribal assembly—presumably comprised of *hunni* and nobles—selected a war chief who conducted the campaign. It is also probable that during periods of war the Goths may have organized their military commands into units of ten, a hundred, and even a thousand men, the latter under a *comites* (later, count) or, perhaps, a *dux* (duke), but this is by no means certain. If combat units of any size were to be supported logistically, some larger organizational unit or units would have been required to provide this function.

Manpower

The size of the Gothic armies of the third and fourth century was clearly not as large as the ancient commentators would have us believe. Eunapius, for example, recorded that the Gothic army that crossed the Danube in 376 C.E. prior to the battle of Adrianople consisted of 200,000 warriors. A century earlier, in 267 C.E., Trebillius Pollio gave the number of 320,000 as the size of the Gothic army that crossed the Danube. While it seems probable that by the fourth century the Goths were among the most numerous and powerful of the Germanic tribes, it is unlikely that they could muster more than 12,000 to 15,000 warriors under arms. Delbruck's analysis of the Gothic army's route and rate of march prior to Adrianople concluded that the Gothic host probably had 15,000 fighting men, another 45,000 noncombatant men, women, and children, and, perhaps, 10,000 slaves, or a body of people 70,000 strong.

Tactical Organization

The fighting power of Gothic combat units was probably quite good. Unlike the earlier Germanic tribes, many of the Goths who fought at Adrianople had served within the Roman army in one capacity or another. Goths had been serving in Roman units for more than a century and were as well armed as the Roman soldier. It was this opportunity to serve with (and fight against) the Roman imperial army that permitted the Goths to develop a powerful and highly skilled class of warrior nobles and retainers under the leadership of a war chief. As a consequence, the combat leadership of the Gothic army was experienced and tough.

Oman argues that, of all the Germanic tribes, the Goths were the first to place their main military reliance upon the horse. To the Goth, it was more honorable to fight on horseback than on foot. Gothic heavy cavalry relied upon experienced horsemen armed with the lance and sword. However, horses and military equipment were expensive, and it is unlikely that the Gothic cavalry was a large combat force. It seems logical as well that some Gothic cavalry had served in the Roman cavalry squadrons and were thoroughly familiar with Roman cavalry doctrine. Gothic cavalry used the saddle, but there is no evidence of the existence of the stirrup.

Equipment

Most of the Gothic army was infantry. Unlike the infantry of its earlier Germanic ancestors who had fought as light infantry with javelin and spear, Gothic infantry was well-armed heavy infantry. The infantry carried the shield and sometimes a pike. Its major arms were the short sword (*scramasax*) or the long cutting sword, the *spatha*. Some infantry carried the *francisca*, a single-bladed battle axe that could be wielded or thrown and could easily split Roman armor, shield, and helmet. As best can be determined, the Gothic infantry did not fight with body armor, although it is likely that some Roman shirt mail must have made its way into the Gothic army. The Goths, like their ancestors, fought in the fluid wedge formation designed more for its ability to be led by the *hunno* (village chief) than for its military effectiveness.

The army of the Goths moved with and around its wagon-forts or *laager*. These wagons carried the army's food supply for the soldiers and their families and whatever logistical items were required for campaigning. At the end of the day, the wagons were drawn into a circle to form a wagon-fort behind which a camp could be constructed. The wagon-fort served as a base from which to launch raids of small parties or a defensive position from which the entire army could fight. In dire circumstances, the Gothic army could fall back upon the *laager* in retreat to regroup its forces or offer a last point of resistance. The way in which the *laager* was used by the Goths strongly parallels the functions the Roman field camp served for the Roman army.

The Roman experience with the Goths had generally not been a pleasant one over the century leading up to the battle of Adrianople. In a number of instances, the Goths had massacred Roman armies and ravaged the provinces of the empire. Their peculiar habit of cutting off the right hand of Roman provincial farmers—the hand needed to work the plow—was particularly irksome. On balance, it was the Romans who had won more battles and killed more Goths than the reverse. At Adrianople, the Goths redressed the balance.

THE BATTLE OF ADRIANOPLE (378 C.E.)

The disaster that befell the Roman army on the plain of Adrianople was the ultimate consequence of a chain of events that began almost six years previously, in 372 C.E., when a fierce Mongoloid people, the Huns, entered European history. For some unknown reason, this nomadic people began migrating westward from the steppes of Central Asia. They invaded the lands of the Scythians in the region between the Volga and the Don, and then invaded the lands of the Alans. After two years of continuous war, the Alans were destroyed. What survivors there were wandered westward through the lands of the Goths.

The Huns continued their advance, crashing into the lands of the Ostrogoths. Under the Ostrogoth chieftain, Ermanaric, the defenders fought well against the invaders, but to no avail. In one battle Ermanaric committed suicide rather than surrender, and his successor, Withimer, was killed in a later engagement. Under the leadership of two chieftains, Alatheus and Saphrax, thousands of Ostrogoths fled westward into the lands of the Visigoths. Athanaric, leader of the Visigoths, planned to resist the Huns, but most of his people were panicked by the fleeing Ostrogoths and joined the mass migration under the Visigoth leadership of Fritigern and Alavivus toward the Danube and the Roman frontier. Eunapius, a contemporary historian, noted that the numbers of Goths that reached the Danube was 700,000 to 1 million, of whom more than 200,000 were warriors. These figures are clearly impossible. It is more probable that Delbruck's figure of 70,000 to 80,000 is more realistic.

In 376 C.E., Athanaric, a leader of the Visigoths, appealed to the Roman emperor to allow his people to cross the Danube to the safety of Roman territory. Valens knew Athanaric well, for this wily soldier had led 10,000 Goths in the service of Procopius, the usurper that Valens had had to destroy. Nonetheless, Valens granted the request for the passage. He hoped to settle the Visigoths as farmers on devastated land in Thrace and to recruit them for future military service. It was an old Roman formula. To protect against any treachery from so large a tribe, Valens agreed to the passage of the Visigoths only if they surrendered every male under military age as hostages (slaves, really) and surrendered their weapons as well. Late in the year the crossing began. The Goths were starving, and in some cases, the Visigoths were compelled to sell their children for dog meat to eat. Faced with this exploitation by Roman officials, the Goths began to hide their weapons from Roman inspectors, eventually reaching the other bank with a considerable armory.

At some point, the tide of Ostrogoths arrived at the Danube and, although they had no permission to cross, crossed the river anyway. The Roman officials were too busy trying to deal with the Visigoths to pay much attention. Fritigern and Alavivus were trying to cooperate with the Romans, but the ill treatment of their people was more than they could bear. Soon, Fritigern sought an alliance with the Ostrogoths. Lupicinus, the Roman military commander in Thrace, was fearful he would lose control of the situation. He invited Fritigern and Alavivus to a banquet and attempted to assassinate them. Alavivus was apparently killed, but Fritigern escaped with his bodyguard and "arose the Goths in arms" against their Roman tormentors. Shortly thereafter, Fritigern attacked Lupicinus and defeated him at Marianopolis (Shumla, in eastern Bulgaria). Fritigern then joined forces with the Ostrogoths Alatheus and Saphrax.

Fritigern turned his fury upon the Romans. He joined forces with another body of Goths and attacked Adrianople, a hopeless task since the Goths possessed no siege train. Fritigern and his tribe descended on the interior of Thrace and laid it waste. Jordanes's description of the Gothic fury is a classic piece of ancient literature:

> Without any distinction of age or sex, they went forward destroying everything in one vast slaughter and conflagration: tearing infants even from their mother's breasts and slaying them, ravishing their mothers, slaughtering women's husbands before the eyes of those whom they thus made widows, while boys of tender and adult age were dragged over the corpses of their parents.

Valens made a hasty peace with the Persians and sent reinforcements to Thrace. His three generals—Saturninus, Trajan, and Profuturus—drove the Goths northward and blockaded them in a marshy region south of the mouth of the Danube. Here, at the battle of Salices (the Willows), the Romans and Goths fought for almost seven days with no decisive outcome. The Goths fell back behind their wagon *laager*, and the Romans tried to starve them out. News that fresh units of Goths had crossed the Danube forced the Romans to lift the blockade of the camp, and the Goths streamed into Thrace. Curiously, Fritigern was assisted by Alatheus's Ostrogoths, the Alani, and even units of Huns, whose original movements had prompted the migration of the Goths in the first place.

By 378 C.E. Fritigern had struck some sort of alliance with the other tribes in the Danube area, and these tribes may have placed themselves under Fritigern's military command. At the same time, the Goths seem to have succeeded in convincing the Germanic tribes of the upper and lower Rhine to join the revolt, and in the spring of 378 C.E., the Franks and Alemanni launched serious incursions into Gaul. This forced Gratian, Valentinian's son who had succeeded his father after the latter's death, to remain in Gaul and deal with the revolt. He crossed the Rhine and killed 40,000 Germans at Argentaria (Colmar). But the raid cost time, and Gratian was unable to answer his uncle Valens's call for help against the Goths.

Valens moved his court from Antioch to Constantinople to be nearer to the theater of operations. He appointed Sebastianus, an Italian general, to deal with the problem in Thrace. Relying upon mobile task forces of trained infantry and cavalry, Sebastianus inflicted a series of defeats on the Goths and their allies. By early August, the bulk of Fritigern's forces were brought to bay in their wagon *laagers* on a hill located in a valley, ten miles or so from the city of Adrianople. The Goths were joined, curiously enough, by a force of Gothic mercenaries who had served in the Roman army. Probably 90,000 to 100,000 souls stood on that hill; probably no more than 20,000 were warriors. Sebastianus advised Valens to starve out the enemy and to await the arrival of Gratian's reinforcements before bringing the enemy under attack. Valens, perhaps jealous of the military reputation of his nephew Gratian, rejected the advice of his field commander and moved his army from Constantinople with the intention of going over to the attack as soon as possible.

August 9, 378 C.E., dawned hot and humid, much as it still does on the Adrianople plain in the summer, with all indications that the temperature would exceed 100 degrees Fahrenheit by noon. On the hill in the center of the valley, Fritigern sent his cavalry out to forage for the troops and their families that were disposed in and around the Gothic wagon *laager*. The running skirmishes and ambushes with the Romans had taken their toll in exhaustion and hunger, for the need to keep on the move to avoid the Roman main force had made it difficult for Fritigern to secure sufficient food for his army and their camp followers. Sometime around noon, Gothic scouts detected the approach of the Roman army as it moved out from the city of Adrianople and reported their approach to Fritigern. He immediately launched outriders to locate the foraging Gothic cavalry and return with it to the wagon-fort.

Early that same morning the Roman emperor, Valens, parked his baggage wagons under the protective walls of Adrianople and set his army on the overland trek in search of the Gothic camp. Ancient commentators place the size of Valens's army at 60,000 men, two-thirds of which was infantry and the remainder light and heavy cavalry. More modern analysis suggests that the Roman army probably did not exceed 35,000 to 40,000 men and horse. After a march of some eight miles, Valens spotted the Gothic camp sometime around noon. Valens had badly neglected his advance security precautions, and it is probable that the Roman advance guard simply stumbled onto the Gothic positions by accident. In fact, the Roman army had not even deployed from column of march into line before sighting the Gothic encampment. This incredible failure in tactical intelligence was compounded by Valens's additional failure to provide adequate security on his flanks or rear. Startled by the unexpected presence of the Goths, Valens ordered his army to deploy immediately for battle. Despite having marched all morning in the scorching heat without any rest or midday meal, the Roman army began to move into position for a fight.

The right-wing cavalry had been in the van of the army, and it rapidly deployed on the Roman right, using its horses and attached skirmishers to protect the deployment of the infantry. The cavalry formed a screen across the front of the line. The left-wing cavalry had been riding rearguard prior to contact and was ordered into position on the Roman left. This required some hard riding to cover the distance from the end of the column to the left flank. When the left-wing cavalry arrived, it did so in some disarray, with horses exhausted. The Roman infantry, hot, thirsty, hungry, and generally exhausted, straggled up the hill to gain the position in front of the Gothic *laager*. The deployment from column to line proceeded much more slowly than normal. When contact between the two armies occurred, much of the Roman infantry was still not in position, but strung out in column.

As the Roman army deployed in front of the Gothic camp, Fritigern must have been tempted to strike before the legions were fully arrayed for combat. Except for some light guard units, the bulk of the Gothic cavalry under Alatheus and Saphrax was off foraging. Fritigern had sent riders to contact them at the first sign of the Roman approach, so he had every reason to expect that his heavy cavalry would return in time to join the engagement. Without the cavalry at hand, however, Fritigern reasoned that an attack was risky. He sent ambassadors to Valens urging negotiations. Valens, for his part, had stumbled into the Gothic army unprepared, and his army was not ready for battle. Accordingly, Valens agreed to the talks to buy time for his army to move fully into position before engaging the enemy.

As so often happens in war, an unforeseen event provoked the battle at a time of neither commander's choosing. Fritigern set fire to the crops and grasslands in front of the *laager* to further delay the deployment of the Romans. The heat and smoke confused the atmosphere of the battlefield. As Valens's ambassador approached Fritigern's camp to continue the discussions, a unit of the ambassador's escort suddenly opened fire with a hail of arrows on the Gothic position. In the heat and confusion of the moment, other Roman skirmisher units positioned in front of the still deploying legion infantry attacked the front of the wagon *laager*. Within minutes, there was panic on both sides as the Goths met the attack and counterattacked from behind their wagons, chasing the skirmishers back to their own lines. The Roman skirmishers and their Gothic pursuers smashed into the Roman infantry as it was still in the process of forming for battle. At precisely this moment, units of the Gothic cavalry (actually they were probably an Alani cavalry battalion) returned to the battlefield and, "from the mountains like a thunderbolt," attacked the cavalry on the Roman right wing with tremendous shock (Figure 16.7).

Taken by surprise by both their own fleeing skirmishers and the sudden

Gothic cavalry assault, the Roman line wavered, flexed, and then held. The legionnaires rallied, and outside the wagon *laager* a violent battle raged. With the attack of the Gothic cavalry, Fritigern committed his infantry against the Roman center and left. On the right, a furious cavalry engagement commenced. Ammianus described the cavalry battle thus: "Then the two lines of battle [the Gothic horse and the Roman right-wing cavalry] dashed against each other, like the beaks [rams] of ships, and thrusting with all their might, were tossed to and fro, like the waves of the sea." The Roman right met the Gothic cavalry assault and held its ground against the initial assault.

By this time, the cavalry units on the Roman left wing had been able to form their units for the attack after their mad dash from the rear of the Roman infantry column to their posi-

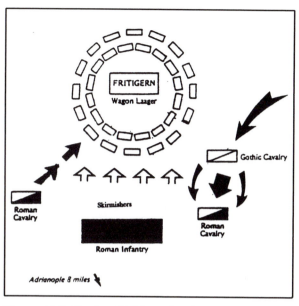

Figure 16.7 Battle of Adrianople, Phase I: Gothic Cavalry Arrives and Engages Roman Cavalry. Concept by Arther Ferrill, *The Fall of the Roman Empire* (New York: Thames and Hudson, 1986). Reprinted with permission.

tion on the Roman left wing. The left-wing cavalry went over to the attack and pressed its assault right up to the wagons, probably with the intent of riding around the *laager* to find a place where a penetration might be possible. In front of the wagons the Roman cavalry was met by Gothic infantry and a hail of arrows and missiles from behind the *laager*. The Roman left advanced so far forward that it broke contact with its supporting infantry still forming up in the Roman center and created a gap between itself and the infantry. Fritigern rushed his infantry into this gap, severing and isolating the Roman cavalry from its vital infantry support. Fritigern pressed more infantry into the attack, this time from all sides, turning the Roman left and pressing the cavalry back against the left of the Roman infantry in the center until it broke, and the Roman horse were driven from the battle. The Gothic attack was so violent that the Roman infantry was "pressed upon by the superior numbers of the enemy, that they were overwhelmed and beaten down, like the ruin of a vast rampart." Roman infantry was so compacted that, as at Cannae, they could not lift their swords or shields to protect themselves.

Fritigern had turned the Roman left (Figure 16.8). Now he moved to exploit his advantage and rushed cavalry and infantry into the gap. Gothic troops worked their way behind the Roman infantry and pounded it against the anvil of the wagon *laager*. Now the Roman right began to give way against the combined cavalry and infantry attack. It still held its ground, but the collapsing

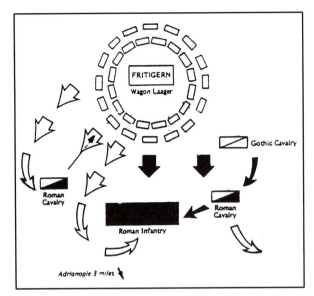

Figure 16.8 Battle of Adrianople, Phase II: Gothic Infantry Encircles Roman Left; Roman Center Surrounded. Concept by Arther Ferrill, *The Fall of the Roman Empire* (New York: Thames and Hudson, 1986). Reprinted with permission.

infantry center pressed against it. Pressed from all sides into a ball, the right wing came under a hail of archery fire. Suddenly, the Roman cavalry shattered, broke apart, and the remnants fled in panic from the field. The Roman infantry, much of it still unformed for battle, was left to the mercy of the combined Gothic infantry and cavalry attack. As the Goths pressed the attack,

> the different companies became so huddled together that a soldier could hardly draw his sword, or withdraw his hand after he had once stretched it out. And by this time such clouds of dust arose that it was scarcely possible to see the sky, which resounded with horrible cries; and in consequence the darts, which were bearing death on every side, reached their mark, and fell with deadly effect, because no one could see them beforehand so as to guard against them.

Then Fritigern committed his reserves, an "enormous host" from behind the wagon *laager*. Ammianus recorded that "they beat down our horses and men, and left no spot to which our ranks could fall back to deploy. . . . The battle developed into a frenzied slaughter."

Valens himself, so one account noted, was trapped in the center of his army and took refuge among some reserve battalions that "stood firm and immovable," fighting on into the night until eventually overwhelmed by superior numbers. Another account had Valens carried from the field wounded. He and some soldiers took refuge in a small house that the Goths set afire, killing all within it. Whatever the truth, the battle of Adrianople had turned into a locus of horror for the Roman army. By the end of the day, the ground was "covered with streams of blood . . . until one black pool of blood disfigured everything, and wherever the eye turned, it could see nothing but piled-up heaps of dead and lifeless corpses trampled on without mercy."

The casualties at Adrianople were horrendous. More than two-thirds of the Roman army, perhaps has many as 25,000 men, met their deaths. The emperor himself was killed. Of equal import for the future was that the cream of the Roman senior general leadership—men like Trajan and Sebastianus— were also killed. Thirty-five tribunes, experienced men who were almost impossible to replace, were slain, as were many *cohort* commanders. Almost the entire command leadership echelon of the cavalry battalions was lost, as were the Master of the Horse (equivalent to an army-level Field Marshal), the High

Steward, and a former commander-in-chief. The loss of military talent was staggering. Not since Cannae had a Roman army been so badly beaten nor had so many trained and experienced legionnaires and officers been lost.

The battle of Adrianople is often regarded as a major turning point in the development of the Western way of war, for it was at Adrianople that the almost invincible force of Roman infantry was defeated by the superiority of Gothic cavalry. It was the defeat at Adrianople that, some have maintained, demonstrated the newly discovered battlefield supremacy of cavalry over infantry, thus marking the beginning of a new era in Western warfare in which cavalry reigned supreme for a thousand years.

Yet, the Roman defeat at Adrianople was essentially due to tactical stupidity on the part of poor field commanders who exposed the unpre-

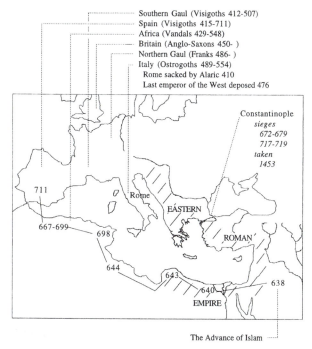

Figure 16.9 The Fall of the Roman Empire. Adapted from Alfred Bradford, *With Arrow, Sword, and Spear* (Westport, CT: Greenwood, 2001). Reprinted with permission.

pared and exhausted Roman infantry to surprise cavalry attack. Moreover, there was nothing in the quality of Gothic cavalry nor in their method of employment that was in any sense revolutionary or a departure from the standard combat doctrine of the Roman army itself. What was important about the battle of Adrianople was not the defeat of the Roman army itself but the influence of that defeat on the larger military-social order of the Roman imperium. With the cream of Roman infantry destroyed, future Roman emperors relied increasingly upon the wholesale recruitment of barbarian cavalry to fill the imperial armies, until the Roman army came to resemble little more than a collection of barbarian warlords in the pay of a foreign political system. When, finally, the political order itself collapsed, all that was left were the tribal warlords. It was from these tribal military fiefdoms that the new social order, eventually known as feudalism, grew, and with it emerged the mounted knight that dominated European warfare for a thousand years.

THE COMMANDERS

Valens, the Roman commander at Adrianople, was appointed by his brother, Emperor Valentinian I (364–375 C.E.), to be emperor of the Roman

East where he served until 378 C.E. when he was killed in battle at Adrianople. Valens had been a member of Emperor Julian's military guard and had considerable military experience in Syria, Mesopotamia, and the Balkans, the latter in conflicts and negotiations with the barbarian tribes. The father of Valens and Valentinian was a Pannonian rope-maker who had served in the Roman army, rising through the ranks and coming to the attention of Emperor Julian who appointed him to military command. Despite Valens's military experience, he was not highly regarded as a soldier. The historian Ammianus says of him that he was "a procrastinator and irresolute. His complexion was dark, the pupil of one of his eyes was dimmed, but in such a way as not to be noticed at a distance; his body was well-knit, his height neither above nor below the average; he was knock-kneed, and somewhat pot-bellied." Yet, Ammianus tells us, he was a "faithful and steady friend, a strict upholder of both military and civil discipline."

The most important criticism of Valens's personality as a commander was his tendency toward half-measures and acceptance of compromise solutions. In short, he lacked decisiveness and will. And yet at Adrianople, he rushed rashly into battle instead of waiting for the reinforcements that were on the way. Valens was killed at Adrianople, and his body was never found. Two versions of his death are offered by Ammianus: (1) he was killed in battle and perished with the masses of his men, lost in the heap; (2) he was wounded and taken to a nearby house that the Goths surrounded and set afire. However he died, Ammianus is clear that Valens was hardly a superb battlefield commander. He says scathingly of the man that "he was equally ignorant of war and literature."

Fritigern, war-chief of the Goths, is a shadowy figure as far as the ancient historians are concerned. We know only that he was an experienced soldier, that he had served in the Roman army as commander of a Gothic tribal contingent, and that once, while he was in negotiations with the Romans, they tried to assassinate him. After Adrianople, Fritigern led his tribal horde across the Danube and down into Greece, burning and killing as they went. Later, the Goths secured Roman permission to settle on the western bank of the Danube, thus escaping the wrath of the Huns to their back, where they became *foederati*. After this point, Fritigern disappears from history.

Gaius Julius Caesar Octavianus (63 B.C.E.–14 C.E.), known to history as Caesar Augustus, was born at sunrise on September 23, 63 B.C.E., in a house at the easternmost corner of the Palatine in Rome, an area known locally as "the Oxheads." Augustus was born into a well-off, but not rich, old plebeian family. The boy's father served as a praetor and later was appointed governor of Macedonia. Augustus's mother, Atia, was the daughter of Marcus Balbus and Julius Caesar's sister, Julia, so that Julius Caesar was Augustus's great-uncle. Caesar seems to have taken an interest in the young Augustus very early on, and when the boy was twelve Augustus delivered the *laudatio* at the bier of his grandmother, Julia. Caesar seems to have been especially moved by the young man's speech and took an even greater interest in him from this moment forward. Too, Augustus was Caesar's only living male blood relative, which to a Roman was sufficient reason to establish a close familial bond.

Young Augustus was drawn to his famous and audacious uncle and asked to be allowed to accompany Caesar on his African campaign against the surviving Pompeyans. The old man was willing, but Augustus's mother forbade it, claiming Augustus was too sickly. At the time of Caesar's murder Augustus was nineteen years old. Only the exceptional affection that Augustus felt for his uncle can explain Augustus's deep hatred of those who had struck the great man down. From the moment the news reached him Augustus vowed that he would make it his life's work to wreak vengeance on those who had killed his uncle. And so he did.

Of all the great captains of antiquity Augustus Caesar is, perhaps, the most complex. There was nothing about his background or early life that marked him for greatness and much that worked against any future hope of it. Although he was born to a respectable plebeian family, it was not one accustomed to holding high office or providing opportunities for its sons beyond the usual advantages accruing to such families. A sickly child, Augustus was plagued by illness all his life. As an adult he frequently fell ill, often on military campaign, forcing him to relinquish command to his lieutenants while he languished in his tent. On several occasions he came very close to dying. He was, even by Roman standards, a short man whose vanity prompted him to wear thick-soled shoes to make him seem taller. He lacked physical strength and endurance, although it was said that his body was perfectly proportioned. He was by most accounts very close to his mother as a boy.

Throughout his life Augustus was plagued by anxiety attacks, some serious enough to land him in a sickbed. It may be safely suggested that some of his attacks of illness on campaign, often coming on the eve of battle, were caused by extreme anxiety. Surely Mark Antony thought so and believed him a coward. Augustus's sleep was often interrupted by nightmares, and all his life he was a believer in the portents of dreams. Each spring he would be visited by dreams of terrible happenings that caused him to worry for the rest of the year that they might occur. One of these dreams recurred regularly. Even though he spoke often of his other dreams, Augustus never revealed the content of this particular nightmare. Whatever it was, this particular dream caused him every year to sit for one day in a public place with his eyes closed and his hand outstretched like a common beggar, to the great wonderment of the Roman people. He was a gambler all his life and loved to bet on boxing matches and play dice. He detested the ostentatiousness of Roman life and once had his daughter's newly constructed villa destroyed because of its outrageous luxury. And yet he had a passion for fine furniture and would stop at nothing to possess a piece he fancied. His own official residence was modest by Roman standards, and he slept in the same small bedroom for forty years on a low bed with a plain coverlet.

Augustus cared little for his personal appearance and often went about for months without his hair or beard trimmed. When he did agree to have his hair cut, he often had two or three barbers work on him at the same time to get the torment over quickly. He rejected fine clothes and went around in crude homespun woven for him by his wife. He preferred common food and frequently dined alone at odd hours. Alcohol went easily to his brain, and he rarely drank more than a cup of wine each day. At his summer villa in Caprae he kept a huge collection of skeletons and bones of extinct sea and land creatures, his "Giant Bones" as he called them. Among his more morbid fascinations was his obsession with the legacies of his friends left to him in their wills. Augustus cared not a whit for the money left by these friends and always renounced his claims in favor of the family heirs. But he was greatly concerned about what the deceased had to say about him. It was as if only in death could he be certain of their affection.

Augustus was certainly no intellectual by Roman standards and received only the usual education for a man of his social station. His Greek was so poor that his uncle sent him to Greece to improve it. The experiment failed, and Augustus never used the Greek language easily. He was, however, an excellent student of rhetoric and practiced speaking daily even when on campaign. Yet he rarely spoke extemporaneously, preferring instead to write out his speeches and to read them or even have someone else read them to his audience. He chided Mark Antony, one of Rome's greatest orators, as a man who "wanted to be wondered at rather than understood," whose writing reeked with "the stench of far-fetched phrases." He practiced his writing skills like all good writers, authoring a number of prose works on various subjects, including a book, *An Encouragement to the Study of Philosophy*. He wrote poetry, a short collection of epigrams, and a Greek tragedy titled *Ajax*.

Given Augustus's personal habits, physical health, psychological dispositions, and social background, it is difficult to believe that this young man rose to become the most powerful person in the Roman world. His reform of Rome's political institutions, its army, its financial system, its laws, its roads, the creation of the imperial province system, the civil service, and the rebuilding of Rome itself all stand as among the most magnificent achievements of Roman civilization. And it is to Augustus that the West owes the establishment of the structure of the Roman imperium, the central institution of Western civilization for more than 500 years.

No great captain of the ancient world ever achieved what Augustus achieved. He set in motion a series of new ideas and institutions that unified the entire Mediterranean world, binding it together with common language, law, legal machinery, monetary instruments, military units, and governmental structures so that the empire of Rome became synonymous with the civilization of the West itself. In the process Augustus created the common culture of the West, first by extending Roman and Italian culture to the provinces and then by permitting what was valuable in the provinces to make its way to Rome, transforming Roman and Italian culture in the process. Augustus's imperial structure became a vast vessel in which a true Western culture arose and prospered, transforming the then known world in the process. Even centuries after Augustus was gone and the empire in the West had been dead for a thousand years, the history of Europe and its national disputes and security issues continued to center about the legacy that had been left to the national entities by Rome, as it does to this day in a number of circumstances. Without Augustus's vision and practical sense there would have been no Roman Empire. Without the Roman Empire, there would have been a very different culture of the West, and the history of the world itself would have been very different indeed.

LESSONS OF WAR

Strategy

1. Be cognizant of the geographic dimension of strategy. Adrianople was a battlefield for fifteen times over a period of 1,500 years because of its geographical location. Geography is not the sole determinant of strategy, but even in an age of modern high-technology weapons and capabilities, geography remains a major consideration in the development of strategy.

2. Armies are genuine creatures and reflections of the social orders that give them life. This is true as well for all forms of government. In military terms, a society cannot give what it does not have. The study and analysis of the adversary's social condition is a major component of strategic analysis.

3. When conducting military operations in coalition with another power, be sure that the other partner can be relied upon to deliver on his commitments for troops and supplies. Otherwise, an army faces great risks. Julian failed to monitor the willingness and ability of his ally, the king of Armenia, to keep his commitments, with the result that Julian and a Roman army died in the desert.

4. Remember Fabius! The strategy of delay has its place in war and often works. The Persians used it successfully against Julian in Iraq in much the same manner as Fabius had used it against Hannibal. Sometimes the simplest strategic technique is the most effective.

5. Beware of wars in unconventional environments. Roman forces were bogged down in a guerrilla war in Armenia for four years because their political goals could not be achieved by military means. Political wars are best solved by political means. Rome and Persia eventually settled the conflict over Armenia by political means, that is, they partitioned the country. Always seek to achieve your political goals by nonmilitary means first. It is always cheaper.

6. Military strategy functions best when closely linked to political strategy. The Roman military strategy of defending the empire's long borders

could only succeed if Roman political strategy was able to prevent a hostile coalition from striking simultaneously on two fronts. In the absence of political success, the probability of military success was greatly reduced.

7. Remember Hadrian's strategy: when overcommitted, admit it and readjust the security frontier to accommodate reduced military capability. Avoid strategic overreach.

8. The perception of power *is* power. This is especially true with regard to military reputation and prestige. The prestige of the Roman army in the eyes of its tribal adversaries was often sufficient to ward off any potential attack. During World War II, the prestige of the British navy helped deter Hitler from attempting a seaborne invasion of England.

9. Always consider the possibility of opening a second front against the enemy. Fritigern used his political authority to form an alliance with the Germanic tribes along the Rhine. By encouraging the Germans to cross the Rhine, Fritigern's strategy forced Gratian to deal with the problem, thus making it impossible for Gratian to reinforce Valens at Adrianople.

Tactics

1. Always consider the effects of weather on the fighting ability of your men. Roman commanders at Adrianople neglected the heat factor in their assessments, with the consequence that Roman troops went into battle exhausted and thirsty from a long approach march.

2. Julian's and Valentinian's campaigns across the Rhine provide an excellent example of the principle that a defensive position is only secure if you undertake preemptive and proactive operations to prevent the enemy from concentrating against that position.

3. Use and exploit tactical intelligence assets. Fritigern used his scouts to detect the approach of the Roman army in time to recall his cavalry. Valens failed to use his intelligence capabilities and had no idea where Fritigern and his army were. Valens stumbled into the Gothic positions by accident and could not exploit the absence of Fritigern's cavalry.

4. Anticipate the unexpected; think outside the paradigm. Valens should have immediately noted the absence of the Gothic cavalry and asked himself, where was it? Valens had contempt for the Goths as adversaries and, as such, committed the mental error of being unable to think in different terms.

5. When necessary, delay battle and play for time to concentrate decisive forces. Fritigern could have struck the Roman army while it was forming for battle. Instead, he played for time until he could bring his decisive cavalry arm into position.

6. To the extent possible, remain in control of events, especially regarding when to initiate battle. At Adrianople, a unit of archers slipped beyond the command and control of the Roman commander and started a battle at a time when neither side was prepared to fight.

7. Always use cavalry in conjunction with infantry, and think about the synergistic effect of combined arms. The individual infantryman is still a formidable threat to cavalry. Valens's cavalry advanced too far without infantry support and was encircled and crushed. The actions of Marshal Ney and of the Scots Grays at Waterloo are examples of the same mistake.

8. Once you have paid the price for breaking through the enemy position, exploit the penetration rapidly and with sufficient force. Fritigern's attack against and through the Roman left is a good example of how this principle can operate.

9. Commit reserves to exploit a breakthrough or, as Fritigern did after enveloping the Roman center, to deliver a fatal blow. In either case, don't be timid. Commit in force.

FURTHER READING

Ammianus Marcellinus. *Roman History of Ammianus Marcellinus, during the Reigns of the Emperors Constantius, Julian, Jovianus, Valentinian, and Valens.* London: G. Bell, 1894.

Ball, Warwick. *Rome in the East: The Transformation of an Empire.* London: Routledge, 2001.

Burns, Thomas S. "The Battle of Adrianople: A Reconsideration." *Historia* 22 (1973): 336–45.

Cambridge Medieval History. Vol. 1. Cambridge: Cambridge University Press, 1952.

Campbell, Brian. *Warfare and Society in Imperial Rome, 31 BC to 284 AD.* London: Routledge, 2002.

Campbell, J. B. *The Emperor and the Roman Army.* Oxford: Clarendon Press, 2003.

Connolly, Peter. *Greece and Rome at War.* Englewood Cliffs, NJ: Prentice-Hall, 1981.

Delbruck, Hans. *History of the Art of War: The Barbarian Invasions.* Vol. 2. Westport, CT: Greenwood, 1980.

Dixon, Karen R. *The Roman Cavalry from the First Century to the Third Century AD.* London: Routledge, 1997.

Dupuy, R. Ernest, and Trevor N. Dupuy. *The Encyclopedia of Military History.* New York: Harper and Row, 1986.

Ferrill, Arther. *The Fall of the Roman Empire: The Military Explanation.* London: Thames and Hudson, 1986.

Fuller, J. F. C. *The Military History of the Western World.* New York: Da Capo, 1954.

Goldsworthy, Adrian. *The Roman Army at War: 100 BC to AD 200.* London: Oxford University Press, 1998.

———. *Roman Warfare.* London: Cassell Academic Press, 2000.

Greenblatt, Miriam. *Augustus and Imperial Rome.* Tarrytown, NY: Benchmark Books, 2000.

Hackett, Sir John. *Warfare in the Ancient World.* London: Sidgwick and Jackson, 1989.

Holder, P. A. *Studies in the Auxilia of the Roman Army from Augustus to Trajan.* London: Oxford University Press, 1980.

Jordanes. *Gothic History of Jordanes.* Translated by Charles Mierow. Princeton: Princeton University Press, 1915.

Keppie, Lawrence. *The Making of the Roman Army: From Republic to Empire*. Norman: University of Oklahoma Press, 1998.

Le Bohec, Yann. *The Imperial Roman Army*. London: Routledge, 2002.

Luttwak, Edward N. *The Grand Strategy of the Roman Empire: From the First Century AD to the Third*. Baltimore: Johns Hopkins University Press, 1979.

Mellor, Ronald. *From Augustus to Nero: The First Dynasty of Imperial Rome*. Ann Arbor: Michigan State University Press, 1990.

Oman, Sir Charles. *The Art of War in the Middle Ages*. Vol. 1. London: Greenhill Books, 1924.

Roth, Jonathan. *The Logistics of the Roman Army at War*. Leiden: Brill Academic, 1999.

Wells, Peter. *The Barbarians Speak: How the Conquered Peoples Shaped the Roman World*. Princeton, NJ: Princeton University Press, 2001.

17 THE EMPIRE OF THE HUNS

[370–468 C.E.]

BACKGROUND

Our knowledge of the Huns is completely dependent upon a few sources in Latin and Greek written mostly by their enemies, the Goths and Romans, with whom they had extensive contacts. The Huns had no written language, and there are no written records of their history. What we know of them begins around 370 C.E. when, for reasons that remain unknown, they began to move out of their traditional homeland north of the Aral Sea and Lake Balkash near the Sea of Azov in what is now western Turkestan and entered what is now the north Caucasus, driving another nomadic pastoral people, the Alans, before them. In 374 C.E. the Huns continued their press to the west, coming into contact with the Goths, an agricultural people settled north of the Danube and in communication with the Romans of the eastern empire. Over the next century the Huns continued their movement westward, scattering the tribal peoples before them and sending them hurtling against the borders of the Roman Empire in both East and West. Within a few decades, the Huns had established an enormous empire east of the Roman defenses of the Rhine and Danube, from where they launched military expeditions against the imperial borders. Serving sometimes as allies of the empire, they also mounted the most significant military challenge to Roman power the empire had witnessed in centuries.

The early origins and history of the Huns remain a matter of speculation. The prevailing theory, although not one without its opponents, is that the Huns were a Turko-Mongol people known to the Chinese as early as the third century B.C.E. as the *Hsiung-Nu*. According to the Chinese historian, Ssu-ma Ch'ien, this nomadic people of skilled horse-archers became a strong nation of confederated tribes sometime around the second half of the third century

B.C.E. when they began to mount attacks against the Chinese states. Chinese records suggest that it was these attacks that forced the Chinese to change their own military practices and abandon the heavy wheeled chariot in favor of a mobile cavalry force equipped, like the *Hsiung-Nu* nomads, with bow, lance, and lasso. The *Hsiung-Nu* were nomads the rhythm of whose existence was regulated by their herds of sheep, horses, cattle, and camels and their seasonal movement to pasture and water. Organized into tribes, they dressed in skins, slept on furs, and camped in felt tents. Their religion was a vague shamanism based on the cult of *Tangri* or Heaven and the worship of sacred mountains and swords. All of these practices of the *Hsiung-Nu* were common to the other nomads of the Asian steppe and are found centuries later among the Huns and Mongols.

The *Hsiung-Nu* were horse-archers skilled with bow, lance, and lasso who utilized the raid and hit-and-run attacks as their military tactics against the Chinese armies that pursued them. Speed, mobility, and surprise have always been the characteristics of nomadic battle tactics, and the nomad rarely engaged the enemy in set-piece battle. Instead, they often raided the enemy force, drawing it after them in a feigned retreat sometimes lasting for days or even weeks until the enemy was exhausted or drawn to unfavorable terrain, at which time the nomad horse-archers would attack.

The *Hsiung-Nu* appear as a force to be reckoned with by the Chinese in the second half of the third century B.C.E., at the time when China had achieved a modicum of unity under the Chin Dynasty. The result of the contact between the two peoples was a state of almost continuous war for two centuries. In 51 B.C.E., the *Hsiung-Nu* fell into a civil war among themselves caused by two rival chieftains seeking command of the tribal confederation. One of these chiefs, Hu-Han-ye, went over to the Chinese and became their vassal controlling the lands north of the Gobi. The other chief, Che-Che, left Mongolia with his tribes and moved far to the west settling near the Aral Sea sometime around 44 B.C.E. Having split the nomad confederation, the Chinese moved to destroy the segment under Che-Che.

In 36 B.C.E., the Chinese sent a large army under their best general, Ch'en T'ang, against the western nomads. Che-Che was captured and beheaded and his tribes scattered over the western Aral steppes. The *Hsiung-Nu* of the west now dropped completely from history. Unlike the history of the eastern *Hsiung-Nu*, which was preserved and recorded by the Chinese, the western branch of the confederation lacked any contact with a literate civilization that could have recorded its history. The record is completely blank for the next 400 years until 370 C.E. when their descendants, the Huns, crossed the Don River and invaded the lands of the Alans.

Even their name, Hun, is uncertain and is derived from the Roman practice of calling them *Hunni*, which may be a corruption of the Chinese *Hsiung-Nu*. Some support for this proposition is received from the Indian practice of calling them *Huna*. We do not know why the Huns left their ancestral home in the steppes above the Aral Sea and moved southwestward. It might have been a collapse in the ecology of the steppe brought on by drought and acidity that made feeding the livestock difficult. This, in turn, may have produced famine. The folklore of the Huns explains the migration as the consequence of an accidental discovery of the lands beyond the Don River by Hun hunters. According to the legend, a party of Hun horsemen was stalking a deer that crossed the Don at a shallow ford. The river had always been the border of Hun territory. Across the river was believed to be a trackless waste where no humans lived. Pursuing the deer, the Huns crossed the river only to discover that the land was rich in dark soil and grass. If the steppe was suffering a famine at the time, the discovery of a new land with plenty of pasture and water could well have proved irresistible to the nomadic Huns. For whatever reason, sometime around 370 C.E. the Huns crossed the Don under the command of their chief, Balamir or Balamber, and invaded the land of the Alans. Over the next forty years, they continued their movement to the west and south, driving the previously settled peoples of the area before them and sending them crashing into the Roman imperial borders. Map 17.1 depicts the movements of the Huns during this period.

Around 376 C.E., reports reached the Roman officers commanding the Danube garrisons that new and unusually large movements of barbarian peoples as far north of the river as the Black Sea were taking place. It was not until large numbers of people, mostly Goths, began appearing on the far bank of the Danube that the Romans began to take seriously the rumors of a new and warlike people who had arrived from the east and were laying waste to the lands of the *barbaricum*. The first to fall under the Hun assault were the Alans,

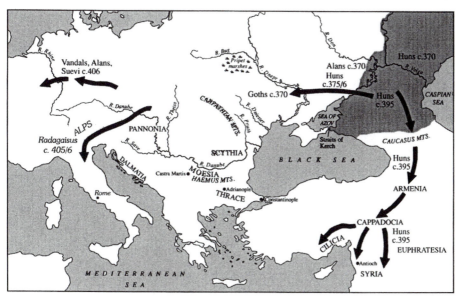

Map 17.1 The Westward Movements of the Huns (370–406 C.E.)

themselves a nomadic people, who appear to have put up a struggle in which vast numbers of them were slaughtered before the nation submitted. Now they were pressed into the military service of the Huns, whose armies attacked the great Ostrogothic kingdom of Ermanaric sometime after 370 C.E. This Gothic kingdom had been only recently formed. Based on a rich agriculture and animal husbandry, the kingdom of the Goths stretched from the Don to the Dniester River and from the Black Sea to the Pripet marshes (see Map 17.1). The initial Hun raids were met with resistance as the Ostrogoths under their aged king, Ermanaric, defended their land. For almost three years the Ostrogoths fought the Huns who, as was their practice, commonly slaughtered the people and burned their houses. The rich villages were destroyed, and the sheer horror of the Hun slaughter so depressed Ermanaric that he committed suicide in despair. Leadership of the Ostrogoths now fell to Ermanaric's great-nephew, Vithimiris, who continued the resistance against the Huns. For a year Vithimiris fought one battle after another only to be defeated again and again, until he himself was killed. With his death, most of the Ostrogoths submitted to the Huns.

The Hun victory brought them to the borders of the Visigoth kingdom ruled by Athanaric, who determined to resist the invaders by building fortifications along the banks of the Dniester River. He dispatched a large force of soldiers under a commander named Munderich across the river and twenty miles to the front to locate and report on the movements of the Huns and to screen the movements of the main Visigoth army preparing its defenses. The Huns realized that Munderich's force was not the main body and ignored it. Riding hard through a moonlit night, the Huns broke contact with Munderich and passed around him, making for a ford on the Dniester twenty miles to his rear. The Huns crossed the river behind Athanaric's main army and struck the ill-prepared force from the rear, completely shattering their defenses and scattering the Visigoths to the Carpathian foothills behind them. At about the same time, Hun armies engaged the other two Visigothic chieftains, Alatheus and Saphrax, crushing their armies and killing their commanders. Athanaric gathered what was left of his army and repaired to a defensive wall between the Pruth and Danube rivers. His efforts availed him nothing, for he was again attacked and taken by surprise and his troops massacred.

The Hun terror had its desired effect, and the panic-stricken Goths now abandoned their lands and, with their families and wagon-loads of goods, streamed toward the Danube where they sought entry into the Roman Empire. Contemporary accounts of the time record that, in the autumn of 376 C.E., 200,000 Goths were gathered on the far side of the Danube seeking to enter Roman Thrace and safety from the Huns. After some delay and negotiation, the Goths were permitted to enter the imperial borders, probably under military pressure when the Romans discovered that a large Hun column was maneuvering north of the Danube and threatened to cross the Danube upstream.

The lesser of two evils was to permit the Goths to enter and to deal with them later. Two years later, in August 378 C.E., the Romans attempted to expel the Goths and suffered a terrible defeat at Adrianople. The Romans were now forced on to the defensive, and the Huns brought large tracts of Pannonia, especially the eastern sections, under their control.

Little is heard from the Huns again until 395 C.E. when they launched their first great invasion of the Roman Eastern Empire with raids that far exceeded the scale of their previous attacks. In the winter of 395 C.E. the Danube River froze, permitting the Huns to cross into the Roman provinces and renew the devastation that Emperor Theodosius I (proclaimed in 379 C.E.) had managed to check by his victories in the Balkans a few years earlier. Thrace and Dalmatia were savagely attacked. But the greatest attack by the Huns came far to the east. Moving over the passes of the Caucasus Mountains, their bands overran Armenia and then made for the richest provinces of the eastern empire. The villages of Cappadocia were burned, and the invaders may even have reached the Halys River. Areas of Syria came under attack, and "the enemy's cavalry thundered along the banks of the Orontes." Great groups of captives and herds of livestock were marched to the north of the Caucasus where they were set to work on the land. The Huns were always short of manpower, and it became a regular practice to set their captives to work on the land. In Armenia the Huns reached the city of Melitene, then overran the province of Euphratesis and into Cilicia. St. Jerome described these raids on the provinces of the eastern empire thus: "Behold, the wolves, not of Arabia, but of the north, were let loose upon us last year from the far-off rocks of the Caucasus, and in a little while overran great provinces." Emperor Theodosius had failed to provide for the defense of the eastern provinces, and much of the Roman army, or at least that part of it that was mobile, was in the West. The result was that there was no regular Roman military force to meet the Hun attack. A eunuch, one Eutropius, hastily assembled what forces he could, including some allied Gothic troops, and finally took the field against them. He failed to bring them to battle decisively, and the Huns withdrew, taking most of their loot with them. Still, at the end of 398 C.E. peace had been restored in the East.

For thirteen years the peace remained undisturbed in the eastern empire, and little is heard of the Huns. At the turn of the new century the Huns launched a massive attack against the empire of the West, staged from their recently conquered positions in the northern Balkans. The Hun assault was first directed against the peoples living between them and the Rhine. In 401 C.E. Alaric, king of the Vandals, left his base in Epirus due to pressure from the Huns and marched on Aquileia and Milan, where a Roman army under Stilicho drove him back. Another battle was fought with Alaric at Pollenza, but it was indecisive and he withdrew. In 405 C.E. another invader, Radagaisus, at the head of a confederation of Ostrogoths, Vandals, Alans, and Quadi broke into Italy and was trapped and defeated at Fiesole, where many of the men starved to death. Next year, hordes of Vandals crossed the Rhine at Mainz, swept over Gaul, and occupied Treves, Rheims, Tournai, Arras, Amiens, Paris, Orleans, Tours, Bordeaux and Toulouse. Simultaneously the Alemanni conquered Worms, Speyer, and Strasbourg. The barbarians had crossed the Rhine frontier of the western empire, and they were never driven back. The Romans, always the pragmatists, settled the tribes in Gaul as allies. The point is that this tremendous surge of the barbarians across the Rhine to enter the western empire was the result of pressure from the Huns. Many of the tribes, especially the Germans, had fought against the Huns and fled to the West only after they had been defeated and there was no choice except Hun slavery.

Attacks by the Huns on the lower Danube provinces resumed in 408 C.E. when Uldin, the first Hun chieftain for which we have a name, crossed the Danube and captured Castra Martis, a fortress lying back from the river in Moesia. Uldin then overran Thrace. When the Romans tried to buy him off, the Hun chief rejected their offer and pointed toward the rising sun, saying that if he wished, he would find it easy to subdue all the land the sun looked upon. The Romans persisted, however, and bribed his followers and subordinates so that many of Uldin's troops deserted him for Roman pay and favor. Over the next four years the eastern empire rebuilt the Danubian defenses and undertook to extend and improve the walls of Constantinople itself against future Hun attacks.

Sometime between 415 and 420 C.E., the Huns undertook a large-scale raid into Persia, where they devastated the land and took thousands of captives. They were met by a Persian army whose own archers were excellent soldiers and who defeated the Huns. Leaving their booty behind to increase their speed, the Hun raiders returned to their northern base. In 420 C.E., Rome went to war with Persia. As the army became more deeply involved in the conflict, the northern frontier was stripped of its defenders, who were needed to press the attack against Persia. With the defenses weakened, the Huns took the opportunity to launch a plundering raid against Thrace. And then the northern frontier was quiet again for almost fifteen years.

If one were to focus only upon the Roman experience with the Huns in the eastern empire one would obtain the impression that they were unrelentingly hostile to the Romans. In fact, the situation between Romans and Huns in the western empire was more complex, at least until 440 C.E. or so. For example, while Uldin attacked the Roman East in 405 C.E., he provided a large contingent of Hun soldiers to aid the Roman general, Stilicho, in the West to defeat the invasion of Radagaisus. It was the Hun troops at the battle of Fiesole that outflanked and trapped the Germans. Later, in 408 C.E., the Romans concluded a treaty with the Huns providing for Hun contingents in the event of conflict with the Germans who had been newly settled in Gaul. This treaty seems to have required an exchange of hostages, one of whom, a young man named Aetius, was sent to live among the Huns where he learned their language and their military skills. Later, Aetius became one of Rome's greatest generals and won several victories over the Huns, not least of which was the battle of Chalons in 451 C.E. It was another band of Huns fighting in the service of Rome that defeated an attempt by Alaric's brother to invade Italy in 409 C.E. In that same year the Romans brought a force of 10,000 Huns to Italy to counter the threat by Alaric, who then abandoned his plan to march on Rome. In 425 C.E. when the usurper John was fighting for his life against the armies of the eastern empire, it was Aetius who was sent to raise a force of Huns to help him. They arrived too late to influence the outcome but were handsomely paid and sent home. It was said that the number of Huns sent home was 60,000. Hun units served as mercenaries and even auxiliaries in both halves of the Roman Empire, sometimes becoming enemies, but always feared and useful as a force of arms.

Attila

Sometime around 423 C.E., a certain Rua rose to the military leadership of the last and greatest confederation of Hun tribes. He shared his position with his brother, Octar, and also had a third brother, Mundiuch, who was the father of Attila and Bleda. We have no information as to what happened to Mundiuch and Oktar, but by 432 C.E. Rua was the sole military leader of the Huns. In that same year Aetius fell into disrepute as a rebel and fled to the Dalmatian coast, where he traveled throughout the provinces of Pannonia to reach the camp of the Huns. Having lived among them as a hostage years ago and used them in his armies after that, he counted the Huns as friends and allies. Rua agreed to support Aetius, but at a price. Five years earlier the Roman province of Pannonia Secunda, including the great city of Sirmium, had been recovered by force by the armies of the eastern empire. In 433 C.E., as a result of the treaty between Aetius and Rua, the province of Pannonia Prima was surrendered to the Huns.

With the help of the Huns, Aetius was able to reestablish his position in Italy, and for the next fifteen years Italy and the western empire remained undisturbed by the Huns. During that time Aetius, in league with the Gallo-Roman landlords of Gaul, maintained themselves in power by using their Hun allies in their conflicts against the Burgundians, the Goths, and the Bagaudae, all of which sought greater freedom from Roman control. The Huns became the main support for the continued Gallo-Roman domination of Gaul until 439 C.E. when the Visigoths massacred the Hun contingents in a battle outside Toulouse. The Huns never came to Aetius's rescue again.

Meanwhile, Rua had turned his attention once more to the borders of the eastern empire. Once more the Huns had chosen their timing well. The Vandals had attacked North Africa and overtaken large areas of the Roman province in 434 C.E. Except for Carthage and Cirta, the entire province had been surrendered. The eastern empire responded by assembling a large naval

and ground force and setting sail to help the western empire regain its lost
territories and protect its main source of grain imports. This, of course,
weakened the Roman defenses in the East. Rua threatened to attack if the
Romans did not turn over to him certain peoples who had fled the Hun
dominion and taken refuge within the imperial borders. The Romans played
for time in negotiations, and just as Rua was preparing to begin his campaign against the Romans, he died. His death greatly relieved the Romans,
but it was short-lived, for Rua was succeeded by his two nephews, Bleda and
the younger Attila, who proved even more difficult to deal with.

Word reached Constantinople that the expedition to recover the African
province had met defeat in the field. The war in Africa dragged on, making
peace with the Huns even more necessary to keep the northern borders of
the empire secure. In 435 C.E. in the treaty of Margus the Romans agreed to pay
Attila and the Huns 700 pounds of gold a year in return for peace. Between
435 and 439 C.E. the Huns kept their word. Attila and Bleda turned inward
and began a war of conquest to increase their empire. Map 17.2 shows the
great size of the empire of the Huns in 440 C.E. at the time of its greatest
expansion. The western boundary of the Huns did not reach the Rhine, for
the kingdoms of the Burgundians and Ripuarian Franks and some smaller
tribal kingdoms lay between them and the river. To the north, sources tell us
that Attila ruled "the islands in the ocean," which historians now agree were
islands in the Baltic Sea. The empire stretched eastward including Scythia
and, perhaps, even the Alans between the Don River and the area west of the
Aral Sea, though this is less certain. All the Germanic and other nations
between the Alps and the Baltic, and between the Caspian (or somewhat

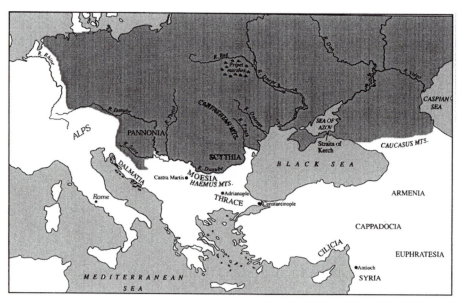

Map 17.2 Empire of the Huns (440 C.E.)

west of it) and an area just east of the Rhine recognized Bleda and Attila as their overlords. The two brothers seemed always to have acted in concert and regarded their empire as a single property, even as they divided it between them, ruling each half separately. We do not know which portion was allotted to each brother.

While Bleda and Attila were expanding their empire between 435 and 440 C.E., peace prevailed on the northern frontier of the eastern empire, even though the emperor failed to deliver to the Huns the agreed-upon 700 pounds of gold each year. In the West, Attila continued the policy of his uncle, Rua, and continued to supply troops to Aetius and the landowners of Gaul until the Visigoths destroyed the Hun army in 439 C.E. The emperor of the eastern empire, Theodosius, instructed that the fortifications around Constantinople be strengthened during this time, that the Danube fleet be increased, and that the northern fortifications along the Danube be repaired and fully manned. Most of this had been accomplished by 430 C.E. so that there was little chance that Attila could respond with violence in light of the Romans' refusal to afford him his annual tribute payment of gold.

Once more, however, events turned to the advantage of the Huns. Word reached Constantinople that Carthage had finally fallen to the Vandals. The Vandal attack on the island of Rhodes now made it possible for them to interrupt the vital grain supply from Egypt. Theodosius came to the aid of the western empire in the spring of 440 C.E., when a large fleet of 1,100 ships with troops commanded by five generals (all with Germanic names!) set sail from Constantinople to rescue Carthage from the Vandals. Within the same year a Persian army under Yezdegerd II invaded Roman Armenia for reasons that remain unknown. What was left of the Roman army was deployed to meet the threat. Once more the defenses of the northern frontier were stripped of troops to meet military requirements elsewhere. Attila's opportunity had come.

The Huns opened hostilities by attacking a small Roman fort north of the Danube. They then crossed the river in force and devastated a number of towns on the southern bank. In a few days the great city of Vininacium (modern Kostolacz) fell into their hands and was razed to the ground. The city remained uninhabited for more than a century afterwards. Next the city of Margus suffered the same fate, while a separate Hun army attacked and overwhelmed the fortress of Constantia. The major disasters of the year were still to come, however. Singidunum (modern Belgrade) was attacked and burned, as was the vitally important city of Sirmium, the hinge upon which the defense of the entire Danube frontier turned. With the destruction of Sirmium in 441 C.E., the Hun campaign came to an end. The densely settled land south of the Danube was filled with walled cities, towns, and fortresses that cramped the maneuver and speed of the Hun armies and, in any case, were difficult to overwhelm. Although the depth of the Hun penetration of the Roman province was not great, the Huns had broken an enormous gap in the fortifications of the Danube frontier. The Balkans now lay at the mercy of the Hun cavalry squadrons. Roman defenses were so thin that the chroniclers noted that Attila had met no significant resistance from the Roman army. In 442 C.E., Attila opened negotiations with the eastern empire to retrieve the gold owed him.

A treaty between the Romans and Huns called for all arrears of tribute to be paid in full and for all fugitives from the Huns taking refuge within the imperial borders to be surrendered. As the year passed, the Persian threat to Armenia receded when the Persians withdrew. More importantly, the great fleet and its soldiers sent to rescue Carthage returned to Constantinople. With his military situation much improved, Theodosius took a stronger stand against Attila's demands, especially as the campaign season of 443 C.E. came around. When Theodosius's emissaries refused to hand over the fugitives to the Huns, Attila's army drove eastward along the banks of the Danube, capturing some Roman forts, and then attacked the city of Ratiaria, the capital of the province of Dacia Ripensis, which was also the base of the Danube fleet and contained one of the state arms factories. The city was overwhelmed and utterly destroyed, its citizens carried off into slavery.

The Hun rear was now secure so that no Roman counterattack could cut the Hun line of communication when they turned into the interior of the imperial provinces. The Hun army rode up the valley of the river Margus (modern Morava) to the city of Naissus (modern Nish), which sat on the right bank of the Nischava River. Naissus was thickly populated and the site of another Roman arms factory. When the Hun armies departed, the city that was the birthplace of Constantine lay in ruins and remained so for another century. The Huns turned southeast and devastated another great Balkan city, Sardica (modern Sophia). The road to the capital was now open, and the Hun armies galloped down the military highway and attacked Phillipopolis. When Phillipopolis fell, the defense of the European provinces was rendered impossible, for it was at this great ancient city that the north-south road from Oescus on the Danube to the Aegean Sea crossed the old highway running from the Bosphorus to the West. By now the Huns were heavily encumbered with prisoners and booty.

At last the Huns confronted the army of Theodosius. The chroniclers tell us that the Roman army was commanded by its best generals, Aspar, an Alan, and the Germans Areobindus and Arnegisclus, who, it turned out, proved to be no match for Attila and his swift columns of horse-archers. The Roman commanders met the Huns in a series of pitched battles outside the capital and suffered heavy defeats in them all. Eventually, the Roman armies were cut off from the capital and forced back into the Chersonesus. The Huns pressed on and reached the sea, only to be confronted by a series of walled fortresses protecting the approaches to Constantinople itself. Unable to mount successful attacks against these defenses, Attila turned his army toward the Chersonesus, engaged the Roman army, and destroyed it. With this result, Theodosius had little choice but to beg for terms.

Negotiations between Roman and Hun began in August 443 C.E., and by autumn the Peace of Anatolius was signed. The terms required that the Hun fugitives be handed over at once, which the Romans, having already killed them, found difficult to meet. Eventually, a few surviving fugitives were found and turned over to meet the demand. The arrears of tribute owed to Attila by previous agreement was reckoned at 6,000 pounds and was to be paid at once. In addition, an annual tribute of 2,100 pounds of gold was to be paid. Further, every Roman prisoner who had escaped from the Huns was now to be paid for at twelve *soldi* a head. The Romans were to agree that in the future no Hun fugitive would be given refuge within the empire. His armies in shambles and the Huns at the gates of Constantinople itself, Theodosius had little choice but to agree. After the conclusion of the Peace of Anatolius, we hear little more of the Huns or their armies. Most probably, internal dissension broke out among them, which may have resulted in the murder of Bleda in 445 C.E. at the hand of his younger brother, Attila. We know nothing about what caused the dispute, only that the consequence left Attila the sole ruler of the empire of the Huns.

In 447 C.E. Attila attacked the eastern empire once more. Again the causes for the conflict are obscure, for the Romans had scrupulously observed the terms of the peace. The attack was larger than the previous one and was accompanied by large contingents of soldiers from the subject peoples ruled by the Huns. This time, however, the armies of the empire were not absent or scattered to other fronts. With the walls of Constantinople having been extended and in good repair, the army of Rome marched out of the city of Marcianople to intercept the Hun army and bring it to battle. The battle occurred near the River Utus (modern Vid), the Romans under the command of the distinguished German general, Arnegisclus. The battle lasted all day and was terribly bloody. By the time Arnegisclus had his horse shot out from beneath him and was killed, thousands of soldiers on both sides had been slain or wounded. The Huns held the field at nightfall, but at a terrible cost in manpower that could not easily be replaced. Marcianople, Arnegisclus's base, fell easily to the Huns, but their armies were too weak to attempt an assault against Constantinople itself. Attila turned his armies toward the Balkans, which they devastated with great ferocity. Illyricum, Thrace, Dacia, Moesia, and Scythia, according to Jordanes, "suffered grievously." Loaded down with slaves and plunder, the Hun armies turned for home to recover and repair. But the world had not heard the last of Attila the Hun.

THE ARMY OF THE HUNS

Like all armies, the army of the Huns was deeply rooted in the society from which it sprang. The Hun society belonged to the lower stages of nomadic pastoralism, the herders of livestock—sheep, cattle, horses, and camels. Most important of these animals were sheep, which provided the Hun nomad with meat and skins for clothes and boots. The Huns wore leggings of goat skins and round caps of leather and cloth. Their jackets were made of the skins of *murinae* or marmots. Why this should have been the case instead of a jacket of sheepskin remains unclear. One explanation may be that the marmot is a wild and wily rodent that must be hunted for its skin unlike the domesticated sheep. It may have been that young warriors had to hunt the marmot as a display and test of skill and the resulting skins made into a jacket as a symbol of their becoming warrior-hunters. Often the marmot jacket was worn under a tunic made of flax, which, since nomads do not grow flax (or any other stationary crop), probably was obtained from the settled peoples living at the edge of the steppe. Like most nomadic tribes, their own economy was insufficient to provide for their needs, and they depended upon these fringe settled peoples for important materials like cloth and metal. Hun women augmented the food supply by gathering roots and berries while the males hunted.

Manpower

The number of Huns was relatively small, and although the chroniclers used the term "horde" to describe them, in fact there was no such entity of great size that existed on a permanent basis. The basic unit of the Hun society was the five- or six-person "family" that lived in one tent. Six to ten tents formed a camp, and several camps formed a clan. Several clans comprised a tribe, the society's largest unit. When formed in confederation for temporary purposes, such as carrying out military expeditions, the Hun confederation or *il* consisted of several tribes. An average Hun tribe probably consisted of no more than 5,000 persons, of which no more than 1,000 to 1,200 were adult male warriors. We do not know how many tribes there were in the Hun nation, but it is likely not to have numbered more than eight to ten. This figure suggests that, despite the claims of ancient chroniclers that Hun armies numbered in the hundreds of thousands, in fact the entire society did not exceed 50,000 to 60,000 people and could produce no more than 12,000 to 15,000 soldiers at maximum effort. It was the military ferocity, speed, and mobility of the Huns rather than their numbers that made them so successful. We ought not to imagine, however, that there was some central location where all the Huns lived together. No nomadic society could feed such large numbers for any length of time. Hun society was highly dispersed, with camps of fifty or sixty people tending their herds and searching for pasture. Even within the camp, individual families or "tents" might wander on their own and gather at the tribe's camp only for important events.

Within the tribe or camp, each household owned its own herds, tents, and wagons, so that the ability to accumulate wealth on any scale was impossible. Males spent all day looking after the herds and hunting for food, while females tended the children, household, and camp and fashioned clothes. There was, therefore, no leisure class of nobles or warriors. The most that might be said of a man was that he was "well-born," the proud boast of Attila, signifying that his forebears were courageous warriors. But the reputation of a Hun warrior had to be earned anew; neither reputation, wealth, nor position was hereditary.

Tactical Organization

The dispersion of the Hun society into several levels—family, camp, tribe, and *il*—meant that there was no permanent leadership structure for war. If we can trust the Roman chroniclers who lived among them, the Huns always distinguished between the chief of a clan, the chief of a tribe, and "the leadership of leading men" (*tumultuario primatum ductum*), who were chosen to lead them in war. Such leaders could be removed if necessary, and their authority ended when the war ended. In peace, the clans, tribes, and camps scattered, so that any permanent or institutionalized system of government or military leadership was impossible. There were, therefore, no permanent kings or even permanent military leaders. This is why the Hun governance of its conquered lands, even at its height under Attila, was only marginally effective and why, after Attila died, the Hun empire disappeared within two decades. Attila's sons could not hold their positions against challengers. Military leadership among the Huns was never hereditary, even among the top warriors.

Initially, there does not appear to have been slavery among the Huns, for slavery made little sense among a nomadic people where food was scarce and tasks simple. We do not hear of Hun slaves, although there were reports that the Huns might have kept captives as slaves to do the work of stable boys and shepherds. This situation changed once the Huns moved westward into the lands of the agricultural peoples where slavery made economic sense to help work the land. Once the Huns came into contact with the Romans, slavery became big business, and there are scores of reports listing the number and prices of Hun captives sold to the Romans for slaves. However, at the height of the Hun empire, this changed. Most Hun manpower at this time was in military service, employed to control the captive peoples and undertake raids against the Roman Empire. As such, there was always a shortage of manpower to work the land and carry out other tasks. The Huns began to carry off their captives not to be resold but to be put to work on the land to produce the food surplus that the Huns, who had never tilled the land but had now abandoned the nomadic life altogether, needed to sustain themselves. Even in war there were limits to how many captive peoples could be pressed into military service for any given campaign. The numbers were limited by the ability of the Huns themselves to ensure the loyalty of these units and the need to keep as many of them as possible on the land producing food.

As long as the Hun tribes and clans remained socially and economically decentralized, they could never develop sufficient political and military coherence to threaten more than the isolated districts of the Roman Empire. But with the successful attacks on the Ostrogoths, which were initially carried out by individual tribes and expanded only when they succeeded, the Huns began to develop the first large confederacy of tribes for military purposes for which we have evidence. Even so, the confederacy did not endure. Many of the raids of the Huns against the West seem to have been undertaken by individual tribes or perhaps by only a few operating in concert to take advantage of a local situation of weakness in some area of the imperial border. It is only much later, with Rua and his brothers, that there is evidence of a large, semi-permanent confederation of Hun tribes marshaled for military purposes.

Such large confederations can only sustain themselves if there is adequate food, and adequate food supplies only became available with the conquest of the Ostrogoth lands. Later, as more military excursions succeeded in producing booty and then even tribute payments from Rome and Constantinople, it became clear to the Huns that warfare and extortion provided the resources to permit their control over a larger number of people and greater area of land. This made possible a larger confederation of tribes to make more certain the successful prosecution of war and to share the spoils. Thus it was that warfare became central to the lives of a small nomadic people for whom war had been, as for most nomadic tribes, a sporadic and even rare occurrence. War, with its plunder, spoils, tribute, gifts, hostages, slaves, and so on brought the confederation into being as almost a permanent social institution. Not surprisingly, the nature of leadership in the Hun society and military order changed radically.

With war came wealth beyond anything the Huns had ever experienced, with the result that a form of semi-permanent kingship emerged in the form of war leaders to command the armies and obtain plunder. The vast amount of tribute in gold paid by the Romans was given directly to the leader, as was the booty taken from captured cities and towns. Previously Hun leaders had ruled together, as did Rua and his brothers and Bleda and Attila. But once Attila's brother was gone, only he ruled the confederacy. More important, when he died his sons claimed to inherit the position of leader as if it were passed through some estate. The fact that the Huns initially accepted their claim to leadership shows how radical the change in Hun governance had become.

The plunder of war was the key to Attila's leadership, for it was his distribution of the spoils that bound his men to him. The old tribal chiefs were replaced by Attila's "picked men," some of whom were not even Huns. Attila replaced the tribal chiefs with his personal vassals in a primitive form of feudal arrangement normally reserved to agricultural peoples. With no land to possess, the Huns invented a feudalism based on the distribution of spoils of war. Not surprisingly, the old limits on the power of the chief were eroded so that Attila became an autocrat with no limits on his power. The old consultations among equals fell into disuse, replaced by the will of the chief to declare and fight wars. Attila was the chief judge of disputes among all the tribes and delivered his verdicts with the power of life and death. He even murdered his own brother without penalty.

Attila's governance of his empire was primitive at best. His "picked men" were mostly responsible for keeping order among the captive peoples and ensuring that food was produced in sufficient quantities and distributed to the Huns. This permitted Attila to supply much larger field armies, and since the Huns remained but a small portion of the peoples within the Hun empire, Attila came to rely upon large numbers of troops from his non-Hun subjects to fight his wars, overseen and controlled by Hun officers. Except for the limited functions mentioned, the Huns did little else in the way of government. They built no houses, churches, bridges, irrigation canals, dikes, or anything else. Whereas the Huns once survived and prospered by herding animals, they had become "a parasitic community of marauders. . . . Instead of herding animals they had now learned the more profitable business of herding men."

Attila's power was a function of his ability to provide his vassals with booty, a circumstance that required almost constant war and raiding as a means of obtaining loot. But wealth is a relative thing, and over time its definition changes so that more is required to fulfill one's needs. After Attila's ability to obtain patronage was reduced, as it was by military defeat and the Roman trade embargoes against him, his ability to rule was weakened. The Romans soon learned to exploit this Hun weakness. They shut down the market towns along the Danube so that the Huns could not trade for important goods, and a complete embargo was levied upon arms. When unrest increased within the Hun empire, the Romans were quick to exploit it with money, support, and promises of aid. Eventually, the social base of the empire itself was weakened, a condition that made recruitment and the supply of large armies difficult. By 450 C.E., the Huns were on the defensive. In 451 C.E. they suffered a terrible defeat at Chalons, and a year later their invasion of Italy had to be recalled due to losses caused by famine and plague. A year later Attila was dead. The empire passed to his sons and within a decade collapsed, with the result that Hun society, deprived of its source of wealth, returned to its old form, and its people scattered throughout the Roman Empire.

Sidonius Apollinaris says of the Hun soldier that he was "below average height when afoot; the Hun is great when mounted on his steed." For the seventy years from the first clash of the Huns with Roman frontier posts until the third decade of the fifth century, the Huns remained unchanged in the manner in which they waged war. Attila's horsemen were essentially the same mounted archers, with only a few changes, who in 380 C.E. had entered the West and fought against the Gauls. Although most Huns still fought unarmored, the nobles seem to have acquired Roman body armor and helmets. Attila's armies carried a siege train within them, but the machines were constructed and operated by Roman deserters or soldiers of fortune, not the

Huns themselves. Most important, Hun tactics and equipment remained unchanged until the end.

The Hun was first a mounted archer, and his horse was his primary instrument of war. Ammianus tells us that the Huns "are almost glued to their horses which are hardy . . . but ugly." To the Romans, these steppe horses looked misshapen, with their short legs and big heads—shaggy and snub-nosed—and seemingly too small to ride. Vegetius in his *Mulomedicina*, his work on veterinary medicine, has left us an excellent account of the horses ridden by the Huns. In his classification of horses in terms of their fitness for war, Vegetius gives first place to the animals of the Huns because of their "patience, perseverance, and . . . capacity to endure cold and hunger." These were hardy creatures, turned out to fend for themselves in winter, with the survivors being gathered up in spring. They were accustomed to cold and frost. Vegetius remarks that they were better than the Roman horse who, "unless it has good shelter and warm stable, will catch one disease after another." Vegetius's description of the Hun horse is complete. They have, he says, great hooked heads, protruding eyes, narrow nostrils, broad jaws, strong and stiff necks, manes hanging below their knees, overlarge ribs, curved backs, bushy tails, cannon bones (upper thighs) of great strength, small pasterns, wide-spreading hooves, hollow loins; their bodies are angular with no fat on the rump or the muscles of the back, their stature inclining to length rather than to height, "and there is beauty even in their ugliness." He adds, "they are quite sensible and bear wounds well."

Fig. 17.1 The Hun Soldier. Adapted from Arther Ferrill, *The Fall of the Roman Empire* (New York: Thames and Hudson, 1986). Reprinted with permission.

We cannot tell from Vegetius's description what *kind* of horse the Huns rode, but we can say with some assurance that it was not the famed Przwalsky horse of the later Mongols with its upright mane and turnpike tail. Nor do we know if the Hun horse, like the Mongol mount, could scrape away snow to find its own fodder underneath and survive on leaves and moss. Hun horses were either cut at the ears or branded to mark ownership. All their steeds were geldings, for a knowledge of castration was essential to nomadic pastoralism. Without it, the stallions fighting over harems of mares and leading them away would have made horse herding impossible.

Sidonius tells us that the Huns were superior horsemen. "Scarce had the infant learned to stand without its mother's aid when a horse takes him on his back. You would think that the limbs of man and horse were born together, so firmly does the rider always stick to the horse; any other folk is carried on horseback; this folk lives there." Figure 17.1 portrays a Hun horseman in full battle kit. The Hun soldier sat upon a saddle fashioned of wood or leather. Once, when he thought himself trapped and facing defeat, Attila ordered his men to make a pile of these wooden saddles to be used as his funeral pyre should he fall in battle. The Huns had no spurs and used leather whips with handles made of wood to urge their mounts to gallop. We are uncertain if the Huns used stirrups, for we have no surviving examples in grave sites. But if they had been fashioned of leather or wood (the Huns had no metal working) they would not have survived in any case. From the perspective of the modern archer, however, it is almost impossible to imagine the Hun soldier's talent with the bow while at full gallop, including the ability to fire his arrows to the rear while retreating (also a Parthian talent, thus, the "Parthian Shot," corrupted in English to be "the parting shot"), without the balance and stability provided by the stirrup.

The Roman chroniclers make quite a fuss about the Huns' shoes, perhaps because the Romans regarded their own military boots so highly. (These boots had been made by the *Ciocciara* people of southern Italy, the former Samnites, for the Roman army since the defeat of the Samnites at the Battle of Caudine Forks around 350 B.C.E. The author's forebears are from this region of Italy.) The Huns' shoes were fitted to the needs of the horseman, not the infantry, and their soles were made of soft and pliable leather to be easily slipped into their stirrups (perhaps) and to give the soldier a good feel for the movements of his mount. The chroniclers report that the Huns were bandy-legged and walked clumsily. Even so, the Huns often fought on foot.

Equipment

The Hun horseman could shoot his arrows to the left and right, forward and backward, with equal accuracy and persistence, even while galloping at full speed, our chroniclers tell us. The basic weapon of the Hun soldier was his bow, which was very accurate up to fifty to sixty meters, with an effective range when fired in volley of 160 to 175 meters. Modern research demonstrates that, at this range, almost 100 percent of the arrows will strike within a box fifty yards by twenty yards, or about the same space occupied by a Roman infantry *cohort*. The Hun bow was a reflexed composite bow 140 to 160 centimeters in length. Its wooden core was backed by sinews and bellied with horn. Seven bone plaques stiffened the ears and the handle, a pair on each ear and three on the handle, two on its sides and one on its top. The string, often silk or rolled animal sinew, was permanently made fast to the bow. This bow or similar ones were common among the nomadic peoples of Asia and remain so to this day. Arrows were tipped with fire-hardened wood or bone, metal being too expensive and unavailable to the Hun nomads unless obtained by trade with the agricultural peoples living on the fringes of the steppe.

The Hun soldier was also equipped to fight in close combat, and he sometimes dismounted to close with the enemy. To accomplish this, he carried a sword. Originally, the Hun sword seems to have been a heavy cutting weapon. Later on it is likely that he may have carried the Roman *gladius* or the Goth *spatha*. Most often the Hun soldier fought with his sword from horseback. An important Hun weapon was the lance. Ten to fifteen feet long, it seemed a clumsy weapon to our chroniclers. But to those who actually experienced its effect in battle, it was a terrible weapon. One soldier, Valerius Flaccus, has left us his impression of the Hun lance. He says, "Stretching out over the horse's head and shoulders, the fir-wood shaft, firmly resting on their [the soldier's] knees, cast a long shadow upon the enemy's field and forces its way with all the might of the warrior and steed." Once more we see indirect evidence of the stirrup, for the lance could not be wielded in this manner without the stirrup. We do not know if the lance was a traditional Hun weapon or acquired later from the Goths and Germans or even the Roman *cataphracti* who also used it. The fact that it was made of "fir-wood" or any wood at all suggests that it was not available on the steppe and was acquired after the wars with the Goths, but we cannot be certain.

The Hun soldier also carried the traditional nomad weapon, the lasso, with which he was well acquainted from his practice of lassoing herd animals. Ammianus tells us that "while the enemy are guarding against wounds from sword thrusts, the Huns throw strips of cloth plaited into nooses over their opponents and so entangle them that they fetter their limbs." Ammianus is not entirely correct here since it is unlikely that the Huns, who did not weave their own cloth but acquired it by trade, would have made lassos from plaited cloth. More likely the lasso was fashioned from strips of leather. The lasso became a powerful weapon in the hands of the later Mongols as well.

Evidence from graves suggests that the Huns wore scaled body armor fashioned of bone while still nomads of the steppe. Cuirasses and armor made of bone plates were also worn by Hellenistic horsemen. Making armor out of bone was a necessity for the Huns who had no knowledge of metal working as far as we know. Pausanias tells of this bone body armor in his description of its use by the Sarmatians.

Fig. 17.2 Bronze Grave Pendant of a Hun Archer

[They] collect the hoofs of their mares, clean them, and split them until they resemble the scales of a dragon. Anyone who has not seen a dragon has at least seen a green fir cone. The fabric [armor shirt] which they make of these hoofs may not inaptly be likened to the clefts on a fir cone. In these pieces they bore holes, and having stitched them together with the sinews of horses and oxen [rawhide lacing], they use them as corselets, which are inferior to Greek breast-plates neither in elegance nor strength, for they are both sword-proof and arrow proof.

Figure 17.2 shows a drawing of a bronze pendant recovered from a Hun grave that portrays what seems to be a Hun soldier dressed in plated body armor, although we cannot tell of what material it was fashioned. Later on the Huns acquired Roman and

Goth body armor by trade or by capturing Roman armories and took to wearing metal armor as a result.

At the beginning of the wars with Rome Hun soldiers wore soft leather or felt caps, but they later acquired Roman and Goth metal helmets. A favorite helmet of the Huns was the German *spangenhelm* with its characteristic nasal guard. Sidonius Apollinaris tells us that the helmets fit easily because Hun skulls were deliberately deformed by tying a band around their heads as children. He tells us that "the nostrils, while soft, are blunted by an encircling band, to prevent the two passages [of the nose] from growing outward between the cheekbones, that thus make room for the helmets for these children are born for battle." Evidence from graves suggests that the Huns practiced skull deformation, but it was probably for cosmetic and beauty reasons rather than for military ones. Hun shields were made of wickerwork to make them light and agile and were mostly round. The Hun shield had to be highly maneuverable to blunt sword strikes while on horseback or to shield the soldier from arrows. Moreover, a round shield offers the soldier greater striking area with the sword by permitting him a greater field of vision and striking area than an oblong (Roman) or even figure-eight (Persian) style shield.

Tactics

Hun tactics, although a surprise to the eastern Romans, were common among all peoples of the Asian steppes. A nomadic tribe is always on the move, consequently the whole group constitutes a ready-made army, easily marshaled, self-supporting, and capable of sudden attacks and moving long distances. In a sense the steppe nomad is always on a war footing insofar as he is always prepared to defend his pasture and animals against the predations of other nomads or to extend them at the expense of someone else. The tactics of the Huns (and other steppe nomads) were the tactics of the hunt. The success of the Huns was not due to any superiority of numbers but to the great mobility of small bands of horse-archers who could move quickly over long distances, concentrate rapidly at any given point, fight a battle, quickly disperse, and reconcentrate at another point. When on campaign, these mounted bands moved across a wide front and were followed by their familes, livestock, and wagons, which could be drawn into a defensive *laager* for protection. Although the troop units were able to move rapidly, the large, heavy, four-wheeled wagons were slow moving and frequently must have been immobile. Descriptions of several Hun battles tell of their wagons being so laden with loot that the army literally found it difficult to move at any pace. In some of Attila's campaigns he seems to have replaced these heavy, four-wheeled wagons with a lighter, two-wheeled vehicle. The hilly and wooded terrain of Europe probably slowed even these lighter wagons to a crawl, with the result that the Hun cavalry units must have often been separated from their wagon *laager* base. This forced the Hun squadrons to live off the land and often to disperse widely to find sufficient supplies to keep the army alive. For this reason, the Huns rarely fought in winter.

Hun tactics have been described as "ferocity under authority," a cyclonic operational tempo that took the form of whirlwind advances against the objective followed by quick retirements, in which whole districts were laid waste and entire populations destroyed. The purpose of the savage ferocity of the Hun attack was to create a psychological state of fear to weaken opposition. The devastation left the rear of the army clear of all potential opposition, which made a quick retreat possible in the face of defeat or heavy opposition. Where the Romans relied upon planning, drill, method, and discipline of their armies, the Huns relied upon fury, surprise, mobility, cunning, and elusiveness. Having moved rapidly to catch the enemy unprepared for battle or having maneuvered to surprise his army by an attack from some unanticipated direction, the Hun army closed rapidly with its adversary usually after a period of archery preparatory fire to inflict considerable casualties.

Once upon their foe, the Huns fought hand-to-hand, first with the sword while mounted and then, if necessary, on foot where the lasso could be employed as well. When dismounted, the Huns seem to have fought in the tactical formation the Romans called *cuneatim*, which reminds us of the *cunei* or the wedge formations that Tacitus tells us were used by the German tribes. We do not know if these *cuneatim* formations were comprised of relatives, family, and clan members as they were for the Germans, but this possibility seems most likely.

Logistics

The weakness of Hun operational practice lay in their poor and often nonexistent logistics system. Their rapidity of movement often forced them to live off the land, which their numbers, though not huge, were sufficient to deplete fairly rapidly, forcing their armies to break up into small groups or to retire. A second problem was their general inability to storm walled cities and fortresses. During Attila's day, some Hun armies carried siege equipment manned by Roman deserters, but it was never available in sufficient numbers to give the Hun army a significant capability to deal with strong defensive works. When confronted with cities, the Huns either gained entrance to them by ruse or betrayal or bypassed them. The Hun method of fighting was admirably suited for the steppe but not as well suited for the topographically more difficult terrain of Europe, with its great numbers of cities and towns.

THE BATTLE OF CHALONS (451 C.E.)

Attila's relations with the West following the defeat of the Hun army under Litorius at Toulouse in 439 C.E. remain obscure. His relations with Aetius remained cordial, as they had been under Rua, and in 445 C.E. Attila was appointed "master of the soldiers of the Western Empire," an honorary position arranged by Aetius (who still depended upon Hun troops or, at least, their neutrality to control Gaul) that brought a large financial stipend with it. In 449 C.E., Attila suddenly changed his course and provoked a diplomatic conflict over an obscure event that had transpired during the campaign of 441 C.E. He demanded that the western empire hand over certain persons and threatened war if they did not. In the previous spring, Attila had signed a third treaty with the eastern empire governed by Theodosius, which made his strategic rear secure from Roman attack. Thus prepared, Attila turned his attention to the West, although the reasons why he did so are unknown and may be as simple as his constant need for more booty to shore up his vassals and troops. Map 17.3 shows the military campaigns undertaken by Attila against the Romans of both empires.

In the early months of 450 C.E., Attila announced that he intended to attack the Visigothic kingdom in Gaul centered on Toulouse, perhaps in revenge for the earlier defeat of the Hun army there. Acting as an ally of Rome, he announced that he was carrying out his war as a friend of Rome (and Aetius), who had fought the Visigoths in Gaul on and off for more than a decade. There is some speculation that Attila may actually have been trying to undercut Aetius by showing Emperor Valentinian, no great friend of the Roman general, that Attila could guarantee Gaul without the help of Aetius. This being as it may, the emperor's sister, Honoria, attempted to reverse her declining fortunes in the court by sending Attila a ring and promising to marry him if he rescued her. Already having decided to attack the Roman West, Attila accepted Honoria's offer, which permitted him to levy a claim

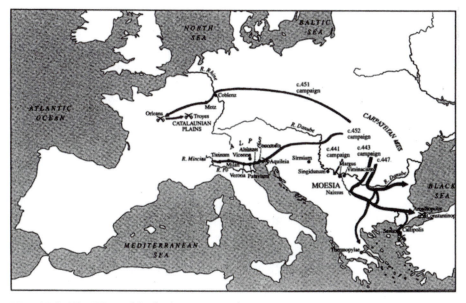

Map 17.3 The Wars of Attila (441–452 C.E.)

for half the empire as a consequence of becoming Honoria's husband. The Romans thought the claim ludicrous and refused.

Events now worked to turn the strategic equation against Attila. Theodosius, the eastern emperor, was thrown from his horse and died on 28 July, 450 C.E. That August, a new emperor, Marcian, was crowned and immediately changed the foreign policy of the eastern empire. He executed the minister who had concluded the treaty with Attila and announced that Rome would no longer send gold as tribute to Attila. Attila's strategic rear was no longer secure. In a series of diplomatic maneuvers that only angered Attila further, the emperor announced that, if Attila threatened war, the armies of Constantinople would meet the Huns with a force equal to the task. At the same time, the Honoria affair only worked to heighten tempers in the Western court, with the result that, by November 450 C.E., there was an open breach in relations between Rome and Attila.

With the threat of war looming on both of Attila's flanks, the wiser course of action would have been to permit matters to calm down and do nothing. But Attila was not to be denied his war. After considering whether to attack the East before the West, he decided to march against the western empire of Rome. Soon after the new year began (451 C.E.), Attila's armies left their log huts on the Hungarian plain and, without foreign allies, began their journey westward, crossing the Rhine near Coblenz after cutting down trees on the river's banks to build rafts. Initially Rome seemed to believe that war was still avoidable, a delusion they quickly abandoned when Attila renewed his demand for half the empire as Honoria's husband! Aetius was put in command of the armies, and he immediately set about attempting to repair the old hatreds between himself and the Visigoths, Burgundians, and Franks in Gaul, whose manpower he desperately needed to fill his ranks.

Events turned ominous for Aetius's efforts, for famine was raging in Italy and supplies and manpower were at a premium. In addition, the legions were in desperately poor shape. The cities of Gaul were already going up in flames as "Attila with his fearsome squadrons spread himself in raids upon the plains of the Belgian. Aetius had scarce left the Alps, leading a thin, meagre force of auxilliaries without legionaries." It was at this point that Aetius was rescued by the arrival of Theodoric, the king of the Goths, who had finally concluded that Attila was the greater threat to his own kingdom and independence and that an alliance of convenience with his old enemy, Aetius, was a strategic imperative. Contingents of Ripuarian Franks, Alans, and Saxons also joined Aetius's army as he prepared to meet Attila. What was at stake was no less than control of Gaul and, with it, the Roman Western Empire.

While Theodoric was deciding whether to join Aetius, Attila struck the first blow. Early in 451 C.E., he set out from beyond the Rhine and marched westward into Gaul. The size of the Hun army is unknown (we may safely discount the figure of 500,000 provided by the chroniclers), but it was considerable. It was a conglomerate force including Huns, Ostrogoths, Gepids,

Sciri, Rugi, Franks, Thuringi, and Burgundians, all serving either for plunder or against their will at the point of a Hun sword. Attila struck for the lands of the Ripuarian Franks just west of the Rhine, using his advance as a platform to make for Orleans, the city at the apex of the Loire River that controlled further movement into Aquitain. Moving rapidly in three columns, Attila's army advanced through Belgic Gaul across a wide front, its right moving on Arras, its left striking down the Moselle River toward Metz, and its center headed toward Paris and Orleans. The destruction was appalling as fire and smoke, murder and rapine swept through Gaul. Rheims, Metz, Cambrai, Treves, Arras, Tongres, Tournai, Therouanne, Cologne, Amiens, Beauvais, Worms, Maintz, and Strasbourg were all sacked and burnt. Only Paris, then but a small town on an island in the Seine, escaped through the efforts of a local farm girl who urged the residents to resist. This girl became the patron saint of the city, Saint Genevieve.

As Aetius's army moved to intercept the invaders, the Huns attacked Orleans. Reports reached Aetius that Sangiban, king of the Alans, whom Aetius had settled in the Orlean region in 442 C.E., intended to betray the city to Attila. Aetius and his army, which now included Theodoric's Goths, moved rapidly to reach Orleans before Attila. Attila won the race and besieged Orleans early in May, pounding the city's walls with rams and siege engines. By the middle of June the city seemed certain to fall to the Huns. One morning a soldier on the walls saw a dust cloud approaching that signaled the approach of Aetius's army. The relief force clashed with the Hun army in a vicious battle in the suburbs and towns surrounding Orleans. Jordanes described the battle: "Driven from street to street, beaten down by stones hurled at them by the inhabitants from the roofs of the houses, the Huns no longer knew what was to become of them, when Attila sounded the retreat. The patrician, Aetius, had not failed in his word; it was the 14th of June. Such was the famous day which in the West saved civilization from total destruction."

The battle ended in a disastrous defeat for the Huns, and Attila broke contact with Aetius's army and slipped away in the night, making for the valleys of the Seine and Aube rivers where the country was flat and open in a region called Campania or Champagne. The Huns were ill-fit for urban warfare, and Orleans had taught them a harsh lesson in that regard. Now, on the open plain, Attila occupied ground more favorable to the Hun horsemen and their swirling tactics. Probably near Mery-sur Seine, Attila set up his rearguard of Gepid mercenaries and deployed the main body of his army, as Jordanes tells us, "on the Catalaunian Plains, which are also called Mauriacian." Aetius had hardly paused to reorganize his units before pursuing Attila. Coming upon the Hun rearguard, Aetius launched a night attack and completely destroyed it in heavy hand-to-hand fighting in the darkness. At dawn, Aetius's army deployed on the plains of Chalons and awaited battle with Attila.

Attila deployed his army slowly and did not leave his wagon *laager* until early afternoon. This suggests that Attila was not completely confident of his ability to win the battle against Aetius, for he had already lost a large number of soldiers. Perhaps he thought that by beginning the battle late in the afternoon, if things went badly he would be able to withdraw his army under cover of night. In any event, Attila took command of the center, where he formed up his bravest Hun troops. On his left he placed the Ostrogoths under Walamir, with the Gepids commanded by Ardaric on his right. He positioned his wagon *laager* to the rear but close enough so that he could, in a pinch, withdraw into it and continue the battle from the cover of the wagons. Jordanes tells us that Attila planned to strike hard at the Roman center, driving it back and throwing it into confusion before quickly retiring to his wagon *laager* as night fell. From there he would decide to go over to the defensive, launch another attack, or simply slip away in the night.

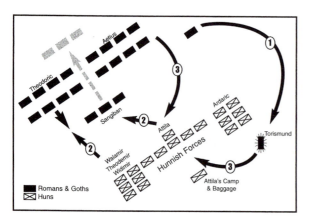

Fig. 17.3 The Battle of Chalons (451 C.E.)

Aetius was an experienced field commander who knew the Huns well, having lived among them as a hostage and employed them in his own armies during his campaigns in Gaul. His experience paid off handsomely, for Aetius seems to have discerned Attila's plan. He drew up his army with the Alans under the treacherous Sangiban in the center, limiting his maneuverability by placing his troops well forward of the main battle line. To guarantee Sangiban's loyalty further, Aetius stationed a squadron of Roman cavalry along with him. On his right he placed Theodoric and his army of Visigoths, while Aetius himself took command of the left wing, which comprised Roman legionnaires, squadrons of heavy cavalry, and Frank infantry that served as the main anchor of the Roman deployment. Also with Aetius was Torismund, Theodoric's son, in command of a contingent of Visigothic cavalry. To prevent Attila from smashing the weak Roman center and withdrawing, Aetius planned to launch two flanking attacks to draw the Huns from their wagon *laager* and then cut them off from it. Around two o'clock on June 20, Aetius opened the battle by sending Torismund and his Visigoth cavalry around the Hun right wing (#1), where it brushed aside the movements of the Hun advance guard to intercept it and seized a commanding height overlooking the Hun flank.

Taken by surprise, Attila sent a contingent of troops to engage Torismund and prevent any attack on the vital wagon *laager.* Then he launched a fierce attack (#2) against Aetius's center, striking Sangiban and the Alans head-on and driving them back through the Roman line. At the same time a Hun brigade crashed into Theodoric's front. Having fixed Theodoric and his Visigoths in place, Attila hoped to penetrate the Roman center and envelop the Visigoth army to the left. The fighting was ferocious as "hand-to-hand they clashed in battle, and the fight grew fierce, confused, monstrous, unrelenting . . . a fight whose like no ancient time has ever recorded," Jordanes tells us. As the Alans fled backward through the Roman line, Aetius's disciplined Roman legions swung their formation as on a hinge, keeping their front first to the Alan flank as they rushed past and then to the exposed Hun flank as they followed the Alans through the gap. Meanwhile, in the Hun rear, a terrible hand-to-hand battle had developed between Torismund and the Huns protecting Attila's *laager*. Here, too, the casualties were horrendous.

With Aetius harassing the flank of the Hun troops that had penetrated the Roman line, the Huns were unable to turn and envelop Theodoric's Visigoths who had held the line against the assault to their front. Somewhere in the melee, along the banks of a brook, the Visigoths were hard-pressed. Theodoric ordered a general counterattack to his front and set out at the head of a brigade to aid his troops near the brook. Jordanes tells us that "King Theodoric, while riding by to encourage his army, was thrown from his horse and trampled under foot by his own men, thus ending his days at a ripe old age." While Theodoric was pressing the Huns back on the right, Aetius had managed to reestablish contact with Torismund, who broke off the attack on the wagon *laager*, shifted his forces, and attacked the Hun line in the rear (#3). At the same time, Aetius ordered his Roman *cataphracti* and Frank infantry into an assault on the exposed Hun flank toward the center of the line (#3). Attila now found himself caught between two forces threatening to trap him in a double envelopment. Theodoric's troops, furious at the death of their king, fought with renewed vigor and "fell upon the horde of Huns and nearly slew Attila." With nowhere to turn, Attila retreated back into his wagon *laager*. Credit is due to Attila for anticipating the possibility of a retreat when he refused to give battle until late afternoon. Now darkness began to set in, and the fighting drew to a close. Attila had guessed correctly, and the end of the day's light guaranteed that he would live another day.

With the darkness came confusion made worse by the absence of moonlight. Hun and allied units were scattered all over the battlefield. As the Hun contingents attempted to find their way back to the *laager*, they crashed into allied units, and small battles continued all night long. Torismund became lost and stumbled into the enemy *laager*, producing a brief but violent skirmish before he could gain his bearings. Aetius had ordered his legions to regroup at the original line and to stand fast under arms all night in anticipation of a Hun surprise attack. Aetius himself went forward to try and reorganize the center of the line that the Alans had abandoned and became lost. "Aetius also became separated from his men in the confusion of night and wandered about in the midst of the enemy. Fearing disaster had happened, he went about in search of the Goths. At last he reached the camp of his allies and passed the remainder of the night in the protection of their shields." As night covered the bloody battlefield, both sides feared that they had lost the engagement.

Jordanes gives us a detailed account of what happened next.

> At dawn on the following day, when the Romans saw the fields were piled high with bodies and that the Huns did not venture forth, they thought the victory was theirs, but knew that Atilla would not flee from the battle unless over-whelmed by a great disaster. Yet he [Attila] did nothing cowardly, like one that is overcome, but with clash of arms sounded the trumpets and threatened to attack. He was like a lion pierced by hunting spears, who paces to and fro before the mouth of his den and dares not spring, but ceases not to terrify the neighborhood by his roaring. Even so this warlike king at bay terrified his conquerors. There-fore the Goths and Romans assembled and considered what to do with the van-quished Attila. They determined to wear him out by a siege, because he had no supply of provisions and was hindered from approaching by a shower of arrows [harassing fire] by archers placed within the confines of the Roman camp.

Attila was trapped. Within the Hun camp, so Jordanes tells us, Attila ordered a great pile to be made from the saddles of his horsemen. This was, he told his officers, to be set ablaze if the Romans broke through, and he would cast himself into the flames and die on the funeral pyre rather than be captured. It was a dramatic gesture (if it occurred at all!) and may have been intended to stiffen the resolve of his men to fight to the last man. Surely burning the saddles of his horsemen would have sent the same message. There was little Attila could do but await the Roman assault.

And then, as so often happens in the history of battles, considerations other than military ones intervened to shape events. Aetius's army had won the day, but the victory had been costly, and it was by no means certain that his army possessed sufficient power to overwhelm Attila's wagons without incurring further heavy losses. Aetius's army was the only Roman army in Gaul, and its destruction would leave Rome at the strategic mercy of its tribal adversaries there, even though some of them, the Visigoths in particu-lar, now fought as allies. The destruction of Attila would also remove the Hun threat to Gaul, removing a major incentive for the tribes to cooperate with Rome in the future. And so, "Aetius feared that if the Huns were totally destroyed by the Goths [Visigoths], the Roman Empire would be over-whelmed." Aetius had to choose between risking his army to destroy Attila or husbanding its strength to serve larger Roman strategic interests in Gaul. Aetius, ever the Roman patrician and who the chroniclers called "the last Roman," chose to tend to Rome's larger interests and permit Attila to escape.

With the death of Theodoric, his son, the young Torismund, had become king. The Visigoths were furious at the Huns for killing their king and wanted to attack. Aetius now displayed his political acumen. He counseled the young Torismund that his interests lay in quickly returning to his own dominions to take up the rule his father had left him. If he failed to return soon, his brothers might seize his rightful lands and mount a challenge to his inheritance. The young king followed Aetius's advice and left for home with his troops. Aetius then told the young prince of his Frank allies that he intended to permit Attila to withdraw. He pointed out that Attila's homeward route would take him close to the lands of the Franks, where the absence of the main Frank army might tempt Attila to raid the kingdom. Moreover, the kingship of the Franks was in dispute between two brothers, one supported by Aetius and the other by Attila. If the Frank prince did not return home to protect his interest, no one could predict what mischief Attila could cause in the kingdom of the Franks. Once more Aetius's advice was taken, and the army of the Franks turned for home.

His withdrawal route now opened by Aetius's political calculations, Attila assembled his wagons and troops and trekked back over the Rhine to his "timber palace" on the Hungarian plain. What his losses were is not known. Jordanes, our main source for this battle, tells us that 165,000 men were slain on both sides, with 15,000 being killed in the fight by Torismund at the wagon *laager*. These figures, of course, are not to be believed but serve the chronicler's purpose in conveying to us a general sense of the great numbers of men that must have been slain at Chalons.

The battle of Chalons is considered to be one of the most important battles in the history of the West. A Hun victory at Chalons would have meant the complete collapse of the remaining Roman civilization in the West and its replacement with a primitive culture of tribes and tribalism. A Hun victory would have removed all the recently settled Germanic and Gothic tribes that had been settled in Gaul from Roman cultural influence, an event that would have accelerated the cultural collapse of the West, replacing it with something akin to the *babaricum* of the eastern empire. In addition, the victory at Chalons permitted the continuation of the ecclesiastical organization of the Christian church, preserving its influence among the peoples of the West. Christianity had yet to triumph completely and had only recently gained a tenuous hold among the tribes. Gradually, the ecclesiastical structure of the Christian church was being superimposed upon the Roman civic governmental structure, with the consequence that civic and religious authority often seemed as one. Over time, this permitted the Christian church in the West to become the chief international authority during the Middle Ages, the only authority that could trace its unbroken descent from Roman times. A Hun victory at Chalons would have plunged the West back into a primitive barbarism and the Christian church into a resurgent paganism, both of which would have destroyed the church's authority and changed the entire course of medieval history. Taken together, then, these considerations made the battle of Chalons one of the decisive moments in the history of the West.

Attila's Resurgence

No sooner had Attila returned to the Hungarian plain than he once more set out to invade the western empire. The reasons for a Hun invasion are not clear. Our chroniclers suggest it was a desire to avenge the defeat at Chalons the year before, but we cannot be certain. In the spring of 452 C.E., Attila crossed the Julian Alps, from which, curiously, the Roman garrisons had been withdrawn by Aetius, and descended upon Italy, directing his fury against the town of Aquileia. The Roman garrisons in the Alpine passes could easily have bottled up Attila's columns and made them pay a heavy price for their passage if not actually destroying them outright. Why Aetius left the passes unguarded remains a mystery. Aquileia's position at the foot of the Julian passes had made it a natural target for invaders throughout history. The city put up a valiant defense and only fell after Attila had to break off the assault and wait for his siege train to arrive from his rear base. When Aquileia fell, it was completely destroyed. So great was the Hun devastation and terror that the city's survivors, so the legend has it, fled to the offshore islands and swamps to escape. On these islands, the city of Venice was founded.

Aetius and the Emperor Valentinian seemed to have been caught completely by surprise, and no Roman army was available in Italy to meet the Hun attack. With no opposition to hinder him, Attila pressed his attack, marching into Venetia and taking Julia Concordia, which he burned to the ground, and then Patavium (modern Padua). City after city threw open their gates to the Hun in hopes of avoiding disaster. In this manner Vincenza, Verona, Brescia, Bergamo, Milan, Ticinum, and Pavia were quickly taken. In every case except Milan and Ticinum, the buildings were saved but the populations were massacred and the survivors enslaved. The northern Italian plain in his hands, Attila drew up his army on the banks of the river Mincio. Across the Apennines lay Rome, and no army stood between it and the Huns. Why, then, did Attila not do what Alaric had done before him and sack Rome?

Three factors may have weighed on Attila's decision. First, when Attila had invaded Gaul in the previous year, northern Italy was suffering a famine. The crops were no better this year, and the devastations of the Hun invasion had mostly consumed what few crops were available. Attila was already short of food, and the lands beyond the Apennines offered no relief to an invading army. Second, famine's companions—plague and other disease—had already set in among the Italian population, and our chroniclers tell us that the first cases of disease had already been reported when Attila reached the Mincio. The battle of Chalons had taken a heavy toll on Hun manpower, always the weak link in their military strength. If disease took hold of their armies in Italy, their position in Europe would quickly become desperate. Third, Emperor Marcian in Constantinople took advantage of the absence of Attila's army from its home base to send an army across the Danube and attack the Hun army that had been left behind to protect the homeland. Attila's attack on the western empire depended upon peace with the Roman East. Now Attila had a war on two fronts, which he could not sustain. Accompanied by Roman officials, Pope Leo traveled to Attila's camp to sue for peace in the name of Rome, an act that greatly increased the influence and authority of the papacy itself. While there is no doubt other factors weighed more heavily on Attila's decision to offer peace and withdraw from Italy, Christian historians have attributed the success of the mission to Pope Leo and the aura of the Christian god, which impressed Attila. This being as it may, Attila withdrew from Italy without ever setting foot south of the Po River. His empire had been shaken to its foundations.

Within a year Attila the Hun, the *Flagellum Dei* or Scourge of God, was dead. He had taken another wife and during the wedding reception had drunk too much. The Huns awoke to the wailing of Attila's new wife coming from his tent. Rushing to his rescue, they found Attila dead, his bride weeping beside him, her face covered with her veil. Attila had bled heavily through his nose during the night (as, indeed, he had done before) and, being drunk, he had suffocated in his sleep. His body was laid out in a silk tent pitched on the open plain. He was buried at night, and those who laid him to his rest (presumably slaves) were themselves slain over his body. After Attila's death, his sons divided up the subject nations of the empire among themselves. Within months, the sons began to quarrel, with the result that a number of great battles were fought between them. The Hun armies were squandered in a pointless civil war. With the Hun military weakness revealed, the subject peoples rose in revolt and in one great battle after another defeated the Huns. The empire flew apart until in the space of a few years it was no more. Some remnants of the Hun armies fled back across the Carpathians, others were given permission by Marcian to settle within the empire. While some Hun units served within the Eastern imperial army, they were never granted the status of allies. Within a decade Attila's great army had disappeared from the face of the earth.

THE COMMANDERS

Attila (406–453 C.E.), ruler of the Huns from 434 to 453 C.E., remains an obscure figure to this day. Even his name is uncertain, a Latinized version of how the Hun pronunciation sounded to the Latin ear. All the descriptions of him were written by his Greek and Roman enemies, the Huns themselves having no written language, and all are unflattering since he was feared and loathed as both a pagan and barbarian. Attila was held in such great fear that he was called *Flagellum Dei*, the Scourge of God, sent by the deity to punish the people for their sins. The Goth historian, Jordanes, has left us a striking portrait of the man. He was, Jordanes writes, a typical Hun in physical appearance—short, broad chested, with a big head, small, deep-set eyes, and a flat nose. His complexion was swarthy, "almost dark-skinned," and he wore a sparse beard.

He was as calculating and cunning as any nomad and was given to terrible rages, although there is some evidence that some of these tantrums were feigned to strike fear in his opponents. Attila was capable of great cruelty, and his armies often slaughtered captured populations wholesale. The Hun practice of slitting throats was a means of instilling fear and eliminating opposition. For all his bad reputation among his enemies, it was said of Attila that he was a fair judge among his own people and very generous with his wealth. He regularly dined on simple fare with wooden plates and cups, while others used captured Roman and silver tableware. Like all nomads he liked alcohol and regularly consumed large quantities of *kumis*, a powerful drink made of fermented mare's milk and blood. He had many wives and fathered many children and was respectful of the nomadic shamans and religious rituals. He routinely consulted the auguries before battle.

The record is mixed as to his ability as a general. In some cases, as when he timed his attacks against the Roman East for when its armies were occupied elsewhere, he appears an excellent grand strategist. In others, as when he invaded the West without sufficient supplies and with the armies of the Roman East poised to strike his main base, he appears to have had no grasp of grand strategy at all. Given that positions of leadership were not hereditary among the Huns, the choice of Attila to succeed his uncle at the age of twenty-eight as commander of the Hun armies suggests that he must have possessed an excellent reputation as a warrior. Tactically, Attila showed signs of brilliance, as at Chalons when he timed the start of the battle to provide him with the early onset of night should things go wrong. In other instances, he seems to have paid insufficient attention to the problems of logistics. He seems to have performed best against mediocre opposition. When he faced talented Roman commanders, he usually met with defeat or achieved only a draw. It is difficult to conclude that Attila was a brilliant field commander. Rather, he was a bold leader of tribal armies that succeeded against marginal opposition. Roman armies of an earlier period would have made short work of Attila the Hun.

Flavius Aetius (395–454 C.E.) was one of the last great Roman generals and statesmen of the western empire, called by one chronicler of the day "the last great Roman." He fought scores of battles in the Roman civil wars and the wars against the barbarians, the latter mostly in Gaul where he used Hun troops as allies to suppress German and Visigoth tribes who had crossed the Rhine to settle in Gaul. As a young man, he spent several years living among the Huns as a treaty hostage, learning their language and military skills. He was said to have been an excellent horse-archer. Aetius was an excellent general, one who always grasped the strategic importance of military events and routinely subordinated these events to larger strategic considerations. Although he tried to stem the flood of barbarians into Gaul from across the Rhine with force, he quickly realized that the task was impossible. Accordingly, he would meet the tribes in battle, defeat them, and then offer them lands upon which to settle, turning them into allies.

His grasp of strategy was equally evident after the battle of Chalons where, for strategic reasons of preserving the military balance in Gaul, he permitted

Attila to retreat back over the Rhine. His tactical performance at Chalons was brilliant, and his success in previous battles reveals an officer who understood the many dimensions of military art and wove them into a tactical tapestry to ensure success on the battlefield. Aetius, like all high Roman patricians, was deeply involved in court politics, and he was in and out of favor many times over his lifetime. In more than one instance, his life was in danger as a consequence of his political involvement. In the end, it was politics, not war, that took his life. Aetius attempted to arrange a marriage between his heirs and one of the emperor's daughters as a way of establishing a claim to the position in the future. Valentinian III was furious and had Aetius murdered during an audience. Capable and daring, Flavius Aetius was the last great imperial Roman general.

LESSONS OF WAR

Strategy

1. A strategic vision is used to guide the application of war, which, without it, becomes merely sport. The Huns possessed no strategic vision. War for the Hun was mostly sport and a way of gaining wealth, not strategic objectives.

2. The Roman commanders, on the other hand, seemed always guided by a strategic vision—defense of the imperial borders—that determined the application of force. This made them more flexible than their enemies in using force and provided them with a long-range vision of the future that they could pursue over time, even in the face of temporary setbacks.

3. It is strategy that drives tactics, never the other way around. Aetius, having defeated Attila at Chalons, resisted the temptation to allow military victory to become an end in itself. Instead, he pursued his strategic objectives and, subordinating military concerns to them, permitted Attila to withdraw with his army intact.

4. Always attend to logistics at the strategic level. Time and again Attila was forced to break off his campaigns due to insufficient logistical support. An army travels on its stomach! It must be fed!

5. Coalition armies derived from vastly different cultures are always a problem to control and coordinate in war. Aetius was successful in holding his coalition of Alans, Visigoths, and Franks together, but only long enough to win the battle. Military coalitions are just that, temporary means to achieve military objectives. When the war is over, the old fissures once more come to the surface. In building coalitions, beware the clash of civilizations!

Tactics

1. The ability of the Hun horsemen to move rapidly over long distances and to concentrate on the objective was one of their greatest tactical abilities.

Almost always outnumbered, they could bring decisive force to bear on local objectives with devastating results.

2. Always be cognizant of the effect of military operations on the psychology of friend and foe alike. The Huns used systematic terror to paralyze the will of the defenders to resist. The behavior of an army at war is crucial to its military effectiveness. Sometimes fear is best subordinated to kindness; sometimes the reverse.

3. The Huns fought for plunder, not glory or honor. As such, they had no psychological difficulty in withdrawing from a fight. On more than one occasion this saved them from disaster and permitted them to fight another day. War is never about honor. It's about winning!

4. Utilize the weather and night to best advantage. Attila began the battle at Chalons late in the day so that the early onset of night would provide him with a tactical opportunity to slow the tempo of battle in case things went badly.

5. Adjust tactics to terrain. The Hun practice of relying on the wagon *laager* worked well on the open steppe but greatly slowed the movement of the armies in the wooded, hilly, and more settled terrain of the West. The Huns would have been better off abandoning the wagon *laager* and using captured cities and towns as their logistics base. Instead they usually massacred the population and burnt the towns. This was a terrible waste of resources.

FURTHER READING

Ammianus Marcellinus. Translated by John Carew Rolfe. Cambridge, MA: Harvard University Press, 1935–1939.

Bury, J. B. *History of the Later Roman Empire.* London: Macmillan 1923.

Brion, M. *Attila: The Scourge of God.* New York: R. M. McBride 1929.

Dupuy, R. Ernest, and Trevor N. Dupuy. *The Encyclopedia of Military History.* New York: Harper and Row, 1986.

Elton, Hugh. *Warfare in Roman Europe, AD 350–425.* New York: Oxford University Press, 1996.

Freeman, E. A. *Western Europe in the Fifth Century.* London, 1964.

Fuller, J. F. C. *A Military History of the Western World.* New York: Da Capo, 1954.

Gordon, C. D. *The Age of Attila: Fifth Century Byzantium and the Barbarians.* 1966.

Grancsay, S. V. "A Barbarian Chieftain's Helmet." *Bulletin of the Metropolitan Museum of Art* (June 1949): 272–281.

Grousset, Rene. *The Empire of the Steppes: A History of Central Asia.* New Brunswick, NJ: Rutgers University Press, 1970.

Harmatta, J. "The Dissolution of the Hun Empire." *Acta Archaeologica Hungaricae* 2 (1952): 277–304.

———. "The Golden Bow of the Huns." *Acta Archaeologica Hungaricae* 1 (1951): 114–149.

Howarth, Patrick. *Attila, King of the Huns: The Man and the Myth.* Carlisle, PA: John Kallmann, 1997.

Ingram, Scott. *Attila the Hun.* San Diego: Blackbirch, 2002.

Jordanes. *Gothic History.* Translated by C. C. Mierow. 2nd ed. New York: Barnes & Noble, 1960.

Maenchen-Helfen, Otto J. *The World of the Huns.* Berkeley: University of California Press, 1973.

Matthews, J. F. "Olymiodorus of Thebes and the History of the West (AD 407–425)." *Journal of Roman Studies* 60 (1970): 79–97.

Nicolle, David, and Angus McBride. *Attila and the Nomad Hordes: Warfare on the Eurasian Steppes.* London: Osprey, 1998.

Otto, J. *A History of Attila and the Huns.* Westport, CT: Greenwood, 1975.

———. *The Huns.* London: Blackwell, 1999.

———. *The World of the Huns: Studies in Their History and Culture.* Berkeley: University of California Press, 1973.

Thompson, E. A. "The Camp of Attila." *Journal of Hellenic Studies* 65 (1945): 112–115.

18 KOREA, THE HERMIT KINGDOM

[612 C.E.]

BACKGROUND

The origins of the Korean people are still a matter of some conjecture. By the fourth century B.C.E. a distinctive Bronze Age civilization extended throughout the Korean peninsula and into Manchuria at least as far as the Liao and Sungari rivers (see Map 18.1). The archaeological evidence of immense tombs, bronze weapons, and rice cultivation tools all indicate control by leadership elites over large labor forces that produced considerable wealth. The key social and political groups were tribal states consisting of walled towns and fortified strongholds surrounded by agricultural lands. The Korean historian, Ki-Baik Lee, has suggested the term *walled-town states* to describe these political entities. These states controlled considerable territory beyond the towns themselves and gave rise to the mountain fortress, the *sansong*, that often encompassed an area of several square kilometers, taking advantage of the mountainous terrain of the Korean peninsula in its design. Natural obstacles were reinforced with six-foot-high dirt walls, while stone walls with wooden gates blocked other avenues of approach. The larger and more strategically placed mountain fortresses were used repeatedly over the centuries by different governmental regimes, and the remains of some of these massive redoubts can still be seen today.

During this same period two new cultures, a Chinese Iron Age culture and a Scytho-Siberian Bronze Age culture, entered Korea, mingling with the existing culture to form a new distinct culture that was transmitted to Japan in the following century. The two most militarily significant technological elements of this new Korean culture were the horse and sharp metal weapons, technology that provided the ruling elites with greater authority and control over their populations. Iron agricultural implements, too, greatly increased the productivity of the land, and the accumulation of wealth so necessary to the development of a genuine civilization increased. With these new technologies, the rulers of some of the walled towns expanded their domains by conquest and diplomacy, forming large confederations some of which bordered upon the northeastern regions of China and the lands of the nomadic tribes of the Central Asian steppes. The Chinese chronicles of the time refer to large Korean political entities based on these confederations of walled-town states (see Map 18.1).

LOLANG   Chinese States and Commanderies
(Seoul)   Modern Names

Map 18.1 Chinese Commanderies in Korea

During the Chinese Warring States period (464–221 B.C.E.), the region between the Liao and Taedong rivers became a contested area. First, the Chinese state of Yan pushed across the Liao River and established a military colony in the Liaodong Peninsula. Yan and its Liaodong territories subsequently became part of the unified Qin Empire at the end of the third century B.C.E., and in 206 B.C.E. came under the control of the Han emperor. During this turbulent period, substantial numbers of refugees from China entered Korea. Through the influence of these refugees and other contacts with China, Chinese political, economic, and cultural influence overlaid the old Korean power structure and culture.

This Chinese influence intensified in 109–108 B.C.E. when Han armies invaded and established four Chinese military colonies (commanderies) on the Korean peninsula at Lolang, Zhenfann, Lintun, and Xuandu. Lolang was the core region of Chinese influence in Korea. It was ruled by a Chinese governor, administered by Chinese bureaucrats, and guarded by Chinese soldiers; its economy was in the hands of Chinese merchants, and a substantial part of its population was comprised of Chinese colonists, many of them retired officials of the Chinese bureaucracy. The area to the south of the colonies remained under the control of native Korean states, although they, as well as the other peoples on the periphery of the Chinese commanderies, were influenced by Chinese culture and accepted Chinese offices, ranks, and other tokens of submission while maintaining some degree of political independence. Beyond the borders of the commanderies these Korean confederations of walled-town states grew in territory and political power. Of these confederations, Koguryo was the most powerful. Beginning in the resource-poor mountains and narrow valleys of the upper reaches of the Yalu (Amnok) River, Koguryo grew in power and territory until it was able to challenge China itself for influence in their common border region.

According to Korean legend, Koguryo was founded in 37 B.C.E. when a certain Chumong led his followers south to the upper Yalu basin. Other evidence suggests that Koguryo may have been the successor to an older confederacy of walled-town states. Whatever the case, it seems clear that the Koguryo leadership consisted of foreign elites who subjugated the indigenous peoples of the Yalu region. Because of its geographical location and its expansionist tendencies, which brought frequent clashes with the Chinese, Koguryo's survival, like that of eighteenth-century Prussia, depended upon its military ability. By the first century C.E., Koguryo had developed into a centralized state led by a ruler who had adopted the Chinese title of *wang* (king). By the fourth century, Koguryo had absorbed the Korean states on its northern periphery and had acquired control of the Lolang commandery as well.

Frescoes from the tomb of Dongshou, the last governor of Lolang, provide a glimpse of the military forces of Koguryo at that time. One of the frescoes shows a procession led by two files of foot soldiers (see Figure 18.1). They wear peaked helmets covering their heads, necks, and ears, jackets of

Fig. 18.1 Soldiers from the Dongshou Tomb Fresco

either plated armor or quilting, and loose, baggy trousers bloused into knee-high boots. The soldiers are carrying halberds over their right shoulders and narrow octagonal shields in their left hands. Behind them march two files of axe-bearing foot soldiers wearing soft caps, bloused trousers and boots, and soft, gown-like jackets. Also visible are similarly attired bowmen, as well as men carrying cloth lanterns, some of whom appear to be wearing plate armor jerkins and carrying their shields under their arms. The flanks of the procession are guarded by eight cavalry troopers wearing helmets similar to those of the infantry, but with tall, horsehair plumes, quilted or armored tunics, and baggy trousers falling to their feet. They carry long spears, and their horses are adorned with armored helmets and covered with either quilting or plate armor reaching almost to the ground.

It was during this period that Koguryo came into conflict with Paekche, a powerful kingdom to the south. By the middle of the fourth century Paekche, like Koguryo, had become a strong centralized kingdom and had absorbed the Chinese southern commandery of Daifang. In 371 C.E. Paekche forces invaded Koguryo, pushing north as far as P'yongyang and killing the Koguryo king. Now in control of all of central Korea, Paekche opened diplomatic contact with the Chinese state of Eastern Jin and with the Japanese, known as the *Wa* to the Chinese and Koreans. In 384 C.E. the Paekche king adopted the Buddhist faith, which his kingdom then transmitted to its neighboring kingdoms and also to Japan, providing Paekche with a powerful ideological system that greatly enhanced its authority and international prestige.

A third powerful kingdom, Silla, emerged in southern Korea in the region east of the Naktong River. During the eclipse of Koguryo power, Paekche and Silla vied for control of the peninsula. A fourth but weaker state, Kaya, developed in the lower reaches of the Naktong. Kaya maintained a vigorous maritime trade with the Japanese who considered Kaya to be their tributary. At the same time Paekche and Silla both sought to gain the support of the Japanese in their rival conflicts, with the result that Japan, too, was drawn into the cauldron of political intrigue and combat taking place on the Korean peninsula. Map 18.2 shows the locations of the rival states.

Faced with military defeat and continuing pressure from Paekche, Koguryo attempted to reform and revitalize its sociopolitical institutions, beginning with the formal adoption of Buddhism as a state religion, the establishment of a Confucian academy, the promulgation of a strong legal and administrative code, and the complete reformation of the military establishment. Building on these reforms, the greatest of Koguryo kings, Kwanggaet'o (391–413 C.E.),

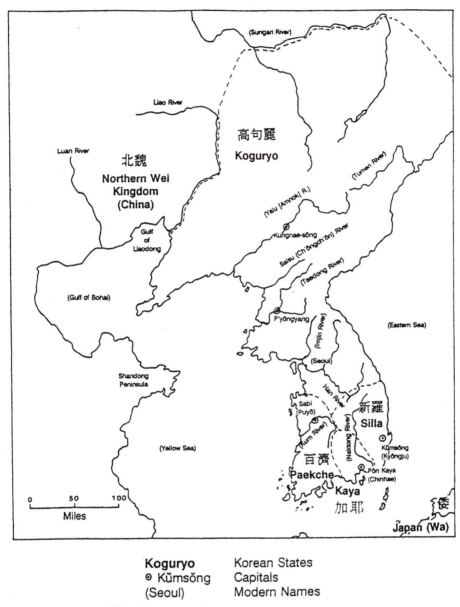

Map 18.2 Korea (Fifth Century C.E.)

whose very name meant "expander of territory," began a campaign of military conquest. Leading his cavalry forces himself, Kwanggaet'o and his army captured the Liaodong Peninsula, once again pressing against the frontiers of China. He subjugated the nomadic people to the northeast, expanding Koguryo's territory deep into Manchuria. He also pressed the borders of Paekche far to the south, thereby incorporating into Koguryo all of the Imjin and Han river basins. He then rode into the southern reaches of the Naktong River, defeating a Japanese army that was then attacking Silla. A memorial stone on the west bank of the Yalu River at the old Koguryo capital of Kungnaesong records Kwanggaet'o's deeds: the conquest of sixty-four walled cities and 1,400 villages. Believing that Koguryo was the equal of China, Kwanggaet'o arrogated to himself the Chinese imperial privilege of assigning an era title to his own reign. This era he called Yongnak or "Eternal Rejoicing." His successor invaded Paekche in 475 C.E., seized the capital, and beheaded the king. Koguryo had reached the zenith of its power, and its king held sway over the territory stretching from well south of the Han River to the Liao and Sungari rivers in Manchuria to the north.

The Three Kingdoms Period

Korea now entered the "Three Kingdoms" period, a time in which Koguryo, Silla, and Paekche vied with one another through war, diplomacy, and intrigue for control of Korea. As part of this maneuvering, all three states plotted and schemed with Japan, the Chinese states, and the non-Chinese peoples of Manchuria and inner Asia for advantage and territorial gain along the borders. This period was marked by shifting alliances, military threats and counter-threats, and the occasional short, sharp, brutal conflict. In the late sixth century the rough balance of power among the Three Kingdoms, the northern and southern Chinese states, and the non-Chinese peoples of Manchuria and the steppes was shaken by events on the Korean peninsula and by the rise of a new player in the game within China proper.

Following the breakup of the great Han Empire, China endured nearly four centuries of fragmentation. Northern China was dominated by the Turko-Mongolian Xianbei people who intermarried with the Chinese and adopted the trappings of Chinese civilization. A succession of regimes led by the partially Sinified Xianbei (the so-called "Northern Sixteen Kingdoms") grappled for control in the north, while in the south the successors of the Han Dynasty kept alive the Chinese cultural legacy of the Yangzi River basin through a succession of regimes known as the Six Dynasties. By 577 C.E., after a series of conflicts and civil wars, the north was reunited by a Sinified Xianbei dynasty calling itself the Northern Zhou.

A leading member of the Northern Zhou court was a certain Yangjian, Duke of Sui. Of mixed Chinese and Xianbei heritage, he rose through the military ranks and court intrigue to become the commander-in-chief of the army of Northern Zhou. He also held the titles of prime minister, grand state master, and "supreme pillar of the state." Shortly thereafter, allegedly at the urging of the eight-year-old emperor, Yangjian was persuaded to take the final step and assume the imperial throne as Emperor Wen of the Sui Dynasty. The young former emperor died shortly thereafter (perhaps murdered), as did fifty-eight other potential rivals for the imperial throne!

Emperor Wen, also known as Sui Wendi, was a man of extraordinary talents and passions, a product, in the words of historian Arthur F. Wright, of the "violent and predatory politics of a divided North China, riven by internecine feuds and racial hatred." The historical record reveals his skillful diplomacy and administrative ability as well as his towering rages and peremptory punishments. Those who protested usually met swift retribution, although on at least one occasion some brave senior advisors remonstrated that it was unseemly for the emperor to personally beat officials to death in the halls of the palace with bastinadoes and horsewhips! Although the instrument of choice could range from the horsewhip to diplomatic negotiation, administrative decree, Buddhist sutra, or the military expedition, Sui Wendi succeeded in unifying the Chinese empire once again. First he concentrated on broadening his political base, reinstituting the old Han Dynasty bureaucratic reforms, offices, and rituals. He then rebuilt the western capital of Changan, renaming it Daxingcheng, promulgated a new body of laws and ordinances—the famous Kaihuang Code—and, while paying due regard to the precepts of Confucius, committed the dynasty to Buddhism, thus restoring religio-cultural hegemony throughout the north.

With his rule in the north now consolidated, Sui Wendi initiated a massive military operation to conquer the Chen, the last and weakest of the remaining southern dynasties. In 588 C.E., after years of logistical, diplomatic, and psychological preparations, Sui Wendi unleashed the Southern Expedition: an eight-pronged amphibious attack against the southern Chinese regime. Overall supreme command of the undertaking rested with the emperor's third son, Yang Guang, prince of Jin and future emperor, supported by able and experienced generals. By the end of the year, China was once again united, and this new, energized Chinese empire collided with the powerful Koguryo kingdom in the long-contested basin of the Liao River.

Just as Sui Wendi was about to rise to imperial glory in the mid-sixth century, the balance of power on the Korean peninsula began to shift as Koguryo found itself under pressure from the increasingly powerful Silla kingdom to the south. Silla allied itself with Paekche, and the two conducted a combined military campaign to eject Koguryo from the strategic Han River basin. Two years later, Silla turned on its former ally and overran the Paekche-occupied lower reaches of the Han. Silla now controlled a wealthy agricultural area with a substantial population base for taxes, labor, and military conscripts, as well as possessed a link with China via the seaports on the west coast of Korea. The Han River valley was the heart of Korea's iron-working industry and was also rich in arable land that could be distributed as fiefs to loyal supporters and relatives. Possession by Silla of the Han drainage basin meant that only two states were left to challenge Silla's power, the Koguryo and the Paekche. But both were now separated by a wide band of territory that Silla occupied and controlled.

Outraged by Silla's treachery, the Paekche king personally led an army against Silla in 553 C.E. to regain his former territories in the Han Valley. The

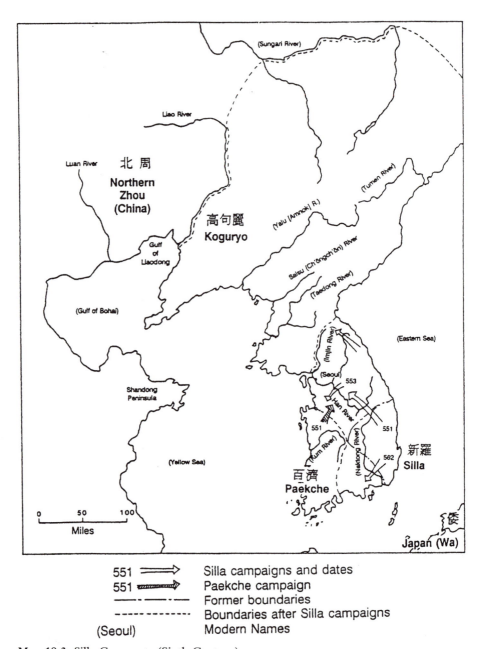

Map 18.3 Silla Conquests (Sixth Century)

attack was unsuccessful, and the king himself was killed. With one of her rivals defeated, Silla now took the opportunity to move southward and put an end to the remaining small state of Kaya. With this victory, Silla armies pushed northeast, further encroaching upon territory that had been dominated by Koguryo. During this period, Japan sometimes organized military expeditions to assist Paekche and punish Silla's aggression against its client state, seeking all the while to prevent any single state from gaining dominance on the Korean peninsula. Although some of these Japanese units actually became engaged in battle, none had any significant impact on reducing Silla's growing ability to control the entire peninsula.

As Silla gradually began to dominate Korea, Paekche and Koguryo joined forces against the common enemy. In the last decade of the sixth century C.E., the two former rivals attacked Silla in an attempt to recapture the Han River basin and sever Silla's trade and communication link with China. The attack failed, and Koguryo began to shift its attention to the north and the growing menace of a reunified China. Initially relations between Koguryo and Sui Wendi's new China had been cordial, with Koguryo continuing the long-established practice of paying tribute to the Chinese or whoever controlled the northern Chinese territories. But once Koguryo began to realize that it was faced with a strong Chinese empire with expansionist ambitions, it began to strengthen its army and defenses.

Historian John C. Jamieson suggests that the actions of the Sui emperors toward Koguryo were motivated by three concerns. First, they feared collusion between Koguryo and the peoples of Manchuria and the steppes that might provoke an attack from along this traditional invasion route. Second, the Chinese feared the rise of a separatist movement in the north that might flourish with Koguryo support. Third, and most likely to provoke a conflict, was the Chinese desire to recover control of the lost territories of the Great Han Empire, to which Koguryo now claimed occupation. With Koguryo unwilling to play the role of submissive tributary to China, and with both powers vying for influence and strategic political advantage among the peoples of the steppes and Manchuria, a clash between the two great states was inevitable.

Just as Koguryo faced threats from two fronts, from Silla in the south and China in the northwest, China also found itself threatened from two directions. China was geographically caught between the powerful state of Koguryo in the northeast and from the steppe peoples, especially the Turks or Tuque (known to the Koreans as Tolgwol), from the north. Koguryo began to send diplomatic missions to Paekche's distant ally, Japan, seeking to buttress its support in the face of hostilities with Silla and China. The result was that two sets of potential belligerents began to coalesce in northeast Asia: a north-south alliance of Turks, Koguryo, Paekche, and Japanese, and an east-west axis of Sui China and Silla. The line of confrontation lay along the Liao River valley (see Map 18.4).

In 598 C.E. Koguryo's King Yongyan (590–618 C.E.), perhaps wanting to establish a secure buffer zone against China, attacked across the Liao River into Liaoxi, the region to the west of the river. Sui Wendi is reported to have mobilized an army of 300,000 men and counterattacked by land and sea. The Sui expedition failed, and Sui Wendi was forced to withdraw his armies back across the Liao River. Both armies remained in place, and their respective

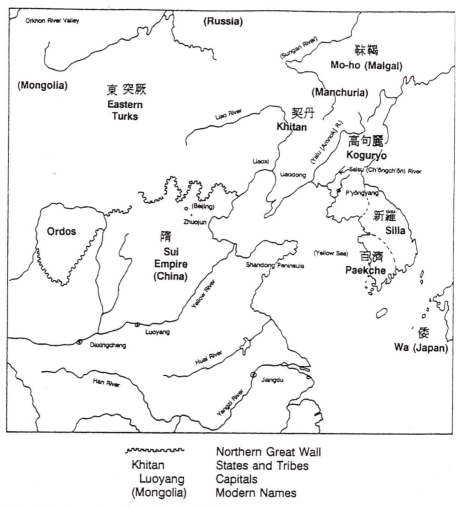

Map 18.4 Campaign of 612: Strategic Setting

governments reopened diplomatic talks. But nations mostly fight for good reasons, and the two countries' long-standing conflicts of interest in the Liao River basin, as well as their rivalry for influence among the northern tribes, inexorably propelled the two states toward other military clashes. Koguryo held fast to her position along the Liao, periodically conducting spoiling raids against the Chinese forces. Meanwhile, Koguryo opened secret diplomatic contacts with the Turks.

Sui Wendi died in 604 C.E., possibly at the hand of his second son, Yang Guang, who had already usurped the position of the crown prince and now came to the throne as Sui Yangdi, Emperor Yang of Sui. He is known to Chinese history as the archetypical licentious and profligate "bad last emperor," a reputation based largely on the annals written during the successor Tang Dynasty. While his true personal characteristics are difficult to discern across the centuries through a haze of partisan history and myth, it is clear that Sui Yangdi pursued a policy of strengthening the nation, expanding and defending the borders of the empire, and constructing great public works. Ultimately he succumbed to the reaction against the high human cost of his building programs and his military campaigns, particularly his single-minded prosecution of the conflict with Koguryo.

Sui Yangdi continued the border policy of his father, dispatching military expeditions against northern Indochina, islands in the China Sea, and nomads on the northwest frontier. These military adventures met with mixed success and brought few lasting gains. With the Japanese, diplomacy was more effective than war. The Chinese were initially offended by the Japanese refusal to accept the idea that their emperor was subordinate to Sui Yangdi. Nonetheless, the two countries were able to establish diplomatic relations. During the subsequent Tang Dynasty, Sino-Japanese relations flourished, with significant cultural impact on Japan.

Sui Yangdi's public works projects also followed the precedents set by his father. When he was still the prince of Jin commanding the Southern Expedition, Sui Yangdi had built an eastern capital at Luoyang, the old capital of the Eastern Zhou and Later Han Dynasties, a major water and land transportation hub and a natural location for the storage and trans-shipment of grain. In 584 C.E., Sui Wendi had begun the construction of a network of canals. Sui Yangdi built ever larger and more impressive canals. Later writers castigated Sui Yangdi for the onerous cost of constructing these canals and suggested they were built so that the emperor could travel in comfort and splendor. In fact, while Sui Yangdi was no stranger to comfort and splendor and canal building certainly imposed a hardship on those mobilized for construction, the canals played an important political and economic role in tying the empire together and providing the means to ship food to grain-poor regions.

The third major category of costly and labor-intensive public works for which Sui Yangdi was criticized by later generations was the repair and construction of walls as defensive works against the nomadic peoples of the steppes. From 607 to 609 C.E., Sui Yangdi mobilized perhaps as many as a million men to work on the walls along the southern edge of the Ordos River, the strategic northwest quadrant of the loop of the Yellow River. Because the Ordos was one of the few places within the vast steppe that could support agriculture, it was of critical importance to the nomads who contended for power in inner Asia. To the Chinese, the Ordos potentially provided a means of controlling the steppe nomads, and even more important, it was the major avenue of approach into the Chinese heartland.

Wall building was one time-honored approach to the nomad threat. War, diplomacy, and treachery were the others, and Sui Yangdi used all these means in dealing with the non-Chinese peoples along the northern borders. From the Chinese perspective, there were four major enemies to be carefully watched: the Koguryo, the Turks, the Qidan (in Korean, the Khitan, a Mongol people who had inhabited the lower reaches of the Liao River), and the Mo-ho (Korean: Malgal), a confederation of Tungusic tribes to the north of Koguryo who had participated in the attack across the Liao River in 598 C.E. Of these, the two most dangerous to China were Koguryo and the Turks. The Turks had arisen in the steppe land of central Asia, and by the mid-sixth century the two major Turkish political groups, or khanates, generally controlled the region from the Persian border in the west to the Liao River in the east. The western khanate drew its strength from western Turkestan, while the eastern khanate was centered on the Orkhon River valley and occupied approximately the same area as modern Mongolia. Had the Turks remained united, it is unlikely that the Sui Dynasty could have stood against them with success. But by the time Sui Wendi had assumed the throne, the two khanates were divided and frequently at war with each other. Both khanates were riven with factionalism, providing an opportunity for Chinese political machinations designed to play one off the other.

Sui Yangdi's suspicions of both the Turks and the Koguryo were heightened in 607 C.E. when he visited the tent capital of Qimin, khan of the Eastern Turks, and discovered the presence of an embassy from Koguryo, evidence that the two states had been in secret contact. Pei Qu, the emperor's trusted strategic counselor, advised Sui Yangdi to demand that the king of Koguryo present himself to pay homage at the Chinese imperial court or face chastisement by a Chinese-led Turkish army. King Yongyan refused to submit, and his refusal provided the pretext for Sui Yangdi's decision to invade Koguryo and end the threat to his northeastern border once and for all. For the next few years Sui Yangdi's efforts were focused on the completion of the extensive canal network. In 610 C.E., the network completed, Sui Yangdi levied war taxes and began to assemble a huge army and logistical train. A disastrous flood of the Yellow River delayed the preparations, but by the first moon of the year 612 C.E., the Chinese emperor was ready to strike Koguryo by land and sea.

THE CHINESE IMPERIAL ARMY

By the time of the confrontation with Koguryo, the Chinese were masters of centuries of military tradition, wisdom, and expertise. The earlier Southern Expedition had reunited China and provided a demonstration of Chinese military expertise in the conduct of large-scale military operations and extensive practical experience in the organization, equipment, transport, and supply of larger military formations in theater-level operations. Sui Yangdi himself, then a prince of Jin, had served as the nominal commander of the Southern Expedition, and though much of the actual planning, leadership, and management of the campaign was in the hands of senior generals, the campaign provided the emperor with considerable military experience. The subsequent border campaigns provided additional practice for Sui Yangdi's commanders and soldiers. Sui Yangdi now stood at the head of what the *Sui History* called the largest Chinese military force ever assembled. The Korean *Samguk Sagi* (History of the Three Kingdoms) claims that the main force numbered 1,133,800. Whatever the actual numbers involved, there is no doubt that it was a formidable army consisting of imperial guards, standing territorial militia units called *fubing*, and conscripts.

Tactical Organization

The core element of the imperial guard was a cavalry-heavy, full-time professional force. The other guard detachments and regional forces were manned by the *fubing*. The *fubing* system developed during the Sui period from the old pattern of military service inherited by the Sui emperors from their Xianbei ancestors. The Xianbei *fubing* consisted of hereditary warriors of the tribal aristocracy. They paid no taxes, nor were they required to perform corvée labor, but they were expected to provide their own weapons, horses, and rations when called to military service. By the time of the Sui Dynasty the *fubing* had become largely Sinified and consisted of troops recruited from each region. Under this system the capital garrison armies consisted of twelve units, four guards (*wei*), and eight army headquarters (*fu*) that constituted the central command structure. In addition, regional military commands (*zongguan fu*) were established in strategic locations throughout the country.

The *fubing* leadership came from the upper ranks of the Xianbei aristocracy and from Chinese military families. The soldiers were recruited locally, given land to farm, and had to perform service at the capital for some period each year, perhaps two months out of every eighteen. At any one time the capital garrison consisted of some 50,000 *fubing* soldiers plus the professional mounted force. The *fubing* system provided a substantial number of trained, readily available military manpower. Divided as they were into small military units, no single detachment was sufficiently powerful to present a threat to the central government. In preparation for the Koguryo expedition, Sui Yangdi also conscripted large numbers of troops and laborers to supplement the *fubing*. Many of these came from Shandong, effectively stripping the province of its working civilian workforce and creating economic hardship. These troops were continually deserting, causing unrest, and even resorting to banditry after having deserted from the military camp. These incidents were extensive enough to slow considerably the final preparations for war.

Early in 612 C.E., the main Chinese army was concentrated at Zhoujun, near modern Beijing. It consisted of two army groups, each comprised of twelve armies. The typical army of the Sui and Tang dynasties numbered about 20,000 soldiers, of which 6,000 or so were utilized in the logistical train as bearers or guards. The remaining 14,000 were divided into a heavy center division of archers, crossbowmen, skirmishers (light infantry), and heavy infantry organized into fifty-man platoons. It is important to note that the Chinese had practiced the "modern" concept of combined arms forces for as long as separate arms of service could be differentiated. The organization of the Sui army set forth in the *Samguk Sagi* is generally consistent with the description offered here as drawn from Chinese sources, but differs in some details. According to the Korean source, each Sui army consisted of four cavalry and four infantry divisions and was commanded by a senior general (*shangjiang*) assisted by a deputy general (*yajiang*). Each cavalry division was comprised of ten squadrons each of one hundred troopers. The infantry divisions were divided into eighty battalions. Each division was commanded by a divisional general (*pianjiang*) and identified by differently colored armor, cap strings, and flags.

Equipment

The infantry formations were made up of heavy infantry, archers, crossbowmen, and skirmishers. Heavy infantry weapons include the *ji*, a halberd-like weapon with a forked or double-headed blade, as well as spears, axes, and swords. Some soldiers probably still carried the *ge* or dagger axe, a wooden haft with a knife-like blade mounted crosswise near the top of the shaft. The *ge* had been a standard weapon of Chinese armies since the ancient Shang Dynasty. The better-equipped heavy infantrymen and crossbowmen probably wore laminar armor, most likely tunics made of metal or leather plates, or laminae, laced together and covering the torso and shoulder. Archers and skirmishers probably wore only cloth tunics, with the skirmishers carrying light shields and wielding short thrusting spears. Light cavalry were primarily archers but may have also carried light spears and swords. The Sui army also included a contingent of Turkish cavalry commanded by Chule, former khan of the Western Turks, who had been established at the Sui court as a potential "anti-khan" in the event the current khan tried to assert his independence from Chinese influence. These Turkish forces were probably equipped in a manner similar to that of the Chinese light cavalry.

According to the *Samguk Sagi* chronicle, the Sui forces that fought at the Salsu River were a specially selected and equipped detached striking force that carried a hundred days' rations for each horse and man, wore laminar armor, and carried spears. The term for spear used in the Korean chronicle is written with a different set of characters from those that indicate "halberds," suggesting that they may have been spears with leaf-shaped metal blades. The Sui army also wore identifiable clothing and carried "military implements" and *huomu*, literally "fire screen," which may have been tough leather shields for protection when attacking fortifications, whose defensive ballistae often hurled fire-pots at the attackers.

Siegecraft

Since the expedition had to cross rivers and attack Koguryo fortresses and walled cities, Sui Yangdi's army included large numbers of pioneers and sappers, bridging equipment, and a substantial siege train. The siege train included various kinds of catapults, collapsible ladders called *yunti* (literally "cloud ladders"), wheeled covered bridges, and artificial tunnels that could be rolled up to the walls of the forts to protect the soldiers from the fall of arrow shot, boiling liquid, and flaming detritus thrown down by the defenders. It was probably here that the *huomu* or fire screens were to be used. During the Han era the Chinese developed elaborate systems for signaling along the walls, which they had erected in defense against the northern tribes. These messaging systems were still in use during the Sui period and included beacon fires for long-range communication, trumpets, gongs, drums, bells, flags, and lanterns for tactical battlefield signaling.

Logistics

In addition to the army, a huge fleet of warships and merchantmen was assembled to provide logistical support to the land force, and an amphibious force was deployed aboard transports and combat ships, vessels presumably similar to those used in the Southern Expedition. The largest of these warships was of the "five-toothed" class and carried 800 sailors and marines. It had five decks towering a hundred feet above the waterline and mounted six fifty-foot booms to smash holes in enemy ships. Once engaged at close range, the marines fired crossbows from ports along the five decks. Other large ships were of the "Azure Dragon" class, while smaller ships of the "Yellow Dragon" class carried one hundred marines each.

THE KOREAN ARMY

Since the records of the Koguryo were lost when a combined Tang/Silla force besieging P'yongyang fifty-six years after the battle of the Salsu River burned the city, little detailed information is available about the organization of the Koguryo army. Some information can be gleaned from the Silla, Paekche, Sui, and Japanese records, however. Since the mountains and valleys of northern Korea were inhospitable to agriculture, Koguryo had traditionally depended upon the hunt and on predatory warfare for economic sustenance. This strategy bred a fierce, cohesive warrior class. Historian Ki-baik Lee uses the term *aristocratic army* to describe the military culture of the Three Kingdoms period. The king was commander-in-chief and frequently took the field at the head of his army. In addition to this "royal army" personally led by the king were other forces called *tang* that could be raised to operate independently. The *tang* probably developed from the ancient tribal war bands, and a strong bond existed between the *tangju* (tang chief) and his soldiers. The commanders and officers were mostly of the aristocratic warrior class whose primary function was to prepare for and conduct war. They were supported by taxes paid by the general population. By the time of the Sui invasion, decades of continuous

Fig. 18.2 Koguryo Heavy Cavalryman

warfare had produced tough, experienced, cavalry-heavy, highly mobile legions. Figure 18.2 portrays one of these Koguryo heavy cavalrymen.

In the kingdom of the Silla, the aristocratic army may have been supplemented by an institution known as the *hwarangdo* (literally, "Band of Flower Youths"), a fraternity of young men—the cream of the aristocracy—who lived together, undertook pilgrimages, and cultivated the arts. While there is some disagreement as to whether the *hwarangdo* was primarily a religious or military institution, many historians believe that the *hwarangdo* had a military function since many of its members later became famous generals. One passage in the *Samguk Sagi* suggests that the leading *hwarang* led groups of young followers (*nangdo* or youth bands) who could be conscripted in time of crisis and who otherwise became "active duty" officers and soldiers when they reached the age of twenty. A Koguryo institution, the *kyongdang*, may have performed a similar function at the provincial level. Like the *hwarangdo*, the *kyongdang* cultivated both military skills and moral values, as well as Confucian studies. Like the *hwarangdo*, the institution of *kyongdang* appears to have been derived from earlier tribal customs involving communal bodies of unmarried youths.

Equipment

After so many years of contact between the two countries, much of Koguryo military equipment as well as some of its organization and fighting doctrine was quite similar to the Chinese, although there were certainly differences. Japanese sources indicate that the basic long weapon of the Korean foot soldier was the *ch'ang*, a spear with a leaf-shaped iron blade attached to a thirteen-foot wood or bamboo shaft. The *ch'ang* was used as a stabbing weapon by both infantry and cavalry and could even be thrown at the enemy. Both infantry and cavalry were also armed with bows. A sixth century C.E. Koguryo hunting scene shows mounted huntsmen using saddles and stirrups, wearing soft, gown-like garments trimmed in fur, and feathered headdresses. They are depicted firing compound laminated bows. Their quivers, worn on the right hip like those used by horsemen of the steppes and later Japanese warriors, are open at the side with the arrowheads resting in a pocket at the bottom and the arrows kept in place by a thong or ribbon. Presumably the arrows were drawn by pulling out and down. Koguryo light cavalry troopers were probably similarly accoutered on campaign, as portrayed in Figure 18.3. These cavalrymen also "swung swords from their mounts as they swooped in on their prey."

Tactics

Korean armies are described as using drums, bells, and gongs as signaling devices. Although there were cases of Korean warriors (probably cavalry officers) engaging in individual combat, the armies usually fought as disciplined units. In battle, the infantry moved up in formation, planted their shields, and fired arrows at their adversaries. When the order was given, the infantry opened lanes in their ranks to permit the passage of cavalry units through their lines as they went into the attack.

While the royal army and the *tang* provided a mobile striking force, the defense of the provinces and provincial fortresses was in the hands of regional units. Each district had at its center a fortress commanded by a *songju* or "castle lord"

Fig. 18.3 Koguryo Light Cavalryman

and garrisoned by locally recruited forces, supplemented by the young members of the *kyongdang*. The larger provinces (*pu*) were governed by aristocratic officials appointed by the king who were responsible for both civil administrative and military functions. The fortresses themselves were probably similar to the ancient *sansong* and walled towns, although the larger fortresses, like those along the Liao River and the city of P'yongyang itself, had stone-faced walls and were of greater size and complexity than earlier versions. These fortresses withstood the initial brunt of the Sui invasion, and their ability to withstand Sui Yangdi's siege shaped the ensuing battle.

THE BATTLE OF THE SALSU RIVER (612 C.E.)

The Sui campaigns against Korea are described in the *Sui History*, but the only source of information for the battle of the Salsu River is the *Samguk Sagi* (*History of the Three Kingdoms*), compiled from earlier sources in 1145 C.E. by Kim Pu-sik. The account presented here follows that account. Information was also obtained from translations by Kim Chong-gwon into modern Korean and an English-language version compiled by Homer Hulbert in 1904, as edited by Clarence N. Weems. The battle of the Salsu River, in which the forces of the Korean kingdom of Koguryo inflicted terrible losses on an invading Chinese army, is considered by many Korean scholars to be the most significant military event of the seventh-century wars between the two kingdoms for control and influence in northeast Asia. The immense cost of the defeat fatally weakened the Sui Dynasty, as it did the Korean kingdom, which eventually disappeared. But the campaigns of which the Salsu battle was a part provided a respite for the consolidation of the successor Silla kingdom, which lived to unify Korea and ensure the survival of the Koreans as separate and unique people.

The campaign of 612 C.E. began in the first month of the eighth year of the reign of Sui Yangdi. The emperor had already carried out solemn preliminary ceremonies and sacrifices and promulgated a punitive decree condemning the duplicity, cunning, and aggression of the Koguryo king. In these decrees Sui Yangdi emphasized the virtue of his dynasty and his own awesome responsibilities as the Son of Heaven and inheritor of the mantle of the ancient rulers of China. Now was the time to carry out the punishment of the evildoers. With a blaring of trumpets, ringing of bells, clanging of gongs, shouting of orders, clatter of hooves, and shriek of bullock cartwheels, Sui Yangdi's vast Chinese army began to move. Each day one of the twenty-four armies shouldered arms and began its march, swinging out onto the road to Korea and leaving a thirteen-mile (forty *li*) interval between the armies. From the fluttering pennons of the lead scouts to the brocade banners of the rearguard, the armored centipede stretched for 320 miles along the dusty road and through the mountain passes to the northeast. The *Samguk Sagi* records that forty days passed before the entire column, the huge imperial headquarters, and the long logistical tail cleared the cantonment area. In a closely guarded carriage at the center of the headquarters and imperial guard detachment rode Sui Yangdi himself, supreme commander of the mighty expedition. In his entourage were Pei Qu, his trusted advisor and chief of strategy; Yuwen Kai, his chief engineer; Yuwen Shu, his favorite general; and his staff administrators, logisticians, and scribes.

Army by army, division by division, the long column slogged along the ancient road to Manchuria and Korea, across the Luan River, through the gates of the northeastern Long Wall, up into the foothills through the ancient "Mountain Sea Barrier" of Shanhaaiguan Pass, and down to the Bo Hai coast road that led into the Liao River valley. Map 18.5 shows the route of march of the Chinese army. In harbors and inlets all along the Shandong Peninsula and the Bo Hai coast, countless ships slipped their moorings, breasted the tidal chop, and sailed out into the Yellow Sea and Gulf of Bohai. Fat-bellied supply ships wallowed north toward the Gulf of Laiodong to feed the army, while the towering "five-toothed" men of war, the Azure and Yellow Dragon ships, and the bluff-bowed transports of the amphibious force set course for Korea Bay and the Koguryo coast.

The slow progress of the mighty force gave Koguryo King Yongyan and his field commander, General Ulchi Mundok, time to prepare for the coming war. They used this time well to mobilize the royal army, the *tang* formations, and the fortress garrisons and to scour the countryside and stockpile food and munitions all along the fortress line. It was now that the *tangju*, the provincial governors, assumed their military roles as commanders and came together to discuss strategy. Reconnaissance units were sent forward to meet the Chinese

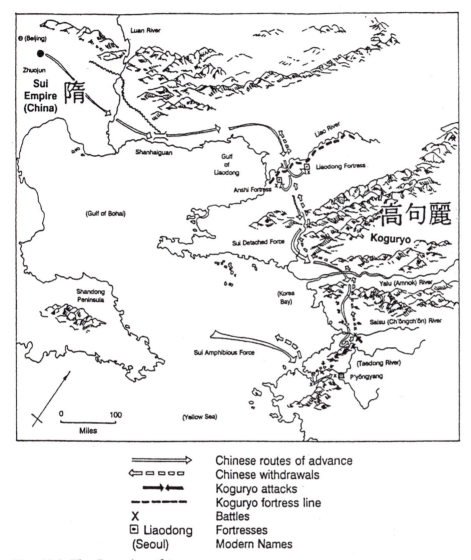

Map 18.5 The Campaign of 612

army and to report on its condition and route of march. Eventually, Sui Yangdi's light cavalry, ranging far to the front of the main force, made contact with the Koguryo Khitan and Malgal scouts. Shortly thereafter, the mounted outpost line of the Koreans was driven inward by the Chinese advance.

By the second month the Chinese army had reached the Liao River. Engineer Yuwen Kai had earlier constructed a three-span portable bridge. This immense fabrication was dragged forward and assembled by Yuwen Kai's pioneers and sappers, only to discover that the final span was too short to reach the far shore! From across the river Korean troops rained arrows down upon Yuwen Kai's combat engineers. Some Chinese soldiers leapt into the water and swam across, but could not climb the steep bank on the far side. They were cut down by Korean archers and spearmen, their blood staining the river shallows. Finally, a single officer, Mai Tiezhang, jumped across the gap from the bridge to the east bank and plunged into the ranks of the Korean defenders. With incredible bravery and ability, he cleared a small area on the far bank by killing the Koreans with his sword. This allowed other guardsmen to swarm up the bank and force a lodgment on the far shore. Although many Korean soldiers were killed in this short battle, the Chinese failed to carry the day, with the result that the Sui engineers pulled the three-span bridge back to the west bank of the river. The solution was obvious, and an engineer named He Zhou was assigned the task of lengthening the bridge. After two days, the Chinese tried again to push the bridge over the Liao River. This time the bridge reached the far shore, and Chinese regulars were able to force their way across and gain the opposite bank. A bloody battle ensued with the Koguryo defenders, in which many soldiers on both sides died. But by the end of the day, the Chinese had their bridgehead across the Liao.

Sui Yangdi's intention seems to have been to strike for the Koguryo capital in the belief that the capture of P'yongyang would bring an end to any resistance and cause the king to give in to Chinese demands. But the road to P'yongyang was perilous, as the Koreans continued to defend tenaciously, fighting delaying actions all along the Liao River before withdrawing into the fortresses. By summer, with the rainy season beginning, Sui Yangdi had invested the Korean fortifications but had not been able to overcome them. Faced with a stalemate and terrible weather, Sui Yangdi pulled his army off the line and into camp west of the Liaodong fortress.

While the main Chinese force awaited the end of the heavy rains, the amphibious force continued on to Korea. Sui Yangdi organized a detached force of nine armies (said to number 305,000 men) to strike directly at P'yongyang. These troops were under the command of General Yuwen Shu and were issued heavy armor, weapons, equipment, fire screens, and rations sufficient for one hundred days. The total weight of all this paraphernalia was so great that, although they faced the death penalty if they discarded any of it, many soldiers secretly buried a large portion of their rations beneath their tents. As the detached force began its march toward P'yongyang, the naval transports of the amphibious force reached the mouth of the Taedong River and began to put 20,000 marines and infantry ashore. The commander of this operation was Lai Huer, senior general of the imperial left-wing guard. The lead elements of the landing force engaged the Koreans and scattered them. Encouraged by this easy success, General Lai moved to exploit the landing quickly by moving 10,000 of his men through the beachhead and into the attack. Unfortunately, only part of the landing force was ashore, and Lai's deputy tried to persuade him to wait until more forces gained the beach. Lai disregarded the advice and pressed ahead.

Korean troops fought briefly with the Chinese point guard of the marines at the gates of P'yongyang and then fell back in a feigned retreat, appearing to abandon the defense of the city itself. The Sui forces entered the capital, where General Lai released them to plunder. As the Chinese troops spread out and became disoriented in the city's narrow streets and alleys, Koguryo commandos came out from their hiding places and fell upon their enemies. Taken by surprise, the Chinese fled from the city. The Koreans engaged in a lethal pursuit, driving the Chinese all the way back to the coast. Humiliated, General Lai ordered his forces to take to their ships and sailed back to Liaodong without trying to link up with the Chinese detached force now approaching from the north. Having met and defeated one wing of the attack, the Koreans now turned to meet the detached force marching on the city.

The armies of the detached force continued southeast, across the Yalu River toward P'yongyang. Rather than attempting to stand and fight the advancing Chinese detachments, the Korean commander, General Ulchi Mundok, refused to give battle and harassed the Chinese flanks. With false promises of a surrender, Mundok lured the Chinese deeper into the country and further from their base of operations. This strategy is called *yudo* or "drawing the enemy in deeply." Although the Chinese won a number of small victories during their advance, they could never bring the Koreans to major battle. After crossing the Salsu River, the Chinese advanced to within ten miles of P'yongyang. The Chinese troops were exhausted from their march and continuous skirmishing with their adversaries. Having buried much of their rations before beginning the march, the Chinese troops now suffered from hunger. Each mile brought them closer to their objective but seemed to weaken their ability to achieve it.

It was now early autumn, and the end of the campaign season was fast approaching. If the Chinese did not force a decision soon, there would be no alternative but to withdraw or lose the army to starvation and the elements. The Koreans played for time. General Mundok pretended to offer the Chinese a surrender in which he hinted that Korea would be willing to submit to Chinese demands. During negotiations he praised the ability and bravery of Chinese generals and argued that, having penetrated so deeply into Korea and successfully withstood so many attacks, they could hardly be faulted for considering their mission to have been essentially accomplished. The *Samguk Sagi* notes that there was discord within the Chinese headquarters as the Sui generals pondered General Mundok's surrender offer. Those who counseled that the Chinese army had achieved its objective of securing Koguryo's submission carried the debate. The Chinese column threatening the Korean capital turned around and began to make its way back north.

After the Chinese column had committed itself to execute a withdrawal, the Chinese began to realize that the promise of peace was an illusion. Once more Koguryo light cavalry began to harry the flanks of the Chinese army. General Mundok sent reinforcements to increase the size of the detachments, fighting a running battle with the Chinese as they withdrew to the north. But Mundok held his main force in reserve, waiting for the right moment to strike. He was waiting for his enemy to reach the Salsu River, which blocked their way to the north. Now Korean engineers did their work. Advanced detachments using some sort of portable barriers, perhaps log rafts stood on end, blocked the small streams leading into the Salsu, lowering its water level. When the Chinese approached the river and began making their way across, the Korean engineers removed the barriers, causing the river to flood and making it much more difficult to ford. General Mundok waited until half the Chinese army had crossed the river before he attacked the rear of the column still on the near bank or caught in the middle of the flooded river. The Chinese units on the far bank could do little to help their comrades, who now came under murderous assault.

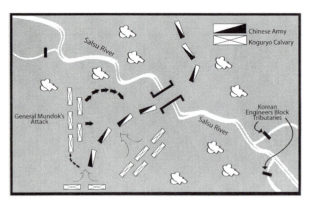

Fig. 18.4 The Battle of Salsu River (612 C.E.)

General Mundok unleashed his army with all the fury and blood lust of his tough, cruel mountain warriors. The rear of the Chinese column was cut to pieces, and only a few survived to plunge into the river in hopes of escape. The Koreans now crossed the river in strength and pursued the head of the column as it fled northward in terror. According to the *Samguk Sagi*, only 2,700 of the 305,000 Chinese troops survived to reach Liaodong, leaving a trail of thousands of pieces of armor and weapons in their wake. Corpses lined the entire line of retreat. Sui Yangdi was outraged at the news of the defeat and sent what few generals and officers had survived the battle home in chains. The approaching cold of the Korean winter made it impossible for Sui Yangdi to mount another military effort at capturing P'yongyang. Worse, if he did not move south soon, the mountain passes behind him would be blocked with snow. With no other choice, the Chinese army began its long march home.

The following year Sui Yangdi raised another army and again crossed the Liao River, only to receive word of a serious revolt near his eastern capital. He dispatched General Yuwen Shu and a substantial part of the army to put down the rebellion. Disruption of the imperial recruitment and logistics system and widespread social unrest forced the Korean campaign to be cut short with no results. By now Sui Yangdi's exactions for public works and war had sparked rebellion at the heart of the empire. Sui Yangdi nonetheless attempted another foray into Korea in 614 C.E., this time penetrating to the outskirts of P'yongyang. Again the Korean king offered the prospect of submission, and once more delayed delivering it. Provoked by the king's intransigence, Sui Yangdi announced yet another expedition to bring the Koreans to heel. But China was exhausted and seething with rebellion and quite incapable of further large-scale military adventures. Sui Yangdi continued to hold the fabric of the Chinese nation together for a few more years. In the end, however, social conditions worsened, and he lost the Mandate of Heaven. Driven from his throne by rebellion in 618 C.E., the emperor sought refuge in his southern capital, where he was murdered by the son of General Yuwen Shu.

The wars had left Koguryo exhausted as well, and revolt and factionalism broke out throughout the country. In 642 C.E. King Yongyan's successor and much of the ruling aristocracy were slaughtered when a military strong-man, Yon Kaesomun, seized control of the government. Over the years the powerful Tang Dynasty that had followed Sui Yangdi launched a series of attacks against Koguryo, which the Korean nation managed mostly to with-stand. Eventually, however, the Chinese proved persistent, and in 668 C.E. the capital of P'yongyang fell to a combined Tang and Silla army, bringing the kingdom of Koguryo to an end.

Korean historians see the half-century of Koguryo resistance against the Chinese as vitally important to the survival of Korea as a nation. Koguryo purchased the time needed for Silla to increase its power so that, when Koguryo succumbed, Silla was able to unify the peninsula and resist Chinese encroachments. Silla established a tributary relationship with China that guar-anteed Korean national existence and a high degree of autonomy, a relation-ship that set the pattern for Chinese-Korean relationships to this day.

LESSONS OF WAR

Strategy

1. Sui Yangdi's campaigns against Koguryo appear at first sight to be a clear-cut case of strategic overreach. Yet, the attempt was continued by the Tang Dynasty for years until its goal of obtaining Korean submission to Chinese will was achieved. In the Chinese view, Korean independence in foreign affairs was vital to its own security insofar as its maneuverings with the nomadic peoples and the other peninsula states threatened Chinese vital interests.

2. The Korean people would have suffered far less had they simply submit-ted to Chinese demands to establish a tributary relationship between the two states. Instead, the Koreans chose to fight. This is an important les-son: what is often perceived by one power to be a reasonable demand can be perceived as a threat to its very existence by another.

3. History is full of examples that parallel the Korean example, of peoples and states that were willing to fight to the death rather than submit to a foreign power. Great powers ought never to underestimate the force of national or ethnic identity.

4. Be wary of advisors who promise easy victory! Pei Qu, Sui Yangdi's princi-pal advisor, was intelligent, steeped in accepted values, and knowledgeable

about some areas of Chinese interests. But he was totally uninformed about Korea, even as he continued to give advice to his king. No one knows everything!

5. Beware of conducting war in foreign lands unless you are willing to occupy and control those areas for a long time. The soldiers and political leaders of Koguryo fought on because they had nowhere else to go. They saw the struggle with the Chinese as a struggle for national survival. Under these conditions, they did not have to win every battle but only to keep fighting. Like modern-day insurgents, they lived where they fought. The conqueror can always go home. The insurgents cannot.

6. Always play to your strong suit. The Chinese could have neutralized the Korean strategy of defending the Liao River line if they had used their control of the sea to operate on exterior lines. For all the glory and reputation of the Chinese navy, China was primarily a land power, weak in naval skills and not proficient in the maneuvering of naval forces. General Lai's amphibious operation against P'yongyang—paralleling MacArthur's landing at Inchon—reveals the Chinese weakness in these kinds of operations.

7. If one is going to detach a sizeable combat force to undertake independent operations, one should always ensure that it has the means to feed and sustain itself. The Chinese detached force against P'yongyang almost starved for lack of rations.

Tactics

1. It is always a matter of intuition whether to play it safe or take risks in battle. As many commanders have succeeded when risking as have failed. Commanders must develop their instincts and sense of proportion and risk in peacetime through the study of history and the conduct of exercises to sharpen and train their judgment.

2. The fate of General Lai's command at the Salsu River reminds us that a fighting withdrawal is one of the most difficult and potentially disastrous of military maneuvers.

3. Any army or detachment conducting deep penetration operations in hostile territory should be prepared in advance to protect its flanks and maintain cohesion and discipline if forced to withdraw under fire. This is always easier said than done.

4. Soldiers will always be the judge of what equipment is worth keeping (and thus carrying!) and what is not. From time immemorial soldiers have disobeyed orders and discarded items they deemed of no value. This being so, it is important to note that they are not always right! The troops of the Chinese detachment that marched on P'yongyang were issued a hundred days' worth of rations, which they promptly buried rather than carry. Once in the field, they almost starved.

FURTHER READING

Bacon, Wilbur D. "Fortresses of Kyonggi-do." *Transactions of the Korea Branch of the Royal Asiatic Society* 37 (April 1961): 1–63.

Bingham, Woodbridge. *The Founding of the T'ang Dynasty: The Fall of Sui and Rise of T'ang, a Preliminary Survey.* Baltimore: Waverly, 1941; reprint, New York: Octagon Books, 1975.

Eckert, Carter. *Korea, Old and New: A History.* Cambridge, MA: Harvard University Press, 1991.

Embree, Ainslie T., ed. *Encyclopedia of Asian History.* New York: Charles Scribner's Sons, 1988. S.v. "Warfare in China," by Edward L. Dreyer.

Farris, William Wayne. *Heavenly Warriors: The Evolution of Japan's Military, 500–1300.* Cambridge, MA: Harvard University Press, 1992.

Gardiner, Kenneth Herbert James. *The Early History of Korea.* Honolulu: University of Hawaii Press, 1969.

Henthorn, William E. *A History of Korea.* New York: Free Press, 1971.

Jamieson, John Charles. *The Samguk Sagi and the Unification Wars.* Ph.D. dissertation, University of California, Berkeley, 1969.

Lee, Ki-baik. "Korea: The Military Tradition." In *The Traditional Culture and Society of Korea*, edited by Hugh H. W. Kang. Occasional Papers of the Center for Korean Studies, no. 5. Honolulu: Center for Korean Studies, 1975.

Lee, Peter H. *Sourcebook of Korean Civilization.* New York: Columbia University Press, 1992.

———. *Sources of Korean Tradition.* New York: Columbia University Press, 1996.

Norman, B., and Joe Wanne. *A Cultural History of Korea: A History of Korean Civilization.* Seoul: Hollym International, 2001.

Rutt, Richard. "The Flower Boys of Silla." *Transactions of the Korea Branch of the Royal Asiatic Society* 38 (October 1961): 1–66.

Schmidt, Andre. *Korea between Empires.* New York: Columbia University Press, 2002.

Tooke, Lamar, and Bill Mendel. "Operational Logic: Selecting the Center of Gravity." *Military Review* (Summer 1993): 3–11.

Twitchett, Denis, ed. *The Cambridge History of China.* Vol. 3, *Sui and T'ang China*, 589–906, part I. Cambridge: Cambridge University Press, 1979.

Wanne, Joe. *Traditional Korea: A Cultural History of Korean Civilization.* Seoul: Hollym International, 2000.

Weems, Clarence Norwood, ed. *Hulbert's History of Korea.* Vol. 1 New York: Hillary House, 1962.

Wright, Arthur F. *The Sui Dynasty.* New York: Alfred A. Knopf, 1978.

19 THE WARS OF ARAB CONQUEST

[600–850 C.E.]

BACKGROUND

The Arab armies are those military forces of Arabian origin that established the empire of Islam through military conquest before being subsumed into the larger Muslim convert population that resulted in substantive changes. The original Arab armies can be said to have existed from 630 to approximately 842 C.E., when the Abbasid caliph, al-Mutasim introduced the Mamluk institution of slave Turkish soldiers who replaced the original Arab contingents in the armies of Islam. Until that time, the armies of Mohammed and his immediate successors were almost exclusively comprised of Arabs from Arabia, and between 633 and 656 C.E. these armies invaded and conquered large segments of the Byzantine and Sassanid empires. Over the next hundred years the Arabs fought three civil wars. The first war replaced the original successors of Mohammed with the Umayyad family who ruled from Syria from 661 to 750 C.E. The Umayyads survived the second civil war (684–692 C.E.) but were driven from power during the third civil war (744–750 C.E.) and replaced by the Abbasid family, who ruled from Iraq and retained the caliphate, although in much altered form, until 1250 C.E. The Arab invasions set in motion enormous changes and produced a new sociopolitical order that eventually included the whole of the Arabian peninsula, all the Sassanid lands, and the Syrian and Egyptian provinces of the Byzantine Empire.

The emergence of Islam in Arabia between 570 and 632 C.E., the dates of Mohammed's life, brought into being a new social, religious, and military force that swept out of Arabia on the wings of the religious fervor begun by the Prophet himself and that collided immediately with the two great powers of the day, the Byzantine and Sassanid empires. The Byzantine Empire ran from eastern Europe, through the Anatolian peninsula, along the Palestinian

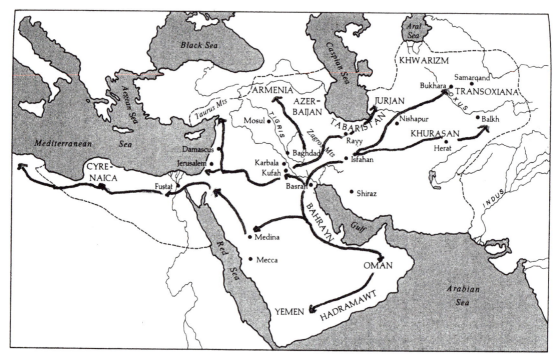

Map 19.1 The Wars of Arab Expansion until the Battle of Tours (732 C.E.). Dashed line indicates limits of the empire.

land bridge, through Egypt on to Libya, to include Syria. The Sassanids controlled all of Iraq and Iran and large areas stretching eastward into central Asia. One of the more remarkable achievements in military history was the conquest of large areas of these empires in less than thirty years by Arab armies that probably never exceeded 5,000 men at any time.

Both empires were fragile, weakened by long wars between them. From 540 to 629 C.E., the Byzantines and Sassanids fought continuous wars in Syria and Iraq. At one time the Sassanid armies washed their weapons in the Mediterranean, occupying Antioch, Alexandria, and Jerusalem only to be driven back by Emperor Heraclius in 623 C.E. The sapping effect of these wars on the empires' strength was exacerbated by religious persecution within the imperial borders. The conflict between Manichaeism and Zoroastrianism, along with the struggles between heretical Christian sects, weakened Sassanid authority, as did the long and bloody persecution of the Monophysites in Egypt by the Christian emperors of Byzantium. Terrible outbreaks of plague and disease struck both empires on and off for half a century, further weakening imperial will. By the time of the Arab invasions, both empires were mere reflections of their former power and relatively easy prey to the wide-ranging *razzias* (raids) of the Arabs.

The Arab invasions were begun by the Prophet himself who, having come to think of himself as God's true messenger, sent demands to the emperors of the Sassanids and Byzantines demanding that they accept him and his message. In the absence of an imperial reply, Mohammed began the holy wars near the end of his life by sending an army of 3,000 men to attack the Byzantine frontier near the Dead Sea. This force was defeated at Muta. Undeterred, Mohammed sent another force against the border the next year and succeeded in occupying some small settlements of Christians and Jews near the northwest Arabian border. Legend suggests he was preparing for yet another attack against Byzantium when he died on June 7, 632 C.E.

In 634 C.E. the Arabs attacked the Byzantine border provinces again, this time with three columns moving through Palestine, destroying a Byzantine garrison en route. At the same time another Arab army attacked Damascus. The Byzantine relief force was engaged and forced to withdraw. In the meantime all of Palestine was left defenseless to Arab raids. A year later Damascus fell to the Arabs. The next year the last remaining Byzantine force in Syria was defeated at the Yamuk River, forcing the Byzantine frontier back to the Amanus Mountains. Two years after Yamuk, Jerusalem and Caesaria surrendered to the Arabs. Between 639 and 646 C.E. Arab armies proceeded to eradicate the last vestiges of Byzantine rule in what had been Roman Mesopotamia, destroying the old unity of the Roman Mediterranean world forever.

To the east, a series of other Arab victories spelled the end of the Sassanid empire. The Sassanids were brought under attack in force in 634 C.E., and within three years Arab armies had pushed to the edge of Iraq. The Sassanids withdrew beyond the Zagros, leaving the door to Persia open. By 641 C.E. a new Arab advance across the Tigris was under way, and within eight years all of Persia was under Arab rule. Arab armies now prepared to push farther eastward across the Oxus, reaching ultimately to India. Far to the West, Egypt and Alexandria became major Arab naval bases, extending the influence of Islam to the Mediterranean Sea. In 661 C.E. with the coming of Umayyads, the Arab assault turned west once again, occupying Tunisia and the coast of Morocco, and at the end of the century, Arab armies crossed into Spain. In less than forty years Arab armies had grown from little more than tribal coalitions to masters of an empire.

The dream of empire had been conceived in the mind of a single man, Mohammed the Prophet, who set in motion the means and motive for the extensive Arab conquest. At the time of Mohammed's birth, Arabia was a harsh land, home to a tangled coterie of rival clans and tribes. Most were desert wanderers based around tribal control of critical oases. Other tribes lived in small towns. Arab society lived by trading and raiding and was patriarchal, bound together by ties of kinship and the sworn duties of the blood feud. The Arabs of Mohammed's day were pagans intermixed with small communities of Jews and heretical Christians. Arab society was almost totally illiterate.

Mohammed was born into this society sometime near 570 C.E. in the town of Mecca of the tribe of Quaraysh. The Quaraysh tribe were traders but drew much of their income from their protection and control of the *Ka'ba*, an ancient black stone worshipped as sacred by the Arabs. Arab pilgrims made annual visits (*hajj*) to worship at the stone, access to which the Quaraysh charged fees. It is one of the more interesting aspects of religious history that Mohammed, the strict monotheist, retained the duty of pilgrimage to Mecca to worship at the old pagan shrine of *Ka'ba* as a central tenet of his new religion of Islam.

Mohammed married the widow of a successful caravan trader and soon was running the family business. At the same time his devotion to his own religious visions grew more intense, and he came to believe that he was the messenger of God. Religious and economic conflict with his own tribe in Mecca forced Mohammed to flee to Medina where, after a short time, he gained converts and was made leader of the tribes there. Mohammed and his followers attacked the caravans of Mecca. This led to war in which Mohammed gained victory in a number of battles. These victories brought his old relatives, the Quaraysh tribe, and other tribal leaders under his rule. This coalition became converts and served as the nucleus of the armies that spread the new religion of Islam.

Mohammed's fusion of religious fervor with the traditional Arab practice of raiding and tribal warfare provided the critical stimulus that motivated the early Arab armies to conquest. A central tenet of Mohammed's new religion was the belief that those who embrace Islam have a sacred right to war upon those who are unbelievers and to conquer and rule them in the name of the true God. The purpose of holy war is not to convert the conquered to Islam, for the faith prohibits forced conversions. It is, instead, the idea of a *jihad*, a holy war to destroy the infidel, war in which God is always on the side of the army of believers. Mohammed himself is said to have proclaimed the doctrine of holy war on his last visit to Mecca. Tradition has it that his last statement to the faithful was that "Muslims should fight all men until they say, 'There is no God but Allah.'"

THE ARMY OF ISLAM

Society

The structure of the Arab army reflected the structure of Arab tribal society. Arab society during Mohammed's day and for more than a century afterward never really developed a stable political order that was worthy of being called a state. There was no state per se and therefore no stable administrative structure of government. Arab society remained what it had always been, a tribal society characterized by personal leadership and appointed retainers that drew no distinction between society, religion, and the army. Indeed, there was never a formal army as such. Instead, there was an alliance of powerful tribal chiefs who led their personal armed retinues in battle. What treasury there was came from gifts and booty obtained in raids. There was no financial system. Government was essentially an enlarged tribal system of negotiated consensus among powerful tribal chieftains, and it was these warrior chiefs who controlled the Arab populace and the army. Government, if it may be called that, was a system of indirect rule through tribal intermediaries. This system of indirect rule plagued the Muslim empire until its end. Power ebbed and flowed from the center of authority, but no caliph ever was able to retain control of the tribal and regional armies for very long. Revolts and insurrections rooted in jealousy, political interests, religious apostasy, and traditional blood feuds went on for centuries.

Some authorities have argued that the invasion of the Byzantine and Sassanid empires by the Arab tribes was comparable with the invasion of the Western Roman Empire by the German tribes with the same general result, the establishment over the long term of a number of separate states ruled by powerful national kings. It seems more correct to say, however, that the Arab invasions were different. Unlike the tribal invasions of the Western Roman Empire, the Arab invasions were coordinated from a single center, Medina, for a specific *religious* purpose, to extend the rule of God's believers over the unbelievers as commanded by God himself. This central leadership, direction, and religious purpose led to a result quite different from that of the Germanic invasions in the West. Instead of conquering, settling, and then ruling the new lands, the Arab conquerors stayed together as soldiers living in garrison cities (*amsar*), military districts (*ajnad*), and even military monasteries (*ribat*) whose members remained celibate. The Arab conquerors remained apart from the societies they conquered and showed little interest in governing the new lands, leaving the old systems, leaders, kings, and governmental officials in place to continue to administer the conquered lands. The military garrisons remained just that, fortresses that accommodated the Arab armies, which could be sent forth on further conquest or used to suppress revolts. This arrangement was possible because the Arab armies, although receiving religious direction from the center, were not really structured armies at all. They were tribal coalitions led by local chieftains comprised of emigrants from Arabia who left their homes to serve as soldiers in a holy crusade. In Islam, all believers were soldiers. There was no Muslim army distinct from Muslim society. Because the Muslims were a holy army and society, living apart from the conquered infidels with their families at government expense until called to further holy war worked well.

The Arabian population that gave rise to the early Arab armies was small and scattered, but routinely carried arms. The tribal leaders lived in houses in towns that were arsenals where the arms of the clan were stored. Tribal conflict over trade routes, personal rivalries, and blood feuds was endemic, and Arab tribes had a long history of fighting. In addition, the early wars between Medina and Mecca during Mohammed's time and the later civil war over his succession provided Arab soldiers and commanders with considerable combat experience. Some commanders and soldiers had gained additional experience serving in the armies of Byzantium and Persia. These early Arab armies were equipped with locally made weapons including swords, lances, shields, and felt armor. Armor seems to have been common, although helmets were not. The sword and spear dominated the battlefield. The horse was in short supply in Arabia, with the consequence that Arab armies did not develop cavalry until much later when adequate supplies of cavalry mounts could be obtained by conquest. What few horses were found in these early Arab armies were so valuable that they were led to the battlefield and only mounted for combat itself. Armed with lances, Arab cavalrymen were too few to play an important tactical role. Usually the cavalry would hover on the flanks of the infantry waiting to exploit any flight or loss of cohesion of the enemy, at which time it would attack. The tactical role of cavalry as a weapon of shock used against infantry was unknown.

Tactical Organization

Under these circumstances it is not surprising that early Arab armies fought mostly as infantry, a tradition that persisted long after they had developed large corps of heavy cavalry. Tribal warfare lent itself to individual combats rather than battle by units, and these early armies probably fought in precisely this manner. Evidence suggests, however, that one of the reasons Mohammed was so successful in the tribal wars against Medina may have been because he taught his soldiers to fight in disciplined formations of infantry. Such formations were, of course, common in the army of Byzantium but were contrary to the general Arab method of fighting. It might be surmised that Mohammed or one of his officers who may have had experience in the imperial army may have adopted the infantry formation and introduced it to the Arab armies.

The Arab armies that attacked Byzantium and Persia may have been infantry armies, but they did not move on foot. Instead, they made extensive use of the camel in transporting their armies to the strategic objective. This provided them with superior strategic mobility, enabling them to bypass enemy strong points and offer battle at times and places of their own choosing. The guiding tactical concept was to move quickly to a favorable position, establish the infantry on the ground, and then force the enemy to attack at its disadvantage. Once the horse became widely available, Arab armies continued their practice of using mounted infantry in a strategic manner. Eventually, the Arab armies produced the best war horse of the day, the Syrian-Arab crossbreed combining the small, strong North African Barb with the heavier Iranian mount.

Once established in their new lands the Arabs attempted to remain an ethnically homogeneous, warlike, and religious society apart from the conquered infidels. But their numbers were very small. Cone suggests that the total size of the Arab armies that left Arabia could hardly have exceeded 5,000 men, whereas the population of the conquered lands probably exceeded 20 million souls! All Arab emigrants lived in garrison cities or military districts and were registered in the *diwan* or "register." The registered soldier was enti-tled to monthly rations for himself and his family and received an annual cash stipend, as did his wife and children. Quarters were also provided for the soldier and his family. In return these religious warriors were available for military service at a moment's notice. As the Arab occupation stabilized, mil-itary calls to active service became relatively infrequent. When called to service, the soldier had to supply his own mount—horse or camel—and military equipment, which included a lance, sword, shield, bow, quiver, and armor—usually some form of mail.

Once registered on the *diwan*, the soldier remained on the roll for life. There was no word for veteran soldier, and no special provisions were made for them. Soldiers too old for service probably provided substitutes or worked for the army administration. Disabled soldiers were registered as cripples and continued to draw some portion of their annual pay and allowance. Arab sol-diers were usually forbidden to engage in agriculture, although in rare instances it was permitted. Such limitations on "fraternization" and economic activity worked against the creation of an Arab "society" in the conquered lands, a task left to the conquered infidels who converted to Islam. In some respects the *diwan* may have been adopted from the military role of the Byzantines, but with a very important difference: the *diwan* was not seen by the Arabs as an institution for the maintenance of the army but as a social institution for the maintenance of Muslims. Stipends were not mere military pay but a right claimed by every Muslim emigrant and his descendants as a reward for par-ticipation in the conquest of Islam over the infidels. Islam was religion, society, and army all in one, and the *diwan* was the mechanism for sustaining all three.

The attempt to sustain a separate Arab identity apart from the infidels was bound to fail in the long run on the grounds of numbers and conversions. Even as military manpower demands increased, the Arabs made no effort to recruit the able-bodied men of the conquered lands into their armies. Captives were often resettled on conquered lands, and some even served as special units (often private guards) or urban police. Gradually, native peoples were per-mitted to lend military service, usually ethnic or racial units serving as separate battalions. But once these captives converted to Islam they could no longer be enslaved, and more and more converts came to serve in the Muslim armies, even as the purely Arab elements remained isolated in their garrisons. Over time the Arab elements of the Muslim armies came to see the military *diwan* as a social stipend, and the Arabs became a smaller and less used seg-ment of the armies as they were gradually submerged into the Muslim armies of disparate peoples who had converted to the new faith.

With gradual assimilation and widespread conversion, the old citizen armies eventually gave way to professional armies manned largely by non-Arab Muslims, although their commanders remained Arabs for many years. The regional armies of the old tribal chiefs survived for centuries but for the most part were confined to their garrisons supported by the *diwan* and were of little use. As the Arabs were submerged in a sea of Muslims, the old tribal consensual style of government became more difficult to operate and proved insufficient to constrain tribal and personal ambitions. The result was two civil wars. The second war (684–692 C.E.) forced the Umayyads to abandon the old ideal of consensual rule completely, and they ruled by force supported by their professional army comprised mostly of Syrian troops. Even so, it was not until the last Umayyad caliph (750 C.E.) that the armies became professionalized, and during the Umayyad period the old Arab armies changed considerably.

Tactics

Under the Umayyads heavy cavalry became increasingly important. Originally, Arab cavalry was divided into armored and unarmored horse, or heavy and light cavalry. The heavy cavalry still comprised only a small number of units and was used mostly as shock troops along Byzantine lines. Light cavalry, when not used as skirmishers and reconnaissance, was used only to complete the destruction of already disorganized or broken units. Surviving records of the period describe the full equipment of the seventh century C.E. Arab cavalryman as lance, sword, shield, hauberk, packing needles, five small needles, linen thread, awl, scissors, horse's nose bag, and feed basket. During the Umayyad period the bulk of Arab cavalry became armored in a transition toward the Byzantine model in mounts, armor, and weapons. Unlike the Byzantines, the Arab armies retained their old infantry traditions. Byzantine cavalrymen, for example, were trained for use as shock troops fighting from horseback only. Arab heavy cavalry was trained in the old tradition of fighting first from horseback (or camel back) and then being able to dismount and fight on foot. Heavy cavalry never became a true arm of decision in Arab armies until much later, and heavy infantry remained the central combat arm. The cavalry would deploy safely behind the infantry formations and sally forth again and again as opportunity permitted to attack the enemy and then retreat quickly behind its own infantry for protection. The idea of cavalry against cavalry in open combat was unknown to Arab commanders.

When the Arab armies encountered the central Asian horse-archer on the rim of the empire they were unable to find a tactical solution to this novel way of fighting. The Arabs did what the Byzantines and Persians had done before them—they hired whole contingents of horse-archers and used them against their countrymen. The new cavalry threat forced a change in Arab cavalry equipment, most notably in the adoption of light felt armor for man and horse to protect against arrows and the introduction of the iron stirrup over the objections of Arab scholars who claimed the device would make soldiers effete by hindering their ability to dismount rapidly in battle. But even with the introduction of the horse-archer, infantry remained the queen of the battlefield in Arab tactical thinking.

The Umayyad period was brought to an end by yet another civil war, and the Abbasids were brought to the throne by rebel armies raised in Iran. These troops replaced the Syrian troops of the Umayyads in imperial garrisons, and the capital was moved to Baghdad. These Iranian troops or *Khurasiani* were mostly horse-archers, and this type of cavalry now became dominant in Arab armies. Although cavalry was now the arm of decision, infantry still played an important role on the battlefield, and close infantry and cavalry cooperation remained central to the new Arab tactical design. These new troops wore clothes similar to the eastern Christian monks and wore beards and long hair. Great reliance was placed upon the bow and lance. The attack was marked by a shower of arrows as the cavalry closed with the enemy at the gallop and firing as it went. Once the troops were in contact, the lance came into play along with other weapons of close combat like the curved sword, mace, battle axe, and short sword of single-edge design.

The Abbasids made no effort to broaden the base of their army or government, relying instead upon those groups and tribes of mostly eastern origin that had brought them to power. The Arab armies were now mostly cavalry armies, and since horses were expensive and training took a long time, it was more efficient for the Abbasids to rely upon the natural horsemen of the *Khurasiani* rather than to outfit and train the Arabs themselves. The heavy reliance upon foreign troops and the failure to extend governmental participation to the powerful regional chiefs resulted in the imperial army being run more like a mafia than a military institution. The caliphs and the army became increasingly isolated from the society, with the consequence that the Abbasids were forced to deal with frequent revolts.

The Mamelukes

During one of the civil wars that threatened to topple the Abbasids, one of the participants, al-Mutasim (833–842 C.E.), outfitted his army with 4,000 Turkish troops whom he had purchased as slaves and then freed for military service under his command. Once al-Mutasim had become caliph, he expanded the practice of purchasing and training Turkish slaves for service in his armies, thereby bringing into existence what Muslims came to call "the Mameluke institution." The essence of this institution was the systematic reliance of the caliphate upon soldiers of servile and non-Islamic origin. The use of other foreign, non-Muslim, ethnic units in the army also increased greatly. The result was that the areas of the empire under direct imperial control were policed by these slave Turks. Over time, most of the major military commands and some important governorships were assigned to Turkish officials as well. Eventually, the Mamelukes executed a military coup against the Abbasids and took control of the caliphate. For the next two centuries the Abbasid caliphs continued to rule from Baghdad, but mostly in name only, while genuine power was exercised by the Turkish military commanders who continued to pay lip-service to the rule of the caliphs. In reaction to this state of affairs, the governors of various provinces, using their regional armies as leverage, broke into open revolt time and again, with one province after another seceding from the old empire by force of arms. By the middle of the ninth century, the old Arab empire had ceased to exist, and with it the Arab "army of God" that had swept over the ancient Mediterranean world wielding the sword of Allah.

THE BATTLE OF TOURS (732 C.E.)

Before the "army of God" disappeared, it succeeded in establishing the Empire of Islam from the Bosphorus to the Pyrenees by destroying the Sassanid empire of Persia and tearing away most of the provinces from the ancient empire of Byzantium. The Arab advance continued along the coast of the North African littoral, reaching the Straits of Gibraltar by 710 C.E. Like other armies before them, the Arabs could not resist the lure of crossing the eighteen-mile-wide strait and invading Spain. In the town of Ceuta, opposite Gibraltar, the Arabs found themselves an ally in Count Julian, who had been sent by the Visigothic king of Spain, Roderick, to meet the Arab advance before it reached the straits. Julian sensed that the future belonged to the Arab armies, and having defeated an Arab probe in strength led by Musa ibn Nusair on the town, offered to throw in his lot with the Arabs.

To demonstrate how easy it would be for the Arabs to cross the straits and attack Spain, he and his men led an Arab raiding party across the straits and conducted a reconnaissance in force in the Algeciras area of southern Spain. The Visigothic monarchy in Spain had been in steady decline due to internal dissension between the nobility and a series of weak monarchs. The Ibero-Roman population had been thoroughly suppressed by its Visigothic overlords and was on the edge of revolt when Roderick ascended the throne in 710 C.E. As had been the case with the Byzantine and Sassanid empires, Visigothic rule in Spain was on its last legs and was easily defeated by the vigorous Arab armies that were now poised to attack Spain.

The next year, 711 C.E., an army of 7,000 men comprised mostly of Berbers and Moors crossed the straits in boats provided by the traitorous Count Julian. The invasion was commanded by a Berber, Tarik ibn Ziyad, who landed at a place the Arabs named *Jabel Tariki*, from which the English-sounding name Gibraltar has come. Unopposed, the army moved northwest. Roderick assembled his army at a place between the Barbate and Guadalete rivers, near the Jand salt lake, and brought the Arabs to battle. Roderick's army is said to have been comprised of 90,000 men, clearly a maximum effort by the Visigoths, while the Muslim army had been reinforced to about 12,000 men. Both sides fought with swords and spears, with armored nobles on horseback being supported by bands of infantry. The Berbers, some of the fiercest horse cavalry troops in the world, had appropriated a good number of horses from local farms and met the Visigoths on horseback. Many of

Roderick's troops were reluctant farmers and serfs pressed into action at the point of the swords of their Visigoth landlords, while most of the Moslem troops were hardened veterans of the North African campaigns. Roderick's armies had already suffered significant desertions on the way to the battlefield. When the Berbers, arrayed in mail and dark blue, face-covering turbans, charged the line, the Visigoth ranks shuddered and broke. Roderick himself lost his nerve and fled from his army, abandoning it to its fate, and was drowned attempting to cross the river. Tarik swept through southern Spain winning another battle at Ecija.

The Muslim advance toward the Visigoth capital at Toledo in central Spain was quick. The Jewish, Byzantine, and Ibero-Roman inhabitants of the region offered no resistance. They had suffered under the oppressive regime of the Visigoths and were not displeased to exchange it for the more tolerant rule of Islam. Some Visigoth warlords tried to oppose the invaders, but there was no coordinated resistance. Other warlords went over to the Muslims in the hope of a future accommodation. In the end, resistance and the kingdom itself collapsed. Over the next few years more Arab troops crossed into Spain, and the remaining cities were subdued or opened their gates. By 716 C.E., the Arab conquest of Spain was complete, and Andalusia, as it was called in Arabic, became the first European province of the Muslim empire.

Throughout their conquests the Muslims were aided by the internal exhaustion and collapse of their chief adversaries. This had been the case in their wars with the Byzantines, the Sassanids, and the Visigoths in Spain. The Muslim invasion of France, however, brought the Muslim armies into contact with a much more vigorous opponent, the warlike Franks. The old Merovingian dynasty of the Franks had maintained a firm grip on Gaul for more than 200 years but was in decline by the time of the Muslim invasion. Real power no longer was held by the Merovingian kings but by powerful men behind the throne. These powerful warlord-vassals were called the Mayors of the Palace. Thus the role of defending the state had come to be assumed by the Arnulfing dynasty and was handed from father to son. One of these mayors was Charles Martel, an illegitimate son, and the principal landholder in north France and western Germany. Martel was the hope of the Franks when, between 717 and 719 C.E., the Muslims in Spain began to launch large-scale raids across the border into France.

In 719 C.E., a Muslim army crossed the border, captured the city

Map 19.2 The Arab Invasions of Southern France (719–726 C.E.)

of Narbonne, and established a base in the area called Septimania on the coastal strip along the Mediterranean Sea between the Pyrenees and the Rhone River. Directly in the path of the Muslim armies was Martel's only rival, Eudo, warlord of Aquitaine. Martel was happy to leave the task of meeting the Muslim thrusts to Eudo, who fought several major battles with the invaders over the next few years, including one at Toulouse in 721 C.E. in which the Muslim commander was killed. In 723 C.E. a new governor, Abd er-Rahman, arrived in Muslim Spain. He immediately launched new raids into Aquitaine and southern France. In 725–726 C.E., the Muslim armies mounted a major offensive to extend their position in Septimania. They captured the cities of Carcasoon and Nimes and occupied all of Septimania, which they used as a tactical platform to launch additional raids up the Rhone Valley as far as Besancon. For the next few years events calmed down in France, and the Muslims made no further effort to increase their position. This respite permitted Martel to campaign in Germany, which resulted in his conquest of Bavaria and some expansion of the kingdom into Thuringia and Frisia. In 732 C.E., the storm broke over southern France as the Muslim armies under Abd er-Rahman, believed to be 50,000 strong, attacked Aquitaine.

Eudo moved to engage the Muslim armies on his home ground, only to be soundly defeated at the battle of Bordeaux by er-Rahman's army of light and heavy Berber and Moor cavalry. Eudo escaped with some remnants of his army and marched to Austrasia to make peace and swear fealty to him. News of the Muslim invasion had reached Martel during his campaign in Germany, where he quickly turned his army around and marched back to France to deal with the Muslim threat. With Eudo's army defeated, only Charles Martel and his army of Franks stood between the Muslim army and their conquest of France. While this was transpiring, er-Rahman and his army had been halted before the fortified city of Poitiers. Er-Rahman left a portion of his army to besiege the city, while he advanced to the Loire River, near the city of Tours, to which he began to lay siege. Martel, meanwhile, had maneuvered southeastward, feeling his way to make contact with the Muslim army around Tours. Er-Rahman's intelligence service detected the movement of Martel's forces moving from the east, south of the Loire. Martel's direction of movement threatened to cut the line of communication of the Muslim army and its large train of captured loot. Here the Muslim commander revealed that his first concern was saving his booty! He hastily dispatched the wagon train of loot to the south, following with a slow withdrawal to Poitiers to protect it from any attack by Martel.

The advance elements of Martel's army made contact with er-Rahman's rearguard

Fig. 19.1 Frank Spear Infantry

as it was protecting the main army's withdrawal to the south. Over the next six days, the two armies engaged in a series of indecisive skirmishes as the Muslim commander continued to withdraw toward Poitiers to link up with the elements of his army he had left there to continue the siege of the city. It is curious that Martel did not exploit the element of surprise when his lead elements initially came into contact with the Muslim army by moving immediately into the attack. Equally curious is that he permitted the enemy to withdraw before him toward Poitiers, a circumstance that could only result in the strengthening of the Muslim numbers as they reached their confederates around the city. However, it might have been that Martel used these six days to have his heralds ride through the countryside calling local men to arms to fight alongside his professional warriors. This might explain how, when the battle finally commenced, Martel's army was larger than the Muslim army.

Fig. 19.2 Frank Cavalry

A more detailed description of the Frank army is presented in Chapter 20. At Tours, Martel's army was comprised of both infantry and cavalry in somewhat equal numbers. The skirmishing and harassment of the Muslim army that had preceded the battle could only have been carried out by cavalry. The Franks had been engaged in war with the Muslims on and off for almost two decades, and Martel surely knew the strengths and weaknesses of his adversary. As a competent field commander himself, he also knew the capabilities of his own Franks. In this regard, he knew that his heavy Frank cavalry, while adequate to the task of delivering shock, tended to be undisciplined once engaged and was very difficult to maneuver. Compared to the experienced light cavalry of the Muslims, his own cavalry was sluggish and difficult to control in mounted attack. The discipline and mobility of the Muslim cavalry, by contrast, made them most effective in the attack, even though they lacked the ability to deliver heavy shock against a foe arrayed for the defense. Muslim cavalry was expert at exploiting any gaps that opened in the enemy's line, rushing through like lightning to attack the rear or turn and roll up a flank. Their mobility was purchased, however, at the cost of any ability to sustain themselves in a defense against European heavy cavalry and even infantry. These must have been among the considerations that went into Martel's decision to dismount his cavalry and have it fight alongside his infantry.

Abd er-Rahman's army was large, although now outnumbered by the Franks, and included many foot soldiers as well as cavalry, for foot troops still played a large role in the Muslim conduct of war. These foot soldiers were likely to have been recent converts to Islam or other peoples who had suffered under the Franks and looked forward to a favorable life under the more tolerant Arabs. It is likely, therefore, that large numbers of Berbers, Arabs, Byzantines, Jews, and Christians all fought side by side in a phalanx of swords and spears equal to the ranks of the Franks. There were probably larger contingents of archers among the Muslims than among the Franks, although they do not appear to have played a decisive role in the battle. The traditional view captured in accounts of the battle of lightly clad Arab horsemen hurling themselves against the heavily armored Frank knights and infantry cannot be accepted. It is likely that these accounts are based on the dress of the Muslim cavalry in turbans and flowing robes, lending the impression that they were unarmored. In fact, it was common Muslim practice to wear their chain mail under their robes and their helmets under their turbans, a habit that made sense in the desert heat. Many of Martel's infantry had been dragooned from the countryside and given what arms they could muster or used farm implements that they brought to the field. The Muslim foot troops were likely to be somewhat better supplied in armor and weapons taken from recently defeated Franks. It is likely, then, that the Muslim infantry was somewhat better equipped in mail and swords than the recently arrived infantry levies of the Franks.

The Christian adversaries of the Muslims were very much aware that the ranks of the Muslim armies were often filled with converts to Islam. And since it was assumed that their own belief in God was a powerful force in the fighting spirit of their Christian soldiers, they assumed the Muslim converts were even more highly motivated. This feeling, along with the multi-ethnic quality of Muslim armies, is captured in the epic poem *Roderick*, which describes the Muslim armies as "A countless multitude; Syrian, Moor, Saracen, Greek renegade, Persian, and Copt, and Tartar, in one bond of erring faith conjoined—strong in the youth and heat of zeal—a dreadful brotherhood."

Martel decided that the best way to deal with the mobility and maneuverability of the Muslim light cavalry was to form his army into a solid phalanx of infantry and dismounted cavalry, perhaps in the shape of a rectangle to defend against attacks from the flanks and rear as well as from the front, and let the Muslim cavalry waste itself against the solid wall of shields, swords, and spears. The most frequently quoted description of the battle of Tours is provided by Isodorus Pacensis, which Sir Charles Oman, the famed military historian, has translated somewhat freely and dramatically to read, "The men of the north stood as motionless as a wall; they were like a belt of ice frozen together, and not to be dissolved, as they slew the Arabs with the sword. The Austrasians, vast of limb, and iron of hand, hewed on bravely in the thick of the fight; it was they who found and cut down the Saracen king." It was a classic battle between infantry and cavalry, such as the Middle Ages had not seen since Adrianople.

Fig. 19.3 Frank Axe Infantry

Our accounts of the battle are woefully incomplete. All

agree that the Muslims opened the fight with the tactics that had won them so many battles before. The Muslim cavalry began a headlong rush toward the Frank phalanx, striking it from several directions at once, seeking to shatter the infantry, penetrate the massed humanity, and cut off pieces of it that could be reduced singly. The Franks held fast as their foot soldiers chopped down horses and men with their swords and axes, taking a frightful toll. As the battle wore on, groups of warriors advanced and entrapped isolated horsemen. Prodding them with their spears, pushing them off their horses, forcing blades through the gaps in their mail armor, and taking anything of value they could get their hands on, these warriors waged a very bloody fight. It was a battle of muscle and endurance as swords smashed against shields and swords and spears tore through the flesh on all sides. It was, of course, the unprotected and poorly trained peasant levies who were slashed, gored, trampled, and crushed until, on both sides, many quit the battlefield.

The Muslims attacked again and again until night brought an end to the slaughter. Sometime in the late afternoon, a wing of the Frank army threatened to envelop the Muslim left, forcing the Muslim army to withdraw into its camp. Just how this might have been accomplished remains uncertain. It is possible that Martel kept a small cavalry contingent in reserve and at an appropriate time, perhaps when the Muslims were regrouping for another attack, sent them against the Muslim left, which, exhausted from its recent assault, refused to engage and retreated to the safety of the camp. Another report suggests that it was Eudo and his cavalry that carried out the maneuver. Somewhere in the slaughter the Muslim commander, Abd er-Rahman, was killed. When word of his death reached the Muslim camp that night, the Muslims decided to break off the fight and withdraw. When dawn broke over the battlefield the next day, Charles Martel and the bloodied Franks could see only corpses and hear only the sound of silence. The Muslim army had slipped away in the night.

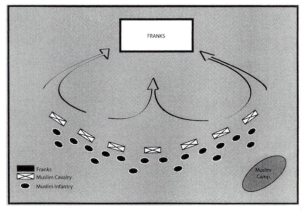

Fig. 19.4 The Battle of Tours (732 C.E.)

Uncertain as to the position of the enemy army, Martel dispatched his cavalry scouts to find the Muslims. When the reconnaissance revealed that the enemy was moving away from the battlefield, Martel decided not to pursue. He had recaptured great quantities of booty in the Muslim camp that he did not wish to leave unprotected. Probably more important was Martel's knowledge that his own undisciplined troops were at their weakest while on the move. His cavalry especially was difficult to control in the pursuit. He had fought the Muslims before and knew that one of their favorite tactics was

Fig. 19.5 Charles "The Hammer" Martel at Tours. From Ward Locke, *Illustrated History of the World* (1885).

to draw the enemy army after it in a feigned retreat, waiting for it to become disorganized, only to turn and attack the pursuers with renewed strength. It is also possible that in a strategic sense Martel wished the Muslim armies to remain in the south, which, after all, were the lands of his chief adversary, Eudo. A Muslim presence there would keep Eudo occupied and leave his ambitions unattended. Martel was satisfied with the victory, for the battle of Tours was one of those rare occurrences in the Middle Ages where an infantry force successfully held its ground against cavalry attack.

The battle of Tours was one of the decisive victories in the history of the West. Fourteen years before Leo III of Byzantium had defeated a huge Arab fleet and army near Chalcedon, blunting the Muslim advance into Europe from the East. Charles Martel's victory at Tours stopped the Muslim advance against Europe in the West. Together these two victories preserved European culture and the Christian religion for several centuries before they faced another serious threat of invasion. Over the next decades Martel and Eudo kept up the military pressure on the Muslim outposts in France, expelling them from Septimania and eventually from France altogether. In 759 C.E. Pepin III, the son and successor of Charles Martel, defeated the last Muslim army in France, forcing it to recross the Pyrenees into Spain, never to return.

Pepin III was the actual uncrowned monarch of France for a decade, as was his father, in the guise of the Mayor of the Palace. In 751 C.E., Pepin ended the mockery that the Merovingian dynasty had become and had himself crowned king of the Franks, with the approval of the Pope. Pepin was an aggressive king and fought many wars in Italy, Germany, and Saxony to increase his holdings and authority. Upon his death, the kingdom was equally divided between his two sons, Carloman and Charles, in accordance with the Frankish custom of succession. In 771 C.E., Carloman died, leaving Charles the sole ruler of the Franks and beginning the reign of one of Europe's great warrior kings. He eventually became known as Charles the Great or Charlemagne.

THE COMMANDERS

Charles "The Hammer" Martel (676–741 C.E.) was one of the greatest warriors of the Franks. His nickname, "The Hammer," may have been derived from the way he "hammered" his enemies and the Catholic Church into obeying his will. He is always portrayed as a mounted knight in battle wielding a pointed hammer as a weapon. As chain mail and plate armor came into wide use, the effectiveness of the sword to inflict deadly wounds decreased. The hammer replaced it as a favorite weapon of the cavalry because its force could deal a stunning or killing blow to the head or easily break bones of the shoulder and arms. Charles Martel was the illegitimate son of Pepin of Herstal, a powerful Mayor of the Palace and the real power behind the Merovingian throne. Upon Pepin's death, Charles was cast into prison by the grandmother of six-year-old Theodoald to remove Charles as a claimant to the throne. In 717 C.E., Charles escaped from prison and assembled an army of partisans to replace the child king. The weak reign of a child and a woman had encouraged wide rebellion in the land of the Franks, and from 718 to 723 C.E. Charles succeeded in putting down a series of rebellions with military force. He then secured the loyalty of these former rebels by awarding them lands and titles confiscated from the Catholic Church. In this way he brought much of Austrasia, Western Friesland, the Neustria, and parts of Aquitaine into the realm.

Over the next decade Charles led his army against Bavaria and Alemannia, the Saxons, and once more against Aquitaine and Provence, always with success. While he was away fighting the Alemanni (Germany) in 730 C.E, the Arab invaders from Spain began to once more extend their gains from Septimania, forcing Charles to return in time to defeat them at the battle of Tours. After the battle at Tours Charles fought other battles to suppress rebellions in the realm, interceded in Aquitaine after Duke Eudo's death touched off a rivalry for his lands, and fought a series of battles against the Muslims in Septimania, defeating them on the River Berre near Narbonne. So great was Charles's power that he did not take the trouble to appoint a successor to King Thierry IV but assumed the full kingly authority, although with no legal right or investiture. But Charles had set the precedent, and it was his son who removed the last Merovingian king and assumed the throne himself.

Charles Martel was a typical Frank chieftain, a man who held his position because he was a proven and capable warrior and field commander. Few medieval kings have fought so many battles against so many enemies with such success. Although he was regarded as an enemy of the Catholic Church for his "secular" practice of giving the Church's lands to his vassals and appointing his generals to ecclesiastical positions, Charles at least agreed, albeit near his death, to sign an agreement promising to protect the Church's lands and prerogatives, and for this he has been remembered in Church chronicles as a good king. Charles's greatest service to the Church was, of course, his victory at Tours and the relentless pressure he and his heirs sustained against the Muslims in France, eventually forcing them back over the Pyrenees. Had the Muslims succeeded at Tours, their advance would have continued bringing with it the lure of Islam's appeal to the lower classes of Europe. Under these circumstances, the survival of the Christian church in the West might have been in doubt.

Abd er-Rahman (?–732 C.E.) was the Muslim governor of Spain beginning in 721 C.E. who planned and commanded a series of raids into France over the next decade. We know little of him except that he was a high-ranking member of the ruling Umayyad family, was a caliph, and had led armies and fought battles in the campaigns of Muslim expansion over the previous years. The chroniclers note that er-Rahman had an excellent reputation as a general and had commanded troops in the African campaign leading to the invasion of Spain. In addition to his cardinal military virtues, Abd er-Rahman is described by Arab writers as a model of integrity and justice, and the first two years of his governance of Spain were occupied by reforms to remove the abuses and corruption of the former regime.

As a commander, he was idolized by his troops and known for his extensive logistical preparations before undertaking a campaign. He was killed at the head of his troops, or so the Muslim chroniclers claim, while Christian accounts of his death suggest that he was cut off by Frank infantry, pulled from his horse, and chopped to pieces. However he met his death, he was so admired that when news reached his army that he was gone, they lost all spirit for the fight and abandoned the battlefield. Abd er-Rahman's just rule lived in the memory of his subjects in Spain, and his son, of the same name, assumed the governorship. In 750 C.E., the Abbasids rose in revolt and destroyed the Umayyad aristocracy. The caliphs were hunted down and beheaded in northern Africa (part of Muslim Spain). The only one of the family to escape was er-Rahman's son, who fled to Spain where he founded a separate state that lasted almost three centuries.

LESSONS OF WAR

Strategy

1. Never let the desire for revenge obscure strategic interests. Martel was ruthless in putting down the various revolts in the empire. But once he had

gained the victory, he offered the rebels a stake in the empire by permitting them to retain their arms, making them his vassals, and assigning them Church lands.

2. Appreciate the virtue of strategic depth. Martel always moved against his enemies as far forward from his core holdings as possible. Thus, he took the fight to the enemy's homeland when he could (Frisia, Alemanni) or as close to his own farthest borders (Tours) when possible.

Tactics

1. Always understand the strength and weakness of your own forces and tailor your tactical plan accordingly. Martel knew his cavalry was slow to maneuver and difficult to control once in the attack. Accordingly, he deployed them as infantry against the Muslim cavalry.

2. Sometimes the best plan is strategically offensive but tactically defensive. Martel moved quickly to engage the Muslim army, but then went over to the tactical defense to take full advantage of his own army's strengths and exploit his enemy's weaknesses.

3. Pursue when you can; always realize the dangers in the pursuit. Martel realized this when he refused to pursue the retreating Muslim army.

FURTHER READING

Cone, Patricia. "The Early Islamic World." In *War and Society in the Ancient and Medieval Worlds*, edited by Kurt Raaflaub and Nathan Rosenstein. Cambridge, MA: Harvard University Press, 1999.

Cone, Patricia, and Martin Hinds. *Gods Caliph: Religious Authority in the First Centuries of Islam*. New York: Cambridge University Press, 1986.

Creasy, Edward Shepherd. *Fifteen Decisive Battles of the World*. New York: Dorset, 1987.

Delbruck, Hans. *History of the Art of War*. Vol. 3, *Medieval Warfare*. Westport, CT: Greenwood, 1975.

Donner, Fred. *The Early Islamic Conquests*. Princeton, NJ: Princeton University Press, 1980.

Esposito, John L. *The Oxford History of Islam*. Oxford: Oxford University Press, 2001.

Glubb, Sir John Bagot. *The Empire of the Arabs*. Englewood Cliffs, NJ: Prentice Hall, 1963.

———. *The Great Arab Conquests*. London: Hodder and Stoughton, 1963.

Goskschmidt, Arthur Jr. *A Concise History of the Middle East*. Boulder, CO: Westview, 1988.

Hourani, Albert. *A History of the Arab Peoples*. New York: Warner Books, 1991.

Kennedy, Hugh. *The Armies of the Caliphs: Military and Society in the Byzantine World*. London: Routledge, 2001.

Lewis, Bernard. *The Arabs in History*. Oxford: Oxford University Press, 2002.

———. *Islam from the Prophet Mohammed to the Capture of Constantinople: Politics and War*. New York: Oxford University Press, 1987.

Mottahedeh, Roy. *Loyalty and Leadership in Early Islamic Society.* London: I. B. Tauris, 2001.

Nicole, David, and Angus McBride. *The Armies of Islam.* London: Osprey, 1982.

Retso, Jan. *Arabs in Antiquity: Their History from the Assyrians to the Umayyads.* London: Routledge, 2002.

Shoufani, Elias. *Al-Riddah and the Muslim Conquest of Arabia.* Toronto: University of Toronto Press, 1973.

The Shorter Cambridge Medieval History. Vol. 1. Cambridge: Cambridge University Press, 1952.

Wellhausen, Julius. *The Arab Kingdom and Its Fall.* Calcutta: University of Calcutta, 1963.

20 CHARLEMAGNE AND THE EMPIRE OF THE FRANKS

[741–887 C.E.]

BACKGROUND

The political map of Europe changed greatly between the fifth and sixth century C.E., the time when the Western Roman Empire disappeared, engulfed in a wave of conquering barbarian peoples from across the Rhine who settled permanently on the imperial lands of ancient Gaul and Roman Europe. The most successful of these peoples were the Franks. Map 20.1 shows the frontiers of the Roman Empire in 300 C.E. along with the homelands of the three major invading peoples, the Franks, Lombards, and Vandals. The land of the Franks was the marshy lowlands north and east of the lower Rhine frontier in what are now the Netherlands and the northwestern part of Germany (see Map 20.1). Roman sources tell us that the Franks were originally a confederation of peoples who spoke a Germanic language. The language itself was a West Germanic dialect, distinct from Gothic (East Germanic) or Old Norse (North Germanic). From a linguistic viewpoint, their most direct descendants are the Dutch and the Flemish speakers of Belgium who mark the boundary between the Germanic linguistic influence and the Romance-speaking Walloons with whom they share the country.

The success of the Franks and their importance to European history is due to their conquest of the wealthy and geographically central provinces of Roman Gaul, though they maintained its Roman administrative structure largely intact. Later, under Childeric, Clovis, and his descendants, the Franks recruited Gallo-Roman soldiers from the Roman *civitates* in Gaul to increase the size of their armies. In the eyes of many, Frankish generals were the heirs to the military tradition of Rome, and their acceptance by the Gallo-Romans as the heirs of Rome was one of the main reasons for the success of the Franks. The name Frank originated with the people themselves and probably

Map 20.1 The Roman Empire (300 C.E.), Homelands of Major Barbarian Peoples

meant something like "fierce" or "courageous" or even "spear." Over time it came to mean "free," probably the origin of our English adjective "frank."

By the eighth century C.E., the Franks were the most important people in European history. It was a Frank who was crowned in Rome in 800 C.E. to become the first Roman Emperor of Germanic origins (Charlemagne). The Franks were the ones who began the reconquest of Spain from the Muslims, who led the Crusades against the Muslims in the eastern Mediterranean, and who spread their culture and style of warfare throughout Europe in the twelfth and thirteenth centuries C.E. So complete was the Frankish dominance of European culture that, to the Muslim mind, Franks and Europe were the same. By the eighth century C.E., the word *Firanja* (from the Latin, "Francia") had entered Arabic to mean "Europe."

The Franks first appear in Roman sources in the middle of the third century C.E. when they are among the Germanic peoples raiding the Roman frontiers. The attacks of the Franks and Alamans between 270 and 290 C.E. were particularly destructive. The barbarians overran almost the entire province of Gaul, forcing the Emperor Probus to restore no fewer than sixty of the 115 towns in Gaul. The attacks included raids by Frankish ships along the channel coast from where they penetrated into the heart of Gaul through the river system, just as the Vikings did six centuries later. Eventually some of the Franks were settled west of the Rhine in the Roman frontier zone, while others remained across the frontier to the east. These Franks were settled in the Roman *civitates* (city-territories) of Trier, Amiens, Langres, and elsewhere as *laeti*, prisoners of war granted land in return for military service. For the next two centuries Franks served in turn as enemies and allies of Rome. By Constantine's time (306–337 C.E.), Frankish regiments were serving in the Roman army, and in 451 C.E. the Franks were the ones who helped Aetius defeat Attila and his Huns at Chalons.

Within a century of their settlement, Franks had risen to high positions in the Roman army. One of these, Silvanus, even seized the throne in 355 C.E. with the help of his Frankish troops and ruled for twenty-eight days before being murdered. It is important to note that, despite their significant presence in the empire, until the sixth century C.E. the Franks were only a confederation of diverse tribes, each commanded by their own war leader, and were not united in any form of overarching political unit under the leadership of a king. The crucial period for the development of the Franks as a unified people was the reign of Clovis (481–511 C.E.). It was this powerful war chief who destroyed the political independence of most of the confederation tribes by killing their chiefs and bringing their tribes under his command. Clovis led his people in a series of successful military campaigns that turned the Franks into one of the most powerful of Germanic peoples. Clovis's descendants became the Merovingian kings and ruled Francia until 751 C.E. when Pepin the Short removed the last Merovingian king and established the Carolingian dynasty.

THE MEROVINGIANS

Our first description of the Franks is provided by Sidonius around 450 C.E., who compares them to monsters, "on the crown of whose pate lies the hair that has been drawn toward the front, while the neck, exposed by the loss of its covering, shows bright. Their eyes are faint and pale, with a glimmer of grayish blue. Their faces are shaven all around, and instead of beards they have thin moustaches which they run through with a comb." He goes on to note that the Franks are a large people, commonly taller and more robust than the Romans.

Between 450 and 480 C.E., the Salian Franks, under their war leader, Childeric, had succeeded in establishing themselves as a powerful military confederation in northern Gaul where they competed with the Britons in the west and Rhineland Franks in the east for dominance. Map 20.2 shows Childeric's campaigns to expand the territory of the Franks. In 481/82 C.E., Childeric's grandson Clovis (481/82–511 C.E.) rose to the leadership of the Salian Franks. Over the next thirty years he carried out a campaign of conquest and national unification that established the Franks as masters of all Gaul. Map 20.3 shows the sequence of Clovis's conquests. These campaigns against the other tribal peoples of Gaul were undertaken by Clovis as the war leader of a confederation of Franks and other tribes, not as king of the Franks, for there was no political unity among the Franks that would lead them to

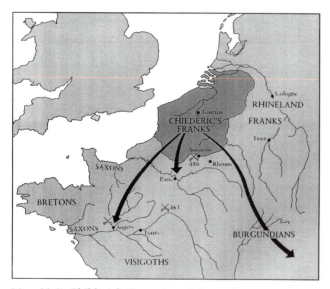

Map 20.2 Childeric's Campaigns (480 C.E.)

consider themselves a nation. The campaigns of conquest required more than twenty years to complete.

It was only after Gaul was subdued that Clovis turned against the rival Frankish tribal chiefs. In 507 C.E. Clovis turned on the Rhineland Franks by persuading the king's son, Chloderick, to murder his father, Sigibert the Lame. Clovis then murdered Chloderick and claimed the loyalty of the Rhineland Franks on the grounds that he had avenged the murder of Sigibert! These events brought the Franks of the kingdom east of the Rhine (called Austrasia) and west of the Rhine (called Neustria) into political union for the first time, with Clovis as their king. The next Frankish chiefs to die were Chararic and his son, whom Clovis had beheaded. Ragnachar and his brother Riccar, leaders of the Franks around Cambrai, were the next to be murdered, this time by Clovis himself, who cleaved them with his battle axe. Rignomer, Ragnachar's other brother, sought to avenge the death of his brothers only to meet his own. All three of these leaders were relatives of Clovis. Clovis then went on a systematic hunt for his potential rivals, many of whom were his relatives, eventually slaying them all and removing any competitor for his throne. No doubt Clovis's military successes convinced some of the other Frankish war leaders to switch their loyalties. Using murder and politics, then, Clovis's greatest political achievement was to unite the divided Franks under a single king and to engender in them a sense of their own national identity.

Gregory of Tours, writing in the *Histories*, sums up Clovis's achievements thus: "Just think of all Clovis achieved, Clovis, the founder of your

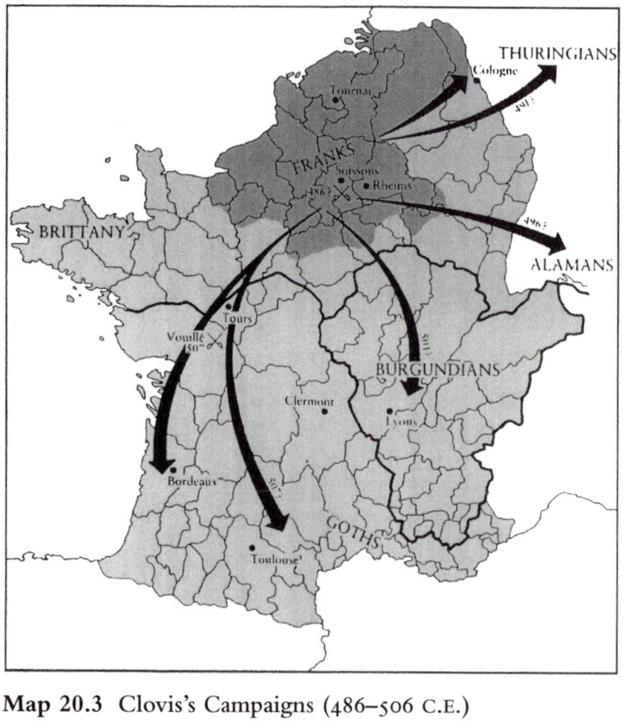

Map 20.3 Clovis's Campaigns (486–506 C.E.)

victorious country, who slaughtered those rulers who opposed him, conquered hostile peoples and captured their territories, thus bequeathing to you absolute and unquestioned dominion over them!" When Clovis died in 511 C.E. his kingdom was divided among his four sons as was the usual Frankish custom of inheritance. Clovis had conquered most of Gaul, but it was during the next half century, under Clovis's sons, that the Franks and the Merovingian dynasty extended their power and influence over much of western Europe and in the process became the dominant successor to the Roman Empire in the West. Map 20.4 depicts the campaigns of conquest under Clovis's descendants.

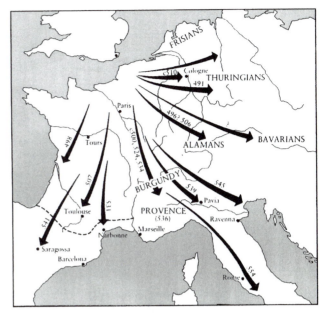

Map 20.4 The Conquests of Clovis's Descendants

By 536 C.E., the Franks had conquered and ruled all of Roman Gaul with the exception of Brittany and Septimania, the latter remaining in the control of the Visigoths. They were more successful than even Rome had been in extending their control beyond the Rhine, where the Eastern Franks were now part of the national confederation. Even so, the kings of the Franks (now known as Merovingians after Merovech, Childeric's father) made no attempt to impose a unified system of government upon their conquered territories. In these territories they appointed local aristocrats to rule in their name, sometimes using their own clan leaders and sometimes keeping former enemies in positions of authority. Within Gaul itself, the basic structure of governmental authority was the old Roman system, which the Franks kept intact even to the point of using Roman officials. In many cases they simply ensconced themselves in the large rural estates (*latifundia*), permitting the former owners to continue exercising their authority to rule the local populations. Four centuries later, this tie between warrior, land, and military service became the basis for the introduction of feudalism throughout Europe.

By the sixth century C.E., the Frankish kings had established their main residences within the Romance-speaking areas of Europe and had begun to accept the notion that the basic divide within their kingdom was between pagan and Christian. It was Clovis, so Gregory of Tours tells us, finally relenting to his nagging wife, who accepted Christianity. The Frank (and thus pagan) version of the story has Clovis praying for victory to the Christian god before a battle with the Alemanni (496 C.E.?). Victory being granted, Clovis converted to the Christian faith. It is also possible that Clovis was already baptized, but as an Arian, a heretical creed, so that his conversion was not from paganism to Christianity, but from Arianism. In any event, Clovis seems to have been re-baptized sometime near the end of his life. We may be fairly certain that the process of Christianizing the Franks was a long and slow one and may not have been complete even two centuries later when, under Charles Martel, the Franks still practiced paganism in the rural areas. To be sure, powerful noble families and substantial segments of the urban populations had converted by then, and we find many accounts of these families establishing monasteries and convents as well as sending their sons and daughters to govern them as abbots and abbesses. But for the most part, paganism still thrived in the rural areas, the success of the Irish monastics who preached among them being less than totally effective.

Until Clovis, the Franks had no institutional kingship. Each tribe had a "king," but he held office because he was the best warrior. In some tribes, the "king" might even step down during wartime to let another, stronger warrior become "king." The tribes would assemble in confederation during wartime and select a leader, called a *duces* by the Romans. After their conquest of Gaul, Frankish tribal war-leaders established themselves in the old Roman districts—"these long-haired kings"—where the Roman officials promptly became their advisors. Over time, the most powerful of these "kings" assumed the Roman title of *rex*. Much of the ceremony of the Merovingian kings comes not from Frankish tradition but from Roman military and imperial ceremony. The Roman practice of raising the new emperor on a shield is but one example. Eventually, the combination of Frankish *regii* and Roman administrators governing the old *civitates* began to be seen as a continuation of the old Roman order.

Under Clovis, many of the other kings were killed or severely reduced in circumstances until he alone held the title of King of the Franks. Unlike the later Carolingian kings, the Merovingians never let go of the military might that was the root of their power. The Merovingians never made the mistake of permitting the Pope and the Church think that royal power came from God via the Church. To the contrary, kings were above the Church, and serious displeasure, exile, or death awaited any churchman foolish enough to challenge a Frankish king on the issue.

State Administration

The administrative apparatus of the Merovingians remains obscure and has come down to us only in its broad outlines. Fundamental to governing the empire of the Franks was the fact that communication was exceedingly difficult. The Merovingian kings attempted to solve this problem by moving their court from one place to another, usually from one rural estate to another rather than from town to town. This permitted some contact between the king and his local officials and had the further advantage of avoiding transportation of large quantities of perishable foods to a central court; rather, the food could be consumed where it was produced. Even so, what we know of the travels of Merovingian kings suggests that they did not wander very far from their favorite habitats. These circumstances forced the Frankish kings to rely heavily upon three types of officials: the bishops, counts, and dukes.

The Christian Church had constructed a hierarchy that closely paralleled the old Roman administrative structure and, in some cases, replaced it completely. In Merovingian times, bishops were usually elected or appointed by local congregations and not from Rome, providing the Frankish kings with sufficient influence to select bishops. For the most part, bishops were important personages in the locality in which they served; at other times they were appointed by the king directly, sometimes as a reward for their earlier careers in his service. In either case, the bishops became important agents in running the state by acting as the king's eyes and ears and administrators.

Keeping an eye on the bishops in the *civitates* was the *comes*, or count. The count was a secular official in charge of a law court to hear and settle local disputes. He was also responsible for tax collection and for assembling local contingents for the army. He, like the bishops, was likely to be a member of a prominent local aristocratic family, although the appointment of outsiders as counts by the king was also common. In some ways the most important local official was the duke, an office that probably has its origin in the Roman *duces* who were military officials in command of troops. The Frankish dukes were also military commanders in charge of units and levies of troops within a given geographical jurisdiction. Not surprisingly, most of the dukes under the Merovingians were Franks, while many of the bishops and counts were Gallo-Romans. Having achieved their power by military action, the Franks sought to keep the military forces firmly within their control. In a contest of wills, the dukes were likely to have more influence than either the counts or the bishops, a reality reflected in the fact that Frankish dukes possessed an array of civil powers in conjunction with their military responsibilities.

From 561 to 638 C.E., the kingdom of the Franks was racked by dynastic struggles, partitions, and reassembly by powerful coalitions of Frankish nobles supporting one or the other royal pretenders. Chlothar II (622–638 C.E.) was probably the last of the great Frankish kings of the Merovingian dynasty. After him came the period known as *les rois fainéants*, the "do-nothing kings," who were eventually replaced by the more Germanic Franks of the Carolingian dynasty. By the end of Merovingian rule, the kingdom had been divided into three parts, each governed by a weak king. There arose within each of these kingdoms a new office, the *Maior Palatii*. Translated as the Mayors of the Palaces, these new officials became even more powerful than the kings themselves. The office seems unique to the Franks, and we cannot be certain when it first appeared, although it is unlikely to have existed before the 650s C.E. Regardless of the formal powers of the office, which included certain ceremonial and judicial functions, in practice the Mayors of the Palaces became the virtual rulers of their kingdoms, with their sovereigns acting more as figureheads. For the next century or so, it was the mayors and not the kings who ruled the kingdom of the Franks. In 751 C.E., Pepin the Short, the son of Charles Martel, himself a Mayor of the Palace, replaced the last Merovingian king and abolished the title of mayor.

From earliest Merovingian times, the kings held an annual assembly in the spring of each year. Often held in March, these assembles came to be called the "Marchfield" or *Campus Martius.* Here would gather the most powerful landowners and military commanders to consider new laws. We know nothing about the process of legislation, but in all probability it involved the usual degree of consensus-building and deal-making, for to a large degree the king was still dependent upon the cooperation of his lords. Another important function of the national assembly was to determine what military campaigns were to be undertaken during the coming campaign season and to raise the armies to fight them. Annual campaigning and territorial aggrandizement was an important force in Frankish political and economic life, as was to be expected in a society of warriors. But by the sixth century C.E., with Gaul firmly in their hands, the expansionary drive of the Franks was checked by the Visigothic and Lombard kingdoms to the west and south. Only in the lands east of the Rhine were there new territories to be had.

By the sixth century C.E., the old Roman taxation system that supported the state had collapsed, and with it the main revenue source of the king. This was the consequence of exempting the new Frankish overlords from the traditional land taxes that had funded the Roman state and from the extension of other tax exemptions by royal favor. One result was that in lieu of taxes, those who owned the land, often military men, had to provide service, most importantly military service, to the king. This practice set the stage for the evolution of the Roman land tenure system into a feudal arrangement, which over the next few centuries became the dominant form of European societal organization. The finances of the late Merovingian and early Carolingian dynasties rested primarily upon the exploitation of royal estates and certain customs duties reserved to the king. The collapse of the Roman taxation system resulted in the disappearance of the administrative apparatus of the state that had been supported by it. With the demise of the administrative apparatus went the incentive to maintain the secular educational system that had educated and trained the civil servants, with the result that there were few trained administrators to help govern the Merovingian state. By the sixth century C.E., only a handful of literate men, mostly clerics, were available to the kings, themselves illiterate, to govern the empire.

By the middle of the sixth century C.E., the Merovingian rulers were kings in name only. Real power rested with the Mayors of the Palaces. The Carolingian dynasty traces its origins to a political alliance between Pepin of Landen, the mayor in Austrasia—the northeastern heartland of the Frank state—and Bishop Arnulf of Metz in the early seventh century C.E. At this time the kingdom of the Franks was once more fragmented into three states, each with its own powerful mayor and ruling Merovingian monarch. Between 670 and 714 C.E., Pepin fought a series of wars with the other mayors, finally achieving a tenuous position of dominance. Pepin's only heir had predeceased him (708 C.E.) so that, upon Pepin's death, war once more broke out.

An illegitimate son of Pepin, Charles Martel, was the only surviving male heir to the powerful family and quickly took control. In a series of military victories, Charles reduced the power of the former mayors and forced them to sign treaties with him. Of the major duchies, only Aquitaine, under Duke Eudo, remained unsubdued. Over the next few years Charles campaigned in Bavaria to bring it and other rebellious duchies under his influence. At this time the Muslims launched a major attack on Aquitaine, forcing Charles to return from Bavaria and meet the threat, which he did successfully at the battle of Tours in 732 C.E. In the next eight years Charles brought Aquitaine and Burgundy under his control so that by 740 C.E. Charles, now known as *Martellus* or "The Hammer," had established himself as *Princeps* of the Franks in control of most of the territories that had been under the Merovingians at the height of their power. The Merovingian kings remained mystical, semi-sacred figures, living links with the pagan past of the Franks, and Charles took great pains to find a Merovingian descendant, Theuderic IV, and place him upon the throne.

CHARLEMAGNE AND THE CAROLINGIAN DYNASTY (741–887 C.E.)

Charles Martel died in 741 C.E., and his power passed to his two sons, Pepin and Carloman. Almost immediately the duchies that had signed treaties with Charles rebelled, forcing the brothers to fight a series of campaigns within Francia itself and later against the duchies on the perimeter, Bavaria, Ale-manni, and Aquitaine. By 751 C.E., relations between the brothers were in an open break over the question of succession. In 748 C.E. Pepin's concubine had given birth to a son, Charles, provoking a conflict with Carloman over his own son's right to the inheritance. In 751 C.E., perhaps to shore up his claim as the sole heir to his father's position, Pepin deposed the last Merovingian king and took his place as the first Carolingian king of the Franks.

The coronation ceremony was held at Soissons, although the details of the event are contradictory, for coronation as such was not a part of the Frankish tradition. The more important event for the future of Pepin's heirs, Charles and Carloman, and the Carolingian dynasty came the next year when Pepin appealed to the Pope to recognize his rule with the title of king. Two years later, Pope Stephen II crossed the Alps to the court of Pepin the Short. Here he anointed Pepin with oil as king of the Franks. Pepin's two sons were also anointed, and the Pope enjoined the Franks "never to choose their kings from any other family." The Frankish law of succession did not recognize primogeniture; the monarchy was elective, as it had been in pagan days, from among the male members of the great warrior families. The Pope's anointing of Pepin's heirs and his instruction that future Frank kings could only come from the Carolingians essentially guaranteed Pepin's inheritance to his two sons. By 753 C.E., therefore, Pepin had outmaneuvered his brother and was in sole command, although Pepin still had the problem of bringing some reluctant duchies under his control.

The Pope's visit to the king of the Franks had other purposes. King Aistulf of the Lombards was encroaching upon Rome's interests in the form of military activity, circumstances that prompted the Pope to look to the king of the Franks for help. Pepin's invasions of Italy in 755 and 756 C.E. were the direct result of the papal visit and the Pope's involvement in the legitimization of Pepin's replacement of the Merovingians. These events created a relationship between the Franks and the Papacy that had long and important consequences for the reign of Pepin's son, Charles, who in 800 C.E. became the first Frankish king to be crowned by the Pope in Rome.

In 768 C.E., while on campaign in Aquitaine, Pepin fell ill. He managed to return to the monastery of Saint-Denis north of Paris, where he died on September 24 at age fifty-four. Like his father, he was buried in the abbey's graveyard. The kingdom of the Franks was once more divided between two brothers, Charles and his younger brother, Carloman. Both men were enthroned on Sunday, October 9, 768 C.E. Resistance in Aquitaine had not ended, and Charles and Carloman planned a joint military campaign against the recalcitrant dukes. The brothers brought their armies together halfway between Angers and Poitiers where, for reasons that remain unknown, they had a severe falling out. Carloman withdrew with his army, leaving Charles to prosecute the attack against Aquitaine by himself, which he proceeded to do with great success, making himself master of the entire duchy. The next few years saw the break between the brothers widen as each maneuvered to attract domestic and foreign allies to his cause. In forging an alliance with the Lombards and the Pope, Charles completely outmaneuvered his younger brother who, at age twenty, died of natural causes in December 771 C.E. Carloman's sons were mere infants and presented no problem of succession. Through negotiation Charles was able to win over his brother's former supporters, effectively putting an end to any resistance to his claim as the sole king of the Franks. Charles reigned over the Franks for the next forty-seven years, during which he fashioned the kingdom of the Franks by force of arms into a genuine empire that encompassed most of the old Roman Empire of the West. Map 20.5 depicts the territory of the Carolingian empire of Charles the Great at the time of his death in 814 C.E.

Charles was twenty-nine when he became king of the Franks and was already an experienced warrior. His father had taken him along on several campaigns when he was just a boy, an experience that had instilled in him a love of the martial virtues and military life. Throughout his life Charles looked

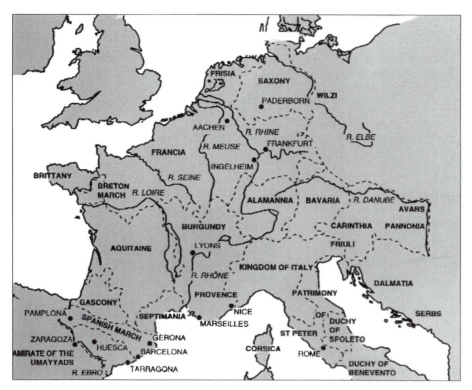

Map 20.5 The Carolingian Empire (814 C.E.)

to the Roman army of the past as an ideal he tried to make his own army emulate. Though the son of a king, he had little education and had read only a few books. In his old age he attempted to learn to write, but to no avail. His signature looks to the modern eye more like a drawing by a young child than writing. And yet he could speak old Teutonic and literary Latin and understood Greek. Two years after Carloman died (771 C.E.), Charles, king of the Franks, received an urgent appeal from Pope Hadrian II for aid against the Lombards, who were invading the papal states. At the head of his army, Charles attacked and took Pavia, assumed the crown of Lombardy, confirmed the independence of the papal states, and accepted the role of protector of the Church in all her temporal affairs. The war with the Lombards was the first of fifty-three campaigns, nearly all of them led by Charles himself, to secure his empire by conquering and Christianizing Bavaria and Saxony, attacking and reducing the threat of the Avars in the east, shielding Italy from the predations of the Saracens, and strengthening the defenses of Francia itself against the raids of the Moors in Spain. Eighteen of these campaigns were fought against the pagan Saxons from 772 to 804 C.E.

In 777 C.E., the Muslim governor of Barcelona requested the aid of the Christian king against the caliph of Cordova. Charles responded not out of religious concerns but from strategic ones, seeking to limit the ability of the

669

Muslims to carry out raids into southern France. Charles led an army across the Pyrenees, captured the Christian city of Pomplona, attacked the Christian Basques with great slaughter, and advanced toward Saragossa. But the Muslim uprisings that had been promised never occurred, and Charles's army was not sufficiently strong to attack Cordova alone. News reached him that the Saxons had broken the peace once more and were marching on Cologne. Charles wisely turned for home, leading his army through the narrow passes of the Pyrenees where, at Roncesvalles in Navarre, an army of Basques attacked the Frank rearguard and slaughtered nearly every man. It was here that the Frank warrior, Hruodland, met his death, the person who, three centuries later, would become the subject of France's most famous warrior epic, the *Chanson de Roland*. In 795 C.E. Charles sent another army into Spain with the result that the Spanish March, a strip of frontier territory in northeast Spain bordering on Septimania and Gascony, became part of Francia. Barcelona surrendered, and Navarre and Asturias acknowledged Frankish sovereignty (806 C.E.). In the meantime, Charles had subdued the Saxons (785 C.E.), had driven back the Slavs (789 C.E.), and had defeated and subjugated the Avars (790–805 C.E.). Finally, in his sixty-third year, the thirty-fourth of his reign as king of the Franks, peace finally came to the empire.

State Administration

All the peoples between the Vistula River and the Atlantic, between the Baltic Sea and the Pyrenees Mountains, including nearly all of Italy and much of the Balkans, were now under Charlemagne's rule. Administering this vast empire, especially one with such poor communications due to difficult terrain, rivers, and distance, was no easy task. At his court in Aachen Charlemagne surrounded himself with administrative nobles and clergymen to help run the empire. These included the seneschal or administrator of the palace, the chief judge or count palatine, the palsgraves or judges of the palace court, and literate scholars, servants, and clerks as could be found throughout the realm.

The empire was divided into counties, each governed by dual authority of a bishop or archbishop to deal with spiritual matters and a *comes* (companion-of-the-king) or count to handle secular affairs. In most cases, these authorities overlapped and served as a check on each other. A local assembly of landowners convened twice or three times a year within the county to discuss the problems of the region and to pass new laws. This gathering also served as a provincial court of appeals for local disputes. Those counties located near the frontiers of the empire where the danger of invasion or war was greatest were called "marches" and had special military governors to govern them. These governors were called *margraves*. All local government was subject to being called to account by the king through his *missi dominici*, literally "emissaries of the master," sent by Charlemagne to convey his wishes to local officials, review their actions, audit their accounts, check on bribery, extortion, and nepotism, and hear any complaints and remedy what wrongs they might. The task of the *missi dominici* was to "protect the Church, the poor, and wards and widows, and the whole people" from tyranny and to report the conditions of the realm directly to the king. These objectives, set out in one of Charlemagne's sixty-five *Capitulare*, literally "chapters," called the *Capitulare Missorum*, grant rights to the people of the realm, a Frankish *Magna Carta* four centuries before a similar document appeared in England.

Charlemagne retained the old Frankish custom of the "Marchfield," the annual meeting of the nobles, landowners, and military commanders to discuss matters of importance. Since, like his Merovingian predecessors, Charlemagne's court moved frequently from place to place—Worms, Valenciennes, Aachen, Geneva, Paderborn, to mention but a few places—meetings with locally powerful personages were held often. It was at these assemblies that the king submitted to his nobles and bishops his proposals for new legislation. These proposals were openly discussed and returned with suggestions. The king would then formulate a proposal and present it for approval, usually by a shouted vote. Hincmar, the Archbishop of Reims, has left us a glimpse of Charlemagne at one of these gatherings. He says Charles "saluted the men of most note, conversing with those whom he seldom saw, showing a tender interest toward the elders, and disporting himself with the young." In short, this was a master politician at work.

Each provincial bishop and administrator was required to inform the king of any significant event in his jurisdiction that had occurred since the last assembly. Hincmar tells us in this regard that "the king wished to know whether in any part or corner of the kingdom the people were restless, and the cause thereof." Charlemagne continued the old Roman custom of *inquisitio*, where the king would summon leading citizens to require that they give testimony about conditions in their districts. They were required to swear under oath that they would provide a "true statement" (*veredictum*, from which the word "verdict" comes) to the questions put to them. In the ninth century C.E., this verdict of a sworn group of inquirers, or a *jurata*, was often used to decide many local issues of landownership and criminal guilt. Out of the Frankish *jurata*, albeit through the Norman and English experience with the institution, would come the jury system of modern times.

Charlemagne is known to history as a just and enlightened king, a verdict clearly deserved and evident in the sixty-five capitularies of Charlemagne's legislation that have survived. This body of medieval law was not an organized system but an extension and application of previous barbarian codes to new circumstances. Their barbarian Frankish origins are clearly reflected in their retention of the old *wergild*, ordeals, trial by combat, and punishment by mutilation. Indeed, death was prescribed for those who relapsed into paganism and even for eating meat during Lent! Even so, many of Charlemagne's capitularies were modern in intent and application. He issued laws concerning sexual behavior, marital relations, agriculture, industry, commerce, finance, education, military organization, and the behavior of governmental officials. He attempted to protect the free peasantry against the spread of serfdom, even as the local landowners ignored his pleas. As a result of the wars against the pagan tribes, even slavery increased for a while.

The commercial structure between western Europe and the Levant and Africa had been disrupted by the Muslim conquest and occupation, with the result that the European commercial middle class declined, leaving no group to compete with the rural aristocracy. The consequence was the development of feudalism throughout the empire. The king himself was dependent upon the income from his own estates, as the obligation of local nobles to pay taxes was replaced by obligations for in-kind service, mostly the provision of knights and troops. Still, under Charlemagne every encouragement was given to commerce. He regulated weights and measures, protected the trading fairs, limited the prices on certain commodities, regulated the arms trade, especially sales to Muslims and pagans, reduced tolls, and built bridges and roads. At Maize a great bridge was constructed across the Rhine, and a canal was planned between the Rhine and the Danube to link the North Sea with the Black Sea. Charlemagne attempted to maintain a stable currency, but the shortage of gold in France and the decline in trade forced him to replace Constantine's gold *soldus* with the silver pound. He also established a system of relief for the poor and taxed the nobles and clergy to pay its costs.

The collapse of the Roman secular educational system that had supported the training of civil servants in the sixth century meant that, during Charlemagne's time, illiteracy was the norm and few, mostly only high-ranking clerics, could read. The lower clergy was mostly illiterate, and Charlemagne himself was illiterate as well. He did, however, attempt to correct the situation by importing scholars from Italy, Ireland, and England to restore the schools in France. They established a school at the palace, which quickly became a center of study and for copying manuscripts. Among the pupils was Charlemagne himself, his wife, his sons, his daughter Gisela, his secretary Einhard, a nun, and a handful of other court officials. Charlemagne was an eager student, and, Einhard tells us in his biography of Charlemagne, "he used to keep tablets under his pillow in order that at leisure hours he might accustom his hand to form the letters; but as he began these efforts so late in life, they met with ill success." Still, he studied rhetoric, dialectic, and astronomy, ordered a German grammar to be constructed, and collected early German poems. He studied Latin with a passion, but spoke German at his court.

When one of the original teachers, Alcuin of York, asked to be relieved of his assignment, Charlemagne made him abbot of Tours in gratitude. There Alcuin set the monks to work to make better and more accurate copies of the Vulgate of Saint Jerome, the Latin Fathers, and other Latin classics. Other monasteries soon followed the example of the monastery at Tours, and the movement spread throughout Europe. Many of the classical texts that have come down to us from these monastic *scriptoria* were preserved for us by the monks of the Carolingian age. Copying manuscripts became a very profitable enterprise, and the *scriptoria* thrived until the invention of the modern printing press in the fifteenth century put them out of business. Thousands of monks then sought a new form of employment and turned to wine making, for which many of them are famous to this day.

In 787 C.E. Charlemagne issued his Directive on the Study of Letters (*Capitulare de Litteris Colendis*) in which he criticized the clergy for their "unlettered tongues" and ordered every cathedral and monastery to establish schools where clergy and laity might be taught to read and write. Two years later he required these schools "to take care to make no difference between the sons of serfs and of freemen, so that they might come and sit on the same benches to study grammar, music, and arithmetic." In 805 C.E. he ordered the establishment of the study of medicine. Under Charlemagne, schools sprang up all over Germany and France. The bishop of Orleans established schools in each of his parishes and forbade the priest instructors to take any fees, what might be the first example of free and general education in Europe. To be sure, these schools could not compete in quality with the great schools of the Byzantines and Muslims in Constantinople and Baghdad, but from their foundations would come the great universities of Europe.

Charlemagne was strongly supportive of the Christian Church but always remained the master of it, even as he used its personnel and doctrines as instruments of government and education, and some of his capitularies take the form of instructions to the clergy regarding the need to reform their behavior. He permitted the clergy their own courts, decreed that a *tithe* or tenth of all produce of the land be delivered to the clergy, permitted the clergy to control marriages and wills, and when he died he left two-thirds of his estates to the bishoprics of the realm. From time to time, perhaps to remind them who was master, Charlemagne required that the bishops make substantial "gifts" to help meet the expenses of government. Charlemagne never permitted the belief that secular authority either came from or was subordinate to religious authority, and though the Christianization of the realm proceeded apace during his reign, at the time of his death whole sections of the empire were still largely pagan.

Out of this intimate cooperation between Church and state came the idea that the empire of the Franks should be transformed into the heir of Rome, a Holy Roman Empire, which would join the sanctity, prestige, and stability of imperial Rome with papal Rome. The popes had long resented their subordination to the political power of the Roman emperor of Constantinople and feared for their own freedom. Any lessening of Constantinople's grip was welcomed. But there were great difficulties in the way. The emperor of Constantinople already possessed the title of Roman emperor, with the full historic right to it, for clearly Constantinople was not only the heir to the empire of Rome, it *was* the unbroken continuation of the empire itself after its fall in the West. No one, certainly not the Church of Rome, had the authority to confer that title upon anyone else, and any attempt to do so risked provoking a war between the Christian East and the Christian West, leaving a weakened empire to be easily conquered by the militant and powerful Empire of Islam.

In December 795 C.E. a new pope, Leo III, was chosen over the vehement objections of the people of Rome who thought him guilty of misdeeds. In April 796 C.E., Leo was attacked by a mob and imprisoned in a monastery. He escaped and fled over the Alps to the court of Charlemagne. The king received him and sent him back to Rome under armed escort, ordering the pope and his accusers to appear before him the following year. In November 800 C.E. Charlemagne entered Rome at the head of a large military contingent. A month later a jury of Franks and Romans agreed to drop the charges against Leo III if he would deny them under oath. On Christmas Day, Charlemagne, dressed in the regalia of the *patricius Romanus*, prayed at the altar of St. Peter. As if planned, the Pope produced a jeweled crown and set it upon Charlemagne's head. Seeing this, the congregation (as if on cue!) proclaimed in the manner of the ancient Roman ritual of the *senatus populusque Romanus*, the senate and people of Rome, "Hail to Charles the Augustus, crowned by God the great and peace-bringing Emperor of the Romans!" His head was anointed with oil, and the Pope saluted Charlemagne as emperor and Augustus, paying him the act of homage reserved since 476 C.E. for the Eastern emperor.

After some anger and various attempts to prevent it, the Byzantines reluctantly recognized Charlemagne as the Roman emperor of the West in 812 C.E. Charlemagne's coronation strengthened the Papacy and the bishops within the empire, if only through the appearance that civil authority derived from ecclesiastical confirmation. Later Popes would build on this idea until, for some centuries, no king in Europe would be regarded as legitimate who had not had his position confirmed by the Church of Rome. Charlemagne's new title strengthened his position against his own barons, and even the pagan tribes on the borders of the empire regarded him as somehow connected to god. The doctrine of the divine right of kings, until now a mere academic debate, took on new meaning until many years later it would become a characteristic of legitimate medieval kingship.

Over the long run, political tensions between East and West contributed to the schism of Greek from Latin Christianity, a breach not yet healed. Symbolically, Charlemagne's desire to make his capital at Aachen instead of Rome underlined the fact that political power had passed from the Mediterranean to northern Europe and that the day had come when Teutons, not Latin peoples, would assume first place on the stage of European history. Above all, Charlemagne's coronation established the Holy Roman Empire in fact, although it would be some centuries before it came to be known as that. It was Otto I who first realized that the nature of Frankish authority had changed. He was the first to see it for what it was, a genuine imperial realm. In 1155 C.E., Frederick Barbarossa introduced the word *sacrum* or "holy" into his official state title, and hence became the first Holy Roman emperor.

THE ARMY OF THE FRANKS

The earliest description of the Franks to come down to us dates from 460 C.E. and is provided by Sidonius Apollinaris, the Roman historian, and differs only marginally from Tacitus's descriptions of the Germans three centuries earlier. The Franks were a Germanic tribal society ruled by warrior chiefs who brought their clans to battle whenever danger threatened. When allied with other clans for wars, these chiefs chose a war leader from among themselves to command them and their clans in battle. The grant of authority lasted only as long as events required, there being no permanent position of king among the Franks. The war chiefs themselves had no power to pass their positions on to their sons. The Frankish custom was to elect chiefs from among the most proven warriors of the most powerful clan families, a tradition that lasted until the time of Charlemagne. Like the other Germanic tribes, the Franks were skilled in war and were formidable combatants. Frankish society was divided into four classes: nobles, freemen, bondsmen, and slaves.

Manpower

From the earliest times all free Franks had an obligation to answer the call to military service when summoned by their war leaders. The call to war could be a general mobilization, the *bannum* or summons, wherein every adult male of the clan, tribe, and nation had to respond. Mobilization in response to a local crisis was called the *lantweri*, requiring only some clans and even conquered peoples to mobilize for war. As the empire of the Franks grew, a general mobilization of the entire people became impractical except under the most dire circumstances. Under the Merovingians and Carolingians, mobilizations were usually localized in the area of threat or in the area from which a military operation was launched across the imperial borders. In these circumstances, the entire population of the locality might be mobilized, augmented by the professional warriors of the standing army. Men who were called to military service (*partants*) were supported with weapons, food, and even the care of their families in their absence by their neighbors (*aidants*). Failure to attend to a general call to arms was punishable by death or heavy fines.

While there is agreement that cavalry came to form the most important element in Charlemagne's armies, there is no agreement as to the proportion of cavalry to infantry. It is possible that the total military manpower available to the Carolingian army under full mobilization and equipment was, perhaps, 100,000 warriors of all types. Under normal circumstances, only a fraction of this manpower base would be mobilized at any one time for a given campaign. Verbruggen is probably not far off the mark when he suggests that a typical field army of Charlemagne's day numbered between 2,500 and 3,000 cavalry and between 6,000 and 10,000 infantry. A force much larger than this would have been prohibitively encumbered by its logistics train. As under the

Merovingians, then, later Frankish armies were still mostly infantry armies, even though they were better armed, armored, trained, and overall better fighters. The army probably marched in divisions, often in parallel columns in approach to contact, with an advance guard, probably cavalry, leading the way and a second cavalry contingent protecting the column as a rearguard. The ability of cavalry to range far forward of the infantry columns no doubt increased the ability of Carolingian armies to forestall surprise attacks.

Cavalry units could move quickly over the ground, and there are even recorded instances of Charlemagne's armies undertaking night marches. Speed and surprise, as well as moving along more than a single axis of advance, improved tactical capability. Still we know little about the actual tactical doctrines of the Carolingian armies. To be sure, cavalry units could conduct reconnaissance, make coordinated flank and rear attacks, carry out ambushes, and support the infantry. Beyond this we know nothing about how infantry and cavalry were coordinated in battle. It is unlikely that Carolingian cavalry could mount a powerful charge (no stirrups), and it may well have been that, once the battle was joined, cavalrymen dismounted and fought alongside the infantry just as they did a century earlier at Tours.

Tactical Organization

The tribal social order of the Franks was clearly evident in their manner of war, where warriors fought under the command of their own clan chiefs and where tactics were very crude as befits an armed force without a centralized command structure. The early Franks fielded only infantry armies and possessed no cavalry contingents at all. Historians find it puzzling that the Franks did not develop cavalry, since their predecessors living in the same area, the Batavians, had been excellent horsemen and had provided the Romans with auxiliary cavalry *alae*. The first account of Frank warfare on horseback dates from 578 C.E., and even here the horse is not used in cavalry charges; rather, the warriors closed with the enemy on horseback only to dismount and fight as infantry, just as they did at the battle of Tours two centuries later. Early Frank infantry wore no armor. Agathias tells us that "they wear neither mail-shirt nor greaves, and their legs are only protected by strips of linen or leather." Frankish tactics were confined to the ambush or frontal assault.

Equipment

The weapons of the Frank infantryman included the *francisca*, the *ango*, the spear, the *scramasax*, sword, *seax*, and round shield. The *francisca* was a single-bladed axe with a heavy head weighing about two pounds, its long blade curved on its outer face and deeply hollowed in the interior. This was not a cleaving axe but a carefully balanced throwing axe similar to the American tomahawk. When Frank infantry was close to the enemy phalanx, it unleashed a torrent of axes against the enemy ranks with terrible accuracy. While the enemy was still stunned by the attack and trying to recover its balance, the Franks would rush among them engaging them in fierce hand-to-hand combat. The bishop of Auvergne describes this tactic when he says, "they [Franks] assemble in dense array and are known for their use of the rapid charge, for they close so swiftly with the foe, that they seem to fly even faster than their own darts [thrown axes]."

Another Frank weapon was the *ango*, a spear with a barbed point meant to be thrown at the enemy from medium range. If the *ango* found its mark it would surely kill. But its basic purpose was not to kill but to lodge itself in the shield of the opponent where the barb made it difficult to remove. The shaft of the *ango* was covered with iron for much of its length, making it impossible for the soldier to lop off the blade with a sideways blow of his sword. The enemy soldier, a long spear stuck in his shield, had limited mobility with which to defend himself in hand-to-hand combat. Once engaged, it was a favorite Frank technique simply to step on the end of the *ango* as it dragged along the ground with its point lodged in the adversary's shield. Stepping on the end froze the movement of the enemy for a few seconds and threw him off balance. These few seconds provided the Frank infantryman with a great advantage, time enough to cleave his uncovered adversary through the head or pierce his breast with sword or spear. While the origin of the *ango* among the Franks is unknown, one cannot help but notice the similarity of its tactical use to the Roman *pilum*, and it is at least possible that the Franks may have adopted their own spear as a consequence of their experience with the Roman armies.

The most commonly used weapon of the Merovingian armies and later Carolingian armies was the spear. The Frank spear had a long blade shaped like a leaf with lugs on both sides of the socket. The metal socket itself extended halfway down the ashwood shaft to prevent the blade from being chopped off the shaft by a sideways sword blow. Contrary to popular belief, the lugs or wings of the blade were not designed to reduce the penetration of the weapon and facilitate extraction. Rather, they were designed to hook the opponent's spear and pull him from his horse or twist the weapon from his hand. The lugs and wings are of no use at all to mounted cavalry or to the use of the weapon as a couched lance. The use of these winged spears by the later Carolingian cavalry suggests that the troopers usually dismounted and fought on as infantry rather than fighting in mounted cavalry charges.

The Frank shield was a small round shield made of wood with an iron rim and central boss. About three feet in diameter, it was constructed of wooden boards between 1 and 1.5 inches thick laid with alternating

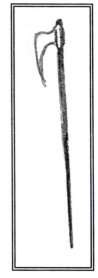

Fig. 20.1
Francisca.
Artwork by
Joel Klein.

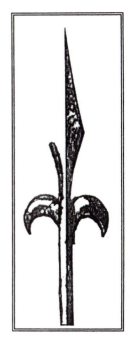

Fig. 20.2 Frank
Winged Spear.
Artwork by Joel Klein.

Fig. 20.3 Frank Round Shield (left) and Frank Kite Shield (right)

grain. A layer of leather sometimes covered the wooden face, and a handle on the back side permitted the soldier a firm grip. This shield was ideal for close infantry combat as it afforded the soldier greater visibility and quicker maneuverability in the defense than either the Roman *scutum* or the later kite-shaped shield. During late Merovingian and Carolingian times the kite shield came into wide use, primarily because it afforded greater protection from spears and arrows for the mounted warrior when slung over his shoulder. The shield was shaped much like an upside-down teardrop, and it extended from the shoulder to the knee with a slight concave hollow to provide some protection to the sides. It was held by a long strap that hung over the shoulder called a *guige*, and sometimes additional straps were worn around the forearm to give additional support and control. The kite shield afforded greater protection for the legs, especially for the mounted warrior. It is likely, however, that most infantry continued to fight with the smaller round shield.

The close-combat weapons of the Frank infantryman were the sword, *seax*, and *scramasax*. The Frankish sword was fabricated by pattern welding, a process of heating, folding, and hammering thin strips of metal into a single blade. It required over 200 hours to manufacture a sword in this manner. The Frank sword was a two-edged, cut-and-thrust weapon some thirty to thirty-six inches in length. Originally the sword hung from a broad belt swung over the shoulder. Later, the scabbard became common. Made of leather and covered with linen and hard wax, with an interior of sheepskin wet with oil, the scabbard provided excellent protection from rust. Equally practical, the scabbard reduced the injuries to the soldier's inner thigh when the sword was drawn quickly. The *seax* was a long, single-edged dagger probably of Asiatic origin, but this is uncertain. Among the Scandinavians this weapon developed into a longer single-edged sword. Among the Franks, however, the *seax* eventually developed into a single-edged dagger of about eighteen inches in length called the *scramasax*. One theory suggests that the name "Saxon" derives from "*seax*-man," a warrior armed with the *seax*. Taken together, then, the weapons of the Frank infantryman included two spears, a throwing axe, a sword, a dagger, and a shield, sufficient weaponry to wreak terrible damage at close range.

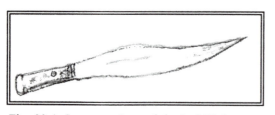

Fig. 20.4 *Scramasax*. Artwork by Joel Klein.

Armor was unknown among the early Franks and only began to make its appearance during the Merovingian age, and then slowly. As was to be expected given the enormous expense, only the wealthier warriors could afford armor and helmets. It was only in the sixth century C.E. that we begin to hear of warriors wearing armor, usually the *brunia* or mail coat similar to those used by other peoples of the time. Scale armor, too, is in evidence but in small quantities among the Franks. At the same time the helmet makes its appearance. The more common type, the segmented *spangenhelm*, may be of central Asian origin

Fig. 20.5 Frank *Spangenhelm*

Fig. 20.6 *Chapel de Fer*

or, as others assert, is a crude copy not of the old Roman helmet but of a type worn by certain classes of gladiators. A second type, the *chapels de fer* (literally, "hats of iron") came into use during the late Carolingian period.

No doubt it was the cost of weapons and armor that limited their use in the armies of the early Frank and Merovingian armies. Some idea of how expensive military equipment was can be obtained from surviving records of late Merovingian times. A helmet cost the equivalent of six cows, a coat of mail twelve cows, a sword and scabbard seven cows, leg greaves six cows, a lance and shield two cows, and twelve cows for a battle steed, a total expense equal to forty-five cows. To put this in perspective, a mare could be bought for the equivalent of three cows, and fifteen mares, the same cost as the forty-five cows it cost to outfit a mounted soldier, was equal to the cost of the herd of domestic animals in an entire village!

One implement of war that came to assume great importance among the Franks was the soldier's cloak made of heavy wool. The cloak was the soldier's bed and his protection against the elements, and he was buried in it when he fell in battle. The traditional cloak of the Franks was dark blue and shaped like a large rectangle that could be folded into a double square and worn so that it reached the feet in front and back while coming only to the knees on the sides. As Christianity gained ground among the Franks, the soldier's cloak took on almost mystical importance. The great Frank saint, Martin of Tours, himself a soldier, began his miracles when he gave his military cloak to a beggar. In Charlemagne's time, these traditional cloaks were being replaced by a new, smaller version sold by Frisian merchants. Ever the old soldier, Charlemagne thought the new cloaks useless. "What is the use of these little napkins? I can't cover myself with them in bed. When I am on horseback I can't protect myself from the winds and the rain. When I go off to empty my bowels, I catch cold because my backside is frozen!"

Logistics

The Merovingian armies had no commissariat. With no logistics train to supply it with food and fodder, the great mass of men moved toward the battlefield, depleting the land of crops and livestock as they went. The passage of an army through friendly territory was often an economic disaster for the peasantry. With no means to sustain itself in the field, the Merovingian army could not deploy in one place for long periods, with the result that much of the army never reached the battlefield at all and, when it did, could not effect a strategic decision. The army of the Merovingians had no strategic endurance. The organizational structure of the society was reflected in the army as well, and there was no proper hierarchy of either civil or military functionaries established to discipline the army effectively. The war leaders of various clan contingents often refused to follow their superiors, one count often thinking himself as good as another to wield command. In the absence of the commander-in-chief himself, say Clovis or Childeric, Merovingian armies had a tendency to come apart after being in the field for only a few weeks, the clan chiefs simply returning home with their men. A military system in which the warrior class lives on its lands spread over the entire country so that the army must be levied, equipped, and assembled for war and travel over large distances is a poor instrument for sustained warfare. Before Charlemagne could fashion his empire, much less sustain it, he first had to reform the military establishment of his predecessors.

There were a number of problems that Charlemagne had to address if his army was to become an instrument of empire. The wars with the Muslims in Spain and the Lombards, both superb and heavily armed cavalrymen, had demonstrated as early as Pepin's time that the infantry army of the Franks was at a great disadvantage without a cavalry arm. Without cavalry, Charlemagne's army could not move fast enough over long distances and with sufficient fighting power to deal with the revolts within the empire and the peoples, particularly the Saxons and Avars, beyond its borders. The need for cavalry was matched by the need for armored men-at-arms to fight both on horseback and as heavy infantry. The Lombard, Saxons, Avars, and Muslims all utilized the mounted bowman that could kill at a distance. Frankish troops serving without mail and helm were at a great disadvantage. Reforming the army meant attracting men of better fighting quality, adequately outfitted and trained for war. The old levy *en masse* of the Merovingians could produce large numbers of men, but most were ill-equipped and poorly trained peasant infantry whose reliability as soldiers was always in doubt. Moreover, the need for speed, and thus mounted men, made the large mass of infantry of the Merovingians a poor military instrument. Charlemagne had to find some way to reduce the numbers of men called to service while increasing the quality, equipment, and fighting ability of those who actually served in battle.

The reforms of the Carolingian army are preserved for us in the military ordinances issued by Charlemagne as capitularies. The first of these military capitularies (803 C.E.) is clearly designed to produce a smaller but higher-quality manpower levy. The ordinance requires that all the great lords take to the field most of the retainers on their lands, leaving behind only a few to care for the estates. This assured that the well-armed, equipped, and trained warrior class would be immediately available for war. Charlemagne then changed the rules of participation for the general populace. Anyone owning four *mansi* of land or more must march to war under the command of his local count or lord. Every man who owned three *mansi* or less was to be paired with another owning a similar amount of land. Between them, one was to report to service, and the remaining other was to pay the cost of his equipment and rations. Owners of even less land were to be joined in fours, one to serve and three others to bear the cost. The counts were responsible for seeing to it that all landowners were placed in one of the above categories. The result of Charlemagne's reform was that the wealthy would always serve in war, while only a third or fourth of the smaller landowners would serve while the others supported the soldier with money, rations, and weapons. Overall the result was a smaller force, but one whose soldiers were much better equipped since the general populace now contributed to the high cost of armor, horses, and weapons.

The general war levy of all Franks remained in place but was applied much differently by Charlemagne. Only those nobles and the landowning populations of an area under attack or from which an operation was to be launched were mobilized. As the royal army moved toward engagement, it would be joined by the knights and foot soldiers of the populations in the immediate arena of threat. Thus, the army grew in size as it advanced, even as its internal lines of communication grew ever shorter and more efficient. Few national calls to arms were ever required under Charlemagne as this system worked relatively well. Even so, the army still had to be fed and supplied while on the march or campaign. Charlemagne created a new logistics system for his armies. The soldiers in Charlemagne's armies were required to bring with them at least three months of provisions consisting of wine, flour, and bacon. Calculations of the three months were dependent on how far from the assembly point a detachment was located. Usually the three months were calculated from the border, with some adjustments made for those coming from far away. Thus, anyone coming from beyond the Rhine for an expedition in Spain could measure his three months as starting from the Loire River, while anyone coming from beyond the Loire for a campaign against the Saxons could count his three months from the Rhine. The point was that each soldier had to have three months' rations as measured from the beginning of the campaign.

Having the soldier provide and carry his own rations helped greatly but was not in itself sufficient. Charlemagne also provided for a wagon train to follow the army. His directives standardized the design and capacity of the carrying carts so that each should be able to carry twelve bushels of wheat or twelve barrels of wine. Each cart was to be furnished with a leather cover to protect its cargo from the weather. The leather cover was to have eyelet holes to pull the leather cover tightly around the wagon, like a pontoon to be stuffed with straw or hay so that it could be floated across rivers. Each cart driver was to be equipped with a lance, a shield, a bow, and a quiver (presumably a sword and dagger as well) to permit the driver to fight as infantry once the enemy was engaged. Lighter baggage was carried on pack-horses, and the whole gathering was followed by a large group of merchants and other providers of services (barbers, whores, surgeons, musicians, morticians, etc.) who saw to some of the army's other needs. Under Charlemagne, military campaigns were planned and organized well in advance so that the army could take advantage of supplies and lodgings along the proposed line of march, all the responsibility of local officials. The old Merovingian habit of plundering the land through which the army had to move to engage the enemy was ended.

To be sure, Charlemagne's commissariat made the army slow to assemble and slow to move. However, for the first time in its history, a Frank army could sustain itself in the field for several months while conducting operations, something no Merovingian army could accomplish. The system provided the army with at least some degree of strategic endurance. Charlemagne was now able to remain in hostile territory for long periods, preventing defeated tribal armies from reorganizing for another fight. In one of his Saxon campaigns (785–786 C.E.), he remained in Saxony building forts and cutting new roads and conducted repeated raids against the insurgents in the depth of midwinter. Charlemagne also made extensive use of the rivers and canals in moving supplies, and in almost every campaign we find him moving his army along two axes of advance not only for sound tactical reasons but also to reduce the size of each army to be supplied and making maximum flexible use of the available river or canal system within the area of operations. The Carolingian logistics system, although primitive by the standards of the armies of Rome and of the ancient Near East, was nevertheless quite an impressive achievement for its day and far surpassed any other in Christian western Europe, at least until the High Middle Ages.

The strategic endurance of the Carolingian army was greatly increased by Charlemagne's systematic use of fortifications and entrenchments, a capability completely lacking in the Merovingian armies. Unlike his predecessors, Charlemagne usually did not evacuate an area he had taken by force. Even when the defeated pledged their loyalty and had given hostages, Charlemagne usually selected appropriate locations (most often a small hill beside a river or stream) and erected palisaded and ditched "burgs" in which he left armed garrisons. Each post was connected to the next by a road, often little more than a serviceable, well-worn path. Behind the line of outposts usually stood a main fortress, which was itself connected to the main frontier road to permit rapid reinforcement by cavalry. The arrangement brings to mind the old Roman frontier fort system that had long ago perished from memory. These fortified "burgs" served their purpose very well and few were taken by assault. Their use constituted a new lesson in the art of war for western Europe, since knowledge of their previous use by Roman armies had long been lost.

Charlemagne's use of fixed fortifications made possible his permanent conquest of new lands. Whereas his predecessors had merely been able to undertake raids and extract tribute, Charlemagne could now forge an empire. The modern cities of Magdeburg, Paderborn, and Bremen can trace their roots to Charlemagne's burgs.

Tactics

None of these reforms would have amounted to much had Charlemagne not increased the combat power and mobility of his army, and this he did by requiring large contingents of wealthy nobles to become mounted horsemen. To increase the fighting power of his infantry, Charlemagne made every effort to improve its arms and equipment. The *Capitulare Aquisgranense* of 805 C.E. required that all men owning twelve *mansi* of land report to the army in a mail-shirt. Since most men did not own this amount of land, only a small part of the army was so equipped; the mass of soldiers were armed with only shield and spear. Another capitulary (807 C.E.) expanded the support of the soldier from three persons to sustain one soldier to six persons to support a single soldier, which resulted in a greater ability to supply the soldier with armor, helm, and sword. Other ordinances directed that the wealthy landowners report in full armor on horseback. Any officer with extra armor or weapons was required to bring them with him for use by others.

Although Frankish noblemen gradually adjusted to becoming mounted cavalry, the best and largest units of cavalry in Charlemagne's army were not Franks at all but the Lombards, the greatest horsemen of Europe. These were Charlemagne's *gasindii*, former Lombard enemies who had been settled on Frank land in return for military service. They were among the best troops in Europe, equipped with sword, lance, helmet, hauberks, and *ocrea* leg greaves, which they probably obtained from the Avars. They were disciplined, well trained, and well led, and they formed the backbone of Charlemagne's mounted force. It was these Lombards who fought and defeated the mobile steppe horse-archers, the Avars, whereas the Frank infantry armies were hard-pressed merely to lay waste the borders of the kingdom. The Lombard horse were as mobile and capable of maneuver as the Avars, and without them Charlemagne would never have defeated these fierce horse warriors.

Because most Frank cavalrymen were landed nobles, they were spread across the realm, a fact that made the mobilization of the cavalry a slow process. To provide the king with a ready-to-deploy mobile force to deal with border incursions or revolts within the realm, the early Carolingians formed a small standing force called the *scara*. Probably an outgrowth of the *socii* or personal armed entourages of the Mayors of the Palaces, Charlemagne's *scara* was comprised of professional warriors who lived and traveled with the court rather than residing on grants of land, a circumstance that made them able to deploy quickly in response to any threat. There seem to have been three ranks within the *scara*, probably based on seniority: the *scholares*, the *scola*, and the *milites aulae regiae*. When operating as distinct units in battle, they were usually placed under the command of the royal *missi dominici* (imperial officers) and fought in close-packed, armored cavalry formations. These formations themselves were subdivided into *cunei*, cavalry units of perhaps fifty to one hundred men. *Scara* units also served as garrisons in the frontier provinces, keeping the peace and responding quickly to incursions or revolts. They were augmented by local full-time warriors called *warda*. These frontier "marches" were governed by *margraves*, a title found earlier under the Merovingians. The *scara* was also the source of military leadership for other units, as its members were often posted to command various clan and tribal units. The introduction of large cavalry units gave the Carolingian armies a maneuver, mobility, and shock capability they never before possessed.

The training of the Carolingian soldier depended upon his status and wealth. All Franks were instructed from an early age on how to use weapons, a common practice in all Germanic tribes where warrior status was the mark of manhood. Young nobles were instructed early in the handling of the horse and the use of the spear, sword, and javelin. *Milites* or mounted warriors practiced with their lances against a dummy target or *quintaine*. There was also training as units, which involved war games (*causa exercitii*) in which units, sometimes from different ethnic tribes, charged each other with wooden weapons in mock battle. We cannot be certain, but it is at least possible that these tribal war games grew out of the Marchfield annual assemblies. Later, of course, they developed into the tournaments of knights.

A description of a Frankish mounted warrior has survived in the work of the monk of St. Gall who, writing sixty years after Charlemagne's death, describes the latter's appearance at the head of his army as it marched on the Lombard city of Pavia in 773 C.E.

> Then appeared the Iron King [Charlemagne] with his crested iron helm [*ferrea galea christatus*], with sleeves of iron mail (*ferreis manicis armillatus*) on his arms, his broad chest protected by an iron byrnie (*ferrea torace tutatus*), and iron lance in his left hand, his right free to grasp his unconquered sword. His thighs were guarded with iron mail though other men were wont to leave them unprotected so that they might spring the more lightly to their steeds. And his legs, like those of all his host, were protected by iron greaves (*ocreis*). His shield was of plain iron without device or color.

The monk goes on to say that "all his men were armed as nearly like him as they could fashion themselves. . . . Iron, iron everywhere."

We are not to believe that the equipment worn by the king was common to most other cavalrymen since the cost of a full armor kit and horse was prohibitively expensive for all but the most wealthy. It is likely, then, that a good number of Carolingian cavalrymen lacked body armor and helmets, at least in the early days of Charlemagne's reign. War against the Muslim and Avar archers, however, convinced the Franks that unarmored cavalry were of limited use so that, by the time of Charlemagne's death when it had become common to tax the citizenry for the soldier's armor, armored cavalry was the rule. Figure 20.7 portrays a mounted cavalryman of the early Carolingian period equipped only with helmet, mail, and spear. The tendency for the mounted warrior to increase his armor continued unabated until the fourteenth century C.E., so it is likely that the mounted warrior portrayed by a chess piece from the late ninth century (about the time the monk of St. Gall was writing) discovered at Aachen, Charlemagne's capital, accurately represents the armor and armament of the mounted warriors of the time.

Fig. 20.7 Frank Mounted Warrior (Ninth Century)

In any event, the well-heeled Frank cavalryman of the day would be outfitted with a metal helmet, most likely the traditional *spangenhelm*, with his body protected with a mail coat or *hauberk* reaching to the mid-thigh that had replaced the old *byrnie*, the leather coat to which metal scales or plates had been sewn. Head and neck were covered with the chain-mail *coif*, which may have been introduced to the Franks by the Avars. Arm and leg defenses were probably chain-mail sleeves that might or might not be attached to the rest of the chain mail covering the body. Later mail *chausses* to protect the legs and thighs would be adopted from the Maygars along with the stirrup. Figure 20.9 depicts two types of stirrups that *may* have been in use by the later Carolingian armies, although we cannot be certain that they were used at all until very much later when mounted combat with the sword and couched lance would have been impossible without the use of the stirrup. The inability to wield the lance or even a spear as a lance or to fight with the sword from horseback without the stirrup has led some analysts to suggest, probably correctly, that the mounted cavalry charge was not a common event in the Carolingian armies. Instead, cavalrymen may have dismounted and fought on foot, like the later English practice of men-at-arms.

Fig. 20.8 Chess Piece Found at Aachen Depicting a Carolingian Warrior

The Frankish cavalryman's weapons included the spear, sword, dagger, and the kite-shaped shield, which afforded the cavalryman greater protection than the round shield of the infantry. The famed *francisca* had by now disappeared from the armies of the Franks, as had the *ango*. Stability of the cavalryman upon his horse was greatly improved when the Franks adopted the

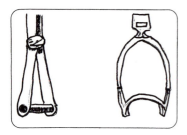

Fig. 20.9 Two Types of Stirrups, Leather (left) and Iron (right)

wood-framed high saddle with a raised pommel from the Avars. The experience of fighting the Avars convinced the Franks of the value of archery, and surviving records tell of units of Frank horse-archers from the Abbey of Fulda, although it is likely that they were really mounted infantry archers who dismounted to fire their weapons. One of Charlemagne's capitularies (813 C.E.) instructs the counts that all infantry they muster for war must be equipped with a lance, a shield, a bow, two bowstrings, and twelve arrows. No one was to report carrying only a club; the most poorly armed man must have at least a bow. We may be fairly certain that archery among the Franks never achieved the level of military importance that it possessed among the English or even the German Alemanni, whose warriors carried bows of yew wood that were taller than a man.

Christianity played an important role in the morale of the army of the Carolingian Franks. Bishops were noble property owners and were required to provide contingents of troops, often under their personal leadership in the field. No Carolingian army went on campaign without its additional complement of clergy to say prayers for victory, recite psalms for the fallen, and act as doctors for the wounded. Morale was also helped by the continued record of success in the field that the army enjoyed under Charlemagne, as well as the opportunities for personal advancement that military service offered. Feudalism had not yet taken complete hold, and advancement through military service was still possible and not as closely tied to the ownership of land and the primogeniture that would eventually develop. Charlemagne attempted to weaken the hold of the traditional "stem dukes" over their tribal clans by relegating them to military service and appointing nonethnic leaders to lead clan military units. He attempted to build the morale of his armies on Christian ideology and solidarity and in more than one instance fought a war of extermination against the pagan tribes. In many areas of the empire the degree of Christianization was small or even nonexistent, and paganism persisted among Frankish clans even after Charlemagne's death. Nevertheless, the role of the clergy was fundamental in war in providing succor and motivation to the troops. Whereas military men dressed in sober fashion, military churchmen relied upon sumptuous robes and extravagant travel carts and canopies to achieve their moral effect.

Siegecraft

Charlemagne was the first Frankish king to equip his army with a siege train, a development concomitant with his appreciation of the important role that fortifications and "burgs" played in keeping his own empire secure. Early Merovingian armies had used battering rams and assault scaling ladders as the major means of reducing a fortress. The Avars introduced the Chinese-style, man-powered mangonels to the Franks, which Charlemagne incorporated into his siege train. It is also possible that the Franks learned of mangonels from their contact with the Muslims in Spain and the Septimania region of France. To sustain itself in the field, the siege train was required to carry three months' rations.

Even given the limitations discussed, Charlemagne's armies were larger, more powerful, better trained, better armed, better able to sustain themselves, and possessed more strategic endurance than any Frank army that had gone before them. In the hands of a skilled field commander and an excellent administrator like Charlemagne, the new army could be used to forge an empire and sustain it long enough to pass it on into the future. No European commander fought so many battles against so many different types of armies and succeeded more during this period of European history than did Charlemagne, the king of the Franks.

THE SAXON WARS (772–804 C.E.)

Charlemagne's wars against the Saxons were the most protracted and bitterly fought of all his campaigns, comprising no fewer than eighteen of the fifty-three campaigns he undertook. The Saxon wars began in 772 C.E., and they continued with various interruptions until the year 804 C.E. The conflict with the Saxons involved features that were not normal components of Frankish warfare—forced mass conversions, large-scale deportations, and massacres of civilians and combatants alike. Though the wars began as conflicts over territory, they became in the mind of the king of the Franks an ideological war between Christian Franks and pagan Saxons. It was one of Europe's first religious wars.

The Saxons were a group of Germanic peoples originally established in the area east of the Elbe and south of the Danish peninsula. After 300 C.E., when the Salian Franks moved across the Rhine into the Roman frontier, Saxon peoples began to drift southwest, and Saxon troops became involved in the frequent tribal wars in the area. In the early fifth century C.E., Saxons, along with Angles and Jutes, migrated in large numbers across the English Channel into the south and east of England. Other groups of Saxons became involved in the tribal struggles for the control of northern Gaul. Most Saxons, however, remained settled east of the Rhine. In the sixth century C.E., the Saxons came into contact with the early Franks who imposed their rule upon them. This governance did not involve an occupation of Saxon territory but a recognition of tributary status and an agreement to provide Saxon troops for the wars of the Franks. Over the next two centuries, Franks and Saxons alternated between periods of war and peace, with the Saxons breaking into open revolt only to be suppressed by the Franks until the next revolt.

In the early eighth century, Saxon raids against Francia sought to take advantage of Charles Martel's preoccupation with his own struggle for power. Upon securing his position, Martel moved quickly against the Saxons, invading Saxony in 718 and 720 C.E. He planned to do so again in 729 C.E., and there were other campaigns in 734 and 738 C.E. Martel's successors fought the Saxons again in 744, 747, and 753 C.E. The reasons for these wars were complex but seem to have involved the movement of an expanding Saxon population southward along the Lippe River. The Lippe River valley had been an important line of communication since Roman times and had been heavily fortified by the Romans to prevent the movement of Germanic tribes into Roman-ruled areas. The Franks had replaced the Romans in this strategic equation, and they had no desire to permit a further Saxon advance southward into the territories that the Franks themselves ruled east of the Rhine.

It was, then, no accident that Charles Martel concentrated his military operations against the Saxons in the Lippe Valley, as did his successors in their wars against the Saxons. Pepin III campaigned against the Saxons in 753 and again in 758 C.E., striking deep inside Saxon territory. The campaign ended with yet another Saxon peace agreement in which the Saxons paid a tribute of 300 horses. This done, the Frankish army withdrew as it always had, and no more is heard of the Saxons until Charlemagne reopened the war against them with a military expedition in 772 C.E.

From the beginning, Charlemagne seems to have had the intention of forcibly Christianizing the pagan Saxons, at the point of the sword if need be. He gathered the annual assembly of Franks at Worms and from there began an unprovoked invasion of Saxony, striking directly at the Saxon fortress of Eresburg, capturing it by force, and then moving on to attack Irminsul. Irminsul was a major Saxon religious shrine, an *idolum* according to the Franks, and held a treasury of religious donations. Charlemagne took the city, destroyed it, and diverted a stream over it so that all traces of the Saxon religious site were obliterated. This is the first time that a Frank king is recorded as having deliberately destroyed a Saxon religious site, and it is likely that Charlemagne wished to humiliate the Saxon gods as much as defeat the Saxons themselves. In this action he revealed his religious motives for the war.

Within a year the Saxons retaliated, raiding and pillaging a church founded by St. Boniface. Boniface had played a leading role in previous attempts to Christianize the Saxons, and he had founded monasteries and churches throughout the area. Charlemagne returned from Pavia a few months later and over the winter (774–775 C.E.) planned a four-pronged assault against the Saxons. The Frank chroniclers tell us that Charlemagne "decided to attack the treacherous and treaty-breaking tribe of the Saxons and to persist in this war until they were either defeated and forced to accept the Christian religion or entirely exterminated."

In 775 C.E. Charlemagne led a large-scale invasion of Saxony. He marched his army eastward up the valley of the Ruhr, capturing a Saxon fort at Syburg before following along the Deimel River to retake Eresburg. He pushed on to the River Weser, effectively traveling across the entire southern frontier of the Saxons. At Braunsberg, the Saxons made a stand and were defeated. Charlemagne now divided his army into two groups. He led one division further east, reaching the Oker River where some subtribes submitted to him. The other part of the army had moved down the Weser only to be ambushed by the Westphalian Saxons in a marshy plain while they were encamped. Upon hearing the news, Charlemagne rushed his army to their relief, arriving in time to prevent a disaster. After a few more local skirmishes, the Westphalian Saxons submitted and gave hostages to the Frank king.

Map 20.6 The Saxon Wars: Charlemagne's Area of Military Operations

The pattern of formal submission and hostage-taking had been for centuries the traditional method of dealing with the rebellious Saxons. Without Frankish troops to enforce the treaty, revolts usually broke out again. The following year, when Charlemagne was forced to attend to events in Italy, the Saxons once more broke into open revolt. The Westphalian Franks attacked Eresburg and Syburg, forcing Charlemagne to return from Italy to deal with the problem. He led an expedition in force to the River Lippe, driving the Saxons from their positions. This time he established garrisons at Eresburg and constructed a new fortress on the river's edge. This became the city of Paderborn. Once more the Saxons signed treaties of peace; once more hostages were given, as it seems likely the previous hostages had, as custom required, been executed by the Franks once the Saxons rose in revolt. In 777 C.E., Charlemagne held the annual assembly at the fortress of Paderborn deep in Saxon territory and spent the year overseeing the construction of additional Frankish forts and garrisons at key points in the valleys of the Ruhr, Diemel, and the Lippe. This had the effect of intimidating many of the Saxon war chiefs into submitting to the Franks. Submission required religious conversion as a matter of course, and scores of forced baptisms were held under the authority of the army of the Franks. Not all Saxons were content to submit, and a group of tribes under the leadership of a certain Widukind withdrew to the north and awaited their chance for revenge.

In 778 C.E. Charlemagne was leading the ill-fated expedition to Spain when Widukind took the opportunity to lead another Saxon revolt. His army struck down the lower Rhine, reaching the city of Cologne and burning churches and monasteries as it went. An army of eastern Franks was ordered to meet the Saxon advance, with the result that somewhere on the banks of the River Eder, perhaps near Leisa, the Frank chroniclers tells us that the Saxon raiders suffered a great slaughter. Upon his return from Spain, Charlemagne spent the next two years reestablishing Frankish influence in the area, a fact that suggests, the chroniclers notwithstanding, that the size and damage done by the Saxon revolt was much greater than the chroniclers report.

In 779 C.E. Charlemagne marched along the Lippe and Weser rivers to subdue the Westphalian Saxons, and in 780 C.E. he again held the annual March-field in Saxony before launching yet another expedition eastward toward the River Elbe. The chroniclers report that thousands of Saxons "accepted baptism" in the wake of Charlemagne's army, which marched to the confluence of the Elbe and Ohre rivers, traversing the whole of Saxony and covering a distance of about 400 kilometers from its starting point. So complete was Charlemagne's domination of the area that he divided Saxony into a number of ecclesiastical regions with secular and monastic clergy being appointed to preach and baptize in each district.

Although one of Charlemagne's detachments had almost been extermi-nated in the kind of attack and slaughter that had gained the early Germans a crucial victory over the Romans in the Teutoburg Forest, for the most part Charlemagne's army met little resistance and easily crushed what it encountered. No one could be certain, of course, if the forced Saxon conversion would hold once the Franks withdrew. In the course of events, Charlemagne was needed in Italy in 780 C.E. and celebrated Easter of 781 C.E. in Rome without news of a Saxon revolt having taken place. In 782 C.E. he returned from Italy and held the annual assembly once more in Saxony where the chroniclers report that "all the Saxons except for Widukind" attended. The conclusions of the assembly led to Charlemagne's proclamation of the first Saxon Capitulare.

The Saxon Capitulare was a body of thirty-four laws prohibiting certain practices among the Saxons and citing the penalties for each. It is dramatic testimony to the draconian way in which Frankish Christianity was imposed upon the Saxons. Most forms of what were regarded as pagan practices or slights on Christian rules were made punishable by death, including eating meat during Lent. Unbaptized Saxons were subject to capital punishment, as were those who practiced burial by cremation. It was the usual Saxon prac-tice to cremate the dead and bury their ashes in mounds. The additional Saxon practices of burning witches alive and eating their flesh and of making human sacrifice were also prohibited. A Saxon caught offering a prayer at a sacred spring or trees was to be executed. The provisions of the Capitulare were resisted, and when Charlemagne returned to Francia a major Saxon revolt broke out under the leadership of the intransigent Widukind. A Frank army was already in Saxony preparing for an attack against the Slavs when the revolt broke out. The commander turned his army against the Saxons, provoking an all-out war.

Saxon Tactical Organization

The Saxons were fierce warriors in the Germanic tradition of individual combat. Their social order was tribal, divided into three classes: nobles, freemen, and the "half-free" or *lati*, in the same manner as the earlier Franks and Anglo-Saxons. Saxon society was organized into regional communities, each of which had its own elected leader. These leaders, also war chiefs, met together annually, each accompanied by twelve representatives of each of the three social classes that made up the population. At the annual assembly new laws were discussed and passed and judgments rendered in legal disputes. Plans for the coming year, peaceful or military, were drawn up for the whole community. Led by their warrior chieftains, the Saxons wore little armor, fighting with spear, sword, shield, and axe in the tradition of heroic individual combat. Although horse-breeding was one of their major industries, they did not use the horse in warfare, fighting almost exclusively as infantry. Some nobles probably could afford armor and helm, but most Saxon warriors fought with undefended head and breast, and protected only by their tunics, although bearing a round, convex shield of linden wood covered with leather. The Saxon shield had an iron rim and projecting iron boss and was indistinguishable from the model used by Frank infantry.

Their most common weapon was the spear with a lozenge-shaped blade some eighteen inches in length. Barbed, leaf-shaped, and triangular blades were also known. The shaft was ash, about six feet long, and the blade held fast with rivets. The sword was also available but not common probably due to expense. It was a broad, double-edged weapon about 2.5 feet long with a sharp point. They used the broad, two-edged dagger called the *seax* like the Franks and used the Danish double-bladed axe, which they wielded with both hands. The throwing axe was unknown among the Saxons. Saxon warriors fought in small, highly cohesive, well-led war bands and may have used the traditional *cunei* (wedge) formations common among German tribes.

The key to the military success of the Franks against the Saxons was that they always enjoyed the advantage of numbers. Frank cavalry could move quickly to gain surprise but was usually unable to effect a decision without its supporting infantry. Alone, the cavalry could be vulnerable to ambush in the same manner that modern armor is subject to infantry ambush if it deploys without infantry. Although the accounts of the ambush are incomplete, something like this seems to have happened in a pass of the Suntel Mountains when Saxon infantry destroyed a column of Frank cavalry. Two Frank armies, one under Count Theodoric, were attempting to join up prior to crossing the Suntel Mountains to engage the Saxons, who were gathering north of the mountains. The army of East Franks under the command of three *missi dominici*, Adalgsi, Gailo, and Worad, reached the crossing point first. Rather than wait for Theodoric to arrive, the *missi* ordered their army to move through a narrow defile cutting through the mountains. The chroniclers

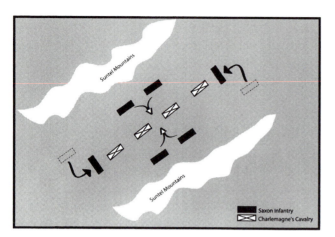

Fig. 20.10 Ambush at the Suntel Mountains (782 C.E.)

tell us the reason was jealousy: the *missi* anticipated an easy victory and did not want to share the glory with the count. The result was a disaster.

The Saxons had discovered the approach of the army of the Franks and lay in wait at both ends of the defile. As the Frank cavalry column moved through the defile, the Saxons closed the door to their retreat by moving a large infantry force behind them. Just as the lead elements of the Frank column were about to clear the end of the defile, another Saxon infantry unit moved across their path, blocking their advance. Unable to maneuver, the cavalrymen dismounted and prepared to meet the Saxon attack. The Saxons attacked from all four directions at once, the main blow falling on both flanks. The battle must have been intense, but relatively short. The Frank cavalry was killed almost to a man, the chroniclers recording that most of the Franks, the three *missi*, four counts, and twenty nobles met their deaths. These numbers suggest that at least 1,500 and perhaps as many as 2,000 Franks were killed.

The promulgation of the Saxon Capitulare in an effort to enforce the Christianization of the Saxons had been a disaster that provoked a general revolt followed by a major military humiliation. Such a catastrophe could not go unanswered. Charlemagne responded immediately by leading a large army into Saxony. Widukind fled to Denmark, leaving the formally converted Saxons to take the blame. Unable to resist Charlemagne's army, the Saxon war leaders submitted, placing the blame for the revolt and ambush on Widukind. Charlemagne was not to be so easily accommodated. He demanded that the Saxons produce the soldiers who had carried out the ambush. With little choice, the Saxon lords handed over 4,500 men who were said to have been at the battle in the Suntel Mountains. The captives were taken to a field beside the River Aller, near the modern town of Verden, and in the course of a single day all 4,500 Saxons were beheaded. Some of the slain had already converted to the Christian faith.

The Saxons were not broken even by a massacre of such proportions, and in the spring of 783 C.E. a more widespread general rebellion broke out in Saxony. Once more Charlemagne personally led his army into battle, this time at Detmold, where the Saxons foolishly tried to defeat the Franks in open battle. The result was a terrible defeat for the Saxons, where "the lord king . . . fought a battle against those who were in rebellion; and many thousands fell on the Saxon side." A few months later, the Saxons met the Franks once more in open battle, this time on the banks of the River Hasse. The Saxons deployed on a small hill directly across the river in their traditional infantry phalanx, inviting Charlemagne and his cavalry to attack. The Saxon tactical deployment seems to imply that they thought that the crossing of the river might separate the infantry from the cavalry, resulting in a piecemeal attack. Or, perhaps, they intended to attack while Charlemagne's army was still engaged in the river crossing. Charlemagne was an experienced field commander, a veteran of many battles, and was not likely to fall into the Saxon trap. Instead, he ordered his cavalry units to cross the river first, while the infantry and probably dismounted cavalrymen held the center fast on the near bank to protect against any Saxon frontal attack. Once the cavalry had crossed the river, they launched a coordinated attack against the Saxon flanks, fixing the Saxon infantry in place. While the Saxons were being harassed by the cavalry, Charlemagne's infantry and some of his now remounted cavalry units crossed the river directly opposite the Saxon center.

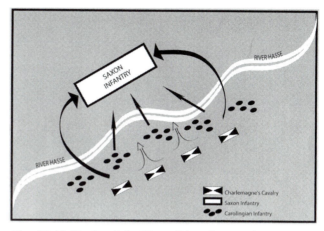

Fig. 20.11 Battle of the Hasse River (783 C.E.)

Once over the river, Frank cavalry and infantry launched a frontal assault against the Saxon infantry phalanx. The fighting was fierce and hand-to-hand, but the Saxons were once more outnumbered. The chroniclers tell us that "the battle was joined . . . and the Franks fought against the Saxons and enjoyed victory, with the aid of Christ's grace; and again many thousands fell on the Saxon side, a much greater number than before." We have no idea how many Saxons were killed that day, but the number must have been considerable. The hill upon which the Saxon positions were located was from that day forward called the Hill of Slaughter.

As harsh as these defeats were, they proved insufficient to crush the Saxons, and a year later, in 784 C.E., Charlemagne was forced to return to Saxony to quell another revolt. He marched through Saxony leaving a trail of death, burnings, and crop destruction in his wake. Poor weather and flooding made it impossible for him to cross the Weser and thus saved the northern Saxons from attack. For the most part Charlemagne faced little resistance, a fact that did nothing to stay the hand of Frankish violence and destruction. In what must have been an act of military desperation, the Westphalian Saxons, who had borne the brunt of punishment, attacked a contingent of troops commanded by Charlemagne's son, Charles. The chroniclers tell us the Saxons were defeated in a cavalry battle, an interesting detail in light of the fact that the Saxons did not usually fight on horseback. It might have been that the Saxon losses of their infantry were so severe that they mounted what few men they had remaining to fight the Frankish cavalry.

The Saxons' defiance even after a year of campaigning may have convinced Charlemagne to continue his campaign throughout the winter of 784–785 C.E. Fighting throughout the winter was unprecedented for the army of the Franks. Charlemagne intended to break the back of Saxon resistance once and for all, and he embarked upon a campaign of unremitting destruction and devastation of the land and its people. The Frank chronicler records that "he [Charlemagne] gave the Saxons a winter of discontent indeed, as he and his *duces* whom he sent out ranged here, there, and everywhere and threw everything into disorder with killings and burnings. By ravaging in this fashion throughout the whole period of the winter he inflicted immense destruction on well-nigh all the regions of the Saxons." The loss of life and property was terrible, and it broke the back of the Saxon resistance.

In March, Charlemagne held the annual assembly at Paderborn and opened negotiations with Widukind, the leader of the Saxon resistance. A deal was struck wherein the Saxons would be converted to the Christian faith. Upon the conversion of their leaders, amnesty would be conferred. Later that year, Widukind himself converted to Christianity, with Charlemagne standing as godfather. The peace was not without its costs. The brunt of the wars against the Saxons had been born by the East Franks who had taken considerable losses. They wished revenge on the Saxons and saw Charlemagne's peace as a betrayal. In 785 C.E., a plot to assassinate Charlemagne was hatched by some nobles of the East Frank nobility, led by a fellow named Hardrad. The plot was discovered, and its leaders blinded. These events only hardened relations between the king of the Franks and his subjects east of the Rhine.

The peace lasted for almost a decade. There was no large-scale movement of Franks into Saxony, so that Frank military outposts remained alien enclaves in a hostile land. Repeated attempts to enforce the hated religious capitularies produced further resentment, as did the enforced levying of Saxon troops to fight in Charlemagne's campaigns against the Slavs. In 793 C.E., the Frank assembly met in Regensburg to hear reports of "a general defection of the Saxons." The next year Charlemagne led a two-pronged attack into Saxony. To avoid yet another slaughter, the Saxon chiefs capitulated. Within a year the rebellion broke out again, this time in response to attempts to enforce the earlier agreement that the Saxons would accept Christianity.

In 795 C.E., Charlemagne ordered the assembly to be held in Saxony and prepared yet another military expedition against the Saxons. He attempted to surround the Saxons by arranging an alliance with the Slavic Abodrites, the Saxon's traditional enemies to the east. The Abodrites had already proved useful in Charlemagne's earlier campaign against the Wiltzi in 789 C.E. While moving to join their Frank allies, the Abodrites were ambushed crossing a river and annihilated. The Saxon victory drove Charlemagne into a rage so that "it [the victory] acted like a goad to the king's resolve, spurring him to the swifter crushing of the Saxons, and provoked him to greater hatred of that perfidious people." Charlemagne launched a campaign of killing, burning, and utter devastation of the countryside. Once more, the Saxons came to terms and surrendered hostages. Within a year the peace was broken, and Charlemagne launched another attack in which he took "innumerable" Saxon lives and captives.

In 796 C.E. Charlemagne entered Saxony at the head of a large army, marching as far as the North Sea coast, where the Elbe and Weser reach the sea, before returning to Aachen. Once more he devastated the countryside and took hostages. Later in the year he entered Saxony again where, as he had done a decade earlier, he planned to remain inside the country and campaign over the winter. He established his main garrison on the banks of the River Weser at a place he named *Herestelle* (literally, Meeting Place of the Army) and deployed units throughout the country to hold down the countryside. Early in the spring of 798 C.E., before fodder for the horses could be obtained and the Frank army could leave its garrison, a group of Saxons captured and killed a number of Frankish nobles including an important royal *missus*. The murder enraged Charlemagne, who then ravaged the whole area between the Weser and the Elbe. Battered by Charlemagne's slaughter and outflanked by his alliance with the Abodrites to their east, the Saxons once more submitted. This was a very important event, since the peace treaty permitted Charlemagne to withdraw from Saxony and travel to Italy in support of the Pope's interests where, in August of 800 C.E., Charlemagne was crowned emperor.

In 802 C.E. yet another Saxon revolt broke out. Charlemagne formed an army from among those Saxons still loyal and sent it against their fellow Saxons across the Elbe River, where "it brought devastation upon them." Charlemagne now embarked upon the "final solution" for the Saxons. As early as 799 C.E. he had begun deporting Saxons and distributing their lands among his soldiers. The dispossessed Saxons were sent as serfs and laborers to other parts of the empire. In 804 C.E., these deportations were increased under the direction of yet another army led personally by Charlemagne against the Saxons. Almost the entire Saxon population resident beyond the River Elbe was rounded up and deported to Francia proper. The Saxon lands were given to the Abodrites. The chronicler records the event thus: "The emperor sent his *scarae* . . . to take the people [Saxons] there away, out of their homeland; and he also removed the Saxons beyond the Elbe from their homes, and he dispersed them within his kingdom where he saw fit." Thereafter, whenever the Saxons are mentioned in the annals, they are shown as contingents fighting in the Frankish armies on the eastern frontiers of the empire. Finally, after almost thirty years, the Saxon wars were over.

Charlemagne's death in 814 C.E. marks the end of the expansionist period of the empire of the Franks. From that time until its demise in 887 C.E., the empire went over to the strategic defensive. One consequence was the decline of its military forces. Frank nobles remained ensconced in their estates, while the recruitment system decayed for lack of financial support. The result was a considerable reduction in the number of good infantry available. Over time, infantry almost disappeared completely among the Franks as the feudal system took stronger root and the mounted knight, bound by obligation to serve his king, became the primary instrument of Frank warfare.

Charlemagne was succeeded by his son, Louis the Pious, who managed to keep the empire intact and resist the raids of the Vikings and Saracens. He died in 840 C.E., and the empire was divided among his sons in the tradition of Frankish inheritance. Although one of his sons took the title of emperor, his authority over his brother kings was a facade. The reality was civil war, in which central governmental authority collapsed under the effects of the war and increased Viking raids. For the next forty years, the empire of the Carolingians struggled against itself, the predations of the Vikings, the invasion of the eastern provinces by the Magyars, and the raids of the Saracens into Italy as they gained effective control of the western Mediterranean after 827 C.E. With the deposition of Charles III, the last emperor of the Franks, the Carolingian empire split into three kingdoms, out of which later came the states of northern Italy, Germany, and the modern state of France itself.

THE COMMANDERS

Charles the Great or Charlemagne (742–814 C.E.) was the illegitimate son of Pepin of Arnulf and Bertrada, the daughter of Chribert, Count of Laeon. Pepin deposed the last Merovingian king of Francia, leaving the throne to his two sons, Carloman and Charles. At age twenty-nine, Charles became the sole king of the Franks and spent the next forty years suppressing the revolts of rival Frankish dukes and extending his realm by military conquest until it was almost as large as the Western Roman Empire had been. During his life Charlemagne engaged in fifty-three military campaigns, leading nearly all of them himself. Besides bringing the kingdom of the East Franks, Bavaria, and Saxony into the Frankish realm, Charlemagne fought and won major campaigns against the Lombards, the Muslims in Spain and Italy, the Avars, Slavs, Vikings, and Maygars. He was a courageous and superb field commander, often personally leading his men into battle.

To provide a more appropriate military instrument to match his strategic vision, Charlemagne reformed the army of the Merovingian Franks, making it smaller, more mobile, better supplied and equipped, and centered on mounted cavalry. This permitted him to move quickly across his realm, taking advantage of interior lines to reach areas under threat. Charlemagne changed the basis of recruitment from the old Germanic levy *en masse* to a system where large landowners were required to provide themselves and a specified number of men for military service in return for an exemption from taxes. Over time the tenure to the land became hereditary and military service replaced taxation completely. Thus, it was under Charlemagne that we see the beginnings of the feudal socio-military system that would eventually characterize the states of Europe over the next five centuries.

Charlemagne's greatest achievement, however, lay in his support for the Christian Church, which eventually displaced paganism completely. In return for his protection, the Popes crowned the Frank emperor, proclaiming him the Christian emperor of the Roman Empire of the West. Thus were joined the secular traditions of ancient Rome with the religious prestige and influence of Christianity, which laid the foundation for the legitimization of the rule of Christian kings into the modern era. From Charlemagne's triumph came the later Holy Roman Empire, which became the centerpiece of the major strategic conflicts and wars from the Renaissance to World War II.

Charlemagne's biographer, Einhard, tells us that Charlemagne was of imposing stature, perhaps six feet four inches tall, to which his bright eyes and long flowing hair added dignity. His neck was short, and his belly protruded, and his voice was not as strong as his size would suggest. Charlemagne, except during affairs of state, had little use for ceremony or extravagant dress and usually wore the dress of the common Frank—linen shirt and drawers, tunic held by a silken cord, and leggings. His thighs were wound round with thongs of leather, and he wore simple laced shoes. He seems to have been healthy all his life, enjoying horseback riding, swimming, and taking the warm baths at Aachen. At age sixty-eight he began to suffer from fevers and acquired a limp in one leg, symptoms that suggest gout. He died at age seventy-two after ruling the Franks for forty-seven years. He was buried in the royal tomb in the church at Aachen. When in the year 1000 C.E., Otto III had the imperial tomb opened, it was said that the great emperor appeared as he was buried, sitting on a marble throne, robed and crowned as in life, the book of the Gospels open on his knees. In 1165 C.E., Charles the Great was canonized by the Christian Church. No contemporary portrait of him has survived.

LESSONS OF WAR

Strategy

1. Charlemagne possessed a strategic vision for the Franks to dominate all the territory in which Franks lived on both sides of the Rhine. Once this was achieved, he altered his strategic vision to include the formation of an empire. Without a grand vision of what he wanted to accomplish, Charlemagne's military victories would have amounted to little.
2. Never fight a war alone if you can forge a coalition of allies to fight it with you. Charlemagne rarely fought a strategic campaign without first securing the overt aid of allies or at least neutralizing the potential opposition of his enemies.

3. A strategic vision without the proper instrument to achieve it is useless. Charlemagne realized that the old Frank methods of war were insufficient for the creation and defense of an empire that stretched across long distances. He reformed the army to ensure that its operational capabilities were congruent to its strategic mission.

4. A successful grand strategy will always permit the achievement of one major objective at a time. Charlemagne never pursued two strategic goals simultaneously. Accordingly, he never was required to fight two wars at the same time.

5. As great a military strategist as Charlemagne was, he was in some respects even a more proficient political strategist. Charlemagne was always cognizant of the importance of political factors in the strategic equation. His coronation at the hands of the Pope gained him more power, prestige, and influence than any of his military victories.

6. Never permit competitors for power to establish themselves. Charlemagne was a supporter of the Church because it was in his interest to be so. He always kept this potential competitor for power under close watch and always made certain that he could control it.

7. It is not always possible to foresee the long-term effects of one's strategic policy. The imperatives of establishing an empire and forging the proper means to do so brought about major changes in the way in which armies could be reliably raised by their kings. Charlemagne's policies set into motion the evolution of feudalism, which ultimately affected the social order and military structure of every European state. Beware the unknowable!

Tactics

1. Always advance along more than one axis of approach if circumstances permit. This facilitates logistics and makes it difficult for the enemy to deal a devastating blow against the entire army.

2. Charlemagne used all means available to sustain his army in the field with necessary supplies. Long before Napoleon, Charlemagne understood that an army travels on its stomach.

3. Adequate supply permitted Charlemagne to create the first army in more than five centuries that had a modicum of strategic endurance. It was this asset more than the fighting quality of his army that permitted him ultimately to gain victory over the Saxons.

4. There is no substitute for speed and flexibility of force. Charlemagne's army could move quickly over difficult terrain and use both infantry and cavalry in relative concert against its enemies.

5. Such qualities, however, are always relative. Against the Saracens in Spain and the Avar horse-archers along the Danube, Charlemagne's armies were comparatively slow and inflexible. Reliance upon a fixed force structure can be dangerous. Learn to tailor your forces relative to the enemy's combat capabilities.

6. Sometimes there is no substitute for cruelty and injustice in achieving military objectives. Charlemagne's repeated slaughter of the Saxons was terribly unjust, but it was militarily effective. However, such tactics must always be weighed against their tendency to work against long-term strategic goals.

FURTHER READING

Bachrach, B. S. *Merovingian Military Organization, 481–750*. Minneapolis: University of Minnesota Press, 1972.

Barbero, Allessandro. *Charlemagne: Father of a Continent*. Berkeley: University of California Press, 2004.

Becher, Matthias. *Charlemagne*. New Haven, CT: Yale University Press, 2003.

Beeler, J. *Warfare in Feudal Europe, 730–1200*. Ithaca, NY: Cornell University Press, 1971.

Collins, Roger. *Charlemagne*. Toronto: University of Toronto Press, 1998.

Einhard. *The Life of Charlemagne*. Ann Arbor: University of Michigan Press, 1960.

———. *Vita Karoli*. Edited by Louis Halpern. Paris, 1938.

Geary, Patrick J. *Before France and Germany: The Creation and Transformation of the Merovingian World*. Oxford: Oxford University Press, 1988.

Greenblatt, Miriam. *Charlemagne and the Early Middle Ages*. New York: Benchmark Books, 2003.

Heer, F. *Charlemagne and His World*. London: Blackwell, 1975.

James, Edward. *The Franks*. London: Basil Blackwell, 1988.

———. *The Origins of France: From Clovis to the Capetians, 500–1000*. London: Blackwell, 1982.

Loyn, H. R., and John Percival. *The Reign of Charlemagne*. London: Penguin, 1975.

McKitterick, Rosamond. *The Frankish Kings and Culture in the Early Middle Ages*. Cambridge: Cambridge University Press, 1995.

Nicolle, David, and Angus McBride. *The Age of Charlemagne*. London: Osprey, 1984.

Oman, Sir Charles. *A History of the Art of War in the Middle Ages*. Vol. 1. London: Greenhill Books, 1924.

Reuter, Timothy. "Plunder and Tribute in the Carolingian Empire." *Transactions of the Royal Historical Society* 35, 4th series (1985): 75–94.

Riché, Pierre. *Daily Life in the World of Charlemagne*. Philadelphia: University of Pennsylvania Press, 1978.

Sullivan, Richard E. "The Carolingian Age: Reflections on Its Place in the History of the Middle Ages." *Journal of Medieval and Renaissance Studies* 18 (1988): 267–306.

Sypeck, Jeff. *The Holy Roman Empire and Charlemagne in World History*. Berkeley Heights, NJ: Enslow, 2002.

Thorpe, L. *Gregory of Tours: History of the Franks*. London: Hammondsworth, 1974.

Verbruggen, J. F. *The Art of Warfare in Western Europe during the Middle Ages*. Oxford: Oxford University Press, 1977.

Wallace-Hadrill, J. M. *The Barbarian West, 400–1000*. Oxford: Oxford University Press, 1996.

———. *The Fourth Book of the Chronicle of Fredegar*. London: Penguin Books, 1960.

———. *The Long Haired Kings and Other Studies in Frankish History*. Oxford: Oxford University Press, 1962.

21 THE VIKINGS

[780–1070 C.E.]

BACKGROUND

Within the Western military experience, perhaps no soldiers have been more maligned in official historical accounts of warfare than the Vikings. Historians of the early Middle Ages universally portrayed them as heartless, cruel, and inhuman, with no respect for the established conventions and civilities of war. And, these early historians quickly remind us, the Vikings were pagans, a fact that accounts in the minds of these historians for their frequent assaults on churches, monasteries, and clerical estates. In truth, however, it is unlikely that the Viking soldier showed any greater degree of inhumanity in war than any other European soldier of the time. The Franks were known for their brutality, which they amply demonstrated in their frequent massacres of the Jews as their armies passed through Jewish communities while traveling down the Rhine to the Holy Land to free Jerusalem from the infidels! Angles and Saxons, those Germanic tribes that left Jutland and Frisia to settle in England and transformed Roman Britain into Germanic England, were also harsh combatants. Safe from Continental influence in their new island home, the Angles and Saxons retained their old pagan Germanic heroic traditions longer than most Continental tribes, a propensity that their early conversion to Christianity did little to dilute. The Viking style of war was no more brutal—and often far less total in its application—than that of any other army of the day. Much of the Viking's bad press was due to accounts written by church historians about a people who were not yet Christianized and who made a habit of plundering church property, not because it was church property but because it was often the richest prize to be had.

The Viking age is usually reckoned as encompassing the period 780 C.E., the year of the first tentative small-scale raids against the English coast, to

1070 C.E., when the last vestiges of Danish rule in England came to an end with the extension of the Norman conquest. The *Anglo Saxon Chronicle* records the first Viking raid on the English coast as occurring in 789 C.E. It is, of course, not surprising that Western accounts of Viking attacks focused upon their raids against England. In fact, however, Scandinavian trading and military expeditions had been taking place along the German coast two centuries earlier. These Viking raids against the Carolingians were what forced the major transformation of the Franks away from their traditional reliance on heavy infantry to a reliance upon heavy cavalry. Only heavy cavalry, it seems, could respond rapidly enough to the coastal raids of the Vikings.

So effective were Viking raids against France that Charlemagne's successors found it reasonable to offer the Vikings a province of their own along the French coast in return for their promise to stop the attacks. The Norsemen promptly took them up on the offer, settled in the province now known as Normandy, and became culturally, linguistically, and militarily French, even to the adoption of the Continental style of horse-borne warfare. Two centuries later, these settled Vikings, now called Normans, crossed the English Channel under the command of their captain, William the Conqueror, defeated Harold Godwinson at Hastings, and established the English monarchy that reigns to this day. It was Vikings, too, that established the first monarchies in Russia at Kiev and traveled down the great Russian rivers to Byzantium, where they formed the personal escort of the emperor, the famous Varingian Guard. The Danes were the ones who established the first professional army in England and established Ireland's most important ports and trading outposts. And it was the Vikings who discovered and settled Greenland and Iceland and who, it now seems likely, may have made landfall in the New World four centuries before Columbus.

We first hear of the Scandinavian peoples in official Roman accounts of the first century B.C.E. when the Romans encountered the Teutones and Cimbri, both Scandinavian peoples who had migrated earlier to northern Germany. Later Augustus Caesar sent a fleet beyond the mouth of the Rhine, north around the coast of Jutland. As a result of this expedition, the Cimbri sent ambassadors to Rome. During Nero's reign (60 C.E.), another Roman fleet traveled to the Baltic, and soon Pliny the Elder was writing in his *Natural History* of a people of great size and fierce courage who lived on a large island in the Baltic that he called Scandinavia. By 100 C.E. Tacitus was reporting in some detail on this same people. Then, for almost 400 years the historical record falls silent until 493 C.E. when Cassiodoris mentions them again. In his *Origin and Exploits of the Goths* he reports that the Goths were really refugees from Scandinavia who left their native home centuries before. Jordanes, writing in the sixth century, refers to one of the northern peoples as the Dani, probably the Danes, and another people thought now to be the Swedes. A century later the Viking raids on England began, with the result that accounts of their raids and their society passed commonplace into the historical literature of the period.

Society

The division of the Scandinavian peoples into three separate nations—the Danes, Norwegians, and Swedes—is an invention of medieval chroniclers and probably did not exist in the minds of the warriors of the Viking age. If the Vikings distinguished themselves from their comrades at all, it was most likely on the basis of the dialect differences between East and West Norse. Perhaps, too, they saw certain communities in this or that part of Scandinavia as being loyal to a certain powerful chieftain who might call himself king. But of whatever significance such differences may have been, they were overwhelmed by a stronger sense of being one people who shared language, religion, law, social organization, art, general culture, and, perhaps most important, the same heroic martial tradition. Certainly, there was no sense of nationhood in the modern sense of the term. The idea of a national identity different from the Norse folk identity came late to Scandinavia. To be sure, the kingdoms established in Denmark at the beginning of the ninth century C.E., and then in Sweden fifty years later and Norway fifty years after that, were more cohesive than the petty military kingdoms they replaced. But there was nothing truly "national" about them. They were simply larger personal aggrandizements of territory, wealth, and power and proved in most instances to be as unstable as the smaller ones they replaced. By 1070 C.E., when the Viking influence in England had finally run its course, there were still only the most embryonic notions of nationality in the kingdoms of Scandinavia, and practically nothing in the way of national institutions of any sort. When the medieval chroniclers speak of the "countries" and kings of Denmark, Norway, and Sweden, then, it must be remembered that only in a very narrow sense did these institutions bear any resemblance to nominally similar institutions extant in western Europe during the same period.

Viking society conformed to the old Indo-European pattern of a social division into three classes—the slave (*pir*), the freeman/peasant (*karl*), and their warrior rulers (*jarl*)—that had appeared throughout Europe and the Middle East as a consequence of the Indo-European migrations two millennia before. Slavery was essential to Viking society, for clearing and farming the harsh northland was difficult, especially so when the farmers left their land on a regular basis to "go a viking," that is, to wander, trade, or fight each other in clan disputes, or to raid the French and English coasts. The slaves were the ones who kept the farms going in their absence. Slaves were lucrative business commodities as well, and the Vikings soon controlled the northern slave trade. Sources of slaves included captives taken on raids against the English and Germans, along with organized slave hunts in the Slavic areas of eastern Europe and Russia. Indeed, the very name "slave" is taken from a confusion of medieval Latin and the vulgate in which the Latin word for "Slav" (*Sclavus*) was idiomatically identical to the Latin word for "slave," or *sclavus*.

The free peasant tilling the land was the backbone of Viking agricultural society, and it was the shortage of good land that stimulated the Viking farmers to set sail across the Atlantic in search of more. It was also the search for land that turned the Viking raiders against England and France into permanent settlers there, where they became farmers once more. Each agricultural clan community consisted of several-score farms (*bygd*) in proximity to other communities. To protect their customary rights and settle disputes, the freemen met in a regular consultative assembly called the *Thyng*. Informally organized, this most typical of Scandinavian political institutions was confined to the locality in which its writ ran. There was no national equivalent of this consultative assembly. Its task was to maintain the customary law, debate the application of new laws, safeguard the rights of the free peasant, and control the constant clan and individual blood feuding by apportioning penalties and compensations.

The elite class of warriors also possessed large estates, and their importance in Scandinavian society (and German society) is signified by the very term for "lord," which is *Hlaf-ord*, meaning "loaf-ward," or "he who controls the bread." In an agricultural society like the Viking culture, this position originally derived from agricultural wealth and only later was attributed to military leaders. The relationship of the elite class of Viking warriors to the rest of Scandinavian society was quite different from that found in northern Europe, where early on powerful lords were able to exercise their authority to form large, almost national, political units and use their military might to enforce a degree of social control to limit clan and individual violence. This development came much later in Scandinavia, with the result that Viking society was fragmented into many local clans, chiefdoms, and individual warrior bands that did pretty much as they wished in the absence of some national authority to curtail them. Individual and clan violence came to be seen as the normal way of life for the Viking, so that unbridled violence became characteristic of Viking society until well into the eleventh century. In these circumstances, military training, fighting, and violent death were commonplace, and a boy learned early how to use his weapons.

Having killed a man in honorable combat was an important mark of status, and some of the Norse sagas tell of warriors who killed their first man at the age of twelve! While most clans were based on blood ties, groups of itinerant warriors, bandits, and criminals often would band together in "artificial clans" based on common interest, loot, and ties of friendship. Many of the early Viking raiding parties were comprised of such artificial clans, often of men banished from certain sections of the land by blood clans for some violent offense. The warriors produced by these social circumstances were first-rate fighting men. As Jones notes, "Take self-confidence and professional skill, add resources, cunning, no nonsense about fair play, a strong disregard for human life and suffering, especially the other man's, and you have a good soldier." It was thus with good reason that the English *Book of Common Prayer* cries out, "From the fury of the Northmen, oh Lord, deliver us."

There were several reasons for the Vikings to begin raiding first mainland Europe and then Ireland and England in the sixth century C.E. These include significant overpopulation throughout Scandinavia, a shortage of adequate farmland in the face of increased claimants, the desire to expand the areas for slave hunting and other trading, the heroic warrior tradition that had become even more prominent as a result of increased freelance violence, and the inability of the great lords to ensure social peace. First and foremost, however, the early raiders were warrior adventurers who came to fight and loot. As one analyst has observed, "Loot is loot in any language, and Western Europe was full of it. Ireland, England, France were the Viking's Mexico, with learning, arts, wealth, and a civilization superior to those of these northern *conquistadors*, and a similar inability to defend themselves from a numerically inferior but mobile and energetic foe." But the

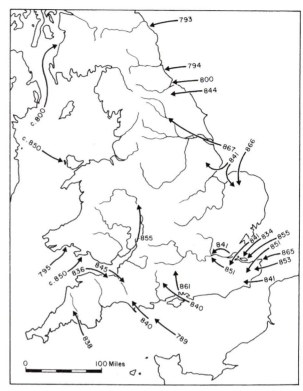

Map 21.1 Viking Attacks on England between 789 and the Capture of York in 867 C.E. Based on a map by Sir Thomas Kendrick.

desire for adventure was, by itself, insufficient, for the lands that the Vikings sought to plunder were across the open sea. Before the Vikings could make good their plans, they required the development of a new military technology to transport them to their objective, the seagoing Viking ship.

The Viking Ship

The reputation of the Vikings as great sailors of the open sea began only in the seventh century with their raids on Ireland and England. Before that point, Viking ships were little more than coastal entrepots or river-going craft. Despite Scandinavia's reputation for fierce weather, in fact most of the coastal areas are accessible by coastal boats almost year round. The west coast of Norway is washed by the Gulf Stream, and the hundreds of offshore islands shelter the inland waters around Denmark and Sweden, making them navigable most of the time. The result was that Scandinavians became excellent coastal sailors but had little experience on the open sea. This changed when, during the sixth century C.E., the long process of experimentation in shipbuilding that had begun in the Bronze Age finally produced a vessel capable of ocean voyages.

Fig. 21.1 Viking Ship

The Viking ship, the Gokstadt-type vessel, was a marvel of technology. The early ships used in the raids on England were fifty feet long, weighed twenty tons, and carried a crew of thirty-five raiders. Within fifty years, a captain of some rank could command a ship of seventy-five feet with a beam of eighteen feet that ran a little over six feet from the bottom of the keel to the gunwale amidships. Her keel alone might run fifty-seven feet and was fashioned from a single oak timber. Clinker built, she was constructed of sixteen strakes of different thicknesses joined by rivets. Below the waterline, the ship's planks were lashed with spruce root lashings and narrow strips of whale bristle, while her seams were caulked with tarred animal hair or wool. These construction materials made the Viking ship very flexible indeed, so that she could pitch and roll in heavy ocean seas without risk of breaking apart. Her mast was thirty-five feet tall with a single, square sail made of strips of heavy woolen cloth strengthened by a rope network and hoisted on a yard of thirty-seven feet.

Steered by a side-rudder oar, the Viking ship was of extremely shallow draft, rarely exceeding 3.5 feet, which gave her the ability to put into shore along any harborless coast or to sail deep inland along shallow streams and rivers. The low height of her sail made it possible for the Vikings to approach land quite closely before the sail could be seen from land. This, and her shallow draft, made it possible for the Vikings to be upon their prey often with less than an hour's warning. Because it was equipped with oars, it has sometimes been believed that the Viking ship was powered primarily by rowing, in the fashion of the ships and galleys of antiquity. In fact, the Viking ship of the seventh century was primarily an oceangoing *sailing* ship, with her oars used primarily for moving up narrow rivers or, more importantly, for pulling rapidly away from the shore to avoid pursuers. If becalmed, of course, the ship could move under oar power, but this would be effective only if it was moving along the coast and had only a short distance to travel.

THE VIKING ARMY

The Viking military tradition was deeply rooted in individual heroic combat between heavy infantrymen. Not surprisingly, this tradition dominated the Viking way of war both at home and abroad. Interestingly, the Viking farmer/soldier was a good horseman, and horses were in common use in Scandinavia, but the animal was not used for war. Horses might be used to transport the soldier to the battlefield (although even this was not common), but there never developed a tradition of fighting from horseback. When raiding, however, it was common for the Vikings to steal every horse they could find, mount up, and range far and wide over the English countryside in search of loot. If forced to battle, the Vikings dismounted and fought as heavy infantry. So strong was the tradition of infantry combat that it affected how battles were fought among the Vikings at sea. Naval battles were never fought in the open sea but always in protected inlets or close to land. There were no naval tactics as such, and ramming and maneuvering were unknown. Instead, Viking captains maneuvered their ships close to one another so that their soldiers could board and fight it out infantry-style on the bloody deck.

Tactical Organization

The early Viking raiders were not princes, kings, or *jarls*, but a middle-ranking type of warrior called the *hersir*, an independent landowner or local chief. Assembled in the command of these captains were the usual collection of adventurers, criminals, and freebooters. It was only later, at the end of the tenth century, that the more powerful *jarls* and chieftains joined the raiding business in search of new land, settlement, and even national identity. The military organization of the Viking raiders was primitive and consisted largely of the traditional Norse war band under the command of a warrior chieftain. The soldiers themselves fought for glory or plunder and, later, for the pay or *Danegeld* of silver coins paid by the English as a fee for not raiding the coastal towns and farms. From time to time an English official would refuse to raise the money to pay off the Danes. To discourage this behavior the Vikings acquired the habit of slitting the nostrils of the recalcitrant official's nose. Unable to raise the money, the official "paid through the nose," thus giving rise to a popular expression in the English language. In general, Viking raiding parties seem to have been the ultimate expression in military freebooting and were usually relatively small, under a few hundred men. For the wars among themselves, however, the Vikings had a more formal military structure that paralleled their social structure. The clans were led by local chiefs who formed their men into *sveiter* or detachments. These detachments were sometimes formed into a *fylking* or battalion under the command of a high chief and fought under a common battle standard.

Tactics

The tactical array of the Viking band was quite limited and seems to have included only two identifiable tactical formations. The first of these was the *skjaldborg* or shield wall, in which warriors arranged themselves in a circle or square close enough together so that each man's shield overlapped that of the man next to him. As each man died, the formation contracted inward, allowing a fierce fight in the defense that could, if required, be to the death. In the offense, the shield wall could have several ranks deployed one behind the other, making it, in effect, a phalanx. Armed with the sword and spear in the defense, the *skjaldborg* was a formidable tactical array against both infantry and mounted attack. At the battle of Stamford Bridge, Harald Hardrada deployed in this manner, ordering his first rank to place the butts of their spears on the ground and aim the points at the horseman's body. The second rank held their spears straight out, aimed at the horse's chest. Within the shield wall, the personal bodyguard of the commander could be used as a mobile reserve to be rushed to any point that threatened to give way.

The second tactical formation used by the Vikings was the *svinfylka* or "Swine's Head" formation. Although the Norse believed that this formation had been given to them by their great war god, Odin, in fact it was more likely derived from the fourth- to fifth-century C.E. Roman legionary formation called the *porcinum capet* or "swine's head." In his *Germania*, Tacitus describes a similar formation used by the Germans called the "boar's head." The Viking version of the formation assembled the best warriors at the front of a wedged-shaped formation, with the first rank formed of two men, the second of three men, the third of four, and so on. The wedge would crash at full run against the enemy line, throwing the full force of the ranks behind it to press through or deep into the enemy line or through a shield wall. Viking tactics were unsophisticated but were often successful because of the courage and ferocity of the Viking warrior, who was always mindful that he was fighting for his reputation as well as for loot.

Equipment

The standard Viking military kit included a conical iron helmet with a nose bridge similar to that worn by the Franks (see Figure 21.2). Some evidence suggests that in earlier times Viking warriors wore more complete and ornamental helmets, but these, like early Viking armor, may have been confined to use by chiefs, more a sign of rank or status than genuine protective combat equipment. The same seems to have pertained to armor. As long as the battles were confined to conflicts among the Scandinavians themselves and were mostly individual combats, Viking armor seems to have been used to a significant extent. But by the end of the eighth century, the old splinted-limb armor of the Viking chieftain appears to have fallen out of favor, so that by the time of the raids against Europe armor was used only sparingly. It may have been that the need to conserve weight aboard ship and to move quickly once ashore led to the thinning down of body armor. When it was used, the type was commonly the mail *byrnie* identical to that used by Harold's troops at Hastings. This mail shirt was short sleeved and ran to midthigh. Sometimes it was slit up the back for greater mobility in wielding weapons. Traditional Viking armor included the *heimskringla*, a body shirt fashioned

Fig. 21.2 The Viking Warrior in Full Battle Kit

of thick reindeer hide that was said to be more effective than the mail hauberk. There is no evidence of lamellar armor in Scandinavia, nor do we find fabric armor of hardened plates. Both these devices are of Middle Eastern origin, and although the Vikings had extensive contact with Byzantium, these armored styles do not appear to have found their way into wide use in Scandinavia.

The Viking shield ("the round war-board") was round and about twenty-four inches in diameter. Made of wood, it often had a metal rim and boss and possessed an Argive-like grip that rendered it easy to maneuver. Later Viking warriors are portrayed as carrying the kite-shaped shield shown on the Bayeau Tapestry in the hands of Harold's men at Hastings. Probably of Norman-French design, the kite-shield may have been more of a fashion since by all accounts the small round shield was easier to use with the sword and, in an interesting application, if slid up the arm, the shield freed the warrior's hands so he could wield the terrible Danish war axe. Unlike the war axe of the Franks, the Danish axe was not meant to be thrown but to be wielded with both hands with such force that it could easily cleave a man, his armor, shield, and helmet, in twain. Since the average Viking was likely to be taller and some-what more physically robust than his opponents in England or France, the heavy Danish axe with its six-foot handle wielded by these fierce warriors was a terrible weapon indeed.

Other Viking weapons included the spear, bow, and sword. If surviving portrayals of Viking warriors can be believed, their spears seem to have been of Carolingian design, with their character-istic broad-leaf blades and wings projecting from

Fig. 21.3 Danish Axes and Spears Used at Stamford Bridge

where the socket joined the shaft. The design is that of a "boar-spear," where the wings act as a hilt to prevent the weapon from penetrating too far into the body. These wings could also be used as a hook to pull a mounted soldier from his mount. The Viking bow was usually made of elm and was about five feet long, accommodating arrows of two to three feet in length, a length that suggests that the bow was drawn to the ear. Although not commonly thought of as such, Viking warriors were excellent archers, the bow being a favorite weapon of the hunt throughout Scandinavia. Still, it was used spar-ingly in battle as would be expected of heavy infantry. Interestingly enough, the Viking bow is remarkably similar to the English longbow of later use, suggesting that the English may have learned a thing or two about archery from the Danes.

The Viking warrior's main weapon was his sword. An object of reverence, swords bloodied in battle were often passed down from father to son, and in some of the Norse sagas swords were even given names. Smelting steel was unknown to the Vikings, but they did know that putting red hot iron in a charcoal fire (often containing bones) would make it harder. This was due to the transfer of carbon to the iron, turning it into steel. Viking smiths made bars of this case-hardened iron, which they cut into strips. These strips were twisted and hammered into the center of the sword blades. Thinner strips of steel were then bent and hammered along the edges of the center blade and hammered flat in a process known as pattern welding. The complete sword blade was then heated and quenched in some liquid to temper it and give it greater strength. Tempering was often done in mud or honey since water turned quickly to steam, drawing off the heat too quickly. Some of the Norse sagas speak of swords that were "quenched in blood," giving rise to the suspicion (unproven!) that some of these swords were tempered by driving them through the body of a slave! Similar notions were said to apply to the manufacture of the Damascene swords of the Islamic warrior. Once again, there is no evidence to support this belief.

A most peculiar Viking military institution was the *berserker* (literally, "bearskin"), a special breed of elite soldier renowned for being transformed by the fever of battle into a fearless killer without regard for his own life. Tales of these warriors stress that when in this battle-trance the *berserkers* possessed great strength and were impervious to pain and wounds. Similar soldiers were called *ulfhednar* (literally, "wolfskin"). Like the old Norse legends of the werewolf (literally, "wolfman"), these elite soldiers were said to become transformed into the animals themselves in some mystical manner, during which they took upon themselves the fighting qualities of the animal. *Berserker* and *ulfhednar* are commonly portrayed in the poems and sagas as usually forming into units of twelve men, where they served as special shock troops. One explanation for their behavior may be that the Vikings had discovered the secret of the *aminita muscaria* mushroom. One authority on this fungus notes that some Norse tribes used the mushroom in religious ceremonies. The mushrooms were fed to sacred reindeer, and the animal's urine collected after it had had time to metabolize the fungus. The animal's kidneys concentrated the mushroom into a powerful natural amphetamine. When the reindeer urine was drunk prior to battle, it had the effect of any powerful amphetamine in that it sharpened the senses, quickened the reflexes, reduced susceptibility to pain and fatigue, and accelerated the solider's mental processes. Whatever the explanation, the behavior of the Viking *berserker* was sufficiently remarkable that its description entered the English language so that, when a person is acting violently, he is said to have gone berserk.

1066 C.E. AND ALL THAT

As Edward the Confessor, king of England, lay dying in January 1066 C.E., three major antagonists watched carefully, awaiting the opportunity to press their claims to the throne of England. What made these pretenders particularly dangerous was that each possessed a large military force and the will to use it in the struggle for succession. One of these was Harald Hardrada, Harald the Ruthless, king of Norway, a ruler of great energy and ambition who wanted to reestablish the Viking claim to the English throne. Hardrada had always believed that he had a strong claim to the English throne, and the death of Edward followed by the shaky and dubious rule of Harold Godwinson, Earl of Wessex, who had seized the throne upon Edward's death, provided Hardrada with the ideal excuse to mount a challenge. He could count on the military help of Tostig, Harold's estranged brother and the king of Scotland. Hardrada's own army was comprised of experienced warriors and was larger than anything Harold could put into the field. It could easily be transported across the North Sea in Hardrada's large standing fleet of Viking longships. In the first week of September 1066 C.E., Harald launched 200 ships from Bergen, each capable of carrying eighty men across the North Sea. Stopping at the Orkneys and the Shetlands, Hardrada rendezvoused with Tostig and his fleet of a hundred ships somewhere off the Scottish coast. The two fleets stopped briefly at the mouth of the Tyne to reorganize, re-form, and prepare for the invasion of northern England.

The invaders sailed south along the English coast. Two days later they raided a settlement near modern Cleveland and, a day later, attacked and burned Scarborough. The ultimate target was York, second only in size to London and the strategic key to control of Northumbria. A few days later, Hardrada's fleet entered the Humber River, proceeded to the Ouse tributary, and anchored at Riccall, two miles east of the confluence of the Ouse and Wharfe rivers. Hardrada debarked a force that has been estimated at between 15,000 and 18,000 men, of which 6,000 to 8,000 were combatants. Of these, perhaps as many as 3,000 were left behind to guard the ships and provisions at Riccall. In two columns, the invaders began the ten-mile march to York.

Morcar, Earl of Northumbria, and his brother Edwin, Earl of Mercia, had begun to raise an army to resist the Viking invasion. Morcar, in command of a force perhaps as large as 3,000 to 4,000 men, moved out of York to Gate Fulford, a location one mile south of the city where the two tracks taken by Hardrada's columns met. The Viking force approached the intersection and was permitted to deploy unmolested. On September 20, the two armies faced each other in the swampy meadow between the river and the raised road. The ground beyond the raised road was fen-like and crossed with

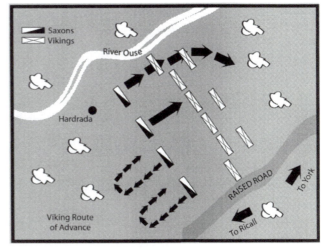

Fig. 21.4 Battle of Fulford Gate (1066 C.E.)

drainage ditches, making maneuver over the ground difficult if not impossible. The English drew up their ranks across the road, with their right flank resting on the river Ouse and their left on the raised road and fen. The Vikings drew up to the front. The battlefield was less than a hundred yards across. More than 10,000 soldiers occupied the ground. The details of the battle are drawn from Viking and English sources, and it is likely that the English were significantly outnumbered.

The English appear to have attacked first, striking the Viking right, pushing it back, and forcing the entire battle line to assume an oblique angle, but without breaking the Viking formations. Hardrada, in command of the Viking left, mounted a fierce attack on the English right, probably taking advantage of his superior numbers. The English line broke, and Hardrada's troops pushed through and began a turning movement, attempting to envelop the English line. To prevent this, the English left seems to have attempted to disengage from the opponents and to withdraw to straighten the line. This provided the opportunity for the Viking right to go over to the attack. Pressed back on both flanks, the English line broke. The *Anglo Saxon Chronicle* recorded that "a great number of the English were either slain or drowned or driven in flight." Some elements were able to reach the safety of York itself.

The city of York was neither stormed nor sacked, and Hardrada imposed only light terms on the population. Winter was not far off, and Hardrada intended to use the city as his main base of operations for his attacks against Harold to the south. The Vikings withdrew most of their army to Riccall for rest and replenishment. Hardrada's problem was his need to obtain supplies from York and the surrounding countryside. By now his army would have consumed what was to be had at Riccall. If he was to move south against Harold he needed food and transport for his army, most particularly for the horses. Negotiations with the administrators of York had gone well enough, and now it was agreed that they would meet on Monday, September 25, with the leaders of the local shires to finalize arrangements. The meeting was to take place at Stamford Bridge, eight miles east-northeast of York.

Harold's strategic position was rapidly eroding. He had been forced to demobilize his army and navy only two weeks before the Viking blow had fallen. The Norse invaders had gained a strong foothold in the north country and were preparing to move south in considerable force by both land and sea. Across the English Channel, Duke William's army awaited only favorable winds to launch an invasion. Harold was caught in the middle. With one invader ashore, Harold had little choice but to deal with it first and hope that the weather might delay William even further. But if time was crucial, Harold could hardly afford to await the southern advance of the Viking invasion force. If his strategy of destroying each invader one at a time was to work, Harold had to go over to the offensive and attack Hardrada's army before it could replenish and reassemble for further movement.

THE BATTLE OF STAMFORD BRIDGE (1066 C.E.)

Harold gathered what troops he could. The housecarls, some detachments not yet demobilized, and a renewed call for the Select *Fyrd* (army reserve) probably produced a force of close to 10,000 men, all mounted for rapid movement. Unencumbered by slow-marching infantry, long supply lines, or cumbersome baggage trains, Harold traversed the 190 miles from London to Tadcaster in about five days, arriving in Tadcaster, ten miles south of York, on Sunday, September 24, thus accomplishing one of the most remarkable forced marches in history. Here Harold's agents learned that most of the Viking force had gone back to Riccall, and most importantly, Harold learned of the time and place of the meeting to take place at Stamford Bridge on Monday. Three courses of action were open to Harold. He could remain within York's walls, strengthen his forces, and wait for Hardrada to attack. This would provide him with the advantage of the defense. Alternatively, he could move quickly up the road to Riccall and hope to catch the Vikings in their camp. Not knowing the strength of the Viking army at Riccall, this plan entailed considerable risk without some sort of naval support and the landing of additional troops to increase his numbers. Finally, he could wait for Hardrada to arrive at Stamford Bridge and ambush him there. Harold decided to attack the Vikings at the bridge. To be successful, surprise was of the essence. Accordingly, Harold ordered the town of Tadcaster sealed off with armed guards along the roads to prevent anyone from informing Hardrada that Harold's army was in Tadcaster. In what must surely count as one of the most egregious failures of tactical intelligence, Hardrada had no idea that Harold was in the vicinity. As far as Hardrada knew, Harold was still in London.

The chroniclers are divided as to whether Harold moved into York Sunday night or Monday morning, but it is certain he was in the city very early on Monday morning. Harold moved through the city and, still early in the day, advanced his army along the Roman road out of York toward Stamford Bridge eight miles away. Harold halted his army at Gate Helmsley, a place on the road behind a small hill a mile short of the bridge. From the crest of the hill Harold could see the Vikings assembling casually on both sides of the bridge over the Derwent River as they awaited the negotiators from York. Harold had moved his army almost 200 miles in five days and placed it directly in front of the enemy, without the enemy being aware that it had even left London. This achievement ranks as one of the most brilliant maneuvers in the military history of the Middle Ages.

One-third of the Viking army had been left behind in Riccall. It was a hot day, and many of Hardrada's men had come to the peaceful parley at Stamford Bridge without their helmets or leather *byrnies*. Not expecting the possibility of a fight at Stamford Bridge, Hardrada had no plan for dealing with the battle when Harold assembled his army, marched it over the brow of the hill, and down the hillside leading to the flat plain by the Derwent River, catching Hardrada completely by surprise. Moments before, Hardrada's men had been scattered along the riverbank. Now, some without armor, helmets, and shields, they were under fierce attack. The direction of Harold's approach had cut off the Vikings from their line of retreat, forcing Hardrada to cross the bridge and assemble his army as best he could. He deployed a small detachment of soldiers on the north side of the river directly in the path of the English advance to act as a rearguard and to delay the enemy until Hardrada could get most of his men across the bridge and assembled for battle on the other side. Once his main force was safely across, Hardrada dispatched messengers back to Riccall to assemble and bring reinforcements. In the meantime, Harold pressed the English attack on Stamford Bridge to gain a foothold on the opposite bank.

In numbers and quality, weapons and armor, the armies were well matched. In skill, valor, and experience it was difficult to choose between them. Although little is known about them, the Vikings and the English apparently had some companies of archers in the field, but for the most part both armies fought on foot. Although the Vikings had a long tradition of horsemanship, neither they nor the English had perfected the use of the horse in battle, unlike the Viking Normans in France who quickly took to the Frank custom of fighting from horseback. The battle of Stamford Bridge was, by all accounts, an infantry battle.

The Viking rearguard fought ferociously and dearly purchased the time for Hardrada to extract his forces from the trap. The English *Chronicle*, written more than a century later, described the fighting at the bridge. "The Norwegians fled from the English, but there was one Norwegian who stood firm against the English force, so that they could not cross the bridge nor clinch victory. An Englishman shot with an arrow but to no avail, and another went under the bridge and stabbed him through the coat of mail. Then Harold, king of the English, crossed the bridge and his levies went forward with him."

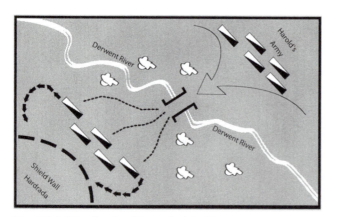

Fig. 21.5 The Battle of Stamford Bridge (1066 C.E.)

As the Viking rearguard fought to the last man to buy precious time, Hardrada deployed his men in a shield wall on a ridge dominating the meadow, about 300 yards from the river. Despite the valor of the Viking rearguard, the English eventually gained the bridge and poured over it into the meadow on the other side. The English re-formed their ranks and attacked up the ridge. Fortune often favors the brave, and this time it favored Harold. Viking and Saxon armies usually had only very small contingents of archers who sometimes opened the battle with a volley or two and then engaged no further. This day, a stray Saxon arrow struck Harald Hardrada dead in the throat, bringing an end to the Viking world's most celebrated warrior. With their brave commander dead on the field, Viking morale sank. Tostig grabbed the famous banner of Hardrada, the Landravager, and assumed command. Hoping to take advantage of Hardrada's death, Harold offered Tostig and his men quarter. Tostig refused, and the fight went on.

The fighting must have been vicious close combat with many casualties taken on both sides. Now Tostig was struck down. With both commanders killed, it is likely that their respective bodyguards had also been slain to a man. Even with their senior commanders gone, the Vikings continued to fight. At last the reinforcements from Riccall arrived commanded by Eystein Ore. Exhausted by the forced march, the Vikings nonetheless threw themselves into the fight, which went on for four more hours. The commander of the Viking relief force had crossed the Derwent River downstream and advanced on the same side that Hardrada's men were making a valiant stand. Had he not crossed the river at all but come straight up the road from Riccall, he might have taken the English in the rear at a key time in the battle. But it was not to be, and by late afternoon, the leader of the relief force was also killed. By the end of the day, most of Hardrada's army had been annihilated and the survivors driven off toward the waiting Viking fleet at Riccall.

Harold pursued the Vikings with "reddened hand," that is bloodily. The *Anglo Saxon Chronicle* tells us, "The English fiercely assailed their rear until some of them reached their ships: some were drowned, others burnt to death, and thus perished in various ways so that there were few survivors, and the English had possession of the place of slaughter." At some point Harold called off his army and the slaughter ceased. What few Vikings were left alive were taken aboard the captured Viking ships for the trip home. Only twenty-four of the 300 ships originally used to transport the invasion force were needed to carry them back to Norway.

Harold's position following the battle of Stamford Bridge was dangerous. The Viking threat had been removed, but at great cost. While no exact figures are available, it is safe to say that almost a third of Harold's housecarls were probably killed and wounded in the battle, along with a significant number of the Select *Fyrd*. Along with the *thegns* and housecarls of the northern earls lost at Gate Fulford, a significant portion of the total available English combat force was not available for further action. Moreover, the English coast was still defenseless, and no fleet stood in the way of the Norman army under William assembled in Normandy and preparing to cross the English Channel. Harold and his army, although victorious, were 200 miles from London and even further from the south English coast, terribly out of position to repulse a Norman landing. Yet, if fortune held, Harold might still escape his predicament. It was late September, and if William did not undertake the crossing of the channel within the next two weeks, the weather would prevent him from having another opportunity until next summer. It was not to be. On October 1, 1066 C.E., in the midst of a victory celebration in York, word reached Harold that on the morning of September 28, three days after Harold's victory at Stamford Bridge, William of Normandy had landed on the Sussex coast.

The Viking defeat at Stamford Bridge brought a practical end to the Viking attempts to conquer England. In 1069 C.E. the king of the Danes made one further attempt at conquest. The Viking army won a significant victory at York, but they soon fell to slaving and looting, allowing the Norman commander to rally his troops and, using reinforcements under William the Norman, drive the Vikings back to the coast. A year later the Danish king himself landed in England only to find the situation so unpromising that he opened truce negotiations with William that resulted in a permanent peace that summer. The Viking fleet sailed for home, never again to return to England.

The battle of Hastings (see Chapter 22) is regarded as one of the decisive battles of English history, as indeed it was. But it was the battle of Stamford Bridge that, perhaps, made the English defeat at Hastings almost inevitable. The need to confront Hardrada at Stamford Bridge cost Harold valuable time, time in which he might have raised more troops, soldiers who could have fought at Hastings. Had there been no battle at Stamford Bridge, Harold might have been able to attack the Normans at Hastings within a few days of their landing rather than having to wait almost a fortnight to engage the enemy, time that permitted the Normans to bring all their forces and equipment ashore unmolested. Or, alternatively, Harold could have forgone the attack on the Normans at Hastings and used the time to assemble a vastly larger army, affording him the advantage of numbers against the Normans as well as permitting him the choice of battlefield. In either case, Harold's chances of defeating the Normans would have increased considerably. As it was, Harold was trapped as the main actor on the stage of history. In less than three weeks, two people saw their fates altered forever, along with that of their kingdoms. The defeat at Stamford Bridge brought an end to the Viking influence in England just as a few days later the defeat at Hastings would bring an end to the Saxon domination of England.

THE COMMANDERS

Harald Hardrada (1015–1066 C.E.), also known as Harald the Ruthless or "The Thunderbolt of the North," was among the most famous of all Viking warriors, whose death at Stamford Bridge is seen by historians as marking the end of the Viking age. He was a man of enormous physical build, with a huge skull, a sweeping moustache, and a misaligned eye. For thirty-five years, ever since he was wounded at the battle of Stiklarstadir (1030 C.E.) at the age of fifteen in the service of his half-brother Olaf's claim to the Norwegian throne, his life was "never free of turbulence and war." His valor and skill at arms were legendary, as were his deeds and reputation as a captain of armies.

Brought off the field at Stiklarstadir with severe wounds, he healed in a lonely farmhouse until escaping his enemies by going to Sweden and then on to Kiev, where he served in the army of king Yaroslav. Kiev had been founded by the Danes as a trading station from which they could conduct slaving operations against the Slavs, whose captives provided a source of lucrative income.

Hardrada remained in Kiev for four years, taking part in Yaroslav's campaign against Poland in 1031 C.E. Shortly thereafter, Hardrada assembled a personal warrior retinue of 500 soldiers and sailed to Byzantium where he entered the personal service of the emperor in command of the famous Varingian bodyguard. He remained in Byzantium for almost a decade, a professional soldier who saw service in many theaters. Records establish that Hardrada took part in conflicts in the Greek islands, Asia Minor, the Caucasus, Palestine, Sicily, and Bulgaria. Here he showed himself to be fierce, resourceful, cunning, and resilient, the epitome of the Viking who lived by rapine and war.

Hardrada returned to Norway around 1045 C.E. where he immediately laid claim to the throne of Magnus the Good, who had recently died. This touched off a war with the Danes that waxed and waned for seventeen years in which Hardrada took part in many raids and battles. With the coming of peace with the Danes, Harald cast about for other avenues of adventure. In 1066 C.E. he invaded England to press his claim to the English throne after Edward the Confessor had died, only to meet his death at Stamford Bridge when a stray arrow struck him in the throat. Harold Godwinson, who defeated Hardrada at Stamford Bridge, said of him, "a small king that, but he stood bravely in his stirrups." Hardrada was buried with his men in the field at Stamford, only to be reinterred a year later in the crypt at St. Mary's Church in Norway, which he himself had founded.

LESSONS OF WAR

Strategy

1. In devising a strategic plan for national defense, remain cognizant of all players in the game. Avoid the almost irresistible temptation to focus on the most immediate threat to the neglect of others. Harold's focus on the prospect of invasion from France led him to completely overlook the prospect of an invasion from any other quarter. When the invasion came from Norway, Harold was taken completely by surprise and had no plan to deal with it.

2. Remember that military forces are always more the result of societal and political forces than an objective assessment of what is required to deal with perceived threats. Harold's force structure was always inadequate to deal with a threat of invasion by either Hardrada or William. Yet the structure remained unreformed because of sociopolitical and cultural forces that the logic of objective threat analysis could not overcome.

Tactics

1. Speed and mobility are among the most important elements in achieving tactical surprise and should be mastered by every tactical commander. Harold moved his army from London to York so rapidly that he was able to completely surprise Hardrada at Stamford Bridge and destroy his army.
2. Always post tactical security. Hardrada did not expect Harold's army at Stamford Bridge, so he did not utilize tactical security to prevent surprise attack. As long as you are conducting military operations in another country, it is always wise to assume that there are no secure areas.
3. When deployed in a secure area, always ensure that the troops are sufficiently equipped to go rapidly into battle. At Stamford Bridge Hardrada permitted his soldiers to assemble without helmets and armor. When the attack struck, his men were at a great disadvantage.
4. Even in modern times the death of a field commander can have paralyzing effects on the will of an army to fight. Hardrada's army collapsed when he was killed at Stamford Bridge, as did Harold's when he was killed at Hastings. A commander should not needlessly expose himself to the risk of being killed. He may lose more than his life. He may lose the battle.
5. Always employ your intelligence assets. Harold was able to surprise Hardrada because his agents learned the time and place of the enemy meeting. Remember: knowledge is power.

FURTHER READING

Berg, Richard. "1066: Year of Decision." *Strategy and Tactics* (November–December 1986): 11–22.

Brooke, F. W. *The Battle of Stamford Bridge.* East Yorkshire, UK: East Yorkshire Historical Society, 1956.

Butler, Denis. *1066: The Story of a Year.* New York: Putnam, 1966.

Cambridge Medieval History. Vol. 6. Cambridge, UK: Cambridge University Press, 1955.

Delbruck, Hans. *The History of the Art of War.* Vol. 3, *Medieval Warfare.* Westport, CT: Greenwood, 1975.

Douglas, David C. *William the Conqueror.* Berkeley: University of California Press, 1964.

Dupuy, R. Ernest, and Trevor N. *The Encyclopedia of Military History.* New York: Harper and Row, 1986.

Fuller, J. F. C. *Military History of the Western World.* Vol. 1. New York: Da Capo, 1954.

Gabriel, Richard. *The Great Battles of Antiquity.* Westport, CT: Greenwood, 1994.

Harrison, Mark. *Viking Warrior.* London: Osprey, 2000.

Lemmon. C. H. *The Field of Hastings.* London: Budd and Gillatt, 1960.

Linklater, Eric. *The Conquest of England.* New York: Doubleday, 1966.

Maclagan, E. *The Bayeux Tapestry.* New York: Penguin Books, 1943.

Marren, Peter. *1066: The Battles of York, Stamford Bridge, and Hastings.* New Brunswick, NJ: Pen and Sword, 2004.

Norman, A. V. B. *The Medieval Soldier.* New York: Crowell, 1971.

Oman, Sir Charles. *The Art of War in the Middle Ages.* Vol. 1. London: Greenhill, 1924.

Patrick, Stephen B. "The Dark Ages: Military Systems Profile, 500–1200." *Strategy and Tactics* (March 1993): 4–18.

Sawyer, Peter. *The Oxford History of the Vikings.* Oxford: Oxford University Press, 2001.

Speed, Peter. *Harald Hardrada and the Vikings.* Austin, TX: Raintree/Steck-Vaughn, 1993.

Tetlow, Edwin. *The Enigma of Hastings.* New York: St. Martin's, 1974.

22 NORMANS AND SAXONS

[1066–1087 C.E.]

BACKGROUND

As Edward the Confessor, king of England, lay dying in January 1066 C.E., three major antagonists watched carefully, awaiting the opportunity to press their claims to the throne of England. What made these pretenders particularly dangerous was that each possessed a large military force and the will to use it in the struggle for succession. While none of the adversaries knew it at the time, the outcome of the struggle for the English throne would shape the history of England for the next thousand years. Edward the Confessor (1042–1066 C.E.) came to power after the Viking line of English kings begun by the Danish invader Canute had come to an end in a series of dynastic wars. Edward's lineage included English and Norman blood, and during the dynastic wars Edward was sent to Normandy for protection. After the death of the last direct Viking claimant to the English throne, Harthacanute, Edward was called to England as king.

Edward's Norman lineage and the strong presence of Norman advisors at his court angered some of the Saxon lords, chief among them Godwine, Earl of Essex, and his sons. After a brief period of civil revolt against the king, Godwine and his sons were reinstated at court. In 1053 C.E. Godwine died and his son, Harold, became Earl of Essex. Harold's mother was Gytha, Canute's sister, a fact that explains Harold's Viking claim to the throne and the fact that four of Godwine's sons had Scandinavian names. Harold's brother, Tostig, ruled the area of Northumbria. When in 1065 C.E., Tostig's fiefdom rose in revolt, Harold was forced to recognize a new earl, thereby gaining Tostig's undying enmity and forcing him into the hands of another claimant for the throne, Harald Hardrada (the Ruthless). Hardrada, king of Norway, was a ruler of great energy and ambition and wanted to reestablish the Viking claim to the English throne. Accordingly, he, too, watched events in England as Edward lay near death. Finally, there was William the Bastard, seventh duke of Normandy, a descendent of Viking raiders and the pretender who felt he had the strongest claim to the throne of England because Edward the Confessor had supposedly promised it to him. As Edward lay near death, each of these contenders began to implement his respective strategies.

On January 5, 1066 C.E., Edward the Confessor died, and Harold moved quickly to seize the throne. On the very day that Edward was laid to rest at his new church and abbey at Westminster, Harold had himself proclaimed king by the *Witan* (Grand Council), comprised only of his friends and allies. Moreover, Harold claimed that Edward had consigned the throne to him with his dying words. Harold had taken the first step and seized the crown. The question was, could he keep it? In Normandy, Harold's proclamation was met with anger and outrage. William of Normandy understood that Harold's action amounted to a *coup d'état* that could only be reversed by force of arms. Ever the strategist, William recognized that any attempt to remove Harold constituted a major international undertaking, one that required considerable military and political preparation.

William was the natural son of Robert the Devil, Duke of Normandy, a descendant of the Viking Norse invaders under Rollo the Ganger who settled in the lower basin of the Seine River a century earlier. Rollo had been granted a fief in Normandy by the Frankish king, Charles the Simple. By the time William was born, the fierce Vikings had given up their Norse tongue for the Romance French and Latin of Normandy and had come to regard Normandy as their home. When William was only seven years old, his father died on a pilgrimage to the Holy Land. Fortunately for William, he was surrounded by his father's loyal guardians. Plot after plot was hatched against his life, but William escaped them all. The task of holding on to power was made all the more difficult by his illegitimacy. The sneering descriptions of him by his enemies as "William the Bastard" haunted him all his life. William grew up amid constant danger, with the result that he developed coolness, shrewdness, and ruthlessness as major character traits, all three governed by a sense of planning and caution. William gradually strengthened his position through a series of wars and violent episodes spanning more than a decade. These wars, and a series of lucky happenstances in which some of his more formidable opponents died, had, by 1066 C.E., secured William's position on the Continent to where he could safely undertake a war against Harold with little fear of attack from neighboring states.

With his military position secure at home, William prepared the political groundwork for a war against Harold. In 1064–1065 C.E., Harold went on some sort of mission to Normandy, where he was seized and thrown into prison by one of William's vassals. As the story goes, William rescued him from prison but would not allow him to return to England until Harold had sworn an oath of fealty to William and recognized his claim to the English throne. Perhaps frightened for his life, there is little doubt that Harold swore the oath. Certainly, he never denied that he did. William's claim to the throne came from his assertion (unproven) that his cousin, Edward, had promised it to him before his death. In any event, William now sent emissaries to Harold in England demanding that Harold recognize his oath and permit William to assume the throne. Harold, of course, refused.

William set about undermining Harold's legitimacy in the eyes of the international community, whose support would be crucial in any war against Harold. To this end, he dispatched emissaries to the major courts of Europe to charge Harold with perjury and breaking his oath. Oath-taking and fealty were serious businesses in the Middle Ages, and it seems likely that William succeeded very well in convincing most European kings that Harold was indeed nothing more than a usurper.

In an age when politics and religion were often one and the same, William pressed his case against Harold with the Pope and emperor. Pope Alexander II gave his support to William's cause and sent him a consecrated banner for his army to carry into battle. Emperor Henry IV promised German help should it be needed, and even the king of the Danes, Swein Estrithson, pledged his support to William. None of these powers actually provided any troops or ships; however, their political support lent considerable legitimacy to William's cause. Equally important, that sense of international legitimacy made it possible for William to raise the large army that his invasion of England required. Harold must have certainly been aware of William's efforts to undermine his standing with world leaders, hence it remains curious that Harold permitted William's charges to go unanswered.

Raising an army of 10,000 men to invade England was no easy task, even for someone as resourceful as William. Feudal law did not require William's vassals to provide military service in an overseas campaign. Moreover, the number of soldiers that William could have raised from his possessions would have been but a fraction of what was required to bring Harold to heel. It took William more than a month at three separate conferences to convince even his own vassals to go along with his plan. Most contingents of the invasion force came from mercenaries, soldiers of fortune, and the land-hungry younger sons of the nobility who were attracted to the idea of almost unlimited plunder opportunities in the English realm. The papal sanction behind William's cause probably also did much to aid recruitment. By April 1066 C.E., William began to construct his invasion fleet and to assemble his forces.

The Invasion

The Norman invasion fleet of some 700 ships assembled at the estuary of the Dives River at the town of Dives-sur-Mer. The assembly point was well chosen. It offered some protection from the gales that ravaged the English Channel in the spring and was ideally placed to receive the wheat supplies grown on the plain near Caen. The assembly point was also close to the forests that provided timber for the construction of the ships. The Norman ships were essentially of Viking design. Most were seagoing longships for moving troops, but others were of deeper draught for the transportation of cargo and horses. All were propelled by a single large sail. If becalmed, the longships could be rowed.

William constructed a military camp for his troops at Dives-sur-Mer that may have covered more than 200 acres. Some 10,000 men were eventually assembled for transport to England, along with at least 3,000 horses. William paid for the troops' food to reduce scavenging from the countryside. Although the task force remained in place for more than a month, from assembly (August) through invasion (September), there is no record of any outbreak of disease, a remarkable military achievement for its time.

Although Harold certainly deduced from his political and diplomatic isolation that sooner or later he would have to deal with an invasion from William, it is not clear that he was yet aware of the preparations going on across the English Channel. When, as the *Anglo-Saxon Chronicle* noted, Harold did mobilize the army and fleet in May, it was to deal with the threat posed by his renegade brother Tostig, not William. Tostig had been in exile in Flanders since being removed from his Northumbrian earldom a year earlier. In Flanders he assembled a flotilla of sixty ships and began to harass the coasts of Sussex and Kent. Harold responded with a general mobilization and moved a small ground force toward Tostig's landing in the south. Tostig moved his ships northward, where he met strong resistance to his coastal raids. He traveled to Thanet, where he was joined by a troop contingent that was staging from the Orkneys. Since the Orkneys were under Norwegian rule, the arrival of these troops suggests strongly that Tostig was already in league with Harald Hardrada, the Norwegian king. After several landings were repulsed, Tostig was reduced to twelve ships. Finally, he abandoned the coastal raids and sailed farther north to spend the summer under the protection of the king of Scotland.

Tostig's attempt at invasion had apparently provided Harold with the excuse to mobilize the army and navy against what certainly was now a clear threat from William's invasion force. The Saxon fleet was in terrible disrepair, and many ships had to be outfitted anew from private and commercial shipping. In July, with the new fleet ready, Harold deployed it along the south coast to await the attack of the Norman fleet. The mobilization law allowed Harold to keep the fleet and the army in the field for no more than sixty days. William's efforts at political coalition-building on the Continent began to pay dividends. Good political relationships along the French coast permitted William access to or control of all the important ports and harbors in northern France. As a consequence, William could launch his attack from any port or combination of ports, forcing Harold to spread his defenses to cover the entire English south coast.

For almost six weeks William's army and ships remained in Dives-sur-Mer, while Harold's army and fleet guarded the shores and strong points of southern England waiting for the Norman invasion that wouldn't come. Official chroniclers of the invasion state that William did not invade because the channel winds refused to blow in the right direction, making an invasion impossible. On the other hand, William had gone out of his way to make his preparations as public as possible, including capturing English merchants, showing them around the camp, and sending them back to England to report on what they had seen. William was certainly aware that Harold, by law and circumstance, could not sustain the English army and navy in the field much beyond September, and it is entirely possible that he delayed his invasion until, as happened on September 8, Harold was forced to recall the fleet and send the General *Fyrd* home. Out of supplies and money, Harold's housecarls returned to London, while the fleet ran into heavy weather and much of it was lost. By mid-September, southern England was virtually defenseless.

With the channel now free of English ships, William moved his ships from Dives-sur-Mer eastward about 160 miles to the port of St. Valery-sur-Somme. There was more chance of a southerly wind here, and the distance across the channel to English soil was shorter than from Dives-sur-Mer. William was prepared to begin the invasion at the first opportunity, when Harald Hardrada suddenly made his bid for the English crown. Harold had so concentrated his efforts on locating and repulsing William's invasion that he failed to notice the other menace gathering across the North Sea. The dreaded invasion of England had finally come, but not from across the English Channel. Instead, the blow was struck from across the North Sea (see Map 22.1).

Harald Hardrada, king of Norway, launched 200 ships from Bergen, each capable of carrying eighty men across the North Sea, in the first week of September 1066 C.E. Stopping at the Orkneys and the Shetlands, Hardrada rendezvoused

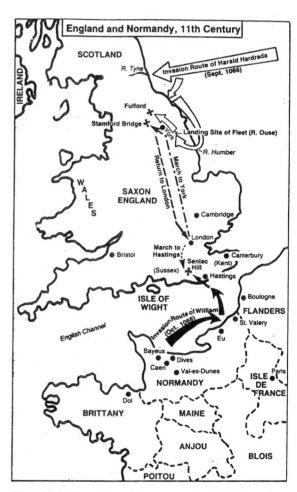

Map 22.1 Operational Deployments of William, Hardrada, and Harold (Eleventh Century C.E.). Courtesy of Dennis Kauth. Reprinted with permission from *Strategy and Tactics* (November– December 1986).

with Tostig, Harold Godwinson's brother, and his fleet of one hundred ships somewhere off the Scottish coast. The two fleets stopped briefly at the mouth of the Tyne to reorganize, re-form, and prepare for the invasion of northern England. The invaders sailed south along the English coast. Two days later they raided a settlement near modern Cleveland and, a day later, attacked and burned Scarborough. The ultimate target was York, second only in size to London, and the strategic key to control of Northumbria. A few days later, Hardrada's fleet entered the Humber River, proceeded to the Ouse tributary, and anchored at Ricall, two miles east of the confluence of the Ouse and Wharfe rivers. Hardrada debarked a force that has been estimated at between 15,000 and 18,000 men, of which 6,000 to 8,000 were combatants. In two columns, the invaders began the ten-mile march to York.

Morcar, Earl of Northumbria, and his brother Edwin, earl of Mercia, had begun to raise an army to resist the Viking invasion. Morcar, in command of a force perhaps as large as 3,000 to 4,000 men, moved out of York to Gate Fulford, a location one mile south of the city where the two tracks taken by Hardrada's columns met. The Viking force approached the intersection and was permitted to deploy unmolested. On September 20, the two armies faced each other in the swampy meadow between the river and the road. The details of the battle are not known, but it is likely that Morcar was significantly outnumbered, and at the end of the day, his army was destroyed. The *Anglo Saxon Chronicle* recorded that "a great number of the English were either slain or drowned or driven in flight."

The city of York quickly surrendered, and Hardrada imposed only light terms since he intended to use the city as his main base of operations for further attacks to the south. The immediate effect of the English defeat was that it removed all possibility of Harold being able to count upon these troops in his fight against Duke William. The Vikings withdrew most of their army to Ricall for rest and replenishment. Negotiations with the administrators of York had gone well, and it was agreed by all parties that they would meet on Monday, September 25, to finalize the surrender and exchange hostages. The meeting was to take place at Stamford Bridge, eight miles east-northeast of York.

Harold's strategic position was rapidly eroding. He had been forced to demobilize his army and navy only two weeks before the Viking blow had fallen. The Norse invaders had gained a strong foothold in the north country and were preparing to move south in considerable force by both land and sea. Across the English Channel, Duke William's army awaited only favorable winds to launch an invasion. Harold was caught in the middle. With one invader ashore, Harold had little choice but to deal with it first and hope that the weather might delay William even further. But if time was crucial, Harold could hardly afford to await the southern advance of the Viking invasion force. If his strategy of destroying each invader one at a time was to work, Harold had to go over to the offensive and attack Hardrada's army before it could replenish and reassemble for further movement.

Harold gathered what troops he could. The housecarls, some detachments not yet demobilized, and a renewed call for the Select *Fyrd* (army reserve) probably produced a force of close to 10,000 men, all of them mounted for rapid movement. Unencumbered by slow-marching infantry, long supply lines, or cumbersome baggage trains, Harold traversed the 190 miles from London to Tadcaster in about five days, arriving in Tadcaster, ten miles south of York, on Sunday, September 24. Here Harold learned that most of the Viking force had gone back to Ricall and, most importantly, Harold learned of the time and place of the meeting to take place at Stamford Bridge on Monday. The result was the Viking defeat at Stamford Bridge, explained in the previous chapter.

Harold's position following the battle of Stamford Bridge was still dangerous. The Viking threat had been removed, but at great cost. While no exact figures are available, it is safe to say that almost a third of Harold's housecarls were probably killed and wounded in the battle, along with some significant number of the Select *Fyrd*. Add to this loss the *thegns* (Saxon warriors) and housecarls of the northern earls lost at Gate Fulford, and a significant portion of the total available English combat force was not available for further action. Moreover, the English coast was still defenseless, and no fleet stood in the way of the Norman crossing should it come. Harold and his army, although victorious, were 200 miles from London and even further from the south English coast, terribly out of position to repulse a Norman landing. Yet, if fortune held, Harold might still escape his predicament. It was late September, and if William did not undertake the crossing of the channel within the next two weeks, the weather would prevent him from having another opportunity until next summer. It was not to be. On October 1, 1066 C.E., in the midst of a victory celebration in York, word reached Harold that on the morning of September 28, three days after Harold's victory at Stamford Bridge, William of Normandy had landed on the Sussex coast.

As mentioned previously, on September 12, the wind had begun to shift, and William had ordered his ships moved from Dives-sur-Mer to St. Valery, the estuary of the Somme, to shorten the distance across the channel. By September 27, the wind had shifted sufficiently to attempt the crossing. During the day the troops and horses were loaded aboard, and the fleet was assembled off the coast just before sunset. William's ship, the *Mora*, a huge lantern strapped to its mast, led the way, as the rest of the 700-vessel invasion force followed in staggered rows. At 8:30 the next morning the English coast came into view, and an hour later the first Norman troops disembarked at the town of Pevensey. The fifty-six-mile crossing had been accomplished with the loss of only two ships.

It is unclear why William landed at Pevensey, an old Roman harbor protected by a shingle bank and mud flats. The Norman ships probably beached in the low tide on the shingle bank. The archers debarked first with bows strung to provide cover, followed by the armed knights on foot to strengthen the covering force. Finally, the horses were driven over the rails and into the surf to make their own way to shore. The landing was unopposed. Sometime in the middle of the debarkation, William ordered some of his transport ships to move down the coast and land at Hastings. Apparently some ground troops and knights were ordered to move overland and join the force at Hastings. The whole episode is somewhat confused, but clearly William intended to shift his base of operations from Pevensey to Hastings to provide himself with a more favorable position.

Strategy

Hastings was located on a peninsula and on much more solid ground than Pevensey. Harold constructed a fort on the peninsula as a final defensive position should it be needed. To the west of the peninsula was a lagoon, while to the east river marshes served as adequate barriers to surprise attack. The terrain to the front was generally flat, leading over a small ridge into a thick forest. Through this terrain ran the single road connecting the peninsula with the old Roman road that ran to London. By controlling this road, William had ensconced himself into a secure base of operations from which to launch his army against Harold.

It is interesting to attempt to discern the strategic designs of both commanders at this juncture of events. William could have quickly moved out of the Hastings peninsula and struck directly for London while Harold was still repairing his force in York. London, however, was relatively well fortified (compared to other English cities), and William had no siege machinery with him. A siege would tie down his army outside the city, allowing Harold the freedom of maneuver to strike at a place and time of his choosing. Capturing London, moreover, would not have done much to destroy the enemy's "center of gravity," namely, Harold's army. On the other hand, William could not afford to remain too long within his peninsula base. The remnants of the English fleet had presumably been reinforced with the large number of ships captured by Harold from the Vikings at Ricall. There was a danger that Harold would move into position and block the land exit from Hastings, while the English fleet bottled up the Norman army on the peninsula and prevent its withdrawal or replenishment by sea. Under these conditions, William risked being trapped until he ran out of supplies, while the English army, now faced with a clear enemy, had sufficient time to draw to it every last fighting man in England.

Harold also faced a dilemma of limited alternatives. He could return to London, reconstitute his army, and then force William to battle. Or, as he was replenishing his army, Harold could have used his fleet to blockade William, and then used his ground forces to ravage the countryside, thus depriving William of local sources of supply. The problem with both alternatives is that the countryside that had to be destroyed was in Sussex, Harold's home base, and its destruction at the hands of its own lord would surely provoke popular revolt. Never one to procrastinate, Harold decided to move directly against William at the soonest possible moment, bring him under attack, and destroy the Norman invasion force before it had a chance to escape from the peninsula.

Harold and his army moved back to London from York, covering the 190 miles in five days. In London, he ordered the army replenished and sent out a call to arms. Reports reached Harold that William was ravaging the Sussex countryside. Impatiently, Harold waited only five or six days to gather his forces before setting forth for Hastings on October 11. Two days later, on the evening of October 13, Harold arrived at Caldbec Hill—the assembly point called the Hoar Apple Tree—one mile from the edge of the Andredsweald Forest and eight miles from Hastings. It is worth noting that Harold averaged nineteen miles a day on his march to Hastings rather than the forty miles a day he had averaged on his march to Stamford Bridge. The march to Hastings was made with mounted and unmounted men, whereas the march to Stamford Bridge had been made only by mounted men. Upon reaching the Hoar Apple Tree, Harold was joined by contingents of the local *Fyrd*, and the army made ready for battle. Once again, Harold had achieved surprise. On the evening of the thirteenth, his army was moving into position to attack, and William of Normandy still had no idea where his enemy was.

THE SAXON ARMY

The origin of the military system of the English armies that fought at the battle of Hastings can be generally traced to the military systems of the Angles, Saxons, and Jutes that began to arrive in England sometime before 548 C.E. In that year there is a written record that an unnamed king of the Britons invited three shiploads of Saxon warriors to come to England and help protect the Britons from the raids of the Picts and other tribal bands. In return for military service the new arrivals were given grants of land in the eastern part of the country. Thus, the first Saxons to settle on English soil came as *foederati*. Later, as more and more Saxons arrived, they gradually came to outnumber (at least in the eastern regions) their original Celto-Romanic employers, revolted against their masters, and gradually spread throughout much of Britain.

Three major streams of immigrant invaders of Britain can be identified: Saxons, Angles, and Jutes. Jutes had some connection with the Franks in the Rhineland and settled mostly in Kent, the Isle of Wight, and possibly Hampshire. The Saxons settled in Essex, Wessex, Middlesex, and Sussex, all names whose ending is a corruption of the suffix "sax." The Saxons traced their lineage to north Germany and Holland. The Angles comprised the final strain of immigrant invaders. Originally from the area of south Denmark, the Angles settled in West Anglia, the Midlands, and the north of England and came to constitute the common stock of the majority of people in England by 1000 C.E.

Society

The period from 500 to 900 C.E. might well be described as the "heroic age" of the English tribes. All three groups, but especially the Saxons, were organized in warrior bands similar in structure and function to those found in Germany and described by Tacitus in the first century. The central place of the warrior band in the tribal culture strongly shaped the larger societal order that had gradually emerged in England by the time of William's invasion. A leading figure in the Saxon social order was the *thegn*, originally a warrior companion of the war band chief, who received horses, spoil, and other booty from his chief as a reward for bravery in battle. As the warrior bands settled down across the English countryside, the *thegn* received land in the same manner. A *thegn* of the band owed military service (*fyrdfaereld*), help in building fortresses (*burhbot*), and bridge repairs (*brycegeweorc*). If the *thegn* refused to comply with military service, he paid a fine of fifty shillings. Land grants were organized into *hides*, approximately the land equivalent required to support one family. The amount of land offered to a *thegn* was generally held to be about five *hides* or 120 acres.

The relationship between the warrior chieftain (later, lord) and his *thegn* was not nearly as strong or legally precise as the feudal relationship between a lord and his vassal. The relationship was far looser, and the obligations more limited. The land grant was given to the *thegn* as a reward for prowess in battle and could not easily be revoked for violation of obligations. The looser social bonds made it more difficult for the warrior clan chief to lay claim to his *thegn's* resources or to require military service. For the most part, the *thegns* were already well on their way to becoming primarily a landed class (as opposed to a military class) by the time of the Norman invasion. Within thirty years of the battle of Hastings, the obligation for military service was already being replaced in England with the obligation to provide only financial support—*scutage*, or "shield money"—with which the king could purchase professional soldiers.

Equipment

The Saxon tribal order retained an emphasis on its old weapons for centuries. The basic weapon of the Saxon soldier was the spear, as it had been for the old Saxon god of war, Woden. The spear was made of ash and attached to a lozenge-shaped spear point. The Saxon warrior referred to himself as *aescberend* or spearbearer (literally, "ash carrier"). The spear was used as a stabbing and thrusting weapon, although occasionally shorter and lighter spears were used for throwing. Swords were common, but not the primary weapon, and many of the blades may have been imported from the Franks. The sword evolved into a double-edged, round-point, cutting or slashing weapon. The axe was not commonly used, and where it was, the throwing axe, *francisca*, was wielded and not the two-handed Danish blade axe. The typical Saxon shield was round and made of yellow linden wood with a strap and Argive-like grip. The mail shirt was known but seems to have been mostly limited to the wealthy. More common was the leather corselet—the *byrnie*—which sometimes had scales or chain sewn over it. Later, the full chain mail shirt was also called the *byrnie*. The Saxon helmet was constructed of bands of metal around a metal headband, meeting in an apex at the crown of the helmet. Between the iron bands were riveted plates of horn.

Fig. 22.1 Interlinked Chain Mail Showing Method of Construction

With only a few changes, the arms and armor of the Saxon warrior of the sixth century were essentially the same as those used at Hastings by English troops 500 years later.

Tactical Organization

In the ninth century C.E., Danish war bands began to undertake frequent raids on the English coast. Small and fast moving, these bands could strike without warning anywhere along the coast and, once ashore, move rapidly inland, often on stolen horses, wreaking havoc as they went. At the time, King Alfred of England apparently reorganized the old Saxon war band system to try and deal with the problem. Alfred required fixed, but staggered, terms of military service from his *thegns* to allow time for planting and harvesting. The old militia system was somewhat more organized into the *Fyrd*, from which general military service was expected, although for short periods of time. It was Alfred who first began the systematic fortification of strong points and towns, a process continued by his successors. These were earthen and pallisaded strong points called *burghs*, and between 911 and 924 C.E. twenty-seven *burghs* were constructed. Even prior to the Danish conquest there were mercenary elements or professional warriors who served for pay within the later Saxon army. These soldiers were paid with the money from a special tax called the *Danegeld*. Originally raised to pay off the Viking raiders so they would not ravage the towns, the *Danegeld* (Dane money) became a permanent tax to be used for military purposes.

The organizational structure of the English army that fought at Hastings was derived in its essentials from the old Saxon army, as it had been modified by its experiences during the Danish conquests. Perhaps the most important structural modification came in 1018 C.E. when the Danish conqueror, Canute, formed the professional corps of the later English army. In 1018 C.E., Canute paid off his men, but kept some 3,000 to 4,000 men on the payroll as a royal bodyguard. It seems likely that Canute's new elite unit was modeled on the military fraternity of Viking warriors that had been previously founded by Swen Forkbeard. This warrior fraternity was comprised of professionals who fought for pay, but who swore loyalty to their king and were held responsible to a strict military code of conduct and honor. Canute's new unit—called the housecarls—were paid from the *Danegeld* and served as a small but well-trained professional army around which other, more traditional elements of the Anglo-Saxon army were organized.

The second element in the English army, the Select *Fyrd*, was the old Anglo-Saxon levy drawn from the *thegns* in much the same manner as it had always been raised. Each estate of "five *hides*" had to provide the lord with one trained and armed soldier or pay a fifty-shilling fine, ostensibly to purchase an alternate. Military service for the Select *Fyrd* was limited to sixty days a year, but it could be called more than once a year if circumstances required. This recruitment system worked relatively well as long as the threat was to English soil, but had limited applicability if an attempt was made to deploy the force overseas. The Select *Fyrd* system lasted until 1094 C.E. when William's successor called it to overseas service and then confiscated the ten shillings for pay with which each man had been provided. He then disbanded the *Fyrd* and sent it home.

The third and largest element in the English army was the General *Fyrd* or militia levy comprised of *ceorls* or free peasants. The militia could be called to military service for only a day and were not paid unless they had to remain on duty overnight. In practice, it was usual to call them to service for a few days at a time. The general levy was based on the "hundreds" or districts within each shire, and it is possible that the decimal system of organization may have been in use. The militia was usually mustered within the boundaries of the shire in which the raid or attack was occurring and was not generally deployed outside its native shires, or at least not usually far beyond its shire borders. The troops of the General *Fyrd* were essentially modestly trained peasants armed with the shield, spear, and club. Occasionally, the helmet or mail shirt may have been found, but only rarely. The General *Fyrd* consisted of all-purpose infantry troops that could not be used in any sophisticated manner.

Equipment

The arms and armor of the English army that fought at Hastings were only marginally different from the traditional arms of the Anglo-Saxon army of a half-millennium earlier. For most members of the General and Select *Fyrds*, the basic weapon was the spear and round wooden shield. The richer *thegns* of the Select *Fyrd* might be equipped with the *byrnie* or mail shirt—short-sleeved and to the waist—and a helmet. But many of the poorer *thegns* would have only a leather corselet and no helmet at all. The helmet was generally of the Viking variety, an iron conical cap with a large cross-nasal piece.

The housecarls were the only troops fully armored and armed. They were equipped with the mail *byrnie* that may have extended to below the knee to protect against sword cuts. To make riding possible, the *byrnie* was slit up the front and back. The *byrnie* had only short sleeves, so there was no protection for the forearms. The housecarls usually wore the hauberk under their helmets to protect their necks. The hauberk began as little more

Fig. 22.2 Saxon Horseman and Infantry

than a leather, later mail, extension over the sides and back of the neck that was attached to the rim of the helmet. Later, it developed into a coif or hood. Worn over the head, it was brought forward and tucked into the neck of the *byrnie*. By the twelfth century C.E., the hood and mail shirt were joined into a single garment, and the whole coat of mail took on the name of hauberk.

The housecarls used the kite-shaped shield that had replaced the old round shield among the professionals. The kite-shield was easier to wield and covered a larger area of the soldier's body. The disadvantage of all the shields was that they had to be dropped or strapped over the back when using the Danish axe. The Danish axe represented the only major improvement to Anglo-Saxon arms over the last 500 years, and as its name implies, it was adopted from the Danes. About 1.25 meters long, the Danish axe was a stout, half-bladed axe that required two hands to wield. Unlike the old missile axe modeled on the *francisca* still in use, the Danish axe was not thrown but used to cleave an enemy in twain. The English also used the

bow, but more as a sporting weapon than as a weapon of war. The English bow, like the Norman bow, was a self-bow, that is, a bow constructed of a single, noncomposite material. It had limited range, perhaps under a hundred yards, and was generally useless against armored troops. The English housecarls and some of the Select *Fyrd* were mounted, but only for mobility in moving to the battlefield. The English army that fought at Hastings had not yet learned how to do battle from horseback. Once they arrived at the battlefield, the houscarls and *thegns* dismounted and fought as infantry.

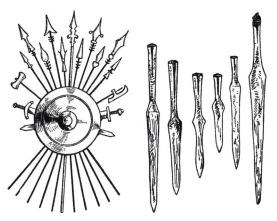

Fig. 22.3 Anglo-Saxon Spears and Saxon Spearheads

Tactics

Two military requirements acted as formative forces in shaping the development of English tactics. The first was the need to develop a response to the amphibious assaults of the Viking raiders who could put ashore anywhere, forcing the English to react on short notice. Second, once ashore, the Viking raiders were highly mobile and could range far and wide across the English countryside before sufficient force could be brought to bear against them. On the Continent, two solutions to these problems gradually evolved. The first was the development of cavalry to the point where it could react quickly to the raids. Unlike other Germanic peoples, however, the Anglo-Saxons never learned to fight on horseback. Consequently, the development of cavalry in England lagged behind that on the Continent. The second solution was to develop fortified strong points and barricaded cities from which local forces could resist and delay the enemy attack until larger forces could be assembled and brought to bear. As with cavalry, the development of the art of fortification in England lagged greatly behind its development on the Continent. It seems fair to suggest that, prior to Hastings, the English had failed to develop a sufficient tactical response to the problems associated with dealing with a seaborne invasion by highly mobile forces, precisely the kind of force William the Conqueror mounted against England in 1066 C.E.

English combat tactics were basic. Armies faced each other across an open meadow and formed the "shield wall," an infantry phalanx of multiple lines arrayed in depth. The degree of compactness of this formation was significantly limited by the infantry's use of the sword and Danish axe, weapons that required considerable room to wield effectively. As one side advanced on the other, the combatants threw their spears at one another, then rushed toward each other and engaged in close combat. Both sides "hacked and hewed at each other over the war-linden" until one side gave way. Tactics were simple, and once engaged, no genuine tactical maneuver was possible. As in other armies of antiquity, the degree of tactical simplicity of the English armies of the day was a function of the low degree of training and military expertise found among the general population from which the soldier was raised.

THE NORMANS

The English army that took the field at Hastings was really no match for the Norman force it faced. William's army was a feudal army, and its military structure reflected its social structure. The entire feudal social order, including the ownership and distribution of property, depended upon the ability of a vassal or lord to provide military manpower to the king. This obligation extended from the bottom through the top of the feudal social order. Although feudalism was decentralized in form, the ability to pyramid military power and gather it at the apex of the political structure created a tendency for feudal societies to develop strong politico-military leaders at or near the apex of social power. Consequently, these leaders could raise and direct substantial armies while, at the same time, creating a sense of nationhood, two factors absent for most of English history through the time of Harold at Hastings. Indeed, it took a Norman victory at Hastings to change the English social order such that it could finally generate strong leaders and a sense of national identity.

Tactical Organization

The centerpiece of the Norman army was its contingent of professional warriors—armored knights outfitted in mail shirts, hauberks, helmets, boots, kite-shield, sword, mace, axe, and lance, all atop a specially bred warhorse equipped with high saddle and stirrups. These latter pieces of military technology had been well developed in Normandy to the point where the Normans were capable of a mounted charge of some speed and shock. Perhaps equally important as any piece of military technology was the fact that the Norman knights were used to operating in concert on the battlefield, and their expertise in horsemanship gave them a flexibility that the English lacked.

The second combat arm of the Norman army was its infantry. Much of the infantry that fought at Hastings contained mercenary soldiers and, as such, was professional. The rest of the infantry consisted of retainers, squires, and attendants of the knights and had at least some semi-professional military quality. Good-quality infantry permits its commander to use it in various ways and as part of a larger tactical plan. William used his infantry at Hastings in precisely this way.

The archers comprised the third element of the Norman army. Archers required considerable training and, like much of the infantry, were professionals. The self-bow was not terribly effective against the armored soldier, but a good

Fig. 22.4 Norman Knight

Fig. 22.5 Norman Archer

number of English troops were unarmored and, therefore, vulnerable to arrow fire. In addition, there is sufficient evidence to conclude that the Normans brought with them the newly developed crossbow. How many of the 1,500 or so Norman archers were equipped with the crossbow, however, remains unknown.

Tactics

Norman tactics were more complex than those of the English, if only because they had more combat arms to coordinate and employ. In a fixed battle, the archers advanced toward the enemy and took it under long-range missile fire. The objective was to harass, frighten, and kill as many of the enemy as possible. If the archers were able to thin the line, the enemy might then be immediately attacked with heavy cavalry in an effort to split its formation and gain a position within it. If a sufficient gap did not appear, the infantry could be used in line attack to engage the enemy in close combat. Often, as hand-to-hand combat became more intense, the enemy formation might break or the infantry might penetrate it. At this point a cavalry attack might succeed in driving a wedge into the enemy line that could be gradually expanded until the enemy broke apart or a flank was turned. Whatever choice of tactics might be used, the Norman army had at its disposal a number of tactical employments that the English army did not possess.

The Normans excelled in two additional military capabilities that the English lacked: amphibious warfare and castle building. The Normans were the first European people since the Romans to pay any serious attention to the ability to transport an army and its provisions by sea in order to insert a military force into a theater of operations, a legacy, perhaps, of their Viking origins. In the case of William's invasion, approximately 10,000 men and, perhaps, 3,000 animals were transported on approximately 700 ships and landed successfully on a hostile shore ready to do combat with the enemy. The Normans were also skilled at castle building, an art that had until Harold's day generally eluded the English. After the battle of Hastings, William moved quickly through England suppressing the remaining opposition and constructing fortified castles in his wake. These castles became the symbol of the Norman military presence in the country, and Norman forces within them could sally forth and defeat any remaining opposition to Norman rule. Eventually these castles were transformed into stone buildings and became the seats of power for the new Norman feudal barons granted vast estates in England.

Manpower

The exact size of the armies that fought at Hastings remains a matter of some conjecture. However, Sir Charles Oman and Major General E. R. James each made independent studies based on a number of factors, and both came to strikingly similar verdicts about the size of the combatants. Oman's study completed in 1907 estimates William's army at about 12,000 men, while James, also writing in 1907, puts the figure at 11,000 men. It should be noted that the numbers refer to William's *total force* based on the number of men and horses that could be transported by William's fleet of 700 ships. The usual assortment of camp followers, merchants, grooms, attendants, and soldiers left behind to guard the ships and garrison the wood fort at Hastings can reasonable account for 3,000 men. Therefore, William probably had at his disposal approximately 8,000 men on the battlefield at Hastings.

Lieutenant Colonel Lemmon, an English officer who lived in the Hastings area and made extensive studies of the battlefield, suggests that William's force was comprised of 1,000 bowmen, 4,000 infantry men-at-arms, and 3,000 mounted knights. Christopher Gravett offers the view that William's army was divided into three contingents. The largest contingent was the Normans under command of William himself. The Norman force was comprised of 800 bowman, 2,130 infantry, and 1,070 knights for a total force of 4,000 men. The Franco-Flemish contingent under the command of William fitzOsbern and Eustace of Boulogne comprised 1,500 men, including 300 archers, 800 infantry, and 400 cavalry. The Breton contingent was led by Alan Fergant, and had 400 archers, 1,070 heavy infantry, and 530 cavalry, for a combined force of 2,000 men. In all contingents the horsemen were organized into *conrois*, a form of military organization based on multiples of five. These groups may have numbered twenty-five or fifty men to a unit.

Opposing the Normans was the English force under the personal command of Harold. The numerical strength of Harold's army is even less clear than the strength of the Norman force. At full strength Harold would have been able to place at least 3,000 housecarls in the field. In addition, the *thegns* and their personal detachments could easily field 6,000 men, while the General *Fyrd*, at maximum effort, might have provided upward of 10,000 men. However, it is clear that the number of Englishmen who stood at Hastings was nowhere near this number. In the first place, the *Fyrd* militia that was mobilized would have been drawn only from the shires near Hastings. Since Harold was moving into the area to contact the Norman army, it is unlikely that, of this potentially small force, no more than a fraction were aware of the summons to arms in time actually to deploy to the battlefield to be of much use. Gravett estimates that no more than 700 or so general militia were present at the battle. In addition, Harold's army had just arrived from Stamford Bridge, almost 200 miles distant, where it had fought a major battle. Given the losses in the battle and the losses through

Fig. 22.6 Hastings from the Bayeux Tapestry

"friction" on the march (on average, approximately 17 percent of force), it is unlikely that Harold had more than 2,000 housecarls ready for action at Hastings. The remainder of the force was comprised of the *thegns* and their detachments. Harold's total force probably numbered about 8,000 men. The ridge upon which the battle was fought is approximately 1,100 yards long from end to end. Assuming each English soldier occupied one yard of front to wield his weapon, Harold could cover his front with only 1,100 soldiers. Harold had enough men to form a shield wall seven ranks deep.

THE BATTLE OF HASTINGS (1066 C.E.)

It is likely that Harold had planned to conduct a surprise attack against William in much the same manner as he had attacked Hardrada at Stamford Bridge, but he arrived in position too late in the evening. This left him with two options. He could rest his troops just briefly, then push on the remaining seven miles to Hastings and conduct a night attack against the Norman camp. This would have required an approach march along a single road in the darkness without any prior reconnaissance, a feat that even a modern army equipped with night vision devices would find difficult. Harold could have chosen instead to rest his troops for part of the evening, then begin an approach march so as to time his arrival at dawn at the Norman camp. But Harold's men had just conducted a fifty-mile forced march that day and were exhausted, and it is unlikely that, had they marched all night to position themselves for a dawn attack, they would have had much resolve left for the assault itself. Harold was forced by circumstance to forgo both options and to debouch his army on a ridge across the London road, the only exit from the Hastings peninsula.

With the chance of surprise gone, Harold had little choice but to fight a defensive battle of attrition. William's army was equipped with contingents of heavy cavalry, and any battle on open ground conceded considerable advantage to the highly mobile Norman knights. Harold suspected as well from the condition of his own troops that William's army was numerically larger and in better fighting trim. If Harold was to defeat the Norman army, he would have to force it to attack him in a strong defensive position until it wore itself out. If this attrition tactic was successful, the time would come in the battle when the Norman army might be so weakened by losses that an English counterattack might carry the day and drive William back into the sea.

Harold chose to stand on what is currently called Senlac Ridge, a piece of ground 1,100 yards long and 150 yards wide that straddled the only exit road from Hastings. The battle of Hastings was actually fought seven miles from Hastings itself, the largest town in the area. In fact, the ground in front of the ridge upon which the battle took place was known to the English as *Santlache* or "Sandy Stream." After the battle, the Normans turned a cruel pun on the English word *Santlache*, calling the battlefield *Senlac* in French or, quite appropriately in light of the slaughter that occurred there, "Blood Lake."

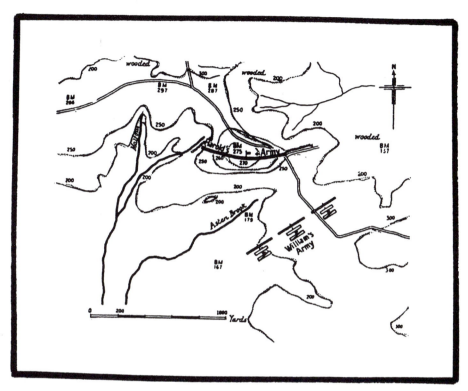

Map 22.2 Battle of Hastings, Topographical Map (1066 C.E.). Adapted from R. Ernest Dupuy and T. N. Dupuy, *The Encyclopedia of Military History* (New York: Harper and Row, 1986).

Harold chose his ground well (see Map 22.2). The front of the ridge gently sloped away to a broad meadow below, across which the Norman force was deployed. The meadowland below the English right was cut with a stream and a shallow marsh, making the ground spongy and difficult for cavalry. Harold's flanks were well protected by the terrain, which dropped away very steeply. The drainage patterns from the high ground on the ends of the ridge had cut the land into ravines. The flank approaches were further blocked by thick brushwood. The road that ran over the ridge dropped off sharply along a thin neck of land to the rear of Harold's position and entered the thick Andredsweald Forest, thus securing Harold's escape route. Harold established his command post on a small hillock on the ridge summit and unfurled his two standards, the Dragon of Wessex and his personal banner, the Fighting Man. The position was well suited to the defense, with a narrow front and secure flanks. Harold's choice of terrain provided William with the single choice of a direct frontal assault conducted uphill.

It was fortunate that Harold had not decided upon either a night or dawn attack, for the result would likely have been disaster. As Harold's troops moved into the Andredsweald Forest to the Hoar Apple Tree assembly point the night before the battle, they were discovered by Norman scouts, who galloped back to Hastings and informed William that the English army was moving toward him. The camp was placed on full alert for the entire evening. Had Harold undertaken a night or dawn attack, he would have found the Normans fully prepared to meet it. As things were, William had decided early on that he would move from his base at Hastings and search out the English army to bring it to battle in open country, where his cavalry would have the advantage. Very early in the morning on October 14, William moved his army up the Hastings-London road in search of Harold and his army.

The *Chronicle* seems to imply that William achieved tactical surprise against Harold when it says that "William came against him by surprise before his army was drawn up in battle array." We cannot be certain if the two armies saw each other as Harold was beginning to deploy on Senlac Ridge or, which seems most likely, if Harold had already occupied the ridge and was still moving his troops into position when the Norman army came into view. Since neither side attempted to prevent the other from deploying into battle array, it is unlikely that William's "surprise," if indeed it occurred at all, had any significant effect. Surely it did not force Harold into deploying on the Senlac Ridge. The terrain itself limited William's tactical options, hence seems purposely chosen by Harold.

William's army approached the battlefield deployed in column and, at approximately eight o'clock in the morning, began to deploy in front of Harold's position. The Bretons, who formed the largest non-Norman contingent, wheeled left and moved over the soggy ground and across the stream that ran through the meadow, assuming a position on the far Norman left. To gain solid ground, the Bretons had to move close to the base of the hill and were within easy bowshot of the English who, unfortunately, had no archers. The center division, the core of the army under William's command and probably twice the size of the other two divisions, moved into position. The last division, comprised of French contingents and commanded by William fitzOsbern and Eustace of Boulogne, moved across the meadow to anchor the Norman right. Although each division varied in size, it was generally similar in its composition of

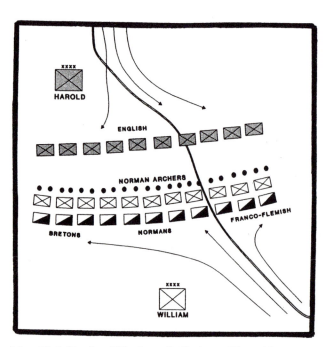

Map 22.3 Battle of Hastings, Preliminary Dispositions (0900 hours, October 14, 1066 C.E.)

forces. Each division possessed a line of archers supported by a line of professional infantry. The striking power of each division, however, lay with its contingents of armored mounted knights. William's army was a genuine combined arms force, and its commander intended to employ the army in a combined arms manner.

The exact nature of Harold's deployment is difficult to determine, but it is likely that the best English troops, the housecarls and better *thegns*, were in the front ranks. The fact that Harold's brothers, Gyrth and Leofwine, were killed relatively early in the battle suggests that they commanded the flanks of the line and were in the thick of battle from the outset. Behind the best troops stood the lesser *thegns*, and in the rear were the levies of local militia. The whole army presented a phalanx of, perhaps, seven-men deep, arranged in a shield wall facing downhill toward the Norman assault. Harold himself was surrounded by his personal bodyguard as he commanded his army from a small hillock slightly left of the English center.

Sometime between nine and ten o'clock, the Norman attack commenced. The line of archers moved gradually up the slope toward the English position until it was within bow range, and the arrow barrage began. The slope of the hill presented a difficult angle of trajectory, and it is likely that many of the arrows passed harmlessly over the heads of the English ranks. The English army had only a few archers, perhaps because the archers were unable to keep up on the forced march to the battlefield. Without archers, there was no one to re-fire the spent arrows and, thus, no return arrows for the Norman archers to reuse. When their quivers ran out of arrows (the later medieval "sheaf" of arrows held twenty-four), resupply was necessary. The arrow barrage proved singularly ineffective in thinning the English ranks, and William ordered his infantry into the attack.

The infantry passed through the line of archers to their front and began the assault up the hill. At some point, the archers had to cease their fire or risk hitting their own infantry. As the Norman infantry advanced, it came under a hail of javelins, spears, and even stones tied to wooden handles hurled at them from the English. The stress of combat and the walk up the hill under fire probably exacted a heavy cost in the energy and spirit of the Norman infantry. The infantry crashed into the English line, and murderous hand-to-hand combat ensued. The two lines were intertwined for some time as the fighting continued, but the Norman infantry could not break through the English line.

William next ordered his cavalry into the attack, probably hoping that the shock of their arrival while the infantry was still engaged might break the English spirit. The knights reached the English infantry line and tried repeatedly to breach it, but to no effect. An occasional knight penetrated the English formation but was quickly dragged from his horse and killed. The fighting was ferocious. On the Norman left the Breton division had been the first to close with the English because it had the gentlest slope to climb. The English

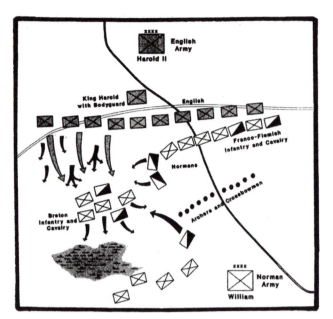

Map 22.4 Battle of Hastings, Flight of the Bretons and the Norman Counterattack (about midday, October 14, 1066 C.E.)

resistance was determined and much more deadly than had been anticipated, and the Breton attack became confused. At this point the Breton knights broke off the attack, turned, and rode headlong down the hill to regroup. In so doing, however, they gave the impression that they were fleeing, and the Norman infantry and archers on the left flank also began to run down the slope (see Map 22.4).

As the Norman center division was just engaging, William noticed the flight of the Bretons on his left. Realizing that their retrograde redeployment had exposed his own left, he wisely disengaged from the attack and fell back in good order. The English right that had repulsed the Bretons, thinking that the Normans were fleeing, lost their discipline and rushed headlong down the hill after the Bretons in an undisciplined counterattack. It was at this point that the rest of William's army began to waver, and the rumor spread that William had been killed. William, having already stopped the Breton's flight, ordered his center division to wheel to his left and engage the pursuing English counterattack in the flank, cutting it off from any support from the ridge. At the same time he personally led the charge of his bodyguard into the meadow, where he threw back his helmet for all to see that he was still alive. With their morale restored, the Normans closed the trap on the English. Fierce fighting drove the English force of several hundred men back atop a small hillock in the swampy meadow, where they were surrounded and slaughtered. Harold watched helplessly from the ridgeline as his men died. The shield wall had contracted under the pressure of William's assault, exposing the flanks and thinning the front line. Harold could only repair the gaps in his shield wall as William prepared for another assault.

It must have been close to midday when William ordered a second attack against the English position. Again the archers began the bombardment, and again the infantry attacked the English line. The mounted knights smashed into the English but could not break the line. It was probably during this second attack that Harold's brothers, Gyrth and Leofwine, were killed. William himself joined the center division in the assault and had his horse cut out from underneath him. Fortunately, his bodyguard was able to protect him from further harm until a remount could be brought up. At the end of the attack, the English line held firm, and the Normans withdrew to their original positions.

Both sides rested and regrouped their forces. William's attacks had not breached the English line nor forced a decisive result. But they were taking their toll on the English strength, which seemed to grow weaker with each attack. Norman losses were mounting also, but William's army was slightly larger than Harold's, and in a battle of attrition William had the numerical advantage. It was probably late afternoon when William ordered yet another attack. William of Poiters recorded that William resorted to a ruse to draw the English troops from their position. According to this account, units of knights broke off the attack and turned headlong in flight down the slope, causing some English infantry to follow in hasty pursuit. The knights then wheeled about, struck the disorganized infantry in open field, and slaughtered them. William of Poiters recorded that this stratagem was used twice during the afternoon fighting, presumably on different parts of the field.

English losses to this stratagem would not have been crucial. For the most part, only the undisciplined militia levies would have been stupid enough to fall for the trick. As the afternoon wore on, the English line was diminished in numbers, but it was comprised mostly of the best troops. To be sure the losses from the close attacks had taken their toll on the housecarls, and there might have been some degradation in the quality of the force. But by midafternoon the English line still stood its ground. At no time during the day had the Normans gained a foothold on the ridge. The results of the previous attacks had produced hundreds of bodies strewn across the front of the English line, presenting the Normans with yet another obstacle. The knights had been in the saddle most of the day, and their horses were exhausted. Many of the knights were fighting on foot because their mounts had been killed.

Harold's army had been subjected to essentially the same pounding that British units later were to suffer at Waterloo. In the later battle, the British squares were similarly subjected to destructive missile fire (bullets) interspersed with the shock of cavalry attack. Harold could withstand further attack, but sooner or later he would have to give way. Deprived of any ability to maneuver, Harold's best hope lay in remaining where he was, thus forcing the enemy to absorb significant losses during its attacks. Like Wellington at Waterloo, Harold could hope for some reinforcement from the remnants of his army and the general militia that was finally catching up with him from his London march, but these were not likely to be numerically significant. His other hope was to hold on until nightfall. His choices, therefore, were not unlike Wellington's, who supposedly opined near the end of the day, "Give me night or give me Blucher."

Sometime near five o'clock in the afternoon, William assembled his entire army for one last assault on the English position. This time, however, he ordered his archers to increase their angle of fire to rain down a storm of arrows upon the packed rear ranks of the English militia levies. The idea may have been to shock these untrained troops into doing something rash more than to increase the kill rate or to disrupt the cohesion of the unit and ham-

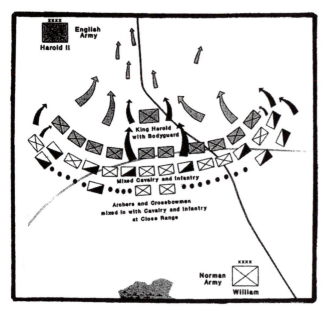

Map 22.5 Battle of Hastings, Final Norman Assault on Senlac Ridge and the Death of King Harold (about 1600 hours, October 14, 1066 C.E.)

per movement from the rear ranks into the battle line. The higher angle of fire also allowed the archers to continue firing during both the infantry and cavalry assaults. As the arrow storm commenced, the Norman infantry closed with the English line, closely followed by the cavalry. As the daylight faded, the English line began to break under the attack (Map 22.5).

It was at this point that Harold was supposedly struck in the eye by an arrow and fell severely wounded from his horse. As Harold lay wounded, a group of Norman knights who had fought their way into Harold's headquarters attacked the king and killed him. At the same time, all along the line, Norman infantry and cavalry were gaining some penetration of the English position, and, indeed, significant inroads had been made into the English flanks. Just as word spread that Harold was dead, the English soldier could clearly see as well that the enemy was within his position in some force. English morale broke, and although small handfuls of housecarls fought on to the end, the Normans overran the ridge. As the English fled down the back of the ridge for the safety of the forest, a disorganized pursuit occurred, only to be broken off as the gathering darkness caused a number of knights to tumble from their horses over the uneven and steep terrain. As night fell, the Normans were in possession of Senlac Ridge, and the English army was no more. William did not know it at the time, but his victory had gained him all of England.

One version of the battle of Hastings by the chronicler William of Malmesbury says that Harold was not struck by an arrow but was killed when a troop of Norman knights hacked its way into Harold's headquarters. Malmesbury identifies the knights as Ivo de Ponthieu, Clifford the Younger, Mountfort, and Eustace of Boulogne. According to Malmesbury, these knights killed Harold with their swords. One knight, probably Ivo, went on cutting off Harold's limbs after he was dead. For this piece of unnecessary savagery, William expelled Ivo from the Norman army and sent him home in disgrace. However Harold died, the incident serves to draw attention to the fact that medieval armies were very much creations of their leaders. The death of a commander was often sufficient cause to lose a battle or even sufficient reason to terminate an entire campaign or the war itself. One of the most

distinguishing characteristics of modern states and armies is the institutional-
ization of power and authority so as to free them from dependency upon a
single leader or commander. In the Middle Ages, political and military
power was largely personal, a characteristic that also made it highly unstable
and fragile.

The battle of Hastings was a decisive event in British history, for out of
the English defeat came the Norman conquest. William was crowned king of
England on Christmas Day 1066 C.E., and within a year William of Normandy had crushed what few embers of resistance were left. A guerrilla war
sputtered on, but to no avail. William established fortified castles throughout
the land and ensconced his barons within them. The old Anglo-Saxon social
order gave way to the more strongly articulated social system of Continental
feudalism, and with it came the rise of a strong king and effective mechanisms of centralized government. Slowly, but far more rapidly than before,
the English began to think of themselves as one people. A sense of British
nationhood was born.

No conqueror had ever gained England in a single stroke. The Romans
and the Vikings had to fight hard for small pieces of the country, and neither
had ever controlled the entire population. William's victory at Hastings was
followed by a rapid and complete consolidation of power that came to be known
in history as the "Harrowing of the North," in which as many as 1 million
Saxons were killed! Two reasons accounted for this political consolidation.
First, although Harold was king, England had never been ruled by a native
king able to engender a sense of national identity. The old Anglo-Saxon social
order, with its emphasis on clans, tribes, and war bands, was premodern in
nature and incapable of overcoming parochial loyalties in favor of a national
sovereign. Second, William filled the political vacuum as easily as he did because
all the significant competitors for power were killed on Senlac Ridge. Of all
the chiefs of the English army, only Esegar and Leofric are recorded to have
escaped, and both were wounded. Harold and his brothers were dead, as
were the cream of the housecarl military elite. The best of the *thegns* were
also dead, and what few remained were rendered penniless by the seizure of
their lands. Almost the entire English army was destroyed, and no military
force capable of resisting William was available in the land. In one swift blow
William of Normandy, forever known to history as William the Conqueror,
had completely decapitated the English political and military system. In its
stead, he laid the foundations of the modern state of Great Britain.

THE COMMANDERS

Harold Godwinson, Earl of Wessex (d. 1066 C.E.), was the second son of Earl
Godwine of Wessex, head of the most powerful family in England. Controlling large estates, the Godwines could raise large numbers of soldiers, which they
used from time to time to check the power of the English king. Leadership

of the family passed to Harold after Earl Godwine's death in 1053 C.E. The eldest son, Sweyn, died the year before during a pilgrimage to Jerusalem. Harold gained military experience in several skirmishes with rebels in the west and in one major campaign in 1051 C.E., which led to his banishment. Several years later, he and his family returned to England by force of arms. Harold, then, had some experience as a soldier but appears never to have commanded a major army until his battle against Hardrada at York. It must be said, however, that his performance at Stamford Bridge in moving his army from London to the battlefield and achieving complete tactical surprise was the hallmark of a great general, one willing to take risks. The same can be said for his performance at Hastings, which, after all, was a near thing for the Normans. Had Harold not been killed at a crucial juncture of the battle, it is not beyond the realm of possibility that he might well have carried the day. He seems, in the end, to have been a gambler both on the battlefield and in the realm of politics, which he seems to have managed with considerable skill during the succession crisis. It is, perhaps, a fitting tribute that this young man, the last Anglo-Saxon king of England, met his death fighting for his throne and country.

William the Conqueror, William the Bastard, Duke William II of Normandy, and *King William I of England* (1027–1087 C.E.) was the son of Robert of Normandy by the daughter of a local tanner. William was the direct descendent of Rolf the Viking who, after a long career of raiding the French coast, was recognized by Charles III ("the Simple") as the legitimate ruler of the lands that he occupied along the Normandy coast. The Viking lineage had remained intact, and little more than a century separated the establishment of the Vikings in France under Rolf and the birth of his most illustrious descendent, William. When William was seven years old, his father died at Nicaea in 1035 C.E. while returning from the Holy Land. As a young prince, he was faced with the revolt of his barons, and he barely survived his youth. At the age of twenty, with the help of the French king, Henry I, William defeated his barons and brought them firmly back under his control (1047 C.E.). He fought other border wars against individual enemies but by 1051 C.E. was firmly in control of his duchy.

Chroniclers record that William had a masterful character and an indomitable will. A man of steel, he could be brutal or lenient depending upon the circumstances in which his interests were to be pursued. He was a good administrator and established a strong civil order in England after his conquest, including a reform of the law governing property (*The Doomsday Book*). He was an excellent and experienced soldier who was easily given to command. His sense of strategy was superb, and he often won his objectives by intimidation rather than battle. When necessary, however, he used devastation as a cruel weapon, and he showed neither remorse nor feeling for the people and peasants he killed. The *Anglo Saxon Chronicle* says of William that "he was a very stern and violent man, so that no one dared to do anything contrary to his will." It was William who established the English administrative state after Hastings and secured the kingdom against the later assault of the Danes.

William is one of the most remarkable persons of medieval history. He was tall and sturdy with a commanding soldier's presence and was a talented and resourceful general. Interestingly, he was also a genuinely pious man, and although his secular politics were often ruthless and cold-blooded, his ecclesiastical policies were notable for their justice and even-handedness. At Hastings, William showed his courage by leading the charge against the Saxon flank at great risk to his own life. But this was not the modern world of war where generals "led" from the rear. It was the ancient world, where a man's claim to bravery had to be tested again and again. At Hastings and elsewhere, William met the test.

LESSONS OF WAR

Strategy

1. Be aware of the moral or ideological dimension of strategy. William was able to build a stronger coalition of forces against Harold because of the widespread perception, aided by the endorsement of the Pope, that William's policy goals were moral. In the modern age, national populations, especially in democracies, seem to demand that national policies be cast in moral or ideological terms.

2. Among Harold's most glaring failures was his failure to counter the erosion of his moral position and legitimacy in the international arena until it was too late. Elements of power, like legitimacy and moral soundness, are difficult to measure in the empirical sense. Yet, they often have great impact on events. A nation allows its own ideological or moral position of legitimacy to erode at great risk.

3. Even after a strategic plan has been formulated and implementation begun, do not neglect the opportunities provided by events to attract additional members of a political coalition to your policies. William continued to expand his supporting coalition even after military preparations for the invasion of England were well under way.

4. The purpose of coalition building in a strategic plan is to increase the military power and options of the major players in the coalition vis-à-vis the adversary. By carefully tailoring his policy so that the military and political aspects of his plan supported one another, William was able to expand his military capabilities. William's successful political approaches to other duchies on the French coast allowed him to gain access to their ports and harbors. This, in turn, allowed him to position his fleet at a debarkation point closer to the English coast. In addition, since Harold could not be sure which port William might use, Harold was forced to spread his naval forces thinly to cover all possibilities.

5. At its most basic, international politics is about interests and not personalities or morals. The Holy Roman emperor and the Pope supported William, despite the fact that everyone involved recognized the invasion as a plan for the organized plunder of a nation, because it was in their interests to support it. It is wise never to rely upon moral restraints or the goodwill of powerful personalities to hinder the impetus of national interests in the execution of national policy. In the words of Henry Kissinger, "It is a foolish antelope who advertises to the lion how tender its flesh is."

6. Attempt to discern the overall political situation of your adversary, most particularly, the degree to which your adversary has domestic political support. William did not appreciate Harold's political position until long after the battle of Hastings. As a result, his policy of political consolidation after the battle met significant resistance and took much longer than planned.

Tactics

1. Make constant use of patrolling and tactical reconnaissance. Harold might well have succeeded in surprising William at Senlac Ridge had William not sent out patrols that discovered Harold's movement into advanced positions the day before the battle.

2. Always strike for the enemy's "center of gravity," which, in most cases at the operational level, is the enemy's armed force. William had a number of operational options that he could have employed after landing unopposed at Hastings. He chose to wait and strike at Harold's army as the surest way to achieve his larger strategic aims.

3. Proper use of the terrain and the tactical defensive can be important force multipliers, especially so for a smaller force. Harold's army was smaller than William's and lacked a number of important combat capabilities that William possessed. Harold chose to fight a battle of attrition from a strong defensive position to offset William's significant military advantages. It almost worked.

4. Employ all elements of your combat arms in concert. Once William stopped committing his archers, infantry, and knights piecemeal and used them in concert for the final assault on Senlac Ridge, he carried the day.

5. Even in modern times the death of the enemy commander can have paralyzing effects on the will of an army to fight. Harold's death shattered the morale of the English army at Hastings. If the opportunity presents itself, attempt to slay the enemy commander. There is nothing personal in this.

6. Maintain control of the attack and position yourself where you can control events. William maintained excellent command and control and field position during the assault on Senlac Ridge. When the Bretons broke and ran, he was in good position to intervene, stop the retreat, and turn it around into a counterattack against the English pursuers.

FURTHER READING

Bennett, Matthew. *Campaigns of the Norman Conquest*. London: Osprey, 2001.

Berg, Richard. "1066: Year of Decision." *Strategy and Tactics* (November–December 1986): 11–22.

Butler, Denis. *1066: The Story of a Year*. New York: Putnam, 1966.

Cambridge Medieval History. Vol. 6. Cambridge, UK: Cambridge University Press, 1955.

Cravett, Christopher. *Hastings 1066: The Fall of Saxon England*. London: Osprey, 1992.

Crossley-Holland, Kevin. *The Anglo Saxon World: An Anthology*. Oxford: Oxford University Press, 1999.

Delbruck, Hans. *The History of the Art of War*. Vol. 3, *Medieval Warfare*. Westport, CT: Greenwood, 1975.

Douglas, David C. *William the Conqueror*. Berkeley: University of California Press, 1967.

Dupuy, R. Ernest, and Trevor N. *The Encyclopedia of Military History*. New York: Harper and Row, 1986.

Fuller, J. F. C. *Military History of the Western World*. Vol. 1. New York: Da Capo, 1954.

Harrison, Mark. *Anglo-Saxon Thegn: AD 449–1066*. London: Osprey, 2001.

Hollister, Charles Warren. *The Military Organization of Norman England*. Oxford: Oxford University Press, 1965.

Lemmon. C. H. *The Field of Hastings*. London: Budd and Gillatt, 1960.

Leprevost, Thierry. *Hastings 1066: Norman Cavalry and Saxon Infantry*. The Hague: Heimdal, 2002.

Linklater, Eric. *The Conquest of England*. New York: Doubleday, 1966.

Maclagan, E. *The Bayeux Tapestry*. New York: Penguin Books, 1943.

Nicolle, David. *The Normans*. London: Osprey, 1998.

Norman, A. V. B. *The Medieval Soldier*. New York: Crowell, 1971.

Oman, Sir Charles. *The Art of War in the Middle Ages*. Vol. 1. London: Greenhill, 1924.

Patrick, Stephen B. "The Dark Ages: Military Systems Profile, 500–1200." *Strategy and Tactics* (March 1993): 4–18.

Stenton, Frank M. *Anglo Saxon England*. Oxford: Oxford University Press, 2001.

Tetlow, Edwin. *The Enigma of Hastings*. New York: St. Martin's, 1974.

Walker, David. *William the Conqueror*. Oxford: Oxford University Press, 1968.